S0-ACC-259

SUCCESSFUL RESTAURANT DESIGN

SUCCESSFUL RESTAURANT DESIGN

THIRD EDITION

Regina S. Baraban

Joseph F. Durocher, PhD

WILEY

JOHN WILEY & SONS, INC.

This book is printed on acid-free paper. ∞

Copyright © 2010 by Regina S. Baraban and Joseph F. Durocher. All rights reserved.

Published by John Wiley & Sons, Inc., Hoboken, New Jersey

Published simultaneously in Canada

No part of this publication may be reproduced, stored in a retrieval system, or transmitted in any form or by any means, electronic, mechanical, photocopying, recording, scanning, or otherwise, except as permitted under Section 107 or 108 of the 1976 United States Copyright Act, without either the prior written permission of the Publisher, or authorization through payment of the appropriate per-copy fee to the Copyright Clearance Center, 222 Rosewood Drive, Danvers, MA 01923, (978) 750-8400, fax (978) 646-8600, or on the Web at www.copyright.com. Requests to the Publisher for permission should be addressed to the Permissions Department, John Wiley & Sons, Inc., 111 River Street, Hoboken, NJ 07030, (201) 748-6011, fax (201) 748-6008, or online at www.wiley.com/go/permissions.

Limit of Liability/Disclaimer of Warranty: While the publisher and the author have used their best efforts in preparing this book, they make no representations or warranties with respect to the accuracy or completeness of the contents of this book and specifically disclaim any implied warranties of merchantability or fitness for a particular purpose. No warranty may be created or extended by sales representatives or written sales materials. The advice and strategies contained herein may not be suitable for your situation. You should consult with a professional where appropriate. Neither the publisher nor the author shall be liable for any loss of profit or any other commercial damages, including but not limited to special, incidental, consequential, or other damages.

For general information about our other products and services, please contact our Customer Care Department within the United States at (800) 762-2974, outside the United States at (317) 572-3993 or fax (317) 572-4002.

Wiley also publishes its books in a variety of electronic formats. Some content that appears in print may not be available in electronic books. For more information about Wiley products, visit our web site at www.wiley.com.

Library of Congress Cataloging-in-Publication Data

Baraban, Regina S.
   Successful restaurant design / Regina S. Baraban, Joseph F. Durocher.—3rd ed.
      p. cm.
   Includes index.
   ISBN 978-0-470-25075-4 (cloth)
   1. Restaurants—Design and construction.   I. Durocher, Joseph F., 1948-   II. Title.
   TX945.B36 2010
   647.95068'2—dc22

                                           2009015923

Printed in the United States of America
V10016335_121719

CONTENTS

PREFACE

My husband, Joseph Durocher, died in July 2009, after a long battle with cancer and shortly after we completed this edition of *Successful Restaurant Design*. It was truly a labor of love, as was his teaching at the University of New Hampshire, New York University, and Cornell University. All who knew Joe admired his dedication to his family, his students, and his work—and his grace, fortitude, and dignity in living with cancer. With love and gratitude, I dedicate this edition to his generous and extraordinary spirit. Joe wrote the following Preface and Acknowledgments, presented here with a just a few minor tweaks—as he often commented with a twinkle in his eye, I was the editor in our partnership.

—*Regina Baraban*

Back in 1989 we never imagined that we would be writing a second, much less a third edition of *Successful Restaurant Design*. But here it is. Over the past two decades, much has changed in our world—and the world of restaurant design. When we first signed our contract for this edition, we told our acquisition editor that the manuscript might be smaller than the one we submitted for the first edition; how wrong we were. As we researched this edition, it seems that every time we turned over a leaf we found more information below. In part, the capacity to dig deep and get all of this research done has been helped by wider use of the Internet. What we soon learned is that the Web made it possible for us to reach out to the world for information about restaurant design. For the first time, we are including mini-cases

from abroad, and works by U.S. designers/architects who have been working overseas. So this third edition is truly a global view of restaurant design.

Since the first edition of *Successful Restaurant Design* was published, thousands of students, designers, architects, and restaurateurs have used this book as a classroom text or as a professional reference. As we have said before, this is not a technical manual, nor is it one of those lavish coffee table books filled with color photography and few words. Our goal since the beginning has been to demonstrate an understanding of how a restaurant is conceived, what the critical design elements are, and how you put them together—both back and front of the house. The integration of the front-of-the-house design with the back-of-the-house design is central to *Successful Restaurant Design*.

The interest in food and restaurants has never been hotter. While economic conditions affect the profitability of any restaurant, the relentless media coverage of restaurants, celebrity chefs, and cooking shows has spurred interest in food and restaurant operations like no other time in history.

Among the new material in this addition is a whole new set of mini-case solutions. Changes such as increased global design efforts, sophisticated use of technology to order food and speed delivery, and creative concept development that delivers both operational efficiency and innovative design are just a few examples that reflect the design directions showcased in these stories. Our hope is that they will pique your interest and foster further discussions about how to go through the process of restaurant design.

Suffice it to say, this is a book about design. But the success of any restaurant rests squarely on a three-legged stool—design, food, and service. The three must pull together, and if one of the legs is broken—well, you know what happens. We talked with some designers who had created truly impressive designs, but the design could not overcome an overbearing host/ess team, inconsistent food quality, or an excessive amount of time waiting to be served. It is our hope that the content herein will help the various members of the restaurant design team to pull all the elements together for a successful result.

MORE ON THE WEB AT SUCCESSFULRESTAURANTDESIGN.COM

Visit our website at www.successfulrestaurant design.com to stay current with additional color images and information that is updated regularly. You'll find supplemental color photography and links to the design and architecture firms covered in the text, as well as links to industry associations and suppliers.

ACKNOWLEDGMENTS

Grateful thanks to our terrific editors at John Wiley & Sons, Inc., our publisher since our first edition. We must also thank all of the designers, architects, restaurateurs, and photographers who provided us with invaluable insights, information, and images for inclusion in the third edition of *Successful Restaurant Design.*

We are particularly indebted to all who contributed time and materials that were used in the "Mini-Case Solutions" and "Speak Out on Design" chapters. Their input ensures that the third edition of *Successful Restaurant Design* will be the most current representation of the art and science of restaurant design.

A special thank you to graphic designer Eric Wentworth of Winter Crow Studio, who saved the day with his high-resolution sketches and drawings when we were in a pinch.

When we wrote this edition, we each had day jobs: Regina, a magazine editor, and Joe, a tenured professor at the University of New Hampshire. We appreciate how our families and friends accepted our repeated laments, "Would love to, but we're awfully busy." You hung in there, and now we can all celebrate. To our daughters, Debra, Lori, and Gail, and their families, let's drink a toast to our grandmothers and grandfathers.

CHAPTER 1

WHERE DESIGN BEGINS

The restaurant can be compared to any complex system that depends on all its parts to function correctly. Metaphorically speaking, it is like a desktop computer. What people see are the monitor, keyboard, and central processing unit (CPU) box, along with peripherals such as printers and scanners. The keyboard is a simple input device, while the monitor and printer are output devices. What makes the computer work is the seamless, complex interaction of the internal hardware components of the CPU and the software—both the operating system and the various programs. If any of the hardware or software components fails to work properly, the computer crashes.

The same holds true for the individual parts of a restaurant. The front and back of the house are meaningless without one another. All spaces in the restaurant should be considered not only on their own terms but also with respect to how well they perform in relation to the whole. This means that the front and the back of the house (even if they are designed by different parties) must work together seamlessly.

All too often, however, the two halves of the restaurant are designed by separate people looking at the space from different doors: the foodservice consultant from the back door and the interior designer or architect from the front. Each ends his/her involvement at the swinging door between the two spaces.

The truth is that both sides of the door are influenced by the restaurant concept and by one another. If the front of the house is not designed to support the back of the house, or the back of the house is not designed to carry out the concept expressed in the front of the house, then the operation suffers. For instance, picture a classical kitchen with a full battery of ranges, ovens, steamers, broilers, and so on,

all geared to produce a comprehensive menu for a gourmet restaurant. A typical quick-service layout—including an ordering queue—would be an obvious mismatch with this classical kitchen and would result in financial disaster for the restaurant.

Another mismatch example is the inclusion of a bank of deep-fat fryers in the kitchen of a café serving spa cuisine. The deep-fat fryers are a costly and space-wasting mistake because fried foods are infrequently found on this type of menu.

Unfortunately, mismatches occur often because the restaurant concept and the menu are not fully developed prior to design programming. The secret to a good relationship of concept, menu, and design is to conduct a careful market study and menu analysis before determining specific design elements in either the kitchen or the dining area.

The secret to a good relationship of concept, menu, and design is to conduct a careful market study and menu analysis before determining specific design elements in either the kitchen or the dining area.

Successful restaurant design should be based on a complete feasibility study that covers the following 10 areas:

1. Type of restaurant
2. The market
3. Concept development
4. Menu

5. Style of service

6. Speed of service

7. The per-customer check average

8. General ambience

9. Management philosophy

10. Budget

Only when these 10 points are fully defined can an integrative design—resulting in a good match of front and back of the house—be realized. These points should be considered at the start of a project, before arriving at layouts and specifications. During the design process, subtle changes can be made to the feasibility study. For example, during the process, ownership discovers that the monthly lease cost for the pad on which the restaurant will be built has increased 10 percent due to a hot real estate market. Obviously, the budget will need to be adjusted to reflect this increased fixed cost, but subtle changes to the menu—which will lead to a high check average intended to cover the additional monthly cost—may need to be made. A helpful source of average restaurant performance statistics is the annual Restaurant Industry Operations Report, published by the National Restaurant Association and Deloitte & Touche, LLP.

The Type of Restaurant

One of the first decisions made about any foodservice space concerns the type of restaurant. Defining restaurant type is not easy. On a simplistic level, one might say, "I want to open a sit-down restaurant." But what exactly does that mean from a design perspective? For example, that sit-down restaurant could fall within any of the following categories:

• Freestanding or within an existing structure

• Independent or chain

• Eat-in only or with a takeout station

• Theme or nontheme

• Ethnic or generic

• Combination

The type of restaurant can also encompass market segment classifications such as quick service, coffee shop, hotel dining, family restaurant, entertainment restaurant, and corporate cafeteria. The direct correlation between the type of restaurant and choice of kitchen equipment is obvious. A Chinese restaurant, for example, calls for different equipment than a seafood family dinner house. Every Chinese restaurant needs, for example, specific ranges designed to hold woks. But front-of-the-house design elements are not nearly as easy to determine. A Chinese restaurant may hint at a particular color palette and design theme, but not all successful Chinese restaurants are festooned with red dragons and smiling Buddhas (Figure 1.1).

The Market

The importance of conducting a thorough market analysis before embarking on a restaurant design cannot be overemphasized. The most spectacular design, the most delectable food, and the finest service can fail to save an establishment that doesn't meet the needs of the marketplace. A good market analysis looks at four main components: potential customers, competition, location, and the economic environment. They are all interrelated, but each should be thoroughly analyzed.

Potential Customers

Identifying the demographic and psychographic profiles of potential customers is crucial for restaurant design success. Demographic information can be fairly easy to obtain. Data such as family income, age distribution, education levels, and home ownership describe part of the picture about potential customers. Such data are available from the U.S. Census Bureau and local economic development offices. A number of online services sell data for any market. Users can choose the exact size of the geographic market from which they intend to draw customers and receive the data via mail or over the Internet. Many recent designs have been targeted to the markets referred to as Generation X, who will range in age from 29 to 49 in 2010; Generation Y—alternatively called the Millennials, the Echo Boomers, or the Internet Generation—will range in age from 10 to 32 in 2010. They have expensive tastes, love going out to restaurants, and are ideal targets for high-designed restaurants where decibel levels are off the charts and ambient light levels are low.

Figure 1.1
Subtle thematic references can, at times, be more effective than overdone clichés. Here, the artwork and table settings in an Asian restaurant designed by Anthony Eckelberry set the stage for diners.
(Photography by Anthony Eckelberry)

However, design teams should not forget the enormous bubble of Baby Boomers (Figure 1.2), who are nearing retirement. Those who have planned well for retirement will have more time on their hands and will seek out restaurants where they will feel comfortable. Lighting levels should be higher in restaurants that cater to Boomers. Care must be given when designing the menu to ensure that the print offers sufficient contrast with the paper so that in dimly lit dining rooms, Boomers can still read the print. Excessive background noise makes it difficult for many Boomers to hear conversations around the table.

The psychographic information—which reveals consumer behaviors—tells an even more compelling story than the more simple demographics. Psychographics reveal how often the targeted customers actually dine out and how much they spend when they dine away from home, and identifies the type of restaurants they frequent. Some of these data can be obtained through consumer surveys, although those are costly. Credit card companies such as American Express sell detailed data on the purchasing habits of consumers, broken down by geographic markets.

In some situations, the customers to be served at one meal are totally different from those served at another. This is particularly true of hotel restaurants (Figure 1.3). In all-suite hotels, for instance, breakfast is usually included

in the price of the room and served almost exclusively to hotel guests, but lunch usually draws a local business crowd. Many popular restaurants in urban areas serve lunch to a neighborhood business clientele and dinner to a far-flung group of patrons who journey to the restaurant from around the city.

In such instances, design needs to suit diverse groups of customers if the restaurant is to succeed. A room designed as an attractive backdrop rather than an imposing statement can accommodate different tastes. Changing certain elements for each meal period, such as tabletop appointments or lighting levels, can also alter the mood of a room. Flexibility is a crucial design factor in both kitchen and dining areas for establishments that serve a wide spectrum of customers.

The impact of the Web on restaurant design will continue to grow. Customers, be they local, tourist, or business travelers, increasingly use the Web to preview restaurants prior to making a reservation. The Web affords potential customers an opportunity to preview the menu—food and beverages—including photos of individual plates of food. Additionally, multiple views of the restaurant interior (and exterior shots where the seating areas or architectural elements are a signature element of the design) have a major impact on informing potential customers.

The plethora of food shows on television—be they local programming, Bravo, or the Food Network—have kindled interest in upscale food preparations and created celebrity chefs, in a way that no other media ever could. Consumers are also introduced to new cooking techniques, as was the case in the second season (2006) of Bravo TV's *Top Chef.* One of the contestants frequently relied on molecular gastronomy techniques to create his dishes. The hit program *Iron Chef America,* with roots in Japan, has also enlightened Americans about myriad "secret ingredients" and, without question, gave celebrity status to the competing chefs. Twenty-five percent of the grading for each contestant is based on the design of the dishes that were presented.

A final consideration is generational differences. Suffice it to say, the Gen Xers (for the most part) are heavy users of technology. Some of them seem to be connected at all times—be it on their cell phones, laptop computers, or the next new chip-based technology. As long as Moore's Law—which roughly says that the number of transistors that a single microchip can hold doubles every 18 to 24 months—is true, new technologies will need to be considered as a part of the design process. These new technologies will impact customers and designers alike.

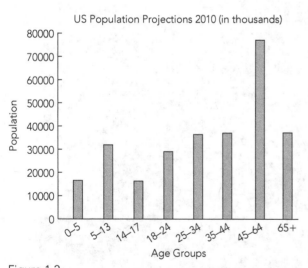

Figure 1.2
This U.S. Census Bureau population estimate for 2010 projects potential customers per age group. When looked at over time, population projections can also anticipate potential labor shortages.

Figure 1.3
Table 45 in the Intercontinental Hotel at the Cleveland Clinic was designed by Bill Blunden to attract medical professionals for breakfast and lunch meetings, and families who want to be close to a patient for evening meals. The multiple spaces appeal to different parts of the day.
(Photos by Scott Pease)

ETHNIC, RELIGIOUS, AND CULTURAL EXPECTATIONS

One must consider the ethnic and religious beliefs of the various groups within the target market. Failing to do so could produce a restaurant design that has a limited audience. For example, barbecued rib restaurants do well in the Southeast; however, the market would be severely constrained in certain areas around Detroit where a population of more than 200,000 Muslims—66 percent of whom are first generation—live, work, and dine out. The Muslim taboo on alcohol should also inform restaurant design in those same areas. A sensitivity to Feng Shui should be considered where the market includes a large population of Chinese customers.

The fastest-growing ethnic population is of Hispanic decent. In areas with a high density of Hispanics, this fact should help shape both the restaurant's menu and its design.

THE COMPETITION

Sizing up the competition is critical to a good market analysis. It starts with identifying both the primary and secondary competition. Primary competitors are those restaurants located in close proximity that offer the same or similar type of food and service as the proposed restaurant at a comparable price point. In rural settings, identifying the primary competition is easy, but in suburban and urban settings, this can be challenging. For example, a proposed restaurant in the northern Chicago suburbs will compete with all of the similar restaurants that lie along the driving route of commuters as they head home from work.

Secondary competitors encompass the different types of restaurants located nearby. Even widely divergent types—quick-service and gourmet, coffee shop and entertainment extravaganzas—should be considered potential competitors. However, the major secondary competitors are those restaurants that have a check average and style of service similar to a proposed restaurant.

Both data gathering and data analysis can be complex. Studies should indicate the financial health of competing restaurants and their volume of business. Shopping the competition by checking out their parking lots and observing their waiting area during meal periods can provide important details about an operation's popularity.

Every effort should be made to find out what developments are planned for the neighborhood in question. In some cases, choosing to locate a restaurant close to others is a good strategy. The chain-restaurant row adjacent to suburban malls is one example of where clustering restaurants tends to work well. The challenge is to create a unique identity for each establishment.

The chain-restaurant row adjacent to suburban malls is one example of where clustering restaurants tends to work well. The challenge is to create a unique identity for each establishment.

For example, consider a strip of roadway where a Red Lobster is followed by a Bugaboo Creek, an Olive Garden, and a regional seafood restaurant. Each has roughly the same check average and style of service; the distinctions are in menu offerings and design. In the case of Red Lobster, the seafood theme is played down and the decor is simple and unobtrusive. Olive Garden plays up its Italian theme with grapes on the menu and colors of the Italian flag. Bugaboo Creek's heavy wood elements, rough edges, and animatronics appeal to families with young children. To stand out from Red Lobster, the regional chain restaurant has a lavish seafood display in its entryway; a cue to customers that they will be eating fresh fish. The display also supports retail seafood sales for at-home preparation. In this case, additional thematic elements, like wallpaper imprinted with nautical images, can further differentiate this seafood restaurant from Red Lobster.

What looks like a hot market today when only two restaurants are open could quickly turn cold when eight more family casual restaurants open their doors within 24 months of each other. The wise design team will gather data on any commercial property in the area that could accommodate a restaurant and keep close tabs on the appropriate government office that oversees building permits or land-use regulators in an effort to project what the future competition could be like.

LOCATION

"Location, location, location," the adage coined decades ago to express the key to business success, remains as true as ever. The ability to recognize a location that is suited to a particular type of restaurant is a crucial market factor. Location is typically defined as a geographic place. The close proximity of that place to a targeted customer base makes it desirable.

Location also gives clues to customer demographics and, in some cases, customer psychographics. For example, the sleek design of the Chinese-inspired Buddakan restaurants in Philadelphia and New York City would likely fail miserably if transplanted to Omaha, Nebraska, because rural Midwesterners look for different kinds of dining and design experiences than trendy New York City restaurant goers.

Architecture is influenced by location as well. Freestanding restaurants in the middle of Manhattan or Chicago are rare. Moreover, different regions call for different architectural styles. The pitched roofs found in New England are there to keep snow from collecting on the roof. Typical southwestern architecture uses adobe—an indigenous material—to insulate the building from the hot summer sun. The point is to avoid grafting architectural style onto an unsympathetic environment.

Successful restaurant architecture works in context with its location (Figure 1.4). In renovations of an existing structure with architectural merit, it seeks to embrace the elements of that structure in the design rather than cover them up. Examples of this are Farallon in San Francisco, where the Pool Room dining space incorporates the vaulted ceiling with its original circa 1925 mosaic ceiling depiction of mermaids that capped the former two-story space above a pool that is still located in the basement of the building.

The geographic location also affects kitchen design decisions. In many urban settings, for instance, food can be purchased daily, but in more remote areas, larger storage

Figure 1.4
Architecture in context: As an homage to the noted architect Louis Sullivan, architect Warren Ashworth incorporated an overscaled arch on the entry to the restaurant.

(Peter Wynn Thompson Photography)

facilities are needed to hold food for a week or more, so extra storage space must be factored into the floorplan.

Location also affects the availability of utilities. Urban restaurants typically have access to natural gas for cooking, some can access a city-generated steam supply, and electricity is available at several voltages. However, in rural areas, a restaurateur may have access only to bottled gas—which puts out 25 percent less heat than natural gas. Electric equipment that runs on 110-volt or 220-volt single phase should pose no problems in any location, but a 3-phase 220-volt power supply is not available everywhere; upgrading that service can be costly.

Traffic patterns should be taken into consideration when picking a location for a new restaurant. For example, a restaurant that targets breakfast customers is best located on the inbound side of the road heading into a city or other concentrated employment area, such as an industrial park. Conversely, a restaurant that targets dinner guests or people looking to pick up a home meal replacement after work can benefit from a location on the outbound side of the roadway. The ease with which drivers can exit and return to limited-access highways is also important.

ECONOMIC CONDITIONS

Finally, a market analysis should consider regional, national, and, in some cases, international economic conditions. The economic climate tends to influence restaurant longevity. In volatile times, planned obsolescence can be the key to a restaurant's success. In the early 1980s and 1990s, for example, the economic picture was such that restaurants designed for a short but popular lifespan gained a competitive advantage. In these cases, front-of-the-house design elements were chosen primarily for their up-to-the-minute look, not for their enduring value. But by the mid-1990s, economic stability and prosperity encouraged more durable designs whose high style did not eclipse comfort. In this millennium, the economic conditions have been on a roller-coaster ride beginning with the downturn (a.k.a. mini-recession) that began in 2000 and was driven down further by 9/11 and the military incursions overseas. Clearly, opening a restaurant during an economic downturn could have a negative effect on a restaurant's chances for success. As can be seen in Figure 1.5, economic conditions are somewhat cyclical. While unexpected social or political occurrences cannot be predicted, the general trends of the economy can be forecast out to 24 months with high accuracy.

Market indicators such as housing starts can help pinpoint the economic strength of a given area. Traffic counts maintained by state transportation departments are valuable for rural and suburban restaurants. Because most customers use their cars to reach restaurants in nonurban locations, increases in traffic count tend to foretell increases in restaurant sales. The trends of the bond market should also be considered. As the cost of capital increases, the prudent restaurateur looks for architecture and design that helps minimize capital costs.

Another point to keep in mind is that the market is cyclical. A drop in interest rates can be a great time to upgrade equipment or undertake a renovation.

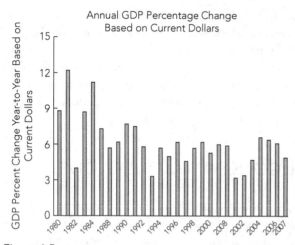

Figure 1.5
The gross domestic product (GDP)—an important indicator of domestic economic conditions—is somewhat cyclical as can be seen in this figure. Opening a restaurant during an economic downturn can be a challenge for even the best designed restaurants.

Communities that rely heavily on a single employer can pose problematic economic challenges. When the main employer downsizes, less discretionary money is available for dining out, and those who are still employed tend to tighten their belts to save for the time when they might be laid off. Urban restaurateurs should be similarly concerned if their operation appeals to a single business segment, like Wall Street brokers or advertising agency personnel.

CONCEPT DEVELOPMENT

With a clear understanding of the market, one can begin to develop the restaurant concept. The answers to four initial questions yield vital background information:

1. What experience does ownership have in the restaurant business?

Owners with a great deal of experience are better able to work with a complex menu, service, and design concept. Those with little experience are better suited to a small operation with a limited menu and simple decor. That said, some celebrity chefs with multiple restaurants in their portfolio, or profitable chain restaurant companies with many restaurant brands, can contradict market conditions.

2. For a restaurant renovation, is the goal to freshen the look of an ongoing business or create an entirely new personality?

A renovation can be as simple as adding a coat of paint, changing ceiling tiles, and installing new wall sconces. More significant design alterations are required to change the personality of an existing restaurant into an entirely new concept. The simple renovation may be small enough to absorb into the ongoing operating costs. Creating a new personality for a restaurant requires a greater capital investment, which may necessitate increasing revenues through price increases.

3. For a new restaurant, is the building freestanding or part of an existing structure?

When building from the ground up, both exterior and interior architecture can be easily planned to support the concept. Creating a concept for a restaurant built within an existing structure can be more challenging because the space limits the designer's flexibility. In this case, it often makes sense to develop a concept that is compatible with the existing architecture. For example, it would be difficult to create a 1950s diner theme in a cavernous loft space punctuated by columns.

4. If ownership has not established a firm concept, then who will develop the concept—interior designer, architect, restaurant manager, or foodservice consultant—or will many parties collaborate?

While input from many players can be valuable, it can also lead to confusion or a loosely defined concept. For example, the chef may want to focus on the tabletop, with dramatic lighting that highlights artfully arranged platters of food in the center of each table. The manager, seeing a greater contribution margin coming from the bar, may want to downplay the food end of the business and position the bar as the heart of the concept. The interior designer may seek to create a strong visual impact by spending the budget on dramatic architectural elements like a soaring staircase or dramatic entry.

QUESTIONS TO ASK BEFORE
DEVELOPING THE CONCEPT:

• What experience does ownership have in
the restaurant business?

• For a restaurant renovation, is the goal to
freshen the look of an ongoing business or
to create an entirely new personality?

• If a new restaurant, is the building freestanding or part of an existing structure?

• If ownership has not established a firm concept, then who will develop the concept—
interior designer, architect, restaurant
manager, or foodservice consultant—or will
many parties collaborate?

A concept is multifaceted and involves every aspect of the operation. It can revolve around a theme that has easily identified in-your-face visual elements—a seafood theme with hanging lobster traps or a Mexican theme with cacti and oversized sombreros, for instance. However, other theme restaurants reflect a subtler approach—suggestions of a theme that give diners a feel for what they are about to get but leave a bit to their imagination. A display of fresh seafood coupled with architectural elements reminiscent of a cruise ship hint of the meal to come. Beginning in 2007, Red Lobster undertook a major redesign of their restaurants with a new look intended to evoke the Maine Coast. This change was matched with extensive television advertising in an effort to communicate to the market that Red Lobster was changing the way it operated.

The adobe walls, pottery, tiles, and courtyard fountain of a Mexican villa-style building prepare the diner for a south-of-the-border experience without screaming the message. Oversized Japanese Suiboku paintings on the wall clearly suggest an Asian food experience. These kinds of thematic references often engender a sense of realism, while the stronger reference can be perceived as pure kitsch. In many cases, theme is expressed both in the interior and on the exterior of a restaurant (Figure 1.6).

In other instances, historic recreations evoke an authen-tic sense of place. Period design can range from a turn-of-the-century hotel dining room to an Art Deco cruise ship motif to a 1950s diner. Ingenious use of design can help an unadorned modern building take on the character of another era, and genuine restoration or renovation can transform the restaurant into a kind of living museum. For example, in the restaurants at Williamsburg, Virginia, and Sturbridge Village, Massachusetts, the costumed waitstaff, original 18th- and early 19th-century architecture, and authentic period cuisine transport customers back to colonial times.

Strong themes have become the core concept for many chain restaurants. Hard Rock Cafe depends heavily on celebrity memorabilia to create its sense of theme. The entertainment concept of the Rainforest Cafe is supported with "boulder"-lined walkways, tropical flora, and periodic visits by animatronic creatures from the wild.

Concept can also revolve around a nontheme—an idea, an image, a shape, a pattern, an architectural style, or a central element that pulls together the concept. In Manhattan's classic Four Seasons restaurant, designed by Philip Johnson in 1959, the modern architectural backdrop of the Seagram building, designed by Mies van der Rohe, influenced every aspect of Johnson's cool, clean, timeless interior design scheme.

In many popular restaurants, the concept combines a food idea with a design idea. Pick a patriotic name and theme, and it makes good sense to roll out a menu that incorporates regional American cuisine. Similarly, a restau-rant called Catch of the Day creates the expectation of a seafood restaurant—although if it sits next to Fenway Park in Boston, the name could imply an after-the-game menu.

Sometimes the food concept is dominant, and design functions as a backdrop for the chef's art. These establish-ments utilize such devices as partially open kitchens to allow patrons a view of the cooking process. Dining rooms are often designed in neutral palettes that permit the plate presentation to be the main attraction.

Exterior architecture often becomes an integral compo-nent of the concept itself. Historically, elements such as Dairy Queen's gambrel roof, Howard Johnson's orange roof, and the ubiquitous golden arches of McDonald's exemplify architec-ture as a symbol of the restaurant. Vernacular roadside archi-tecture literally portrays the concept (Figures 1.7 and 1.8).

Exterior architecture often becomes an integral component of the concept itself. Historically, elements such as Dairy Queen's gambrel roof, Howard Johnson's orange roof, and the ubiq-uitous golden arches of McDonald's exemplify architecture as a symbol of the restaurant.

Figure 1.6
Theme is critical to Bembos in Peru, designed by José Orrego Herrera, where the exterior expresses the bright colors and high energy found in the interior.
(José Orrego Herrera)

Figure 1.7
This Rainforest Café exterior suggests that a different kind of experience awaits inside.
(Photo by Joseph Durocher)

Figure 1.8
The exterior of the Hilltop Steakhouse, in Saugus, Massachusetts, with its faux gambrel barn roof and its seven-story Hilltop Steakhouse sign, is a form of vernacular architecture.
(Photo by Joseph Durocher)

THE MENU

Menu planning is integral to restaurant development. Some chefs and owners feel that the entire operation should revolve around the menu. However, all too often the menu is not planned in advance of the concept and the design. In fact, the chef is frequently brought on board long after construction is under way. The chef's input can improve both front- and back-of-the-house design; likewise, his or her absence can lead to subsequent problems.

It also helps if various members of the design team know something about menu planning. The first fact to consider is that, ultimately, diners mandate what stays on the menu, regardless of restaurant type. Owners, chefs, and foodservice consultants may have a penchant for certain types of foods, but if they do not tailor their preferences to customer demand, the restaurant may soon be out of business. Restaurateurs who believe that they are in the business of educating customers about cuisine will find themselves fighting a long uphill battle. This is why operators often change at least 50 percent of the menu within the first six months of operation and why selecting equipment that affords flexibility in menu planning is important.

Unquestionably, menu offerings affect consumer behavior and affect the decision of whether to eat at or return to a particular restaurant. Menu changes, albeit costly, can become necessary for many reasons. The menu may not conform to the production or service capabilities of the facility. A health-conscious clientele might place an overwhelming demand on the one overworked steamer that cooks seafood and vegetables, while several fryers sit unused. Regardless of the reason, a change of menu—and, hence, of kitchen or front-of-the-house design—should always be factored in as a possibility during the planning process.

Food may not be what brings people to a restaurant the first time. The lure might be an eye-catching exterior design, a great media review, or a word-of-mouth recommendation. However, food is, in large measure, what keeps people coming back—and anything that can be done to improve customer perception of that food is important. Diners want hot food hot and cold food cold, for example. Anything that gets in the way of this basic goal will lose customers. Servers prancing through the room with uncovered plates of artfully arranged foods may be a great merchandising technique, but it will backfire if the food isn't hot when it arrives at the table.

THE SPEED OF SERVICE

Speed of service and turnover rate are closely allied. Quick-service operations have the highest turnover rate—that is, guests occupy a seat for the shortest time. Tables should turn over every 15 to 20 minutes in quick-service restaurants. In cafeteria operations, customers take more time to get their food and the turnover rate is a bit slower: 15 to 30 minutes. The full-service dining experience, particularly in expensive restaurants where multiple courses are cooked to order, is the lengthiest; customers wait the longest for their food and spend the most time eating it. Turnover can range from about 30 minutes in a roadside diner to 4 hours in a gourmet establishment.

The amount of time a customer spends in a restaurant—both in getting food and in eating it—has design implications for both the front and back of the house. If customers are expected to dine on gourmet fare for an hour or more, then comfortable seating, such as upholstered armchairs, and an à la carte kitchen are in order. Conversely, if faster turnover is desired, then hard-surfaced chairs will help move guests out of the dining space as quickly as possible. Furthermore, the kitchen must be laid out, staffed, and fitted with equipment that speeds the preparation and service of food to the guests.

The type of point-of-sale (POS) system can markedly affect a restaurant's turnover rate. With today's POS systems, the ordering process and payment should be streamlined. Order-entry stations located throughout the dining area enable servers to place an order without traveling to the kitchen. Handheld order-entry pads coupled with credit card swipe and printer units can increase turnover rates even more. If the handhelds are linked to the table management system along with bar and kitchen printers and are part of a two-way communication system, speed of service is maximized. With kitchen printers, the entries are significantly easier for the kitchen staff to read—which, in turn, shortens the time it takes to prepare an order and decreases the chances of mistakes.

With the most sophisticated POS systems, pop-up menus mandate servers to include all the information needed to complete an order, like the degree of doneness, choice of accompanying side dishes, or the type of salad dressing.

Some restaurateurs have even placed order-entry units in the hands of guests. As the cost of these decentralized systems drops, more restaurateurs will incorporate them into their restaurants when high turnover rates are desired, thus increasing space in the front of the house.

Speed of service is too often overlooked in the planning process. In one case, a group of owners, new to the restaurant business, approached the development of their pro forma statement without considering speed of service. They began with the following information:

Menu: continental
Style of service: leisurely plate and cart service
Number of seats: 235
Lunch turns: two per day
Dinner turns: five per day

Based on their projected fixed expenses, the owners determined that they would need $74,000 per day in revenues. To achieve this, they calculated a per-check average by dividing the total daily sales by the total number of customers served:

$$\frac{\$74,000 \ \text{required daily revenues}}{\#\ \text{of lunch covers} + \#\ \text{of dinner covers}}$$

The resulting $45 check average was considered appropriate for this type of operation, and thus the project proceeded.

Neglecting to consider speed of service caused grave problems, however, because the restaurant could not meet the projected turnover rates and provide the leisurely dining experience expected with a $45 check average. In other words, to meet the projected turnover rates, either the tables would have to be turned in less than an hour, or the total serving time for lunches would have to stretch over 4 hours and for dinners, over 10 hours. Management had failed to recognize the amount of dining time necessary in this type of establishment.

THE PER-CUSTOMER CHECK AVERAGE

It is essential to consider the check average in concert with the other elements that contribute to the design concept. Here are two questions that need to be addressed:

1. Will a low check average dictate more turnover and thus a sturdy, low-maintenance design?

Low-priced menus usually lead to higher customer counts, creating the need for fast turnover. However, this must be considered in the context of the market. For example, an inexpensive quick-service operation might work nicely when located next to an industrial park where employees from various companies take half-hour lunch breaks that stretch over a two-and-a-half-hour lunch period. But if the quick-service restaurant sits next to a single manufacturing plant where the production line shuts down completely and everyone gets one hour for lunch, the chance of realizing multiple turns is minimal.

Where multiple turns are forecasted, durable, low-maintenance design makes sense because of the potentially higher volume of business. Where only one turn is projected, a low-cost design package is critical because the revenue stream cannot support a high-capital budget.

2. Is the cost of capital low enough to cost justify the high design costs associated with high check averages?

When the cost of capital is low, it is easier to cost justify building a large, upscale restaurant with more expensive menu items. Low capital costs also make it possible to upgrade the design without having to increase check averages.

The cost of the meal carries with it design expectations in the mind of the customer. People don't expect a $4.50 meal tab in a luxurious environment replete with rich materials, nor do they expect to pay dearly for fine cuisine in a room that looks like a 1950s diner. Check average and speed of service must be carefully monitored and matched for successful results.

THE GENERAL AMBIENCE

Before arriving at specific design solutions, define the type of atmosphere desired for a given restaurant. How should the customer feel in the space? Energized, ebullient, ready to eat and move on? Relaxed, at ease, comfortable enough to linger for hours? Stimulated? Cheerful? Nostalgic? Serene? Pampered? Protected? On display?

Obviously, different types of restaurants evoke different types of feelings. The feeling of dining in a homey neighborhood coffee shop differs from the feeling of dining in a high-designed corporate cafeteria, a gourmet establishment, or a theatrical grand café. These feelings are a function not only of food and service but also of interior design and architecture.

THE MANAGEMENT PHILOSOPHY

Management philosophy helps dictate design philosophy. In the case of the chain restaurant, for instance, the philosophy of corporate-level management is to maximize profits for the shareholders, who are looking forward to the next quarterly report. However, as reported in the article "To Woo Europeans, McDonald's Takes an Upscale Turn," by Julia Werdigier, in the August 21, 2007, issue of the *New York Times*:

Sophisticated? McDonald's?

The Golden Arches are going upscale. Aiming to create a more relaxed experience in a sophisticated atmosphere, McDonald's is replacing bolted-down, plastic, yellow and white furniture with lime-green designer chairs and dark leather upholstery. It is the restaurant chain's biggest revamp in more than 20 years and, together with its franchisees, it plans to spend more than 600 million euros, or $828 million, remodeling 1,280 of its European restaurants by the end of this year.

. . . The changes are paying off. In the first half of this year, combined sales at Europe's 6,400 restaurants rose 15 percent to $4.1 billion, compared with a 6 percent increase in America, where McDonald's has 13,800 restaurants, and sales totaled $3.9 billion.

Design updates can clearly impact sales even in the largest chain operations where design updates to all of the restaurants in a region can approach a billion dollars. Because of this, chain restaurants tend to be pragmatic, derivative, and safe in making a redesign decision. System-wide design updates are often delayed as the cost of renovation and lost sales during renovation on hundreds or thousands of restaurants can reflect negatively on the corporate balance sheet. On the other hand, the entrepreneur looking to attract a young, sophisticated clientele may take a chance on innovative design and architecture. Restaurateurs looking for the long-term growth of their business may invest most on design in the hopes of creating a classic design statement "with legs."

For some owners, the throwaway restaurant is appealing. These are people looking to get into the business for a minimal investment, reap the revenues that often accompany a newly opened restaurant, then get out before the bottom line crashes. They then take their money and invest it in a continuing series of new, short-lived restaurants.

THE BUDGET

The budget is nearly always a limiting factor in the design of a restaurant. A big design budget is only as big as the market will bear, and not even the best-financed project can afford wasted design dollars. However, adherence to a tight budget means little if the dining room looks tired and worn after two weeks of operation or if management can't afford proper maintenance procedures.

Budgetary planning has inherent contradictions. Every owner wants to stretch design dollars as far as possible and not go broke before opening day. A restaurant is, after all, a business. However, modern consumers, many with a mind-set hungry for new visual experiences, increasingly view design as part of the value equation that they expect from restaurants.

The main problem with budgeting is that design is expensive. Further, good architecture takes time, and time is money. Of course, design is a relatively unimportant backdrop for food and service in some successful restaurants, and the charm of other totally undesigned bistros stems from their visual chaos. Such successes, however, are rare. Even simple interiors and rooms that appear to reflect time-worn patinas have often been designed—for a fee. Likewise, kitchen design is no free lunch, but back-of-the-house design investments can buy a layout that increases productivity and efficiency and returns more to the bottom line.

The costs of front- and back-of-the-house design vary wildly with location, type of restaurant, intended life span, and other factors. Basically, the owner pays for both goods and for services. Goods translate into furniture, fixtures, and equipment (FF&E). Services include fees for the schematic design concept, as presented in floorplans, elevations, renderings, and other architectural plans. Services also include the writing of FF&E specifications but not necessarily purchasing. Some design firms prefer to remain purely service oriented and leave the procurement and installation process to purchasing agents.

There is no uniform method of charging for design services. The design firm's fee may be based on square-foot costs, a percentage of total project costs, a consulting fee at hourly rates, or other methods. Many variables influence fee structures but, as a rule of thumb, most firms charge a fixed fee based on the scope of the job and on the total project cost.

There is no uniform method of charging for design services. The design firm's fee may be based on square-foot costs, a percentage of total project costs, a consulting fee at hourly rates, or other methods.

Some firms that provide purchasing services charge a percentage markup based on FF&E prices. Owners should beware of design thrown in "free" by equipment or purchasing houses whose profit comes from markups. The motivation may be to overequip the space in an effort to increase the markup profits.

Budget planning must begin in the early stages of the design process. The owner should develop an initial budget as a guide and agree on a final budget before any design contract is finalized. As the project progresses, the budget must be carefully monitored. Projects always have hidden costs, and renovation often presents more expensive surprises than new construction. In truth, any number of factors may drive up the costs of one or more elements of the construction budget, so contingency dollars should be built in.

A crucial aspect of budgetary control is how design dollars are allocated. Adding one dramatic design treatment in an otherwise simple room, for example, can elevate an ordinary interior to something special. However, other design elements may hike the design budget considerably but have little impact on customers.

The best practice is to invest money where one gets the biggest bang for the buck and to spend the most on items that customers come in contact with. Good design doesn't always mean expensive design, but fine furniture and finishes cost money. Applications like faux finishes can help control costs but, in an upscale restaurant, it is advisable to mix faux with fine finishes to create a balance. Sometimes it costs less to hire a muralist or furniture maker to create custom applications than it does to purchase fine art or furniture.

A good designer knows how to prioritize and how to take from one area and give to another in order to adhere to the total FF&E budget. If surprises raise costs so high that the budget needs to be adjusted, the designer should inform the owner immediately. There's no excuse for running out of money midway through a project.

EXPECTED RETURN ON INVESTMENT

The design and construction budget must also relate back to management's expected return on investment (ROI). Any restaurant owner hopes for the highest ROI possible, but those owned by an investment group will probably expect the highest return—frequently in excess of 20 percent of their investment per year. The independent, however, may be using funds from noninstitutional sources so their expectations of ROI could be quite lower. If a restaurant is owner-operated with family pitching in on the labor front, they may forego salaries for a period to help the profitability of the operation.

Another factor in ROI can best be seen in a multiconcept chain. In some cases, earnings from one unit or concept within a chain can be used as seed money to launch another restaurant within the same chain or a new concept. Such an approach is most appropriate to privately held restaurant companies, although it is used in some publicly traded companies.

CONSTRUCTION MARKET

Construction costs have risen steadily over the past decade, and there can be rapid rises in costs for certain materials when natural disasters occur, like Hurricane Katrina that struck in 2005. Labor and cost of materials are the two major contributors to restaurant construction project costs. Figure 1.9 tracks the Producer Price Index (PPI) for Materials and Components for Construction and shows that prices for all construction products: wood, concrete, steel—began a sharp rise in 2003. In times where prices rise quickly, it is important to add inflation factors into the construction budget estimates. The real estate downturn in the middle of the last decade significantly curtailed residential construction; however, commercial construction did not really feel the downturn until late in the last decade as measured by the Work-on-the-Boards Index published monthly in *AIArchitect*.

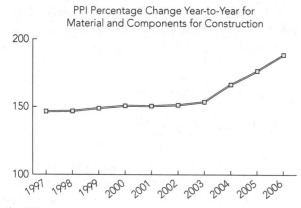

PPI Percentage Change Year-to-Year for
Material and Components for Construction

About PPI
The PPI-Producer Price Index is published monthly by the US Bureau of Labor Statistics. A base of 100 was set in May of 1982. In 2003 this price index began a rapid climb.

Source: http://data.bls.gov/cgi-bin/surveymost?pc

Figure 1.9
An upswing in the Producer Price Index can, if not considered, lead to budget overruns for a project with a long lead time. Interim price spikes in material can arise from other than economic conditions (e.g., weather, earthquake).

Another factor that influences construction costs is based on where the restaurant will be built. The initial cost is the land or space rental. A second cost consideration is the variance in labor costs in different areas of the country. The *RS Means Building Construction Cost Data* publication that is updated yearly offers excellent insights into the relative difference in construction costs in various parts of the United States. Unit and square foot costs are also given so that accurate estimates can be made for a construction project.

THE SYSTEMS APPROACH

MARKET SEGMENTS VERSUS SERVICE SYSTEMS

How will the customers be served? Will guests help themselves at buffets, queue up as in a quick-service line, or be served at the table on individual plates or platters of food?

Will a combination of service styles be offered such that guests help themselves to some items while servers deliver others? The answers to these questions dictate specific spatial considerations in the design plan.

For example, full-service restaurants can have many styles of service: plate, platter, cart, buffet, or any combination of the four. Plate service, in which food is plated in the kitchen and then passed over to a waitperson who serves finished plates to the guest, requires the least amount of tabletop and dining room floor space. Platter service, in which food is assembled on platters and frenched (served onto a waiting dinner plate in front of the diner) requires larger tables and more floor space so that the server can manipulate the platter between the guests.

Cart service requires the most space, as the guéridons (service carts) must be moved around the dining room and kept at a safe distance from tables when flambé cooking takes place. When buffets are integrated in a tableservice restaurant, space for the buffet, circulation paths to and from the buffet, and space so that staff can restock the buffet must be considered.

Restaurants can be classified in many ways. Historically, classifications are based on check average, theme, type of cuisine, or market segment. Segmentation by market (Table 1.1) and food category (Table 1.2) are the most commonly used classifications in the foodservice industry.

But, from a design perspective, the market segment called hospitals is not at all descriptive and is only marginally helpful in the concept development. All hospitals feed patients in their room and probably have a cafeteria for the employees. But the similarities may end there.

A single hospital could also include an à la carte restaurant in space that is leased out; a quick-service court also in leased space or in a series of "outlets" run by the hospital foodservice; a buffet in the cafeteria; machine feeding for 24/7 availability; and even banquet facilities that double as in-service training space during the day.

Similarly, elementary school foodservice could consist of the standard straight-line cafeteria, a scatter system of individual food stations where students help themselves, or a quick-service system such as McDonald's. Each of these types has different design implications, and the term *elementary school foodservice* does not give a clear picture of the operation.

Using the service system classification, the designer can accurately identify styles of service and types of food delivery systems. If, in the preceding example, the school board

TABLE 1.1 MARKET SEGMENTS AND THEIR COMMON SERVICE SYSTEMS

• Full-service restaurants	À la carte, family style, tableside, buffet, takeout, delivery
• Quick-service restaurants (fast food)	Fast food, takeout, delivery, drive-through, buffet, satellite
• Fast-casual restaurants	À la carte, fast food, takeout, delivery, buffet, satellite
• Elementary and secondary schools	Fast food, buffet, cafeteria, satellite
• Employee feeding	À la carte, fast food, takeout, banquet, buffet, cafeteria, satellite
• Hospitals	À la carte, fast food, takeout, banquet, buffet, cafeteria, tray, machine, satellite
• Hotels and motels	À la carte, family style, table service, fast food, banquet, buffet, tray, satellite
• Colleges and universities	À la carte, fast food, banquet, buffet, cafeteria, machine, satellite
• Military	À la carte, family style, fast food, takeout, buffet, cafeteria, machine, satellite
• Recreation facilities	Fast food, takeout, cafeteria, machine
• Convenience and grocery stores	Takeout, buffet, satellite
• Nursing homes	Cafeteria, tray, machine, satellite
• Transportation	À la carte, fast food, tray, satellite
• Retail stores	À la carte, fast food

TABLE 1.2 FOOD CATEGORIES

- Asian
- Chicken
- French
- Italian
- Latin American
- Mexican
- Middle Eastern
- Pizza
- Sandwich
- Seafood
- Steakhouse
- All other food categories

calls in a designer and says, "We want to put a foodservice operation in our new elementary school," then the designer has little insight into the characteristics of the design. If, however, the board says, "We want a quick-service operation featuring healthy fast food in our new elementary school," the designer has a well-established frame of reference to help determine which type of food delivery system is optimal. Similarly, the designer doesn't have much to go on if a restaurateur says, "I want to open a steakhouse."

The designer knows more if the restaurateur says, "I want to open an à la carte service restaurant with a steakhouse menu, salads prepared at tableside, and a buffet-style dessert bar."

So it is the service systems (Table 1.3) that truly shape the design of a restaurant or other foodservice operation.

Describing a foodservice operation using a process-oriented approach can be more appropriate in the concept development of a restaurant than building the concept solely on a market of food category.

The term *service system* is loosely defined as the means by which food is prepared and delivered to the customer. At times, a foodservice operation combines more than one service system. This is called a complex service system. Each of these service systems needs its own set of subsystems to back it up. Subsystems include such functions as purchasing, fabrication, preparation, and assembly, to name a few. The functions performed and the layout of the subsystems vary with the type of service system or systems in a particular operation.

A general description of each service system appears below. While the variations to each may further inform the concept, the service systems will have the greatest impact on the final design. An understanding of each of the service systems is important because subsystem design flows from them.

TABLE 1.3 SERVICE SYSTEMS

Service Systems

- À la carte
- Family style
- Tableside
- Quick service (fast food)
- Takeout
- Delivery
- Drive-through
- Banquet
- Buffet
- Cafeteria
- Tray
- Machine
- Satellite system
- All other service systems

À la Carte

In à la carte service, a waitperson takes orders from individual customers and presents them to the chef for preparation. For the most part, the preparation is done to order and, in every case, the food is plated specifically for a particular customer. À la carte service is frequently found in upscale restaurants, executive dining rooms, hotels, coffee shops, and other full-service operations. (It is sometimes referred to as table service, which does not convey information adequate to developing an effective design scheme.)

In the kitchen, high heat and quick-cooking equipment—like charbroilers and flattop ranges—are needed to support the cooking of sautéed, broiled, or fried individual portions of food. In addition, a steam table is needed to hold foods and sauces prepared in bulk.

Tableside

The key element in tableside service is the preparation or assembly of foods at tableside on a guéridon (cart). Raw or partially cooked food ingredients are brought to tableside where they are finished, plated, and served. Most often, tableside service combines with à la carte service, with one or two special tableside menu items, such as a Caesar salad or a flaming dessert, actually being prepared at tableside. A rechaud or butane burner is needed to cook or warm

items at tableside. Tableside service was a key service style in such venerable restaurants as Lutèce and La Côte Basque in New York City, and while many restaurants have moved away from this style, it is still a stalwart for operators who aspire to classic French haute cuisine.

Tableside in a dining room with multiple levels will not work as smoothly as one on a single level because it limits the movement of carts. The ventilation system must also be sufficiently upsized to remove the extra smoke and smells of tableside cooking. The timely coordination of foods coming from the à la carte stations of the kitchen and the tableside preparations must be timed perfectly.

One of the keys to successful tableside service is to measure and assemble all of the ingredients before they are taken to the dining room. This *mise en place* ("everything in its place") requires additional refrigerated storage space in the kitchen.

Quick Service

Customers queue up in either a number of lines or one serpentine line to place their orders. Typically, the counter worker takes the order, assembles the food, and receives the payment. This style of service is further characterized by speedy food delivery and the use of disposables. Chain and independent restaurants, elementary and secondary schools, employee feeding, hospitals, colleges and universities, the military, and recreational facilities are common market segments that include quick-service systems.

Most fast feeders batch-prepare foods. Warming equipment that maintains the quality of the prepared foods plays an important role in the kitchen. Many items are partially prepared and then custom finished when ordered. Freezer storage is critical, along with oversized dry storage to hold large supplies of disposables. Dumpster space is essential to hold the large volume of trash generated.

The front of the house needs enough space for customers to queue up and place their orders. Behind the order counter, space needs vary. In some cases, the order taker must handle cash as well as assemble orders. In other restaurants, different people handle cash and order assembly. In some, 80 percent of the sales will be made at drive-through windows.

The fast-casual is an upscale twist on traditional quick service. In many fast-casual operations, the ingredients are prepared fresh daily, so there is greater reliance on refrigerated rather than freezer space. Also, items are frequently prepared to order rather than being assembled ahead of time. Examples of this can be found in Mexican restaurants such as Moe's Southwest Grill and Chipotle, where each item is prepared individually to the customer's specifications. In these operations, the precooked or presliced ingredients are held in a steam table or refrigerated pans. The counter person draws portions for assembly, while the customers walk along the queue watching the items being made.

BANQUET

Banquet-style service typically involves a predetermined menu that is usually prepared and plated en masse. Payment for the meal is arranged in advance. In some instances, the starter course may be preset on the tables. Banquet service is offered through the catering departments of full-service restaurants, noncommercial feeders, and hotels as well as in catering facilities.

Bulk food production equipment is typically found in a banquet kitchen. This type of kitchen can benefit from mechanized equipment used to pre-prepare foods. Walk-in refrigeration is important to hold raw foods and plated foods that are ready for service. Heated holding equipment is required for holding plated hot foods. In large banquet operations, heated carts are positioned around the banquet serving area before the course is served in order to speed service. Warewashing equipment dedicated solely to banquet operations is frequently incorporated into complex foodservice operations.

FAMILY STYLE

Food is brought to the table on platters, which are placed directly on the table for self-service. This style is seen in full-service establishments. Chinese restaurants, in particular, favor family-style service. Designers find that extra tabletop space is needed to hold the multiple dishes involved. Family-style service is also seen in some hotels, where plates of food are placed in the center of a banquet table, allowing customers to rotate the lazy Susan to make their choices.

Heaping platters of nachos and wooden schooners bedecked with sushi are also examples of family-style serving vessels. The theater of these offerings can be a great merchandiser, but extra space on the tabletop is essential.

BUFFET

Buffets depend on holding stations where diners or servers choose from the displayed items. In some cases, servers may assist in the portioning for control reasons. Buffets can be a straight line or scramble configuration. In the straight line, customers proceed in a logical flow from the beginning to the end of the line. In the scramble system, customers approach the buffet at random points. Hotel restaurants, especially for Sunday brunch, salad bars in full-service restaurants and noncommercial dining facilities, and sandwich stations in college cafeterias are some examples of where buffets are used.

Some buffets incorporate stations where foods are prepared to order or in small batches. This approach usually requires special cooking equipment—for example, butane gas burners, an alcohol-fired rechaud, or an induction cooktop.

TAKEOUT

Takeout service relies on heat stable and leakproof disposable packaging. Food is either batch-prepared and then packaged, or prepared to order and packaged as it comes off the fire. Food may be packaged in a partially cooked or raw state for completion at home. That usually means cooking in a microwave oven, although an increasing number of disposables are intended for heating in a conventional oven.

Seating is not required for takeout, but sufficient space is needed for customers to wait for their food. Takeout service is an integral part of many quick-service restaurants—be it counter or drive-through—and represents most of the food sales in the convenience and grocery store market segment. In some places, reach-in refrigerators that hold bottled and canned drinks add to the check average, as do snack items, which are displayed for impulse purchasing near the POS.

Boston Market was an early and successful home meal replacement (HMR) operator. It offered customers comfort food like rotisserie chicken, turkey, and meatloaf accompanied by well-displayed side dishes and cornbread before the market term *fast-casual* was in vogue. Hot foods were typically batch-prepared and displayed in a steam table.

Some HMR operations offer packaged meals displayed in refrigerated cases (Figure 1.10). To maximize sales, HMR outlets may also offer desserts, beverages, and appetizers to

Figure 1.10
HMR depends on visual appeal to sell food. Here, the deli display cases help merchandise pre-prepared foods.
(Photo by Joseph Durocher)

accompany a main course. Over the past decade, much of the HMR market has been captured by grocery stores. HMR needs a high volume of traffic to be profitable. With an increase in dual-income families and longer working days for managers and executives, HMR warrants consideration in future restaurant designs.

HMR needs a high volume of traffic to be profitable. With an increase in dual-income families and longer working days for managers and executives, HMR warrants consideration in future restaurant designs.

DELIVERY

Delivery service relies heavily on telephone orders, with an increasing number of restaurateurs accepting delivery orders via the Internet. Prepared food is delivered to customers via bicycle in urban areas and motor vehicle in suburban areas. The success of delivery systems depends on population density sufficient to warrant the transportation costs. Delivery service systems are typically matched with takeout systems in a chairless storefront operation and combined with tray service in hospitals, hotels, and nursing homes. Sturdy, leakproof, insulated packaging is important to delivery operations, as is heat-retention equipment that works well with the chosen delivery vehicle.

Sturdy, leakproof, insulated packaging is important to delivery operations, as is heat-retention equipment that works well with the chosen delivery vehicle.

From a design perspective, the restaurant must have a comprehensive telephone ordering system that maintains customers' files. With the help of caller ID, a customer's past purchase records, address, and phone number are displayed when the order taker begins processing the order. The optimal system allows customers to charge their orders, thus eliminating the need for delivery persons to carry large amounts of cash. On the production side, menu items must be quick to prepare, and the cooking equipment must be capable of cooking foods rapidly and consistently, with little attention from the kitchen staff.

CAFETERIA

Pure cafeteria service differs from buffet service in that customers select foods that are portioned by counter staff. In some cases, the foods are portioned and displayed for pickup; in others, such as with hot foods, the items are portioned by a server as requested. Diners assemble food and utensils on a tray. Cafeteria flow is generally cold items first, hot food items second, and beverages last. Whether the layout is a straight line or a scramble system, this type of service is the backbone of noncommercial foodservice and is often combined with a buffet-style salad bar.

Cafeterias work most effectively with a high volume of traffic. In the kitchen, volume production and holding equipment is necessary. Cafeteria operations frequently feature lower-priced food items in sauces, so equipment such as tilting fry kettles, steam-jacketed kettles, and deck ovens are often found in cafeteria kitchens. In the front of the house, the steam table and warming cabinets are essential design elements.

TRAY SERVICE

Tray service involves the delivery of preordered, fully assembled meals. Temperature maintenance systems are often incorporated with the tray or delivery cart in order to keep hot foods at proper serving temperatures from the time of assembly to the time of service. In other cases, hot foods are rethermalized just prior to service. This style of service is employed in hospitals, hotels, nursing homes, and airliners.

Hospitals, nursing homes, and some flights are typically supported with tray service provided by a high-volume kitchen fitted with equipment capable of preparing foods in large batches. Tray assembly areas take up a great deal of space in such operations, and more floor space is needed to store carts and extra trayware. In hotels, tray-service food is prepared to order in the hotel restaurant or room service kitchen and delivered to each guest's room. In any tray-service operation, space is needed to hold carts in between meal periods, and easy access to elevators or delivery docks is essential.

MACHINE SERVICE

Machine service refers to coin- or mag-stripe-operated vending, in which a limited assortment of preportioned or mechanically portioned food or beverages can be obtained at any time. Staffing is required only to fill and clean the machines.

Equipment and product security are important design concerns for this type of operation. If a dining area is provided, it must incorporate low maintenance, highly durable tables and chairs, and dispensers for napkins, plasticware, and condiments. This type of service is a must in 24/7 operations such as health care and colleges and universities.

SATELLITE SYSTEM

In a satellite system, foods are prepared in bulk at one kitchen (called a commissary), then transported to finishing kitchens and assembled for service at those sites. This style of service is most commonly found in schools and health care facilities, although such operations as Domino's Pizza prepare rounds of dough in a commissary, truck it to satellite stores, and turn it into pizza there. Dunkin Donuts has also gone to a commissary style of operation for their pastry and sandwich offerings. In addition, some full-service restaurants with many points of sale utilize satellite systems for some or all of their items because of the economies and control available through a commissary kitchen.

Volume production equipment is required in the production areas of a satellite operation. If foods are to be transported chilled, special tumble chillers or blast chillers are needed to quickly cool cooked foods. Walk-in refrigerated space is essential for holding foods ready for distribution. Transportation equipment, whether to in-house service points or distant points, must be considered as an integral part of the overall system design.

THE KEY RESTAURANT BUILDING BLOCKS: SUBSYSTEMS

Each of the service systems just discussed is supported by numerous subsystems. One way to picture the process is to think of the service system as a wheel and the subsystems as its spokes (Figure 1.11). Every service system includes its own unique set of subsystems. The layout and design of each of these subsystems relates to the chosen system or systems

Figure 1.11
The subsystem wheel depicts each of the functional areas needed to support any type of service system.

found in the restaurant. To further define the restaurant concept, it is important to identify the needed subsystems before the project moves forward to the design phase.

PURCHASING AND RECEIVING

The nature of purchasing and receiving food affects restaurant layout. Numerous factors must be considered before arriving at spatial allocations for receiving areas. Here are some questions to consider:

1. Will the food be purchased from many suppliers, all of which require time at a loading dock, or primarily through a one-stop-shopping distributor?

Delivery space can be minimized when the majority of products are purchased from a single vendor. With multiple vendors, a small loading dock can become a choke point during delivery time. For large operations, a raised loading dock—ideally, fitted with a height-adjustable loading ramp—can speed the delivery of large loads if they are delivered by vehicles with high tailgates. Investigate the type of delivery trucks used by local vendors for guidance in designing the loading dock and access area. Deliveries made by 18-wheelers require far more maneuvering space than those made in a panel truck.

2. Will purchases arrive as individual cases or on a pallet?

In some large-volume operations, pallets move directly from the receiving dock to the production areas, with no intermediate stop in the storeroom. An adjustable loading ramp or lift is essential when foods arrive on pallets. In smaller restaurants, foods arriving in single cases typically are moved to a storage area accessible to the receiving area and kitchen.

3. Will food and supplies be purchased and stored in a company warehouse?

Many chain restaurants coordinate purchasing functions through a central purchasing office. If the "purchased" food and supplies come from a company warehouse, the space needed for the purchasing and receiving functions can be minimized. If the warehouse makes deliveries to units each day, the amount of required storage space can also be minimized.

4. Will purchases be made online or will distributor sales representatives (DSRs) visit the operation to take orders?

Online purchasing requires access to the Internet and a secured area for computer equipment. If DSRs drop by to take orders, the purchasing manager must have space in which to meet with them. The purchasing area should include space to maintain records on purchases and store samples of the tableware, flatware, and glassware used in the various service areas.

STORAGE

In order to design successful storage subsystems, the designer must understand the frequency of deliveries and the issuing policy of the restaurant: location, size, and type of storage spaces as well as their access requirements flow from this information. If deliveries arrive daily, the storage spaces can be significantly smaller than if deliveries arrive weekly. The volume of business also has a direct impact on the amount of space needed for storage.

Another consideration is the relative mix of dry goods, refrigerated foods, and frozen foods. Some types of operations use far more canned goods than others. Some may rely heavily on fresh foods, with little use of canned or frozen. All of these decisions have design implications. Here are additional questions to consider:

1. Will cooks work from open storage?

From a design perspective, it is essential that the open storage adjoin the production areas so that cooks need not waste time moving between spaces. Security is a major concern with open storerooms, so entrances to storage areas should not open onto the back loading dock or be located close to employee locker rooms if they are provided.

2. Will cooks have a par stock of some ingredients issued to their work areas, with special items drawn as needed from the storage areas?

This type of policy ensures that a par level of items like spices, salt, sugar, and other commonly used ingredients is maintained at the point of use in the kitchen. Expensive ingredients, or ingredients used for a particular preparation, are drawn from a controlled storage space.

3. Will a storeroom manager assemble the primary ingredients for the cooks?

This policy keeps the cooks out of the storage areas except when they pick up a cart loaded with ingredients for a particular meal. In such cases, the primary storage areas need not adjoin the preparation areas.

4. Does the potential exist for exterior walk-in refrigeration?

Walk-in refrigerators and freezers, when equipped with adequate locking equipment, are secure spaces that need not be located inside the restaurant building. When fitted with a weather cap, these exterior refrigerated spaces can help to minimize building costs. In some cases, a walk-in can be positioned so that its access door connects through an exterior wall of the restaurant.

5. Will deliveries arrive at times when the restaurant is not staffed?

If the answer is yes, a receiving space with an exterior and interior access door will allow deliveries to be made securely. This space needs to be planned at the same time as the receiving area. If an exterior walk-in is available, it can be fitted with an exterior door and a cage to allow for off-hour deliveries.

FABRICATION

This subsystem includes those areas where food is first handled, or placed into process, prior to the pre-preparation stage. In classical kitchens, before the advent of preportioned meats, fish, and poultry, fabrication areas were commonly used to break down primal cuts of meat; in effect, the kitchen included a butcher shop.

Fabrication areas have become particularly important for large operations located in high-rise buildings. Follow the delivery of lettuce as an example:

Several cases of lettuce are delivered to a ground-floor loading dock. The lettuce is then moved to a ground-floor fabrication area, where the heads are unpacked, washed, and stored in large plastic containers for subsequent distribution to upper-level preparation areas. Without the fabrication subsystem, the cases of lettuce would be delivered upstairs for handling, then the empty cartons and wrapper leaves sent back to the ground floor for disposal. The fabrication area helps streamline the process and cut back on vertical transportation costs. Here are some questions to ask:

1. What items will be fabricated on site?

In many cases, fabrication is limited to protein items. Regional chains can create signature cuts used by all units by moving the fabrication function to a central commissary. However, filleting whole fish close to the time of service is still one of the best ways to ensure highest quality.

2. Will a separate fabrication area be needed, or will the function be performed in the same space used for pre-preparation?

If the spaces are to be shared, most of the fabrication will have to be done during third-shift hours when the preparation crew is not working.

Cutting strip loins and other wholesale cuts into steaks in a display fabrication area is an integral part of the merchandising process in some steakhouses. In other restaurants, a glass-walled refrigerated room allows diners to view the meat-grinding and burger-forming process; passersby can view thousands of pounds of rib roasts and strip loins in an aging refrigerator through a window that opens onto the street.

PRE-PREPARATION

In the pre-preparation subsystem, foods are made ready for the final phase of preparation. For example, pre-preparation may include breaking the lettuce into salad-sized pieces and storing them in containers until ready for assembly on salad plates. Pre-preparation may be the *mise en place* work that is done for tableside flambé preparations. Pre-preparation may also include mixing, rolling out piecrusts, and assembling pot pies that are ready to go in the oven when ordered. A carefully planned pre-preparation area can speed final preparation in an à la carte kitchen and improve overall productivity in any kitchen. Before this space is designed, the answers to the following questions are needed:

1. Has enough space been allocated to prepare vegetables separately from protein foods?

Whenever possible, the sinks used to wash lettuce and vegetables should be separate from those used to defrost meat or scale fish, or in which the ice from a crate of chicken melts. The concern is cross-contamination. Salad and vegetable ingredients that are eaten raw can easily be contaminated and cause food poisoning if prepared on improperly sanitized surfaces previously used for meat, fish, or poultry.

2. Will pre-preparation be manual or mechanical?

Mechanized equipment can be cost-justified if it saves a sufficient amount of food and labor costs, or if it saves space. For example, a vertical cutter-mixer can produce hundreds of gallons of emulsified house salad dressings in one hour. The per-gallon cost for raw materials is far below that of brand-name dressings. Another example is a floor mixer that can quickly and evenly mix ingredients for meatloaf. A 30-pound batch of ingredients would take 10 to 15 minutes to mix by hand but only 60 seconds with a mixer. Additionally, the mixed ingredients can be put back under refrigeration or in the oven quickly, so there is less time for bacteria to develop than if they were prepared by hand.

3. Will pre-preparation for several kitchens or stations take place in a given area?

Centralizing the pre-preparation of numerous items can save time and space needs in the preparation areas. For example, the hot foods and bakery stations can both use the floor mixer mentioned above: hot foods with a paddle attachment for the meatloaf and the bakery would use the same machine to knead dough with a dough hook, or pie pastry with a pastry knife attachment.

PREPARATION

The preparation subsystem (also called production) involves the final cooking or assembly of food (Figure 1.12). Every kitchen has a cold-food preparation area and a hot-food preparation area. Preparation may refer to the station where the pre-prepared salad ingredients are portioned onto the salad plates or the cooking stations where the marinated ribs are broiled or the scallops are pan-fried or where ingredients are cooked in a display kitchen.

This subsystem can also extend into the dining room. A display kitchen where chefs cook and assemble dishes for service is one example. Another is the Sunday brunch setup where the chef cooks individual orders of eggs or omelets

Figure 1.12
In the Mongolian Wok station in this University cafeteria, protein ingredients are added by the staff after students assemble veggies and other mixings.
(Photo by Joseph Durocher)

on gas or induction burners. Here are but a few of the questions that must be asked when planning preparation areas:

1. What's the menu?

Nothing affects the design of preparation areas more than the menu.

2. Will any of the preparation areas be in view of customers?

The answer to this question will influence the type of equipment that should be chosen, particularly the exterior finish of the equipment. Display kitchens must also incorporate hidden garbage containers and have surfaces that are easy to clean.

3. How many preparation areas will there be?

A simple foodservice system typically includes only a cold-food and a hot-food preparation area. However, in a more complex system, one might find a bake shop, banquet preparation, takeout preparation, and more.

HOLDING

Once cooked, food items may be held awaiting service. Some foods need to be held hot, while others remain under refrigeration. Holding areas are often divided into two sections: holding for food prior to plating, and holding for plated dishes. Consider a banquet for which 400 boneless Guinea game hens are roasted. A holding cart is needed to hold the hens before they are plated. The holding cart is also used to hold the dauphine potatoes and medley of vegetables that will be plated with the hens. The sauce used as a bed under the hen must also be held. This holding cabinet is positioned at one end of the assembly line, while four carts capable of holding 100 covered plates each are positioned near the other end. In this example, the holding carts are perfectly suited to a banquet-style serving system.

Each service system requires its own custom holding configurations. These questions must be answered when planning for holding:

1. What styles of service will be employed?

As seen in the banquet scenario above, five large holding carts are needed to support a banquet for 400. For quick-service, à la carte, satellite, and other systems, different holding equipment is required.

2. What is the maximum number of meal components that need to be held at one point in time?

If the maximum number of banquet meals is 400, then five carts should be sufficient. In a quick-service burger operation, the holding areas must be sized to hold the maximum number of burgers and fries needed during peak service periods.

ASSEMBLY

Once cooked, foods need to be plated or assembled for plating. In an à la carte operation, the assembly subsystem is adjacent to the preparation and holding areas. The lobsters come out of the steamer and go directly onto the plate and out to the customer (Figure 1.13). In a cafeteria or buffet operation, many foods are prepared and delivered in bulk to the assembly area located behind the serving line, then individually plated for the diner or set up for self-service.

Here, too, it is important to identify the style of service. Banquet service requires a large area for assembly. In à la carte service, the prime menu ingredient may come off a broiler and be combined with accompaniments that were batch-prepared and held in a steam table. In this case, each meal is plated individually, so the assembly area for à la carte service will be much smaller than in the banquet operation.

SANITATION AND SAFETY

Warewashing, pot and pan washing, and interim and after-hours cleaning are part of the sanitation subsystem. Sanitation is frequently overlooked in restaurant design. Hand sinks, soap, and adequate hand drying must be easily accessible to all employees. Storage for mops, buckets, and cleaning supplies should be kept separate from food supply storage. A slop sink is essential, or floor mops will be cleaned out in the same sink used for washing greens. In addition, the decision to specify an expensive conveyor

Figure 1.13
The pickup area of the kitchen shown here, next to the assembly area, is where foods are often held under heat strips awaiting pickup by servers. The circulation in front of the pickup station affords staff the space to assemble all of the items needed to serve each course.
(Photo by Joseph Durocher)

dishwasher or a more moderately priced rack machine should be based on a careful analysis of the type of operation and the expected volume of tableware per cover.

Safety must be thought of in terms of food, employees, and physical structure. Food safety frequently intersects with sanitation. However, an increasing number of operators have upgraded security to ensure that foods are not deliberately tampered with prior to service. Employee safety addresses equipment issues and prophylactic measures that decrease the chances of physical injury. Physical structure safety includes fire detection, alarm, and suppression along with ventilation. Consider these questions:

1. How many preparation areas are planned?

At a minimum, one hand sink is needed for each work area. Don't forget that front-of-the-house staff also need a hand sink.

2. Will protein foods arrive as preportioned frozen or fresh?

Frozen items often need little or no handling before they are placed into preparation. However, fresh items frequently must be processed to get them ready for preparation. In such cases, equipment and supplies to sanitize an area are essential. Color-coded cutting boards help minimize the chance of cross-contamination when protein foods are fabricated or pre-prepared on site.

3. Will the cooking equipment be clustered in one area, or will foods be cooked in several locations throughout the restaurant?

If the cooking equipment is grouped together, then the ventilation and fire suppression configuration is quite straightforward. If several cooking areas are physically separated, the ductwork and fire suppression connections can look like a plate of spaghetti above the ceiling tiles.

ACCOUNTING

Accounting subsystems—typically comprising order entry, printers, and cash and credit control devices—must be carefully integrated with the design of the operation. The components should be chosen based on the needs of the particular restaurant operation, that is, number of seats and menu items. Too often, sophisticated and expensive accounting subsystems are specified for small restaurants that actually need a less elaborate scheme. Sometimes this equipment becomes an unsightly and noisy intrusion on the dining experience. Here are a few accounting questions to consider:

1. Which kitchen/bar stations will get order printers?

Order printers ensure that production stations receive orders as quickly as possible. They also provide an important internal control service. Designers should ensure that cabling is run from the order-entry units to the remote printers.

2. How many order-entry stations will be needed?

This information suggests the number of front-of-the-house service stations to plan for. If servers work from a cash-and-carry system, a cash drawer will be needed for the head cashier only. However, if each server is assigned a cash drawer, the system cost increases and invariably results in fewer stations.

3. Will wireless systems be used upon opening or possibly in the future?

If wireless order-entry and credit processes will or may be used, it is a good idea to run wire for the wireless antennae before the walls are closed in.

The following three sections are subsystems for the front of the house but are included here as they relate to the back of the house.

SERVICE

Service stations can be fixed or mobile. A generous number of stations that are complete service support units support the speediest and most attentive service. Stations that are a long distance from the kitchen need a more complete station than those that abut the kitchen, where backup is within a few steps. Most servers would agree that a service station that houses all of the tableware needed to reset tables for an entire shift is optimal. This requires a unit that holds the flatware, glassware, and napery for each station. Further, one that has a water supply and ice bin for filling water glasses and a hot plate for backup coffee helps service flow. Without these stations, servers have to travel back and forth from the kitchen to set and reset their tables. In addition, if a guest drops a utensil or is served a dirty utensil, the support station provides a quick replacement (Figure 1.14).

CUSTOMER SUPPORT

This ranges from the napkin and sweetener station in a takeout coffee shop to a foot-operated hand-washing stations in a rib joint. In both cases, they offer an extra level of convenience for the customer. In a donut shop, the station should include waste receptacles. Providing disposable utensils and napkins on this station in a takeout sandwich or salad operation frees counter staff from having to include such items, and new prestacked dispensers improve sanitation (Figure 1.15). Operations that offer a bottomless cup of coffee can provide a complete coffee station where customers help themselves.

In quick-service operations, the trash bins where customers deposit their waste are important support stations, as are the conveyor belts in cafeterias where diners leave their trays. The design of support stations closely follows the type of service.

Figure 1.14
A fully stocked side station can help increase turnover and improves customer satisfaction and server efficiency. This service station at Hard Rock Cafe in Chicago incorporates a sink, backup reset supplies, and an espresso machine.
(Photo by Joseph Durocher)

Restaurants that will be targeted toward families must plan for a space to store readily accessible high chairs and booster seats. Diaper-changing stations are essential in men's, women's, and unisex restrooms. Trash cans, sanitizing wipes, and hand sanitizer dispensers at a changing station are welcome additions.

SUPPORT STATIONS

In the kitchen, support stations may include all areas located near food pickup where the waitstaff obtain such items as serving trays and soup spoons. In some kitchens, preportioned salads are dressed by servers, who remove the salads from a reach-in that is filled by the kitchen staff from the back and accessed by the service staff from the front. If these functions are overlooked in the design, servers will run around the kitchen trying to find a tray—while the plated foods get cold—and then serve a teaspoon with the soup.

SUMMARY

The initial information-gathering process that must be done before the actual design phase begins is critical. A successful design begins in the planning process and integrates the front and back of the house. Careful consideration of restaurant type, the market, concept, menu, style of service,

Figure 1.15
These dispensers minimize contamination of food contact surfaces and save staff time.
(© 2007 Dixie Consumer Products LLC. The Georgia-Pacific logo and all trademarks are owned by or licensed to Dixie Consumer Products LLC.)

speed of service, per-customer check average, general ambience, management philosophy, and budget leads to the best design solutions.

Answers to the questions outlined here will provide the design team with important insights into critical operational elements that must be incorporated with the final design. Without an understanding of these operational components, both kitchen and interior design can negatively affect the functioning of the restaurant.

CHAPTER **2**

INTEGRATIVE DESIGN

The design process begins with an idea. That idea may be the dream of a mom-and-pop team to own a family-run restaurant, a chef looking to open his or her signature establishment, a team of college graduates who band together to open a restaurant themed around their favorite PlayStation 2 game characters, or a multinational chain seeking to enter a new market segment: steak, seafood, Mexican.

The design team will take those initial ideas and work to develop a workable plan from a marketing, financial, service, architectural, and design perspective. It is at this point that design and architectural drawings are developed. In some cases, renderings and scale models will be developed. Computer walk-throughs or sophisticated three-dimensional renderings of design elements round out the ways in which the design team could express a restaurant design.

THE DESIGN TEAM

The design of a successful restaurant does not come from the mind of one person. Rather, it reflects the efforts of a host of professionals (Figure 2.1), all of whom provide vital pieces of the picture, from kitchen equipment selection to architectural detailing to tabletop design to the integration of heating, ventilating, and air conditioning (HVAC) systems. Of course, ego is a factor to be reckoned with. Both owners and designers often view the restaurant interior as an extension of themselves. To owners, it's the manifestation of their personality; to designers, the manifestation of their

talent. Quite often, chefs (who may also be owners) regard the kitchen as their private domain. Problems surface when individuals operate wearing blinders that prevent them from making objective design decisions. Ideally, sensitive or damaged egos don't get in the way of professional collaboration.

Each professional also takes a different view of where the design process begins. Some say that it starts with the menu, others with the market, and still others with the architecture. Traditionally, however, the process of foodservice design should begin with ownership. Ownership plants the initial ideas in the minds of the "design team," which, in turn, translates these ideas into a total concept and, subsequently, into a physical design.

The key team members should be involved from the beginning. Depending on the size and scope of the project, key players typically include the owner (or owner's representative), architect and/or interior designer, and foodservice consultant.

As the project develops, the design team is likely to grow. Particularly for large-scale projects, a financial consultant may get involved early in the design process. Ideally, the chef and restaurant manager will also offer input during early concept discussions. These three players will become more involved as the project develops. The financial consultant oversees the budget and raises questions when a design suggestion could lead to potential cost overruns. The chef suggests menu items that support the restaurant concept, and ensures that the foodservice consultant incorporates equipment that supports the menu. The manager, who is held responsible for all operational aspects of the

Figure 2.1
This schematic shows a sample design team
for a major restaurant project.

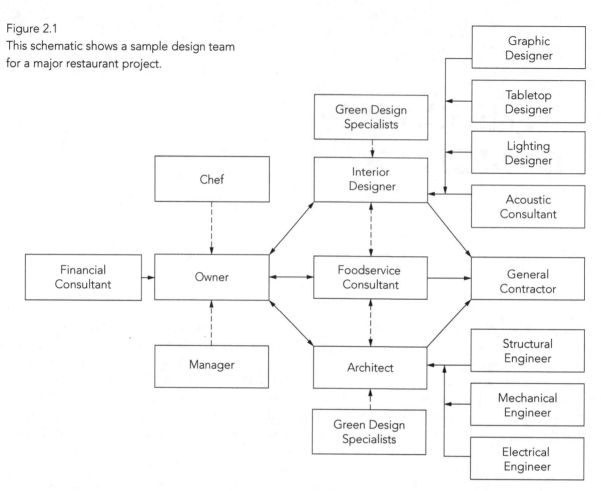

In this design team, the owner takes on the role of team leader. The manager, chef, and financial consultant serve as advisors to the owner. Green design consultants work with all members of the team, particularly interior designers and architects. The dashed lines between members of the team are meant to show their advisory role with each other.

restaurant, recognizes the design elements that could negatively impact efficiency or operating costs.

Other design team members may include the electrical engineers, lighting design consultants, acoustic consultants, graphic design consultants, tabletop consultants, and green design consultants. Sustainable design has fast become an important consideration for restaurants, and even if the team does not include a green specialist, they should consider the U.S. Green Building Council's Leadership in Energy and Environmental Design (LEED) guidelines and those of the Green Restaurant Association.

In the most inclusive scenario, the restaurant's employees and customers give input to the design team. Increasingly, companies have used social networking sites on the Internet to get consumer opinions. The Second Life web site, for example—a virtual world on the Web—has become a popular place for some independent restaurants to gather consumer feedback on proposed projects. When Starwood Hotels launched their *aloft* brand, the hotel giant created a virtual home on the Second Life web site to solicit feedback and comments from consumers that helped to shape *aloft's* new design prototype. It seems likely that chain restaurants will follow suit and use similar techniques to test the waters in cyberspace during the design phase of new projects.

Problems arise when no clear leader emerges to guide the design process. The owner should establish a team leader, someone with a balanced perspective of the many factors involved in the design of the restaurant. This individual coordinates the planning process, disseminates ideas, and has ultimate responsibility for the execution of those ideas. The team leader should be familiar with all aspects of the operation, from menu items to actual design and construction.

Often, the owner takes on the role; after all, the owner has ultimate fiscal responsibility for the restaurant. In today's marketplace, however, many owners actually have little or no experience running a restaurant, so they often farm out the individual responsibilities during the planning phase. The owner nevertheless is responsible for integrating the various parts of the planning process into a whole. If he or she cannot take on this responsibility, a different team leader must be identified.

In some projects, the foodservice consultant, interior designer, or architect becomes the team leader. This can cause difficulties as the design process develops because each of these professionals has his or her own priorities. The head of the design team—no matter what her/his professional perspective—must maintain a neutral position and consider all aspects of the operation.

The nature of the project, whether the renovation of a 60-seat independently owned bistro, the new design of a 250-seat chain eatery, or the construction of a 400-seat theatrical restaurant, often dictates the choice of team leader. Many restaurant chains maintain an in-house design specialist to oversee projects, and a foodservice consultant is often the team leader for the remodeling of a kitchen. In new construction, the architect tends to become the team leader. Today, increasing numbers of design firms specialize in restaurant design, coordinating and handling every aspect of the project. In any case, without a strong team leader, the design process can become an uncoordinated and frustrating procedure that yields disappointing results.

It's important to emphasize that, as mentioned earlier, the team does not have a set number of players or a predetermined leader. This is due to the nature of restaurant design itself. Not all projects are the same; thus, not all design teams are the same. The following descriptions of potential team members and the contributions they can make are offered as a guide to assembling the right team for a design project.

OWNER

Owners have ultimate financial responsibility for the project and frequently initiate the concept. They may or may not be experienced in restaurant operations or have training or education in foodservice management. Restaurant owners tend to have aggressive, entrepreneurial personalities and are extremely dedicated to their work. Often, a restaurant is owned by multiple partners, each of whom has different areas of expertise. Limited partnership restaurant owners are minimally involved in day-to-day operations, yet their input during the design phase may be substantial—and potentially disruptive—if they are inexperienced in restaurant management.

Because owning a restaurant is thought to be a glamorous and profitable undertaking that does not require specialized education, it tends to attract newcomers to the foodservice industry. In the past few decades, investors have flocked to restaurant partnerships in the hope of gaining tax breaks from passive investment losses. Celebrities such as Danny Glover, Wesley Snipes, Jimmy Smits, Jennifer Lopez, Robert DeNiro, Denzel Washington, Michael Jordan, and Jay Z have all tried their hands at restaurant ownership. The penchant for restaurant ownership shows no sign of abating any time soon.

Investor-owners tend to rely heavily on their designers to determine the feasibility of a concept and interpret it accordingly. They often want design creativity and allow the design firm to develop original ideas. As well, investor-owners of big-budget projects often employ hospitality accounting firms to conduct full feasibility studies before launching a project.

Some owners possess skills that enable them to function in dual roles on the design team: chef-owners or architect-owners, for instance. These individuals tend to know exactly what they want. They often retain a design firm to execute their ideas rather than to contribute new ideas.

If any owner becomes too ego driven, the design process can falter.

CHEF

The chef (and, at times, other members of the kitchen staff) should be considered an important member of the design team. Chefs look at the layout of the kitchen from an operational perspective. They have the best understanding of what types of equipment are required to produce the menu items. The chef is responsible for efficient food production. If the selection or layout of equipment does not match the menu or the style of service that is appropriate for the restaurant, this efficiency cannot be realized. The chef (who has ultimate responsibility for the smooth operation of the kitchen) should be involved early in the design process, but is frequently not brought on board until the restaurant is nearly completed in an effort to save on pre-opening labor costs. Some teams engage a consulting chef to work with the design team while the kitchen layout is being planned.

Chef-owners—many of whom have become celebrities in their own right—are increasingly common today. These individuals often design efficient kitchens featuring simple yet durable equipment that offers quick cooking with minimal investment. Because they are also responsible for the bottom line of the restaurant, they look for equipment that serves multiple functions, thus freeing square footage for front-of-the-house seating. For example, they tend to specify equipment such as a combination oven that does the job of three pieces of equipment: convection oven, steamer, and steam-injected deck oven.

MANAGER

The manager of the restaurant can add important operational insight to the design process. Managers are frequently brought on board during the construction process and may be called on to act as the owner's representative and to interface with the project team leader on an ongoing basis. It is important for them to understand the overall design scheme and to offer input into that scheme during the planning phase. Experienced managers carry with them a history of restaurant layout and design experiences that can provide invaluable information to the designers. Unlike the chef, managers tend to look at the design primarily from a front-of-the-house perspective. They should be knowledgeable about design issues that can improve market share, internal controls, safety, and sanitation throughout the operation.

FOODSERVICE CONSULTANT

The foodservice consultant designs the back-of-the-house operation and provides space layouts, mechanical and electrical diagrams, and equipment specifications. Firms range from a single individual to large companies with offices around the world. The scope of services may include menu planning, equipment purchasing, engineering evaluations, and management advisory services such as feasibility studies. Large firms, whose staffs include in-house architectural designers and who maintain a network of outside consultants, often provide team leadership. As leader, the foodservice consultant assists the owner in clarifying the concept for the restaurant, helps determine the feasibility of that concept within a given marketplace, and may even be involved in site selection.

Methods of charging include a flat fee based on hourly rates or a percentage of the total project cost. Some equipment supply houses have kitchen design experts on staff who provide design services, but these firms make money primarily by selling equipment. Architecture, design, and foodservice organizations can provide useful information for restaurant design projects.

INTERIOR DESIGNER

The interior designer is responsible for the layout and decor of the restaurant's public spaces. Like the foodservice consultant, design firms vary in size and scope of services. In general, designers develop floorplans, elevations, renderings, reflected ceiling plans, lighting plans, and furniture and accessory plans. They provide color schemes, material and decorative specifications, and all furnishing specifications. Some purchase as well as specify furnishings.

Today, increasing numbers of designers have become restaurant design specialists and take on the role of team leader. In this capacity, they may supervise a total design package from concept development to menu graphics to exterior signage to kitchen design. Other designers take on the role of team leader only for the front of the house. Most interior designers have special training or education in interior design or architecture and, in many cases, belong to the American Society of Interior Designers (ASID) or other professional organizations (Table 2.1). An updated list of design, architecture, and restaurant organizations along with their URLs is available on our web site.

Interior design fees are based on a percentage of project cost, hourly consulting rates, or square-foot cost. If purchasing services are provided, the design firm may charge a markup on furniture, fixtures, and equipment (FF&E) purchases.

TABLE 2.1 ARCHITECTURE, DESIGN, AND FOODSERVICE ORGANIZATIONS

American Institute of Graphic Artists (AIGA)

American Institute of Architects (AIA)

American Lighting Association (ALA)

American Society of Interior Designers (ASID)

Color Association of the United States

Environmental Design Research Association (EDRA)

Foodservice Consultants Society International (FCSI)

Green Restaurant Association (GRA)

International Association of Color Consultants/ Designers (IACCNA)

Interior Design Educators Council, Inc. (IDEC)

International Furnishings and Design Association (IFDA)

International Interior Design Association (IIDA)

National Restaurant Association (NRA)

North American Association of Food Equipment Manufacturers (NAFEM)

National Sanitation Foundation (NSF)

U.S. Green Building Council (USGBC)

World Business Council for Sustainable Development (WBCSD)

For a current list of organizations and their web sites, log onto www.successfulrestaurantdesign.com.

ARCHITECT

Traditionally, the role of the architect was confined to the building structure and exterior design. Over the past few decades, however, most architectural firms have expanded their practice to include interior design as well. Construction plans must be certified by a licensed architect whenever a building permit for renovation or new construction is required. Restaurants designed from the ground up or facilities that require complex redesign of interior architecture, HVAC, or electrical systems may also require the services of an architectural firm.

Architectural input is particularly important when the interior design calls for uncommon structural elements. For example, a grand staircase that flares in two directions as it reaches a second floor is best designed by an architect. If the staircase is to be supported with wires that hang from the floor above, the plans must consider the load of the staircase on both the first and the second floor. While a designer can conceptualize such a staircase, the architect has the expertise to ensure it is safe to use.

Frequently, however, the roles of architect and interior designer are interchangeable. In these cases, which represent the majority of projects today, one individual or firm functions as restaurant designer. Architectural firms often keep interior designers on staff, and interior design firms often keep architects on staff.

The scope of services and methods of charging for an architectural firm whose practice includes restaurant design are basically the same as those of an interior design firm. The differences between the two often lie in design orientation and, at times, technical expertise in specific areas. Architects, for example, tend to deal with space, form, and volume rather than with surface decoration. Interior designers may be more knowledgeable about color and accessories.

GENERAL CONTRACTOR

General contractors (GCs) are crucial members of the design team, but often they are not properly recognized or brought on board early enough. It is the GC who is ultimately charged with converting the architects' and designers' drawings into bricks and mortar.

When GCs are involved with the project during the design phase, they can point out difficult or costly structural forms. For example, if a restaurant design includes curved walls and ceilings, the GC can identify spots where creating such curved elements will substantially increase the cost of construction. They might also point out important timing elements during the construction phase. For example, when building a second-floor kitchen space, the GC might recommend that the installation of one exterior window be delayed until all of the oversized pieces of kitchen equipment are brought in with the help of an exterior scissor lift or crane. While access through a window space is not ideal, the GC might opt for this solution, having experienced the impossibility of moving a large piece of equipment up a narrow staircase. In the long run, this recommendation would improve the final execution of the project and lead to tighter control over the construction budget.

The GC is frequently chosen by a bid process, but the same care given to the selection of other design team members should be extended. Both the quality and the cost of the GC's work greatly affect the success of the project.

As with other members of the team, it's important to take a close look at the scope and quality of the GC's potential contribution before making a final selection. There are times when the lowest price is not the best price.

As well, the GC heads a team of subcontractors who together build the restaurant. It is important to investigate the background and skill levels of the subcontractors, and to ensure that they are in compliance with insurance and immigration laws. The design team leader should also find out if the subcontractors are union or nonunion workers. For example, consider the case of a restaurateur who rents ground-floor space in a new high-rise where the building is being constructed by workers from a number of unions. If the chosen restaurant subcontractor does not employ union workers, work-site difficulties could lead to construction delays.

ENGINEERS

Three types of engineers are traditionally involved in a restaurant design: structural, mechanical, and electrical. They may be on the staff of an architectural firm but, more often, they are called in from private engineering firms as needed. Structural engineers are retained both for renovations and new construction to deal with issues involving the structural integrity of the building. For example, a structural engineer would provide input about installing such elements as a suspended staircase.

Mechanical engineers handle mechanical systems such as HVAC and work on pumping, plumbing, and elevator systems. To conserve energy, mechanical engineers can specify systems that minimize the amount of exhaust air drawn by kitchen hoods. Sufficient makeup air and exhaust fans that can be slowed during nonpeak hours are two energy-saving techniques that mechanical engineers often employ.

Electrical engineers determine the amount of electricity needed for an operation and how best to distribute it. They are often called on early in the design process to determine the cost of new electrical service or expanded service.

In complex designs, all three engineers may be required. Consider a "green" roof garden, for example. The structural engineer will ensure that the skeleton and roof structure can support the added weight. The mechanical engineer will figure out the optimal placement of solar panels to provide low-voltage lighting in the evening. The electrical engineer will create an electric plan to connect the solar panels to the inverter, storage batteries, and the low-voltage light fixtures.

LIGHTING DESIGNERS

Lighting designers are often retained by the restaurant designer to highlight special features of the restaurant—both interior and exterior—deal with technical lighting problems, or program a computerized illumination system. Because lighting plays such an important role in creating restaurant atmosphere, the lighting designer has become an increasingly important team member, especially for complex projects that require intricate illumination schemes. The lighting designer can also provide important insights into the quality of each light source and how it will affect the appearance of design elements, people, and food.

Lighting designers also play a crucial role in sustainable building design. While the electrical engineers produce the spatial plan for wires and other electrical components, it is the lighting designer who chooses the lighting fixtures and lamps that significantly impact the building's electricity use and carbon footprint. An eco-conscious lighting designer will choose warm fluorescent bulbs and long-burning halogen bulbs, for example.

ACOUSTIC ENGINEERS AND ACOUSTIC CONSULTANTS

Sound, be it softening or enhancing, is best addressed by an experienced acoustic engineer or consultant who understands the sound-dampening characteristics of specific building materials. They can work to control the decibel levels within a space and help in the planning and selection of sound systems. They understand how best to deploy speakers to create either an even level of sound throughout the restaurant or to allow different areas to have varying sound levels.

OTHER SPECIALTY DESIGNERS AND CONSULTANTS

Other specialty designers are usually brought on board by the team for big-budget projects or those that require specialized problem solving.

GRAPHICS, ART, AND MENU DESIGNERS

Graphic designers may be called in to design the restaurant's logo, interior and exterior signage, and menu graphics. Branding is an integral part of any restaurant's identity and becomes increasingly important when a single restaurant grows into a chain. Graphic designers should be aware of competitive restaurant graphics to ensure that the work that they propose does not lead to a trade dress lawsuit.

Art consultants are often involved with foodservice facilities that are part of much larger organizations, such as a hotel or a corporate headquarters, and with specialty restaurants that showcase fine art as part of the décor. They may be charged with selecting and purchasing wall art, ceiling art, and sculptural pieces.

TECHNOLOGY CONSULTANTS

Different types of technology consultants may be brought in to assist with a restaurant design project. For example, a wireless expert is needed if management chooses to outfit the space with Wi-Fi access for customers, plus a wireless order-entry and check settlement system for staff. In addition to selecting the technology providers and placing wireless nodes, the wireless expert ensures that the software incorporates firewalls to prevent hacking into the restaurant's computer.

Other types of tech consultants include video experts, who may be used for operations such as sport bars where large-screen televisions are needed. They can help choose the optimal type of screen for a particular setting, and also advise on the number of screens and their placement to maximize visibility for customers.

TABLETOP CONSULTANTS

The tabletop consultant plays an important role for restaurants that emphasize food presentation. Tabletop consultants specify chinaware and also assist as requested with flatware, glassware (including for specialty drinks), and table covering choices.

Tabletop consultants should provide samples of the dinnerware they propose, so that the chef can see how each food item will appear as the guest will see it. It is also important for the chef and design team leader to see how all of the flatware, glassware, and dinnerware will look on the tabletop. If side food items are served on separate dishes, for example, then the table itself needs to be large enough to accommodate the extra dishes.

COLOR CONSULTANTS

Color consultants work with all of the other front-of-the-house team and the chef to ensure optimal color compatibility of all the front-of-the-house design elements. The consultants can provide input on how lighting choices will affect the color of the foods, customers, and interior surfaces. They understand how customers react to colors, the role of color in different cultures, and how color can help to create a brand identity.

FINANCIAL CONSULTANTS

The real estate consultant becomes a team member when real estate is a critical factor in determining whether or not a project will fly. In such cases, the real estate interests in a restaurant are nearly as important as the operational interests.

Another type of financial consultant is the feasibility consultant, who conducts a marketplace study that identifies potential customers, the competition, and the economic conditions of the locale. These consultants can also help determine the market response to prices and assist with the final pro forma statement development and future projections income and expense statements out into the future. Obviously, the cost of developing the restaurant will affect the profitability of a restaurant over time. The feasibility consultant can help determine the amount of capital investment that the proposed concept can justify.

GREEN DESIGN SPECIALISTS

Increasing numbers of restaurant designers and architects follow the precepts of sustainable design—either developing expertise within their own practices, or working with green design consultants. Green specialists are knowledgeable about the ever-changing federal, state, and utility incentives that promote renewable energy or minimize energy use associated with new construction and renovation. They can advise on the building shell and on internal elements. They have a full understanding of LEED principles, sustainable site development, waste management and recycling, means of conserving water, ways to improve energy efficiency, what materials are optimal from an environmental and sustainability perspective, and how to create an eco-friendly interior environment.

The Final Team

In extremely large restaurant projects, all of these specialists and others may be involved with the design process. The complexity of the project has a great impact on the complexion of the design team and the number of its members.

As the design process develops, a clear understanding of the responsibilities of each member of the team should be established. Ideally, the team moves forward as a coordinated entity. If not, a maverick member might attempt to divert efforts from the stated goals, and a team leader may have to stand up and pull the rest of the team along. Interpersonal relations are a big part of the design process, and often the most challenging. It's important to remember that every member of the team, from the owner to the carpenter who nails and screws the structure of the restaurant together, contributes to the overall success of the operation.

Space Planning: Value Engineering

The first concrete planning of a restaurant design should begin only after the team members have thoroughly analyzed the market and have defined the type of restaurant, style of service, concept, systems to be utilized, and the other factors outlined earlier.

The data are then organized into a design program that draws on many considerations, including a classic concept called value engineering, which can be a key component of space planning. The term was coined by Lawrence Miles while he was employed at General Electric in the 1940s and is central to our philosophy of restaurant design. It is generally defined as "an analysis of the functions of a program, . . . items of equipment, building, facility, service, . . . directed at improving performance, reliability, quality, safety, and life cycle costs."

Specifically, the aspects of value engineering (VE) that apply to restaurant space planning include a close analysis of building facilities and equipment with the goal of determining optimum efficiency. Such an analysis is particularly important in an era of celebrity chefs, bigger-is-better kitchens, increased building and operating costs, and increased chain ownership with goals of continually increasing quarterly profit.

Value engineering (VE)—which optimizes flow patterns—is one of the keys to a successful restaurant design.

Value engineering applies to any type or size operation. For multiunit restaurants that depend on a standard design footprint, a VE analysis can substantially affect the returns on initial construction and operational costs. For example, many chains have tagged on drive-through windows to their existing facilities. What a VE analysis of this new service option might tell management is that the amount of space needed for customers in walk-in order/pickup areas should be decreased in future units. This is because many of the customers who formerly walked into the restaurant will opt to use the drive-through instead.

VE can be anathema to the chef whose ego is linked to a showcase kitchen—oversized, overdesigned, and overequipped. That said, if having custom-built, color-coordinated cooking equipment is central to the restaurant concept—for example, in a display kitchen—then they are warranted. However, if an enameled range at an upcharge of 50 percent over an operationally equivalent range won't be seen by customers, then its inclusion in the kitchen cannot be warranted under a VE analysis.

Flow

An important goal of VE is to optimize flow in terms of distance, volume, speed, and direction. Typically, flow patterns are charted for customers, employees, food, tableware, and service (Figure 2.2). Flow patterns must be considered carefully at the start of design programming. Flow must also be considered in parking lots, where entrance and exit along with drive-through lines must be considered. In most municipalities, the points of entry and exit along with traffic flow on the pad must be defined on a site map to obtain a permit.

Distance

For customers, distance from a parking space to the front door of a restaurant can be critical. Where the parking lot of a large, high-end restaurant covers an acre or more of land, a drop-off area, or facilities for valet parking, should

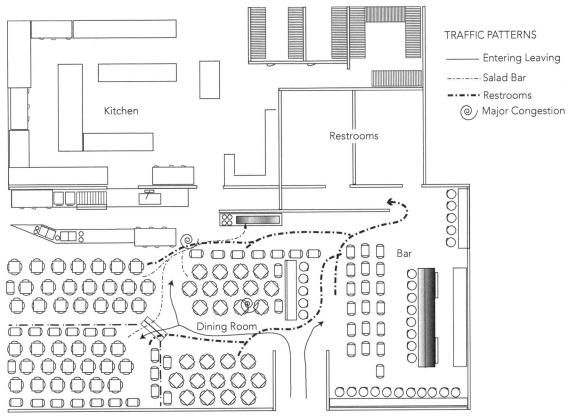

Figure 2.2
Successful restaurants depend on customer flow patterns that cross each other as little as possible. In this figure, there is one major congestion point where the paths of customers going and coming from the salad bar and restrooms cross at a choke point.

be considered. If the restaurant offers "call ahead and take it home" meals—as is the case with many midscale chains—at least one parking spot should be reserved for quick pickups.

Many spatial relationships are important, such as the distance from the dining tables to the rest rooms. If the rest rooms are located down a long corridor or on another floor, they will be inconvenient for customers and could lead to delays in service. In an entertainment restaurant, the distance from the tables to the animatronic elements should be considered because the greater the distance, the less desirable the seat.

Some upscale restaurant floorplans are designed with power seats in mind—tables that celebrities or highly placed business executives consider the best in the house. Depending on the target market, they can be tables that give customers a great view of the action in the dining room, or quiet spots for celebs who want privacy, or a chef's table in the kitchen for foodies.

From a service staff perspective, the distance from the kitchen to each of the tables is important. When the kitchen and dining spaces are on separate floors, distance can become an issue of stamina and safety, as climbing stairs will quickly tire servers who are out of shape. In such cases (and in large single-floor restaurants), service stations with a full backup of supplies for an entire meal period are essential. For optimum efficiency in a busy restaurant, a ratio of 22 seats to a service station—fully stocked with backup dinnerware, water, and ice—is ideal. Distance to an order-entry station is also important, as is the number of servers who will use each station, and the system's ease of use. In too many restaurants, servers have to queue up at order-entry stations because an insufficient number of them have been installed.

Distance from the back to the front of the house and vice versa is a crucial component of the floorplan. For example, a display kitchen can shorten the flow of food from the range to the guest (Figure 2.3), but if the service staff is forced to return to the back of the house to pick up salads, the efficiency of the open kitchen is lost. In Figure 2.2, guests make their own salads, so servers need to go into the kitchen only to drop off soiled tableware and to pick up foods that are not prepared at the display kitchen.

In many restaurants with display kitchens, the pre-preparation for the hot foods is done in the back of the house. The food is then brought to the display kitchen, where cooking is performed within view of the customers. In full-service restaurants with display kitchens, cooking is kept close to the customers so they can watch the drama of food preparation. Artfully arranged salads and desserts may also be visible to patrons and located within easy reach

of the service staff. In this scenario, servers rarely need to enter the back-of-the house kitchen during service time.

A well-designed kitchen not only facilitates the transfer of food from the storage areas to the customer but also the return flow of dirty dishes from dining room to kitchen. Intuitively, positioning the dish return area just inside the return door to the kitchen minimizes the distance that dirty dishes must be carried. However, in some cases, the dish area is pushed deeper inside the kitchen to minimize the sound that could carry over from this area to the dining spaces.

In any restaurant, spatial flow should minimize the places where the paths of customers cross with each other or with staff. If it is unavoidable for traffic patterns to overlap, pathways should be widened. Before finalizing a floorplan, it is important for the design team to visualize the flow patterns of customers and service staff. Figure 2.4 is an

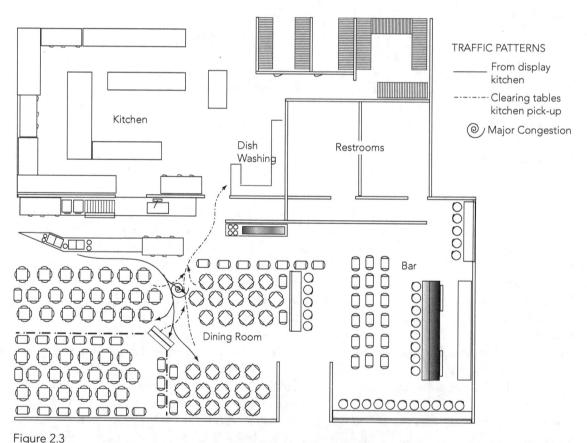

Figure 2.3
Display kitchens can help improve the efficiency of the service staff by shortening the flow of food from kitchen to guest. In this figure, a choke point develops for staff as they move to and from the display kitchen, warewashing, and tables.

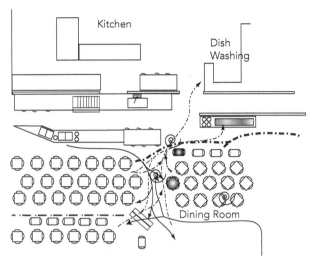

Figure 2.4
Choke points where the paths of staff and customers cross should be avoided. At a minimum, the aisles can be widened to lessen congestion.

overlay of a section taken from the previous two figures. Clearly, the two congestion points are close to each other. While it may be difficult to change these flow patterns, one can decrease congestion by removing the two shaded tables in the diagram, thus widening the aisle space.

VOLUME OF BUSINESS

Initially, volume projections indicate the appropriate size of a given dining area. However, looking only at the overall volume of business over the course of a day can be misleading. A corporate cafeteria, for example, must be designed to handle a large volume of traffic during a short lunch period, so seating and serving areas have to be larger than if the service were extended over three hours.

Another instance of misleading volume projections is a quick-service operation on an interstate highway. Here, volume projections far exceed seating requirements because many customers will take food back to their cars rather than use the restaurant's seating area. However, volume of business does dictate extra restroom space for those travelers who take out food or stop to use restrooms without buying food.

The volume of business must also be considered when planning the parking areas of a restaurant. Local building codes frequently define the required number of spaces based on the number of seats in the restaurant. The codes may also

affect the design of ingress and egress from the parking lot and mandate the installation of expensive traffic lights.

SPEED OF SERVICE

The faster the service, the more the restaurant depends on a well-designed floorplan. Quick-service operations and cafeterias should be laid out so that each area of the restaurant, all food and supplies, and every piece of equipment helps maximize speed. These fast-paced operations should have clearly defined, short lines of flow that do not cross. In many quick-service operations, the parking lot is on one side of the building. Customers enter in the front and exit through the dining room that is adjacent to the parking lot. This circular flow minimizes cross-traffic patterns.

In a fine restaurant, the mannered service is an expected part of the leisurely dining experience, and placement of support equipment is not as important as in high-speed operations. For aesthetic reasons, management might even decide to eliminate service stations from the dining room. Although this lengthens the distance servers travel when resetting tables, the decision could be acceptable in establishments where diners expect a lengthy, slow-paced meal.

DIRECTION

The ideal layout creates a straight-line—or circular—flow that is unidirectional, with no crossing flow patterns. Such a design may prove impossible but should be aimed for in the planning process.

Directional flow issues begin in the parking lot when guests look for a parking space. A herringbone parking space design helps define flow patterns in a way that straight-in parking does not. Once inside the restaurant, elements should flow logically so that guests need not retrace their steps. For example, the reception stand should be close to the entry to allow people to check in and then move directly on to either the bar or the dining room without retracing their steps.

In the back of the house, the flow should move—as much as possible—in a straight line all the way from the receiving dock to the server pickup station. The waitstaff should be able to take the food directly to the guests and eventually bring dirty dishes and soiled table linen directly back to a cleanup area.

THE AMERICANS WITH DISABILITIES ACT

The Americans with Disabilities Act (ADA) of 1990 was passed to provide people with physical challenges access to many public spaces. One such space is the restaurant, which falls under Title III: Public Accommodations. The most visible result of the ADA has been the inclusion of handicapped-accessible rest room facilities and ramps that can accommodate wheelchairs. However, many other ADA design elements must be incorporated in new or modified restaurants.

For example, restaurants must comply with basic nondiscrimination requirements that prohibit exclusion, segregation, and unequal treatment. They also must comply with specific requirements related to architectural standards for new and altered buildings; reasonable modifications to policies, practices, and procedures; effective communication with people with hearing, vision, or speech disabilities; and other access requirements. Additionally, public accommodations must remove barriers in existing buildings where it is easy to do so without much difficulty or expense, given the public accommodation's resources.

Failure to consider the needs of all physically challenged persons can lead to litigation by the Justice Department. In several instances since the ADA legislation was enacted, restaurateurs have been forced to close their establishments because it was cost-prohibitive to make the facilities accessible. It is important to note that ADA regulations are frequently updated, so the design team should stay up to date on current and pending changes to the basic requirements.

There are various sources to help keep the design team current on ADA requirements. Back in 1991, the National Institute of Disability and Rehabilitation Research (NIDRR) funded 10 Disability and Business Technical Assistance Centers (DBTACs) throughout the United States to offer information on ADA compliance. In addition, ADA consulting specialists can be retained to ensure that a design complies with ADA requirements. In some cases, federal tax incentives may be available to help pay for modifications to bring an existing facility up to ADA standards.

Another ADA factor is the need to accommodate physically challenged employees. Sight-impaired employees working in the dish area, for example, may need specially designed dish racks or audible temperature readouts. Minimal design modifications will often enable a restaurant to comply with ADA standards in both the front and back of the house.

Handicap parking spaces are also mandated by the ADA. The number of spaces is determined by the total number of parking spaces provided in the restaurant's parking lot. The ADA also offers specific guidelines on how those parking spaces must be designed and where they must be located. The inclusion of van-accessible parking spaces—which have 96-inch-wide spaces versus the 60-inch-wide standard handicap space—is also advisable because they can accommodate a wheelchair lift.

MOVING THROUGH THE SPACES

With an understanding of how flow impacts restaurant design, it is time to start the space planning process. Space planning begins by looking at the parts that make up the whole of a restaurant. These parts are not the chairs or the artwork or any of the other decor items. Rather, they consist of the spatial areas that together comprise the total front and back of the house.

EXTERIOR

The exterior includes every outside aspect: the parking lot, the building skin, exterior signage, landscaping, and exterior window and lighting treatments. Free-standing buildings with architectural elements that help them stand out from the crowd as travelers whip by at 40 miles per hour have a competitive advantage over the standard box-shaped restaurant with no distinguishing architectural character. The exterior of restaurants located in high-rise buildings consists of interior corridors so signage plays an important role. In shopping malls, public "outdoor" seating areas often comprise the exterior of a restaurant operation, or the exterior may consist of large communal seating areas shared by all of the eateries in a food court.

ENTRY AREA

The entry area begins when customers step inside the restaurant. Its form varies greatly, depending, in part, on whether the restaurant is freestanding or incorporated within a larger building. Climatic conditions also affect the appearance of the entryway. In general, it should look inviting and should help move patrons in an orderly flow from exterior to dining. Doors usually separate the exterior from the entry, but in situations such as a shopping mall or cafeteria, patrons may walk through open portals (which are typically secured at night). Where energy efficiency is paramount, double doors, revolving doors, or air screens are important considerations. The entry area itself includes such elements as the maître d' station or reception area, coat- or bag-check area, a waiting area (often with seating), space for guests to queue up for ordering, and, frequently, the cash-handling systems.

DINING AREA

The dining area begins where the entry area stops, and runs to the kitchen. It frequently interfaces with a beverage service area. Typical elements include seating and server stations, ventilation, and sound and lighting systems.

Architectural treatments such as raised or lowered floor and ceiling levels often help define dining areas. Salad bars, buffet tables, and display kitchens are frequently located in or adjacent to dining areas. Because the dining area is the restaurant's revenue-producing area, it occupies the largest amount of square footage.

BEVERAGE AREA

The beverage area, typically serving alcoholic beverages in full-service restaurants, consists of a front bar and back bar, bar seating, and, sometimes, cocktail seating. Music and video systems are often featured. The size of the beverage area depends on the importance of beverage sales to total revenue. In some restaurants, a single beverage area services dining room customers as well as bar customers, but other restaurants include separate service bars for the dining area.

Wine storage and display is an increasingly important design element in many types of restaurants. In full-service restaurants, wine displays near the entry area or in the beverage area can entice people to purchase wine. In theatrical restaurants, the action of the wine cellar can be part of the show when this area is located in view of the guests. In other establishments, wine displays are used as a decorative

element in the dining room (Figure 2.5). Nonalcoholic beverage stations, such as for coffee, self-serve soft-drink stations, or napkin/utensil pickup, may also be incorporated in the beverage area.

RESTROOMS

Optimally, both front- and back-of-the-house restrooms are included in the restaurant floorplan. However, in some facilities, a single restroom located in the front of the house services both staff and customers. The size of the restrooms depends on the size of the restaurant. While most restaurants include separate facilities for women and men, some may have unisex restrooms. Larger establishments might include makeup areas for women, shoeshine stations for men, and ADA-compliant facilities.

KITCHEN

Nearly every restaurant kitchen can be divided into the functional areas described in Chapter 5. The kitchen is typically a third the size of the dining area, but this ratio can vary greatly according to restaurant type. In many contemporary restaurants, the kitchen, once hidden behind swinging doors, sits in full view of customers. The equipment in a kitchen will vary significantly depending on the type of establishment and its menu.

SUPPORT AREAS

Restaurant support areas include receiving and storage areas (dry, refrigerated, and frozen), plus employee restrooms where appropriate, locker rooms, employee lounge/cafeteria, and management offices. All of these areas are located in the back of the house and are discussed in full in Chapter 5.

Not every foodservice operation incorporates each of the areas mentioned in this chapter. Furthermore, the significance of each functional area varies from restaurant to restaurant. In fact, every restaurant space has unique requirements and characteristics and should be analyzed individually in order to arrive at a successful program. The following discussion looks at spatial requirements for five major service systems: quick-service, full-service, cafeteria, banquet, and take-out.

Figure 2.5
Wine cellars can serve as a focal point in the dining room. At David Burke's Primehouse in Chicago, the wine cellar lines the right-hand wall as guests enter the dining room. The curved-glass front merchandises wine offerings and guides guests to their seats.
(Photo by Joseph Durocher)

QUICK SERVICE

This type of service system is typically characterized by an area where customers queue up to place their orders and a combined food assembly and payment area. In drive-throughs—which have become increasingly important in quick-service systems, payment windows are sometimes separate from food pickup windows.

QUICK-SERVICE EXTERIORS

Exterior signage and graphics are of utmost importance to the quick-service operation. Initial development of the design concept should include a signature ideograph or typeface that integrates with the logo. The logo helps establish a clear identity that communicates instantly to

people whizzing by in their cars (Figure 2.6). Operators tend to carry elements of the logo throughout the entire quick-service environment by emblazoning appropriate surfaces with the name or ideograph as a constant visual reminder to their customers.

Signage often works hand in hand with architecture. For more than 30 years, the golden arches have indicated the location of a McDonald's, as do the signs and architectural elements of many free-standing quick-service operations.

Primary colors and bright lighting are commonly used on quick-service exteriors to further emphasize identity and create an upbeat, high-energy image. Gone are the days when garish quick-service signs were the accepted norm. Today, most signage, while still colorful and well lit at night, does not include flashing lights or other loud elements that are frowned upon by local zoning boards.

Figure 2.6
Roadside restaurants, particularly quick-service operations, have developed logos that can be quickly identified as drivers whiz by. The bold signage, colors, and Swiss cheese wall windows create a strong visual statement at this Bembos restaurant in Peru, designed by José Orrego Herrera.

(José Orrego Herrera)

QUICK-SERVICE ENTRY AREAS

In the quick-service restaurant, the entry is the place where customers divide into queues. The two basic types of queue are: (1) several separate lines, each of which leads to a point-of-sale (POS) station, and (2) a single, usually serpentine line that leads to a single POS station. The lane length of the drive-through queue—as in (2) above—must match the expected volume of traffic that will back up at this station during peak hours. Separate ordering, payment, and pickup stations have been shown to speed the drive-through queue in many operations. These stop-and-go steps keep customers engaged rather than thinking about how long they have to wait. Menu selections, ordering, delivery, and cash handling all take place along the one multistop line.

Inside the restaurant, an obvious disadvantage to the single-line system is that the customer may be faced with being the 30th person in line. The alternate method breaks the queue into perhaps five lines with six persons in each, so the customer's perception is of a much shorter queue that will take less time to get through. In actuality, the throughput (the number of customers served in a given time) is about equal in both systems. What saves time in the single line is a division of responsibilities among the counter staff: one person takes orders and handles cash, while others assemble the order. In multiple lines, a single person takes the order, assembles it, and handles money transactions. An additional advantage of the single-line queue is that it limits the number of registers and amount of front counter space.

Customer-facing order-entry displays help to minimize order-entry mistakes and speed service in both drive-through and walk-in areas. A monitor is stationed at each ordering station for customer viewing. If a mistake is made by the counter worker, the customer can quickly ask that the item be corrected. The counter worker need not repeat the order out loud as the customer can see the order—and any subsequent modifiers—on the monitor. Today, most quick-service operations accept credit cards, and attaching a card swipe to the monitor minimizes peoples' fears that their cards could be used fraudulently. The customer-facing order-entry screen and ATM-style card payment systems should also be considered as a part of the drive-through design for quick-service restaurants.

A relatively new twist on quick service is the fast-casual segment, in which items are prepared to order. Customers see the food prepared in front of them and can customize their orders. In the Chipotle and Moe's Southwestern Grill chains, for example, people walk along one side of the assembly counter while watching and directing the staff member who assembles a burrito, taco, or other item behind the counter.

QUICK-SERVICE BEVERAGE AREAS

Most quick-service operations don't serve alcoholic beverages, but some install beverage bars where customers fill their own cups with whatever cold or hot beverage they desire. Such beverage bars shift the cost of labor associated with filling drinks to the customers. They tend to speed service because the counter staff does not have to pour and assemble drinks along with food items.

QUICK-SERVICE DINING AREAS

Hard surfaces, bright lighting, and primary colors are the traditional design characteristics of quick-service dining areas because these elements facilitate easy maintenance, fast turnover, and upbeat energy. To accommodate aging Baby Boomers or create a classy feeling, these hard-edged design elements are sometimes softened with such applications as artwork, soft accent lighting, and toned-down color schemes. Glass-enclosed greenhouse seating areas and overhead skylights are often used in quick-service architecture to mellow the ambience with natural light and plants. While appealing to customers, these can pose some operational challenges. South-facing enclosures heat up quickly and can go unused during hot summer lunch periods if the air pumped into them is not sufficient cooled. A separate air-conditioning zone can keep greenhouses at an enjoyable temperature, prevent other dining areas from overchilling in the summer, and can prevent the greenhouse from being too cold to enjoy in the winter.

Play areas for children can also be found in many quick-service restaurants. They need to be positioned so that parents can eat while keeping a close eye on their kids. Elements within the play areas must be easy to clean to minimize maintenance costs (and clean play areas will minimize parental concerns about sanitation).

Most contemporary quick-service interiors are divided into several small seating areas, with acoustic ceiling tiles or wall coverings to help mute noise levels. Multiple seating sections allow management to close an area for cleaning during slow periods.

In many operations, the fixed, molded plastic seating typical of quick-service interiors in the past has been replaced by smart-looking café chairs with padded seats and counter seating for single diners. In some places, the increased girth of the patrons has necessitated the upsizing of seating with fewer booths and more free-standing tables and chairs. Burger King was one of the first quick-service chains to move to free-standing tables and chairs, beginning in 1999 with the opening of a renovated facility in Reno, Nevada. The seating change was said to reflect the corporate premise of "have it your way." Since then, many other quick-service operations, particularly those in the fast-casual segment, have followed suit.

In some fast-casual operations, Wi-Fi is integral to brand identity and becomes an important part of the design plan. Wi-Fi customers are typically single diners. They want an electrical connection so that they don't have to rely on their computer batteries. They will also spend more time at their table than will other customers. Some fast-casual operators, like Panera Bread, offer free wireless throughout their operations. To appeal to Wi-Fi users, they have incorporated several cushioned armchairs with a rounded arm desk. This seating option maximizes availability of the regular tables for diners who occupy seating only long enough to eat a meal or enjoy a beverage. On the technology side, the design must incorporate sufficient wireless coverage to allow multiple users to log in at one time.

The design goals for quick-service and fast-casual operators continue to be easy maintenance, fast turnover, and upbeat energy. Today's quick-service dining areas may look more up-to-date, with lighting levels soft enough that patrons don't need to wear sunglasses, but if the interiors are too comfortable or can't withstand the spills and stains of constant turnover, the design has failed. The fast-casual segment also relies on multiple table turns during peak serving hours, so even the cushioned seating often found in this segment should not be so comfy that it will keep customers lingering more than 30 minutes over a meal or snack.

QUICK-SERVICE RESTROOMS

Quick-service restrooms must be designed to handle high-volume traffic. Fast feeders are typically used as roadside or walk-in rest stops, so the restroom volume can be greater than the diner volume. Spaces must be functional and easily cleaned with a minimum of upkeep. The restrooms take such a heavy beating that all design applications should be durable and easy to maintain. Hand dryers are the most sanitary, low-maintenance, and arguably most eco-friendly option for drying hands. Even in restrooms with towel dispensers, they should be included as a backup for when the towel dispenser is empty.

Large-roll toilet tissue and hand towels will cut down on restroom maintenance time. Autoflush urinals and toilets help improve sanitation and minimize offensive smells. Hands-free soap dispensers and auto-operated faucets provide increased sanitation. Outward-opening doors or waste baskets situated near the doors minimize the buildup from hand towels dropped by customers who don't want to use their just-washed hands to open the door.

QUICK-SERVICE KITCHENS

Optimal efficiency is crucial in a quick-service kitchen. Kitchen design for large chain operations has been researched, revised, researched again, and brought to a point where the placement of every element leads to the highest level of productivity per employee hour. Some fast feeders specify custom equipment—designed specifically for their menu—from their suppliers. As with any kitchen, the key is to keep the flow of product in as straight a line as possible and not cross it with the flow of personnel.

For large chains, proprietary time and motion studies help determine the optimal layout of equipment to maximize productivity. Such advanced research is cost prohibitive for single outlets or small chains, where the initial placement of equipment may need to be modified soon after the operation gets up and running. The choice of equipment that can easily be shifted from one location to another and the installation of utility connections that can be easily accessed and flexible in their design helps operators fine-tune their kitchen layouts.

Expanded menus challenge the design of quick-service kitchens. The kitchen once designed to process only frozen fries and burgers now may also be the production facility for fresh produce, soup, or even home-baked breads. For new units, the design is relatively simple—plan the kitchen to incorporate the expanded menu. Adding a convection oven or a vegetable prep area to an existing facility with an already tightly designed kitchen can lead to a back of house that does not optimize productivity.

QUICK-SERVICE SUPPORT AREAS

The storage areas of quick-service restaurants are similar to those in other kitchens. Historically, limited menus placed limited demands on storage areas. As menus expanded, however, and more fresh ingredients were added, storage needs increased. For example, quick-service operators who make and bake their own biscuits must store large bags of flour, whereas they formerly received ready-to-eat rolls. In addition, a great deal of space is required to store disposables.

The offices in quick-service restaurants are usually small—often nothing more than a nook in the back of the kitchen. Because of the sophisticated POS systems in most fast feeders, much of the paperwork ordinarily completed in a full-service restaurant office is instead done at the registers. Frequently, the data is fed to a central data-collection office (not the on-site office), which sends reports back to the individual unit. Employee locker room spaces are limited and employees use the dining space to eat and take breaks.

FULL SERVICE

FULL-SERVICE EXTERIORS

In chain-operated full-service restaurants, the exterior architecture can establish the theme and identity of the restaurant in much the same way as it does for quick-service restaurants. The logo or ideograph displayed on the building's exterior often carries through to the inside, and architectural form becomes a recognizable icon. The idea goes back to 1935, when the first Howard Johnson's roadside restaurant opened, with its ubiquitous orange roof—a roof that became synonymous with the Howard Johnson's brand. A more recent example is the Olive Garden chain, with signage that hasn't changed much since the first Olive Garden opened in Orlando, Florida, in 1982. There's also the Hard Rock Cafe logo, which made its first appearance in London in 1971, and has become a recognizable icon worldwide, although its building shape changes from location to location (Figure 2.7).

Converting existing restaurant structures that were built with recognizable architectural elements presents special problems, especially if the building in question happens to have been a known chain. In other words, to disguise a recognizable architectural form and create a new image may require extensive reconstruction. A bit of cosmetic overlay won't work. For example, the Prince Restaurant, with its "leaning tower of Pisa" out front, would be hardpressed to sell the structure to other than another Italian restaurant operator. Similarly difficult to sell are the log cabin–themed structures that became the hallmark of the Smokey Bones chain. Darden Restaurants shuttered 56 of the underperforming Smokey Bones properties in May

2007 and began proceedings to sell the remaining 73 restaurants, which finally changed hands in January 2008.

Independent full-service restaurants vary widely in their architectural and graphic statements. Depending on the type of establishment and the target market, exteriors range from the undesigned and unembellished concrete or brick box to innovative architectural statements. Here, too, consumers recognize exterior symbols. The aluminum-sided diner, for instance, is synonymous with a diverse, hearty, inexpensive American menu served 24 hours a day. Careful restorations or new knockoffs of this classical design have become late-night hangouts for everyone from the cross-country trucker to the urban club-goer.

In general, most suburban chain operations are situated in freestanding buildings whose architecture (as with quick-service chains) is recognizable. Independent urban restaurants frequently sport distinctive, highly individual façades with features such as floor-to-ceiling windows that afford passersby a view inside, or high-tech video displays that also hint at the electricity and excitement inside. Other places use unusual or overscaled architectural elements to create identity.

An investment in architecture and graphics is an investment in image that can pay off handsomely in the long run. The challenge is to create an individual identity that nevertheless remains in context with its environment, whether a casino promenade or a rural country road (Figure 2.8).

FULL-SERVICE ENTRY AREAS

On average, full-service restaurants have small entry areas that function as pass-through spaces to the dining room. In some establishments, a coatroom is tucked into a corner of the entry area. Restrooms occasionally adjoin this area but in such cases it is important to carefully watch flow patterns to minimize constriction.

In casual restaurants, the entry space often includes a dual-purpose host and cashier station. Upscale restaurants have a maître d' station where guests check in before being led to their table, but the station does not include cash-handling functions. The check-in station must be close enough to the front door so that it can be easily seen, but far enough away so that waiting guests will not block the flow of other traffic in and out of the restaurant. In some international destinations, the maître d' station is located in the center of the dining area, so guests actually pass dining tables on their way to check in. This layout can confuse American diners, who expect to encounter the host stand in the entryway.

Figure 2.7
The architecture of Hard Rock Cafes is different in each location, but the signage creates a recognizable image worldwide. When people see the stylized steel guitar, there is no question about where they are.
(Photo by Joseph Durocher)

Figure 2.8
The exterior of Del Posto's in New York City appears to be an entrance to an apartment building, yet leads directly into the restaurant.
(Photo by Joseph Durocher)

The entry area in chain restaurants may include everything from waiting lines in steakhouses to newspaper vending machines in coffee shops. It is usually an unembellished area where guests wait for a table. In many instances, there is little or no seating, in the hopes that diners will go to the bar for a drink before being called for their table.

In an upscale full-service restaurant, however, the entry area can set the stage for the dining experience to come. The entry is the transition zone between the outside world and the restaurant and, even in small spaces, good design can facilitate the transition with devices such as vestibules or angled entry doors (Figures 2.10a-d). Lighting plays a crucial role in creating a smooth transition between outside and inside. Smell is also important; in the entry, customers begin to get olfactory clues about the meal to come.

In many restaurants, the entry area melds with the bar (Figure 2.9). Barriers are minimized in an effort to draw people into the space and to let them preview the dining experience. Coatrooms are set aside and, in some operations, are placed in remote locations so as not to interfere with the traffic flow or entry aesthetic.

FULL-SERVICE DINING AREAS
Full-service dining spaces continue to show great variety of size, shape, and decor. Large rooms are often broken into dining nooks with levels or barriers that create a feeling of privacy. Mirrors are used creatively to give tantalizing glimpses into other parts of the room or to make a small room feel larger. Comfort is paramount in upscale full-service

Figure 2.9
Here, in a Hard Rock Cafe, the central bar, with its video tower above, is seen by all guests as they enter the restaurant.
(Photo by Joseph Durocher)

Figure 2.10
The look and type of the entry can send messages of what's to come. The intricately designed wooden doors at the entry of Pink Pepper in Chicago suggest a luxe experience within (a). The arched entry of Morimoto in New York City (b), with its cloth banners that swing in the breeze, hints of the Far East.
(Pink Pepper (a): Photography by Anthony Eckelberry. (b)-(d): Photos by Joseph Durocher)

(c)

(d)

Figure 2.10 (*Continued*)
The archway at Per Se in
New York City (c) leads to a
waiting area where diners can
assemble in an English garden
setting before entering the
gourmet restaurant. The eatery
in Portovenere, Italy, is clearly a
pasta restaurant as evidenced by
the window curtains fashioned
from rigatoni (d).

restaurants, where padded chairs, booths, and banquettes are typical seating choices. (Figure 2.11).

The spatial plan of the dining room—and the amount of space needed between tables—should always take into account the traffic flow of the waitstaff and guests. In today's restaurants, POS order-entry systems placed throughout dining spaces and remote printers located in kitchens and bars have diminished much of the waitstaff flow. Handheld computerized order-entry and check payment pads, which are becoming increasingly common, also cut back on service traffic.

In many full-service restaurants, particularly gourmet dining establishments, food is the major attraction. The amount of floor space per seat will vary as a function of the type of seating, size of table, and style of service—plate, platter, or cart. In a restaurant classified as luxe or haute cuisine, the multicourse dining experience could take many hours, and it is important to ensure that customers are not interrupted by distractions. Chairs should be positioned so that other diners or staff won't bump into them as they move about. Temperature levels should be even throughout the meal period. Sound levels should allow for easy conversation, and lighting should enhance the overall experience.

In casual full-service chains and independent restaurants, design is often used as a marketing tool to attract a targeted clientele. Today's theme restaurants are more about

Figure 2.11
At Table 45, a rounded booth provides diners a level of intimacy while also directly engaging them with the kitchen production area. To further increase privacy, architect Bill Blunden encased this space in glass on the kitchen side and entry side.

(Photo by Scott Pease)

creating an experience—one that is bigger and better than the competition—than just recreating a look. Diners and cafés might draw on design elements from the 1940s and 1950s; chain steakhouses often reflect a rustic, wild West aesthetic; and an Italian theme is often conveyed by a green, white, and red color scheme—the colors of the Italian flag. Such design references are part of a comprehensive branding that also extends to the food and the service.

In theatrical restaurants, barriers between dining and drinking are often lowered to create the feeling of one large space and to allow visibility between bar patrons and restaurant patrons, enabling customers to "see the show" from every seat in the house. B.E.D. (Beverage, Entertainment, Dining) took the theatrical front stage when it first opened on New Year's Eve back in 1999. B.E.D. still offers serious cuisine to diners who sit cross-legged and shoeless on beds, which can be curtained off to provide some privacy. At midnight, B.E.D. shifts focus to become an all beverage-service restaurant.

Dark dining, which started in Europe and spread to the United States, is another example of restaurant theatrics. In some, such as the Opaque restaurant in the Beverly Hills Hyatt, weekend diners enjoy a dining experience without sensory distractions. The concept is that the lightless dining room forces guests to rely on their olfactory and tactile sensory organs.

While "razzle-dazzle" is important to theatrical restaurants, bringing customers back a second and third time depends on food and service that complement the design. Design alone cannot ensure success, particularly in hip urban neighborhoods where customers will move on to the next trendy restaurant as soon as it opens unless there is a reason to return.

If there is entertainment on a stage, the dining space is typically one large room, perhaps tiered (which can be a design challenge due to ADA requirements). If the entertainment plays on video screens or incorporates animatronics, all seats in the house should have a view. Videos and animatronics can be strategically installed in many places, making it possible for one restaurant to have several dining spaces of varying size. As well, part of the entertainment might be an open kitchen, an element that became popular in the 1990s and continues to be used in many types of establishments.

In theatrical or entertainment restaurants, illumination levels can be intense, and specialty theatrical lighting is frequently used to highlight the action. High noise levels create action, excitement, and energy, and help develop the feeling of the room. However, ear-splitting reverberation that makes conversation painful has become less common in some places, particularly those that cater to a Baby Boomer clientele.

FULL-SERVICE BEVERAGE AREAS

Many full-service restaurants incorporate bars that are visually separated from the dining areas. The bar often serves multiple purposes: as a drinking spot for customers who may or may not be eating, as a service bar for the dining room, and as a waiting area for diners. It is often accompanied by a cocktail lounge, especially when food is served. Today, some restaurants serve complete meals at the bar, and many offer scaled-down portions for guests looking for an alternative to a big meal. Some bars even have a station that is used to produce small tapas plates.

Bars can range in size, from four-seat waiting areas for takeout diners to mega bars, where dozens of bartenders work at a time. The size of the bar and the number of stations depends on their role in the restaurant. They play a minor role in elegant restaurants that emphasize a fine dining experience, but in many other types of restaurants, the bar is an open, inviting area for drinking or casual dining.

While most full-service restaurants store wine in the back of the house, increasing numbers have wine displays and wine cellars that are integrated with the interior design concept. Space and equipment is needed to store white wines under refrigeration for service. Both red and backup white wines should be stored in a climate-controlled space that keeps the bottles at roughly 58 degrees Fahrenheit. If wines are to be sold by the glass, storage space for the open bottles must be provided—ideally under temperature-controlled conditions.

In many full-service restaurants, the bar attracts its own crowd as well as diners waiting for tables. In such instances, the bar should be designed and positioned so that the bar patrons don't interfere with restaurant patrons. Flow patterns and physical features such as half walls, planters, and other elements that separate these customer groups should be considered.

FULL-SERVICE RESTROOMS

Restrooms in the full-service establishment should be designed with as much care as the dining spaces. When artfully designed and appointed, they are a welcome addition to the dining experience. They can even become marketing centers, with glass wall cases to display branded items such as hats, T-shirts, and other paraphernalia available for sale on site or on the Web.

In addition, there are many ways to extend the dining room design into the restrooms. Flowers, wall covering, hand-painted tiles, and other design elements go a long way toward engendering customer goodwill. Patrons of theatrical restaurants tend to be concerned with personal appearance, and their trips to the restroom often turn into lengthy visits. From a design perspective, additional space must be set aside for mirrors and makeup areas. In entertainment restaurants, the fanciful decor is often mirrored in the restroom design. Music piped into the restroom areas is common in many types of full-service restaurants.

In every type of restaurant, restaurant materials and surfaces should be durable and easy to maintain. Materials used around urinals and toilets must be capable of holding up to frequent cleaning, with few seams that could collect bacteria or mold. Waterless urinals should be considered for installation in "green" restaurants.

FULL-SERVICE KITCHENS

Both menus and kitchens are standardized in most chain operations. While the same layout may not be used in all chain kitchens, the type of equipment is always the same. The independent restaurant kitchen, however, does not follow a standard format. Frequently, batch-prepared foods are held in steam tables, where they are supplemented with foods prepared to order at a grill or fry station.

In the à la carte kitchen, where all food is prepared to order and few foods are prepared in advance, high-heat equipment capable of cooking food within minutes is most frequently included in the design. With few exceptions, kitchen space is tight because restaurateurs strive to maximize revenue-producing, front-of-the-house space. Wherever possible, a single piece of equipment should be used for the production of multiple menu items.

With the exception of restaurants that have display kitchens in the front of the house, most of the food preparation and cooking in full-service operations takes place in an all-enclosed kitchen. The exceptions often include pizza restaurants, whether they are chain or independent—some with wood-burning pizza ovens that become visual focal points. Similarly, many contemporary high-design restaurants feature display kitchens that showcase the chef's art as drama. In these cases, the back-of-the-house kitchen has even less square footage.

Display kitchens must be equipped with easy-to-clean equipment, typically clad with stainless steel or enamel. Cleanliness (an ongoing concern in any kitchen) is particularly important in display kitchens, so undercounter waste receptacles must be programmed into the design.

The display kitchen is usually split into two spaces: the finishing kitchen in the front of the house and the storage and pre-preparation areas in the back of the house. Consequently, the spatial relationship between these two areas is critical. Pass-through reach-ins make it easy to back up supplies from the pre-preparation area and allow finish chefs to draw from a continually replenished supply of ingredients. Theatrical lighting is frequently used to focus attention on such equipment as wood-fired ovens, rotisseries, or char-broilers—all an important part of the show.

Expanded emphasis on food has led to all types of display kitchen areas in theatrical and other types of full-service restaurants—from full open kitchens to large pickup windows. Some of these have seating at or adjacent to the service pickup areas, with little or no separation between the kitchen theatrics and the customers. Recently, the number of new restaurants with display kitchens has decreased, possibly in response to rising energy costs. In enclosed kitchens, the large exhaust hoods required over most pieces of cooking equipment remove heat and air from around the hot food station. In display kitchens, conditioned air—be it cooled or heated—is also removed, adding to utility costs and sometimes causing air to be drawn into the restaurant through the front door.

FULL-SERVICE SUPPORT AREAS

Because full-service menus are usually more complex than those for quick-service operations, they require more storage for the varied types of food items. Less space is needed for dry storage, however, because most full-service restaurants use fewer paper goods.

In the full-service restaurant, the mix of dry to refrigerated to frozen changes as a function of management policy. In some independent operations, fresh foods are used wherever possible. This is particularly important in those restaurants where organic or sustainable foods are an integral part of the concept. Others, including many chain operations, depend heavily on frozen and canned goods.

The type of support facilities and their spatial requirements also depend on the type of restaurant. Steakhouse operations, for example, need sufficient walk-in storage to hold Cyrovac bags of wholesale cuts of meat or precut steaks. In steakhouses where meat arrives in wholesale cuts, such as bone-in strip loin, a fabrication area that includes a band saw to portion the wholesale cuts into steaks is essential. A seafood restaurant that serves a large volume of fresh lobsters requires a holding tank with a water filtration and refrigeration system. In general, the more varied the menu, the more storage space is needed. Fresh ingredients require more preparation space and specialty processing equipment than frozen or canned foods.

CAFETERIA

CAFETERIA EXTERIORS

The exterior of a cafeteria operation usually consists of a building shell that houses not only the cafeteria but also other types of facilities (offices or hospital beds, for example). Therefore, the exterior of the cafeteria traditionally has not been integrated with the overall design program. In some operations, however, the exterior approach to the cafeteria—actually located inside the building—is designed to attract patrons. Floor treatments, artwork, and windows into the serving area can capture the attention of people as they walk by. Large businesses may dedicate an entire floor to the cafeteria, which has its own elevator or elevator access. Thoughtful design treatments, such as menu displays in the elevator or hanging banners over the escalator, can spark interest in the cafeteria and lead people into the space.

CAFETERIA ENTRY AREAS AND SERVERIES

The cafeteria entry area is minimal in size and limited to the space where customers pick up a tray and are introduced to menu offerings. In cafeterias where most patrons are on a meal program, sufficient space is needed to incorporate identification systems. College students, for example, frequently purchase a meal plan and use biometric scanners and ID keypads to gain entry to dining areas. It is important to incorporate a hand-sanitizing station immediately after the biometric sign-in station if thumb or whole-hand checking is used.

Entry areas in the traditional straight-line cafeteria, commonly used until the late 1970s, were larger and longer because they served as holding areas where guests queued up. Today's scramble designs, where patrons do not enter a line but travel to individual food stations, eliminate the need for an entry queue.

The servery is the design feature that distinguishes cafeterias from other types of foodservice. In general, it needs to be large enough to allow a smooth and continual flow of traffic during the peak meal hour, when customer counts swell considerably and patrons' time is limited. In those operations where items are sold individually, a sufficient number of cashier stations immediately before the dining area is essential.

The scramble-system servery was conceived to cut down queuing and to speed customers to particular food items such as hot entrées, grilled meats, sandwiches, stir-fry, dessert, and beverage stations. The marketing advantage of the traditional straight-line design was that customers were paraded past all food offerings and made impulse purchases. Such a design can still work well today in cafeterias that cater to transient customers who are not familiar with the layout of the servery—on cruise ships, for example.

With the scramble system, customers who have learned the layout of the servery can be more selective, so attractively designed food stations are critical. In an ideal design, the queue at each of the hot food stations would be the same length. While the length of a queue is, in part, due to the station's location and food offerings, designers should keep the market's preferences in mind when placing stations and incorporating elements to make them more attractive.

Exhibition cooking and preparation, such as made-to-order grilling, stir-frying, and roast carving, have proven to be popular draws. Again, flexibility in the design of the servery is important. For example, the queue at a single, 30-foot-long, make-your-own sandwich bar can be shortened by cutting the station into two sandwich bars with core sandwich items on both and specialty items—such as vegan selections— placed consistently in each substation. Such a change is possible only if the refrigerated wells that hold the sandwich ingredients are integrated into mobile carts as opposed to being fixed into a counter.

Care must be taken to position food stations so as to maximize flow with minimal cross-traffic. Another goal is the careful placement of food and beverage stations and cashiers. Figure 2.12 is a schematic that depicts a logical flow through a cafeteria servery and into the dining space. Note that the beverage stations are adjacent to the cashiers. This placement minimizes the chance that customers will spill drinks as they move through the servery. Also note that the hot food stations are situated just before the beverage stations. This helps ensure that food is still hot when customers reach their seats.

Efforts have been made to deinstitutionalize serveries, with less emphasis on stainless-steel surfaces and more attention to

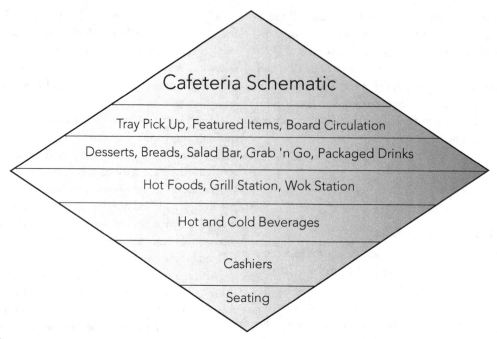

Figure 2.12
Cafeterias should have a logical progression of spaces, as shown here. Cashiers are placed at the dining room end of the servery in cash operations, and in the entry area when all-you-can-eat, flat-fee meal plans or cash meals are offered.

lighting, color, finishes, and textures that improve the look of the food and add warmth to the feeling of the space. Scramble systems depend on well-placed and descriptive signage to educate and direct customers. They are not as effective when serving transient guests because these guests are unfamiliar with the layout and can become confused.

CAFETERIA BEVERAGE AREAS

As mentioned earlier, cafeteria beverage areas are typically placed just before the dining area, where customers stop to pay for the items on their tray. In flat-fee cafeterias—where diners pay in advance for unlimited access to the cafeteria for a given meal period—beverage stations placed near seating areas can help minimize spills that could happen in bustling servery areas.

CAFETERIA DINING AREAS

No longer is cafeteria design typified by institutional green masonry block walls. Today, cafeteria design is often indistinguishable from full-service restaurant design. Elements such as greenery, carpeting, and artwork help stylize the setting. Particularly in corporate cafeterias, vaulted ceilings, textured wall treatments, soft lighting, comfortable seating,

indoor gardens, water elements, and contemporary styling add flair and attitude.

In markets where cafeteria-style operations compete with full-service restaurants, the decor package in the servery and dining areas is upbeat and the service is often interactive. As always, acoustic control is an important design consideration, along with easily maintained surfaces and durable furnishings. Perhaps one of the best ways to keep tables free from clutter is to place easily accessible tray disposal in a convenient location. When tray returns are placed adjacent to the only exit, customers are more likely to return their trays to those locations than when the tray return is placed away from the exit (Figures 2.13 and 2.14). During peak hours both dishwashing machines are used, while during off hours only one machine is needed. This can save labor, utilities, and cleaning chemicals.

Spatially, cafeteria dining rooms are often divided by barriers, levels, or other devices to allow customers a choice of open or intimate dining. Large cafeteria-style restaurants may have dining areas broken into several sections, some of which can be reserved for groups. Semiprivate cafeteria dining areas enable informal meetings to be conducted over a meal or a break period. Private dining rooms should

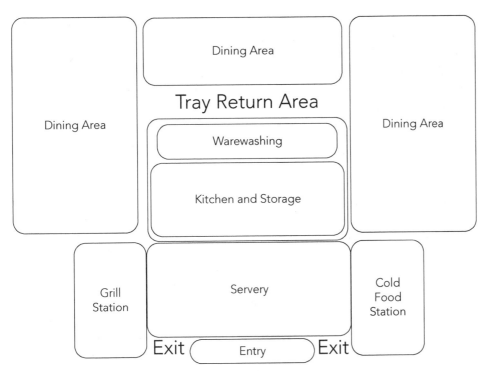

Figure 2.13
In this schematic, the tray return area is central to each of the dining spaces; however, diners near the bottom of the left and right dining spaces need to walk away from the exit to deposit their trays—not an optimum flow plan.

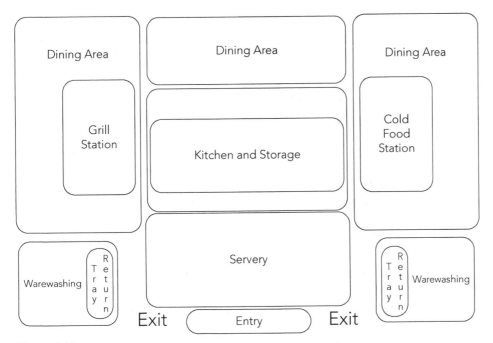

Figure 2.14
Here, the tray returns are adjacent to the exit points. Patrons throughout all of the dining areas can deposit their trays without backtracking away from the exit. The proximity of the warewashing to the service stations can also speed resupply of dishware to each station.

also be incorporated in the designs for hospitals, universities, or corporate cafeterias as optional dining/meeting space. Cafeteria dining areas are often used for special evening functions, so design flexibility should also be part of the spatial plan. Storage areas are needed for chairs and tables when the dining space is converted into a reception area or set up theater-style for a meeting.

CAFETERIA RESTROOMS

Cafeteria restrooms are usually incorporated into the design of the building that contains the cafeteria. Thus, their design is frequently not an integral component of the interior. Like all foodservice restrooms, however, they should be functional and easy to maintain. In meal-plan cafeterias, restrooms should be provided within the cafeteria proper so that customers need not exit and reenter the space.

CAFETERIA KITCHENS

Cafeteria kitchens traditionally have been designed with banks of steam-jacketed kettles, pressure steamers, and deck ovens, all aimed at bulk preparation of large batches of food. Recent changes in menus and servery design have changed the fare and the face of cafeteria kitchens. Pre-preparation is typically done in a remote kitchen, and foods are finished in each of the cooking stations as needed.

For instance, the toppings used in a pizza station are prepared in the kitchen, packaged, and held for use at the pizza station. The same is true of a stir-fry or Mongolian wok station. With foods being finished in each station, there is little or no food waste at the end of a shift. The pizza chef will assemble and bake pizzas only as customers remove slices from the self-service area, and stir-fry dishes are made to order. This practice helps to maximize food quality as well.

Shifting the locus of production out of the kitchen not only changes spatial allocation—requiring more servery space and less back-of-house space—but also creates different demands for cooking and refrigeration equipment in the back of the house. Low-pressure kitchen steamers are replaced with faster and smaller high-pressure steamers in the servery. Large kitchen steam kettles are replaced with smaller trunnion kettles, where soups are heated in small batches as needed.

The floorplan of the cafeteria kitchen depends, in large measure, on the type of organization the cafeteria is in. Hospitals, for example, require separate assembly areas for patient meals. Industrial kitchens may employ a satellite feeding program where foods are prepared in a central location, then served in serveries located throughout a large industrial complex. The larger and more complex the institution, the larger and more complex the kitchen. A smooth, straightforward flow from receiving to preparation to servery pass-through is always the spatial goal. Multipurpose equipment and labor-saving layouts also help achieve an efficient, successful design.

CAFETERIA SUPPORT AREAS

Storage and receiving areas for cafeteria operations are frequently separated from the production areas because most cafeterias are located within a multistory building shell. One receiving dock often serves the entire building, and the storage of foodservice goods may be overseen by the storeroom manager for all departments within the building. In such cases, it is important to incorporate a service elevator that allows for easy movement of goods from the dock to storage areas.

Offices and employee spaces are similar in size and nature to those in a commercial restaurant, although employees typically eat in the dining space (as in quick-service restaurants). Increased office space is required in complex foodservice operations such as hospitals, where multiple styles of service are supported by a single kitchen and support facility.

BANQUET

BANQUET EXTERIORS

Freestanding banquet facilities, typically used for special events, benefit from landscaping that not only entices customers but also affords an excellent backdrop for photo shoots. Landscape architecture should incorporate spaces for wedding services and receptions for the couple who have their hearts set on a close-to-nature experience. Banquet spaces within larger building complexes are ideally located near parking areas to accommodate customers who do not work inside the building.

BANQUET ENTRY AREAS

Banquet entry areas can serve a variety of functions:

Registration. For business events, space is required for registration desks or ID check for guests awaiting entry into the banquet space.

Waiting. The space must be large enough to accommodate guests waiting to be seated.

Reception. Both waiting space and circulation space is needed to enable guests to approach portable bars or for servers to pass drinks through the crowd. In some instances, hors d'oeuvre displays or passed hors d'oeuvres must be planned for as well. In cases where food is offered, an optimal design will provide clear access between the food station(s) and the kitchen or backup stations where pre-prepared foods are available.

Display. Displays of event materials may also have to be planned for when designing banquet entry areas.

BANQUET DINING AREAS

Banquet dining areas must be planned with flexibility in mind. A given space may be used to serve 350 people at a sit-down breakfast or 300 for a lavish luncheon buffet. It might also be used as a plenary meeting room for 450 with full audiovisual support, or as a dinner-dance space for 275 dinner guests.

For example, large ballrooms are often designed as flexible space that can be divided into several smaller rooms. While the ceiling and depth of the ballroom remain the same, the smaller rooms will be narrower. To prevent a "tunnel" effect, ceiling treatments that make the ceiling look lower can be helpful.

BANQUET BEVERAGE AREAS

Most banquet operations use portable bar equipment. The number of bars and bartenders must be sufficient to meet the demands of the group. Generally, one bar setup should be sufficient to service 75 guests. However, if the cocktail period is short, additional bars may be needed to ensure that all guests are served in a timely fashion, even though they will take away from the waiting space and circulation space.

BANQUET RESTROOMS

Unlike restaurant restrooms, where the flow of guests is continuous and even, banquet restrooms must be capable of handling a large volume of periodic use. It is critical to have a sufficient number of stalls and urinals to ensure that banquet patrons can use the facilities quickly. In women's restrooms, areas with flattering lighting allow for a quick makeup check.

BANQUET KITCHENS

Banquet kitchens require volume production equipment, capable of allowing cooks to prepare enough food in a single batch to meet the serving needs of the event. Additionally, there needs to be enough refrigerated and hot holding equipment to maintain foods at temperature. For cold foods, it's optimal to have enough refrigeration space to house carts that accommodate all the plated cold courses. Similarly, kitchen designers must plan for enough heated banquet carts to hold all of the hot plated meals. They also need to allocate enough space in the floorplan to plate meals in an assembly-line format.

BANQUET SUPPORT AREAS

Banquet support areas are often ignored, but they are critical to success. Space is needed to store banquet tables and chairs and risers when they are not in use. Space is also needed to store the myriad pieces of banquet tableware that may be used only periodically. Access space to banquet areas is also important. In the case of dividable ballrooms, double-walled corridors can eliminate noise carryover while providing easy access from the kitchen area to all parts of the dining space.

TAKEOUT

TAKEOUT EXTERIORS

Many takeout operations are housed within an existing facility, so the exterior is not a crucial consideration. However, those that incorporate a drive-through window must consider exterior features. Traffic flow patterns change when a drive-through is added to a restaurant. The area allocated to cars that queue up for the takeout window takes away from parking spaces. Sufficient space is needed for the queue of cars to ensure that they do not snake out onto the roadway. Drive-throughs are most effective when takeout foods can be quickly prepared (or are pre-prepared) and quickly packaged. A second line or a valet delivery to the car for preorders can speed customers through the line. In any scenario, a payment window early in the queue will speed service to all customers.

TAKEOUT ENTRY AREAS

The most important consideration of a takeout entry is to provide easy access to the street. Takeout entry areas should also be planned so as to minimize the impact of the takeout business on dine-in business. This can mean a separate entryway for each type of customer.

Self-serve disposables in the entry area cut back on the time that counter staff would need to pack such items. However, self-service can lead to higher costs and a lot more waste because customers often take more disposables than they need. Bins of utensils can also pose a health hazard as they are handled by staff, who pull them out of large cases and then load them into utensil bins. The alternative shown in Figure 1.15 dispenses individual utensils and does not require staff to handle the utensils at all.

TAKEOUT DINING AREA

By definition, takeout operations do not include dining spaces.

TAKEOUT BEVERAGE AREAS

In many takeout operations, a beverage area set up for self-service is the best option. From a design perspective, this necessitates packaged-beverage display cases that are easy to load and access. For dispensed beverages, the holding capacity and type of cup dispenser is important to consider. The dispenser must be easy for staff to reload and for customers to use. Often, the empty cup is given to the customer along with the rest of the order. This saves labor and prevents customers from taking a beverage that they have not paid for.

TAKEOUT RESTROOMS

As with the dining space, restrooms are typically not needed to support takeout restaurants. However, when takeout is combined with quick service, restrooms are essential.

TAKEOUT KITCHENS

Takeout kitchens can range from a nonkitchen operation supplied with foods prepared elsewhere to a limited kitchen with high-speed cooking equipment. One of the keys to a successful takeout concept is a menu that can be prepared in advance and then cooked or served quickly when ordered. Asian menus are ideal for takeout because the bite-sized ingredients cook quickly in a wok. Rotisserie chicken and batch-prepared side dishes are also suited to takeout because meals can be plated from a ready supply of cooked foods.

TAKEOUT SUPPORT AREAS

Storage areas for packaging materials are essential. Order-taking areas and equipment must also be incorporated into the design to ensure quick and accurate communication of orders among the customer, the order taker, the food preparers, and those who assemble the orders.

SUMMARY

Space planning for any type of foodservice enterprise incorporates common design principles. A well-designed restaurant, however, is one where the design team has carefully attended to the character of the operation and designed spaces so that they work most effectively for the customers, the staff, and management. Time must be spent developing the floorplan and considering, rejecting, and refining spatial options until arriving at the best possible solution.

CHAPTER 3

THE PSYCHOLOGY OF DESIGN

"We shape our buildings and our buildings shape us." Winston Churchill expressed this thought to the House of Commons just after World War II. He was referring to a proposed plan to change the shape of the legislators' meeting room, concerned that a change of physical environment would, in turn, effect change in the legislative process.

Churchill's point—that environment affects behavior—is a well-documented fact, but only recently has the knowledge of social scientists (environmental and behavioral psychologists) been deliberately applied to the practice of restaurant design.

ENVIRONMENT AND BEHAVIOR

Applied research supports the notion that customers' attitudes and behavior are influenced by their interaction with environmental elements. These elements have been referred to as "servicescapes" in academic literature since Mary J. Bitner, in "Servicescapes: The Impact of Physical Surroundings on Customers and Employees" (*Journal of Marketing* 56(2), pp. 57–71), first wrote about the role of environmental factors in 1992. Anna S. Mattila and Jochen Wirtz, in their 2001 article, "Congruency of Scent and Music as a Driver of In-Store Evaluations and Behavior" (*Journal of Retailing* 77(2), pp. 273–289) showed supporting findings that " . . . when the arousal levels of ambient scent and background music matched, consumers' evaluations of the shopping experience were enhanced." From a restaurant design perspective, this finding implies that matching soothing background music—classical, for example—with subtle aromas of roasting thyme and oregano, or jazz with tangy citrus aromas, creates more pleasing servicescapes than Gregorian chants overlaid with the piquant aroma of roasting ancho peppers.

Physical factors could be the light intensity in a room, the temperature, or tactile features of a chair or tabletop elements. For example, consider the chair you are now sitting in. You might be able to read this text for hours because the design of the chair and the texture of the seat covers are conducive to reading. Conversely, you might already feel uncomfortable. The chair could be so comfortable that you want to take a nap, or the angle and hardness of the seat might cause you to adjust yourself frequently, or get up to stretch your legs before coming back to this book. This psychological reaction to physical features is important to the selection of seating in a restaurant, because it can influence guests either to eat quickly and move on or to linger over a meal and choose to stay for an after-dinner cordial.

Seating selection is one of many decisions made by the design team that should reflect a working knowledge of design psychology. The combination of all environmental elements affects how people feel and, consequently, how they act in a given space—how long they stay, how comfortable they feel while they are there, what they remember, and, perhaps, if they want to come back again.

HOW SPACE IS PERCEIVED

In order to analyze the psychological impact of design elements, one must understand the many ways in which people perceive their surroundings. According to the anthropologist Edward T. Hall, in his book *The Hidden Dimension* (first published by Doubleday in 1966), sensory apparatus falls into two general categories: distance receptors and immediate receptors. The distance receptors—the eyes, the ears, and the nose—are used to examine faraway objects and sensations. These receptors allow us to gather information without making contact with an object or person. The immediate receptors—the skin, the membranes, and the muscles—examine the world up close. The immediate receptors enable the experience of touch and the perception of such diverse sensations as temperature, texture, hardness, and shape.

Hall also defines different distance zones because distance from any given object influences the perception of that object. A classic example is the impressionist painting that looks like blobs of color on close inspection but, from a distance, reveals a Parisian landscape. So, too, in a restaurant must the design consider the sensory impact of objects that are close to the guest along with objects that are across the dining room. Hall's distance zones, which are excellent guidelines for environmental design planning, are as follows:

Public distance—12 feet and beyond. The feeling of distance one gets when entering a high-ceilinged restaurant or a large, open lobby. Public distance encompasses the view when walking into the dining area itself or when entering a spacious pickup area in a kitchen.

Social distance—4 feet to 12 feet. Customers feel social distance when they watch the television screen above a bar, entertainers in a nightclub, or the service staff bustling about the restaurant. Similarly, the kitchen staff experience social distance while working in a display kitchen, where guests walk by, or in a bakery station, where workers at other stations can be seen.

Personal distance—18 inches to 4 feet. The feeling of distance experienced when speaking across the table to dining companions. This is also the feeling two kitchen staff members get when working at a double-sided workstation or at a broiler station positioned next to a fry station.

Intimate distance—physical contact to 18 inches. The feeling of being close enough to touch a dining companion, as when seated side by side on a banquette.

It is the sometimes crowded feeling when a diner's chair is bumped by passing service staff or a cook brushes past a coworker in a cramped kitchen.

Another important influence on the way people perceive space is their ethnic background and country of origin. In Europe, for example, people are comfortable in crowded dining conditions, hence the popularity of cozy cafés and beer halls, where tables and people press together in a way that members of other cultures might find stifling. In contrast, the hushed atmosphere of the Japanese teahouse in downtown Tokyo, with its sense of serenity and spaciousness, reflects a totally different cultural orientation. The study of these responses by persons of varying cultures falls within the theory of proxemics, which was developed by Hall. His contention was that perceptions of spaces are, in part, molded by culture and not solely from sensory apparatus.

If management can identify the cultural characteristics of the target market, design can be geared to suit it. In this context, cultural characteristics could indicate ethnicity, urban versus rural preferences, the needs of bicoastal travelers, or the tastes of Baby Boomers versus Millennials. Mark S. Rosenbaum and Detra Montoya, in their March 2007 article "Am I Welcome Here? Exploring How Ethnic Consumers Assess Their Place Identity" (*Journal of Business Research* 60(3), pp. 206–214), identified the importance of how consumers perceive physical and social elements in a consumption setting. From a restaurant design perspective, this would suggest that gilt-edged walls and linen-covered tables with fine china, glassware, and sterling silver flatware would appeal to customers of certain socioeconomic backgrounds while intimidating others.

Additionally, their research discovered that

. . . ethnicity of employees and customers in a setting, a process termed "place likening," and by responding to verbal and nonverbal cues in a consumption setting . . . demonstrate how physical and place identity elements influence responses among Hispanic and homosexual consumers.

There are subtle implications of this research. For instance, the incongruity of black-leather-clad waitresses in microskirts could derail the potential for success of even the most carefully designed full-service restaurant serving haute cuisine. Similarly, design that is intended to appeal to a targeted ethnic group could fail due to the exogenous ethnic makeup of the service staff or even the manager.

Distance Receptors

Visual Space

Visual perspective is affected by the structure of the eye and the angle at which objects are viewed. The retina—the light-sensitive part of the eye—is composed of three areas, each performing a different function. One important function is peripheral vision, the field of vision outside the line of direct sight.

Hall cites the following example of peripheral vision:

A man with normal vision, sitting in a restaurant twelve to fifteen feet from a table where other people are seated, can see the following out of the corner of his eye. He can tell that the table is occupied and possibly count the people present, particularly if there is some movement.

At an angle of 45 degrees he can tell the color of a woman's hair as well as the color of her clothing, though he cannot identify the material. He can tell whether the woman is looking at and talking to her partner but not whether she has a ring on her finger. He can pick up the gross movements of her escort, but he can't see the watch on his wrist. He can tell the gender of a person, his body build, and his age in very general terms but not whether he knows him or not.
(***The Hidden Dimension***, p. 72)

People can perceive all specific details about an individual only when they are directly in front of the retina—providing they are not too far away.

The more designers understand how vision zones work, the more effectively they can manipulate visual space. For example, a diner's field of vision is broader when sitting on a banquette than when sitting in a booth (Figure 3.1). Banquette seating also places customers within personal

Figure 3.1
The field of vision from a banquette seat is wide open, while booth seating provides a feeling of intimacy. This row of rounded booths at Fulton's in Chicago offers a level of privacy, while at the same time allowing diners to look out over the Chicago River.
(Photo by Joseph Durocher.)

distance of each other, unlike when they are seated in booths, particularly high-backed booths.

Guests are more affected by surrounding elements in a banquette and more private in a booth, where the field of vision is narrower. This implies that banquette seating—which provides more visual stimulation—encourages faster turnover and is especially appropriate for a casual restaurant or one with a big open kitchen. Booth seating, because it limits visual stimulation and distractions, provides a feeling of intimacy, and leads to slower turnover of tables, which works well for restaurants that want to attract business diners or romantic couples.

Personal space can be real or perceived, so using angled tables rather than banquettes can eliminate the perception that another customer is in one's personal space (Figure 3.2). In fact, freestanding angled tables can create a sense of intimacy and cut visual distraction throughout a dining room. Increasing the space between tables can also lessen visual distraction, although this is a costly technique. Lighting levels can be modified to further limit the scope of vision,

and light or cool colors can help create an overall sense of spaciousness.

Designers often manipulate visual space with mirrors and reflective surfaces (Figures 3.3a and b). Mirrors expand the sense of space as well as the field of vision. (Used incorrectly or to excess, however, they can cause visual confusion and disorientation such as one can experience in a "fun house" at a carnival.) Mirrored columns or mirrored horizontal or vertical planes can open up an otherwise claustrophobic room while adding sparkle and visual excitement. Here are some mirror solutions:

- *Art mirrors.* These large, framed mirrors typically sit high on a wall to give an overall sense of openness to a space.
- *Mirror strips.* The strips are frequently applied above a banquette or a wall-mounted coffee bar to offer the customers facing the wall a glimpse of the action behind them. Mirrored strips at eye level permit a selective (and secretive) view of the bustling waiters, sparkling tabletops, and other diners to the rear.

Figure 3.2
To decrease visual distraction, designers angle tables to redirect sight lines away from other tables.

Figure 3.3a
Mirror strips allow diners eating at a wall-mounted eating counter to check out the goings and comings behind them at Nanoosh in New York City (a).
(Photo by Joseph Durocher)

Figure 3.3b
The large art mirror at Cafe Descartes (b) in Chicago demonstrates how a mirror can become a décor piece while also expanding the feel of the space.
(Photo by Joseph Durocher)

- *Mirrored columns.* This application allows customers seated in a middle of a room to catch a glimpse of other customers from varying angles.
- *Ceiling mirrors.* Their hard surface reflects a good deal of sound, but they tend to open up a space and offer whimsical views of activity throughout the room.

Another effective means of modifying visual space is to minimize sight lines. A frosted glass or glass brick wall, for instance, limits visual perception. Light and motion can be perceived through the glass, yet a feeling of intimacy is maintained for the diner. In some cases, one-way or reflective glass is used on exterior window walls. Diners can thus look out, but passersby can't look in. However, these reflective windows can, from the outside, give the impression that the restaurant is closed, which is not good for business.

AUDITORY SPACE

Auditory space involves how the ear works and what, exactly, we hear. The ear actually picks up sound from two main zones. Primary audio space, in which one hears and is heard clearly, extends to 20 feet away. Background audio space extends from 20 to 100 feet away. In many dining areas, sounds in the primary audio space must be modified and turned into background noise so that diners can hear table companions and servers and can speak to them without strain. At the same time, they should be conscious of a friendly background buzz. This state has been called convivial intimacy. It means that guests feel secure in their privacy, yet part of a larger whole. One of the greatest challenges is to ensure that none of the seats is overpowered with background noise. Thus, the impact of ceiling speakers, wall-mounted televisions, and sound-producing equipment in the back of the house must be considered.

While some operators pump up the volume in an effort to create a hip young vibe, the backlash can have negative effects on employees and diners and could lead to litigation. The Zagat *America's Top Restaurants 2008* survey identifies noise as the second most common complaint and the Occupational Safety and Health Administration (OSHA) sets standards for employees who work in environments where the sound levels are above 80 decibels (dB), which is the case in many restaurants. The psychological benefit of loud music or a loud conversational buzz should be carefully weighed against the negative aspect of overly noisy interiors.

Control of primary and background auditory space is also important in the kitchen. Kitchens are innately noisy spaces made louder by communications between kitchen workers and the service staff. Sound above 65 dB will force workers and servers to yell so that they can be heard over the background noise. When remote printers are linked to the point of sale (POS), the need for conversation between production and service staff is significantly decreased. Although background noise can add vitality and energy to the kitchen, the sound must be controlled to minimize carryover into the dining area. This carryover sound is of particular concern in display kitchens because of their proximity to dining areas.

While it makes operational sense to place dish machines close to the entry door of a kitchen, such placement can lead to sound carryover into the dining room. A double set of doors, along with added insulation in the wall between the two spaces between the kitchen and dining room, can help minimize noise carryover.

Because the restaurant, by definition, is a noisy environment, acoustic control often involves the skillful application of sound-absorbing materials with the goal of achieving background buzz. Soft materials like carpet, upholstery, wall coverings, and curtains, as well as acoustic ceilings, panels, and banners, all help mute noise levels, but the most effective way to deaden noise is with ceiling treatments (Figure 3.4).

Designers can effectively combine acoustic materials with decorative applications. For example, a treatment composed of fabric-covered baffles that temper noise levels might serve as a unifying design statement that pulls together the entire room. Baffles, which generally are made of glass or mineral fiber bats encased in perforated metal or fabric, are especially effective in high-ceilinged spaces.

For retrofit, the acoustic panel is an efficient and cost-effective choice because installation does not involve structural work. Faced with woven fabric or perforated vinyl, the panels come in a variety of shapes and sizes and are easily attached to walls or ceilings. They can even be formed into the restaurant's logo or other graphic symbols. Similarly, plain acoustic ceiling tiles can be painted to reflect the restaurant's design theme.

Another technique that can be particularly effective in helping soften loud conversation is the use of background music. Here, the principle at work involves masking undesirable noise—voices at other tables, the clatter of dishes, and so on—with the desirable sounds of music suited to the taste of the restaurant's clientele. As noted in Chapter 4, however, it is important to control the level of background music so that it does not become a distraction. Restaurants with live entertainment face a particular problem because live music often becomes foreground music. For guests who wish to listen to the music, this is a pleasing addition to the environment, but for those wishing to converse while they dine or sit at a cocktail table, foreground music can be irritating.

The obvious solution—cutting the size of the dining spaces to quiet primary audio space—is not always effective because sound waves travel through floors, walls, and ceilings. Just because adjacent dining rooms are visually separate doesn't mean that they are acoustically separate. In operations that require a single dining area, careful attention to sound-catching corners, shapes, and spaces can significantly limit reverberating sound.

In some types of operations, such as the quick-service restaurant or the bar-dominated gathering place, little attention is given to controlling primary audio space because high noise levels create movement, excitement, and action—all desirable in these places. Popular see-and-be-seen restaurants throughout the country often share remarkably high noise levels created by hard surfaces such as steel, glass, wood, and concrete. Many also have high or domed ceilings that reflect or focus sound, generating hot spots of high noise levels. It's important to consider that all of these sound-reflecting surfaces and materials can generate reverberation and cause an echo effect. However, as noted earlier, high noise levels can turn off some customers and create a problem for employees.

Figure 3.4
Nothing is more effective for controlling noise than acoustic ceiling treatments. Here, at Cafe Descartes in Chicago, a fire-retardant swag draped in a wavelike pattern adds color and a sense of movement and helps dampen any reflected sound.
(Photo by Joseph Durocher)

OLFACTORY SPACE

The olfactory sense is the sense of smell, which, despite its importance, is frequently overlooked in restaurant design. Smell evokes the deepest memories of all the senses, but how often does the design allow pleasant aromas to waft through the restaurant—aromas that customers will remember the next time that they think about where to eat? As pointed out earlier, how well those aromas meld with other design aspects—such as the type of music—to create a pleasing and appropriate mix of stimuli should be considered.

Given current interest in fresh, whole ingredients, filtering their aromas through the front of the house could have a positive effect on diners. Because an absence of smell obscures memories, the indiscriminate elimination of all olfactory sensation can have a negative psychological effect. The smell of fresh-baked breads outside a boulangerie or of slow-smoked pork shoulder at a barbecue restaurant helps stimulate the appetite and customers' olfactory remembrance of a restaurant. Today, aroma infusers are available for front-of-the-house ventilation systems. The infusers slowly dispense the aroma of fresh coffee, fresh bread, and dozens of other memory-provoking essences.

Another technique to enhance the guest's aromatic experience is tableside cooking. In some recipes, for example, a dash of Worcestershire sauce is added to the heated pan. The accompanying sizzle and the aroma of the vaporizing sauce tantalize palates and prompt others to purchase tableside preparations. This technique is used effectively in Mexican restaurants, where sizzling fajita platters are paraded to the table; in Asian restaurants, where foods are placed on a sizzle platter just before serving; and in teppanyaki restaurants, where foods are cooked on a flat griddle (teppan) in front of diners.

Smells can also create negative feelings. The stale smell of beer or slightly soured mixers tells the customer that a bar lacks a good sanitation program. The smell of a bouquet of lilacs when customers are trying to savor a vintage Bordeaux indicates an ineffective ventilation system—and management's insensitivity to their customers' appreciation of wine. Negative smells can attach to such items as glassware; using a stale bar towel to polish clean glasses can impart an off-odor that will be released when beer or other beverages are placed in the glass. Of course, the smell of garbage in the parking lot sours the stomach.

IMMEDIATE RECEPTORS

TACTILE SPACE

Tactile space includes both what is actually perceptible by touch and what relates visually to touch. A wineglass, for example, is an item that a guest touches in a restaurant, and a coarse fieldstone wall is a surface whose texture engages the visual perception. Tactile space is extremely important because it can psychologically warm a room, which makes people feel comfortable, or it can make a room feel cold, such as when stainless-steel sheeting is used on the walls.

Tactile elements involve people with their surroundings. This is particularly important in modern interiors and in large, high-ceilinged spaces, because both tend to make people feel separate from the environment. Diners often like to feel impressed by the design of a restaurant, but they don't like to feel overwhelmed. Textural architectural and decorative surfaces like fabric, brick, upholstery, and artwork can all keep the environment from feeling distant or intimidating (Figure 3.5).

The touchable items in a restaurant—seating and tabletop elements—have a lot to do with people's enjoyment of the dining experience. The degree of seating comfort, for instance, has a great deal of influence on the length of the meal and should be chosen to suit the facility. Natural materials, upholstered seats, and padded armrests maintain high comfort levels and are recommended for high-ticket establishments. Comfortable seating also helps customers feel content as they sit through the multiple courses—which play a pivotal role between profit and loss in many fine restaurants—for one to three hours.

Tactile sensations can also be negative. No one likes the sticky sensation of plastic upholstery in warm temperatures, the feeling of pitching too far forward in a hard seat, or leaning against a seat back that is uncomfortable. Yet some degree of tactile discomfort can be appropriate for a restaurant that depends on fast turnover, like a quick-service eatery. Here, the seating can be pleasing to the eye but not comfortable to sit in for long. This reflects a common design technique in the quick-service environment: furniture that looks good but becomes uncomfortable to sit in after about 15 minutes.

Figure 3.5
The mesh wall behind the curly branches in David Burke's Primehouse in Chicago adds tactile interest and helps to absorb sound, which mutes what could be an otherwise noisy environment.
(Photo by Joseph Durocher)

Tactile sensations are also important in the kitchen. Well-balanced knives, solid worktables, and substantial cutting boards give kitchen workers a sense of security and comfort.

Turnover in 30 minutes or less is not only essential to the success of quick-service restaurants but also plays a pivotal role in customer satisfaction and the ultimate profitability of such operations. Frequently, cafeterias serve large numbers of diners in a limited period. Comfortable seats can slow table turns and lead to dissatisfied customers who wander around the dining room with trays full of food in much the same way as they hunt for parking spaces for their cars.

In any type of restaurant, the tabletop elements—table surfaces, flatware, glassware, dishware, table accoutrements—play a major role in customer satisfaction. The feel of a perfectly balanced fork, the coolness of a chilled beer mug, and the pleasant touch of a linen napkin add to the dining experience. Even in an inexpensive eatery, the choice of tabletop utensils is critical to diners' enjoyment of a meal because of the direct contact with these items. Tabletop elements, from paper plates to crystal goblets, should always be carefully chosen.

Tactile sensors are finely tuned. The fingers detect smoothness and temperature, and the muscles in the fingers, hands, and arms weigh tabletop items, calculate how well built they are, and determine imperfections in balance or form. The oenophile sipping a 1961 Château Lafite-Rothschild from an improperly balanced wineglass does not fully enjoy the experience, and a five-degree rise in temperature as growing numbers of diners overload the cooling system on a hot day can make guests irritable and hasten their departure.

On the tabletop, as in the restaurant interior itself, avoiding a homogeneous textural weight is advisable. The tabletop could offer a pleasing tactile experience through the contrast of a smooth marble table surface, nubby linen-blend napkins, and cut-crystal glassware. Likewise, a casual restaurant might feature smooth polyurethane wood tabletops with woven placemats and heavy stoneware. Attention to tabletop detail helps create a strong impression of value in the minds of clients. It shows concern for the things people touch and implies a high regard for the food as well.

Tactile space is an important concern with takeout foods. A thin napkin for fried chicken tells people that they will have trouble wiping their fingers when they are through. Flimsy plastic forks and knives encourage people to take two of each and prepare for all of them to break—hardly the message that should be sent to paying customers.

Tactile sensations are also important in the kitchen. Well-balanced knives, solid worktables, and substantial cutting boards give kitchen workers a sense of security and comfort. Nonslip flooring is another crucial design element in the kitchen. The tactile sensation of secure footing is essential to a sense of safety.

Another part of the restaurant where tactile attention is important is the restrooms. We all tend to equate a dirty restroom with a dirty kitchen. By the same token, attention to restroom detail causes customers to feel that management cares about the broader quality of their dining experience. Skillful use of tactile space, for instance, might mix Corian™ or marble surfaces, terra-cotta flooring, attractive dried flower arrangements, and decorative tile walls. Such textural diversity creates a pleasant effect, yet provides surfaces that are easily cleaned and highly durable.

Food, of course, is the most tactile element of all (Figure 3.6). Food presentation works on many levels to impress—or distress—the diner. In addition to food's appearance, mouthfeel—its texture in the mouth and the complete organoleptic experience that includes taste, texture, and temperature—is an element of customer satisfaction.

If presented in a nondescript way, even well-prepared dishes can look unappetizing. Conversely, carrot curls on sandwich plates or sprigs of lemon thyme on poached filets of lingcod go a long way toward creating the impression of good food. A delightful textural balance of foods is literally mouthwatering.

Even in the quick-service environment, tactile cues can create the impression of food value. Packaging design often plays an important part. If the standard ketchup container that spells out the word *ketchup* on one side and names the manufacturer on the other also shows an image of red, ripe tomatoes, the customer is more likely to perceive the value of its contents. The average quick-service container, however, has nondescript surfaces that give little indication of the contents and in no way help sell the product. Home meal replacement (HMR) offerings, however, are packaged in containers with see-through lids that allow the food to merchandise itself.

Corporate branding and packaging can have a significant influence on diners. A study published in the August 2007 issue of *Journal of Pediatric and Adolescent Medicine* clearly showed the psychological impact of branding. In the study, children were given samples of food and beverages from McDonald's. Some samples were in the original McDonald's wrappers, while other samples were in generic wrappers. The children preferred the taste of the food and drinks in wrappers with McDonald's images on the packaging, even though the food was identical in both samples.

THERMAL SPACE

Thermal space relates to temperature. In the restaurant, the most important psychological effect of thermal space is its influence on one's sense of crowding: hot rooms feel more crowded than cool rooms. Consequently, a full restaurant should be kept comfortably cool so that diners do not experience the discomfort of feeling hemmed in.

Figure 3.6
At the Castello Banfi in Montalcino, Italy, this dish of grilled shrimp and chive risotto delights the customer by using the food to give a burst of color and sculptural dimension.
(Photo by Joseph Durocher)

Half-empty restaurants might benefit from warmer temperatures because the warmth helps create a feeling of more people in the room.

Overheated kitchens result in overheated tempers and, ultimately, have an adverse effect on productivity. "If you can't stand the heat, get out of the kitchen" does not carry the weight in a labor-short marketplace that it once did.

Temperature control is a particular problem in the design of ballrooms or restaurants with window walls. Here, the heat loads—from the occupants of the room or the rays of the sun—can periodically overload cooling systems and make the rooms feel uncomfortably warm.

KINESTHETIC SPACE

Kinesthetic space is the psychological (not physiological) perception of space. Physical conditions affect kinesthetic perception. A room that can be crossed in one or two steps creates a different sensation than a room that takes 15 steps to traverse. A 20-by-40-foot room with a 7-foot ceiling feels a lot smaller than the same room with an 11-foot ceiling.

Designers can manipulate kinesthetic space in the restaurant by a variety of techniques—mirrors, barriers, and furniture arrangements—that help achieve a desired psychological effect. A lowered ceiling over perimeter seating, for instance, affords a more intimate dining experience than a high-ceilinged central area in the same restaurant. Tatami rooms with sliding doors also offer a feeling of intimacy, yet when packed with diners they could feel claustrophobic.

Another aspect of kinesthetic space is that the fewer restrictions to movement, the larger the space feels. When comparing two identical rooms with different furniture arrangements, the one that permits the greater variety of free movement is perceived as larger. This principle can be effectively applied in compact urban storefronts, where a wall-hugging seating arrangement keeps the space from feeling cramped.

After explaining how the vocabulary of the social scientist can be applied to the process of restaurant design, we examine next the psychological effects of three crucial design applications: spatial arrangements, lighting, and color.

SPATIAL ARRANGEMENTS

Spatial arrangements should always be orderly, guiding customers and employees in a logical progression from space to space: from exterior to entry zone to dining room, from kitchen to dining room to bar and back to dining room. The restaurant exterior, including signage, parking lot, and landscaping (when applicable), is important because it creates the first impression and gives visual cues about the type of facility within. Spatial features such as large parking lots, the location of doorways, and covered walks between the valet and the entryway can draw diners in or prompt them to go elsewhere.

As for the interior, social scientists divide space into two main areas: barriers and fields. Barriers include walls, screens, symbols, and objects. Fields include shapes, size, orientation, and environmental conditions. In the restaurant, both serve functional and psychological purposes.

Barriers often act as space dividers to create feelings of privacy. For example, a dividing wall can separate the functions of entry and dining, and potted palms can help delineate small, intimate dining areas in a large room (Figure 3.7).

Fields can be thought of as the complete architectural plan: the overall layout of space with its accompanying environmental conditions of climate and lighting. These elements substantially influence how people feel in a space.

A small room helps create a cozy feeling for a gourmet restaurant, and a large room helps engage diners in the see-and-be-seen atmosphere of a theatrical restaurant. The mixed sensation of barrier and field of the open kitchen, and the proximity of work and dining areas, affects both the kitchen staff and the diners.

Shape also has psychological impact. Because people tend to be attracted to curved forms, architects often build large, curved walls. The upward sweep of these curved lines can be uplifting. Restaurateur Drew Nieporent suggests that restaurants "need curves, round tables, and banquettes. People like corner tables and by curving the banquette, you end up with a corner." Many restaurant designs use curved banquettes and other curvaceous shapes to great advantage (Figure 3.8).

Finally, the interaction between spaces—between the outside and the inside, between the front of the house and the back of the house—can help communicate information about the quality of the dining experience and about the food itself. A display kitchen or more subtle kitchen references, like wood-burning pizza ovens or pickup windows, not only signal messages about the food but also allow diners a privileged glimpse of the back of the house. Psychologists maintain that people like seeing what goes on behind the scenes and that those staged regions that bridge the front and back of the house can generate a lot of customer interest. In this context, service staff uniforms also link kitchen and dining rooms and send messages about both the food and the type of establishment. Black jeans and a T-shirt, for example, carry a completely different set of associations from a full-skirted, blue-and-white-checked gingham uniform, the former belonging to a hip, expensive inner-city bistro and the latter to a popular, moderately priced pancake house.

Within the dining area, designers can manipulate spatial arrangements for a variety of psychological effects. A really bad table is never necessary. Terraced floor levels rising back from windows, for example, can provide each table with a view. In a large room, terracing from side to side defines spatial areas and creates islands of intimacy. Other techniques that facilitate comfortable dining and camouflage room size include lowering parts of the ceiling (mentioned previously in respect to kinesthetic space) and enclosing an area with architectural or decorative dividers. The larger the room, the greater the need for such enclosures.

Furniture arrangements can facilitate or retard interaction among people and should be chosen to suit the type of facility. For example, a restaurant that functions as a

Figure 3.7
In this Judd Brown Design of Harbor Grill in Florida, vertical and horizontal barriers and fields help to separate each of the dining areas.
(Photography by Jack Gardner Photography)

gathering and meeting place wants to encourage interaction among guests. Here, face-to-face seating and an asymmetrical bar shape can help draw people together. Other facilitators include uncluttered lounge seating and casual-looking furniture. Conversely, when privacy is desired, widely spaced tables can be arranged at angles to each other to restrict views of other diners. Chairs in a row, barriers between chairs, and linear bars act to retard conversation.

Rooms with a regular layout of tables all neatly lined up in rows seem formal. Tables that are randomly spaced throughout the room, with different sizes of tables mixed together, and rooms divided with barriers lead to feelings of informality and even intimacy.

In the back of the house, equipment arrangements can retard or improve interaction among employees. The equipment itself or divider walls serve as barriers. However, half-high divider walls can help interaction among workers because they allow people to talk to each other. Limiting barriers can also improve supervision. Managers who can easily see every corner of the front and back of the house can more readily supervise employees.

FENG SHUI

Feng shui is the Chinese art of geomancy: the belief that the placement and location of buildings and objects can harmonize or conflict with the natural environment and cause good or bad fortune. Principles of feng shui can be used in site selection and the placement of buildings on the

Figure 3.8
This large curved banquette at Mercat in Chicago offers a level of privacy and is far less rigid than traditional straight banquettes.
(Photos of Mercat by Frank Oudeman)

land as well as the placement of elements within a building and even the naming of a business.

A restaurant with good feng shui is said to be a good place in which to conduct business, and it affords a sense of well-being and equilibrium, while a restaurant with bad feng shui will be uncomfortable for diners and bad for business. For example, a restaurant built on a T-shaped lot across from a triangular pond surrounded by oddly shaped trees is said to have bad feng shui that will cause the restaurant to fail.

Quick-service giant McDonald's incorporated feng shui in a renovation of their franchised Hacienda Heights, California, unit in 2007. The design incorporates leather-covered seats, soft earth tone colors, live bamboo, and water elements all geared to creating a harmonious environment based on principles of feng shui—that would be understood and appreciated by the large Asian community living near this restaurant. This design makeover is in keeping with the McDonald's philosophy of remodeling restaurants to cater to local tastes and to prompt diners to enjoy the environment and want to return.

Many feng shui principles relate to sound design principles in general use. It can be prudent for the design team to consider the positive psychological impact of integrating good feng shui wherever possible.

LIGHTING

Lighting is arguably the single most important element in restaurant design because incorrect lighting can obviate the effectiveness of all the other elements. Lighting is a critical psychological component as well; more than any other design application, illumination creates mood. Lighting can make a room feel intimate or expansive, subdued or exciting, friendly or hostile, quiet or full of electrifying energy. Not only is the intensity of the lighting important but also the light source, the quality of the lighting, and the contrast of light levels in different areas. In the kitchen, lighting intensity must be maintained at a level that does not lead to eyestrain.

Ideally, a lighting design consultant is retained to handle the complexities of designing an effective illumination scheme. If the budget prohibits the hiring of a lighting designer, the architect or interior designer must be well versed in lighting psychology and sensitive to the specific demands of the facility. A bustling cafeteria calls for a bright ambient light level and brightly lit architectural surfaces to help move people through the space. An elegant à la carte French restaurant should have a more subdued illumination scheme to encourage leisurely dining. A source of illumination between diners, like candles or reflected light bounced off the tabletop, draws them together while providing a complementary glow that helps overcome the negative aspects of downlighting.

Remember that restaurant lighting is similar to theatrical lighting; both set the stage for a dramatic production that relies heavily on setting and atmosphere to carry it off. Although the lighting scheme should always respond to the type of facility, the following guidelines for psychologically effective illumination apply to any restaurant.

LIGHTING LEVEL CONTROL

A dimming control system that can modify illumination levels for optimum psychological effectiveness is important to any lighting scheme. The system should be changed in response to the time of day and to create different moods for different occasions. The same room can feel bright and cheerful for breakfast, restful for lunch, animated for cocktails, and romantic for dinner—all due to carefully planned light programming. If the budget permits, an automated

system can be programmed to react to external light conditions and deliver the desired light levels for any time of day or type of function. When possible dimming systems should not be adjusted during dining hours, as this can be distracting to the clientele. Nevertheless, control systems should be clearly marked to facilitate manual lighting level changes, should the need arise.

TRANSITION ZONES

Light transition zones are important so that customers don't feel blinded when they enter from bright sunlight or disoriented when they leave at night. When people step into a dimly lit restaurant from the sunlit outdoors, for example, their eyes need time to adjust before they can see clearly. Light transition zones help eyes adjust before people move on to the dining area and impart a logical psychological procession from outdoors to indoors.

LIGHTING MIX

Sparkle is said to enhance and encourage conversation. Sparkle comes from light fixtures such as chandeliers and multiple small pin lights. It is also produced from certain reflected light, such as light bounced off glassware, mirrored surfaces, and shiny tableware. Especially appropriate for leisurely dining, sparkle seems to create an almost magical effect that makes people feel animated but not restless.

For environmental comfort, and to avoid a homogeneous, boring effect, direct lighting (light cast directly onto an object, without reflections from other surfaces such as walls or ceilings) should be counteracted with indirect lighting. The juxtaposition of direct and indirect lighting can create an interesting yet comfortable effect. Indirect lighting can create small shadow patterns that feel friendly; however, large, dark shadows can appear hostile and should be avoided.

LIGHTING CUSTOMERS

One of the most important aspects of psychologically effective restaurant lighting—and the most overlooked—involves making people look their best. When people feel attractive, they not only enjoy the environment more but also tend to return for repeat visits. If flesh tones look good, food also tends to look good. Both look best under incandescent lamps, but a careful mix of warm (or tinted) fluorescent and incandescent lighting can also provide a rosy, flattering glow. A mix of light-emitting diodes (LEDs) can also create a lighting environment that is complimentary to skin tones.

Strong downlighting, however, is extremely unbecoming to people because it highlights every imperfection, and light sources improperly angled can throw unflattering shadows over faces. Guests also tend to feel uncomfortable when their table is lit more brightly than the environment around them; the effect is something like looking into a black hole. Therefore, people should not be spotlighted as if they were on stage but rather surrounded with soft light. Although strong downlighting centered on the tabletop can be used effectively, designers must install easy-to-aim lamps that can be adjusted when tables are moved.

BLENDED SOURCES

Perhaps the most crucial element of psychologically effective restaurant lighting is balance. If a room is too bright, too dim, too deeply shadowed, or too homogeneously lit, it won't feel comfortable. Achieving the right balance involves not only the correct selection of light sources but also light programming that is sensitive to overall brightness, daylight, and the color spectrum.

COLOR

Color perception is rooted in a physiological response and a programmed response that begins with early childhood. In Andrew J. Elliot and colleagues' review, "Color and Psychological Functioning: The Effect of Red on Performance Attainment" (published in the *Journal of Experimental Psychology: General* 136(1), 2007, pp. 154–168), the authors point out that, "From infancy outward, persons encounter both explicit and subtle pairings between colors and particular messages, concepts and experiences in particular situations," and propose that, " . . . color has different implications for feelings, thoughts, and behaviors in different contexts." With this in mind, we offer the following general guidelines that should be generally applicable.

COLOR AND LIGHTING

Color should always be chosen in concert with lighting because the two are so closely associated. Together, they communicate a variety of psychological messages on both obvious and subliminal levels. Their relationship stems from color perception being a function of the type of light source and the reflective surface itself. In other words, the same color takes on different hues or appears to be a different color when seen under different light sources (e.g., fluorescent or incandescent) or when viewed in direct or indirect light. Light is color itself, whether the source is a tinted bulb, a neon tube, sunlight, or a candle.

LIGHTING AND COLOR

Another consideration is that the source of light affects the perception of color. Some of the light is absorbed, but the light that is reflected is highly charged with the color of the surface material or, in other words, its hue. In addition to hue, brilliance and saturation affect the perception of color. Combined, the Munsell color system gives a graphic depiction of how these three elements interact. The higher the value of the color, the greater its reflectance. The saturation of each value level can be thought of as the purity of the color. Pure yellow has a higher saturation level than a shade of yellow produced by mixing yellow with black or some other less reflective color.

COLOR IN RESTAURANT DESIGN

Light and cool colors recede. This principle can be used in restaurant design to expand a sense of space.

Light and cool colors recede. This principle can be used in restaurant design to expand a sense of space. Conversely, dark and warm colors advance and can be used in large rooms to keep the space from feeling vast and impersonal and to instill a sense of intimacy. Warm colors become excellent highlights as points of color on a tabletop and add to a feeling of elegance.

Bold, primary colors and bright lighting encourage turnover and are appropriate for quick-service and casual restaurants that depend on fast turnover. Extremely high illumination, however, washes out the effects of colors (as well as the effects of texture), leads to eyestrain, and lessens the impact of design detailing.

Muted, subtle colors create a restful, leisurely effect. Pastel color schemes, in addition to making a small room appear larger, evoke a calm atmosphere.

Light colors can also make a room look brighter because the brightness of a color is a function of its hue. Light colors such as yellow appear brighter than dark colors such as navy blue, even when measured brightness is the same. Measured brightness is expressed in lumens, which are absorbed into dark-hued surfaces and reflected from bright surfaces. As mentioned earlier, brightness is also affected by the light source.

Because they carry various associations, colors can evoke a theme, a style, a culture, or a country. Purple, for example, is the color of royalty; green is the color of nature; and red and gold suggest a Chinese influence.

Color schemes should relate to climatic conditions. Simply put, warm colors feel right in colder climates and cool colors feel right in warmer climates. On their own, however, cool colors are generally unappetizing (maybe this is partly why food is never blue). Therefore, even in a tropical climate, cool color schemes should also employ warm accents.

Stylish color schemes reflect trends in the consumer marketplace. Over the past three decades, color palettes have shifted from cool hues like seafoam green, deep blue, and aqua— often combined with burgundy, peach, or rosy terra cotta—to bright, clear colors that found their way into the color palettes of the restaurant designer. Color cycles literally move around the color wheel, gradually shifting from the cool colors to the warm colors and back again, with each trend enjoying a life span of about eight years.

An analysis of colors themselves must be tempered by at least three facts. First, the effect of any color depends on its hue and intensity. Sky blue, aqua, and navy are all blue, but each carries a different association. Second, the perception of color changes with distance. When choosing colors, designers must compensate for the public distance from which customers view a restaurant when they enter. Third, ongoing research by experts and associations has yet to quantify scientifically the effects of colors. On the contrary, color psychology engenders much disagreement. Nonetheless, it can be helpful to consider individual colors and their psychological effects.

RED

Historically, reds suggest aggression, hostility, and passion. A limited number of colors harmonize with red because it is so intense, but the edge can be tempered with gold, wood, brass, crystal, or mirrors. Red and black are a classic combination, with an upscale, stylish association. Some say that red enhances the appetite.

GREEN

Green is associated with nature and general well-being. Because of its link to the outdoors and therefore to good health, it has become a trademark of natural and green restaurants. Green is also linked with "lite" and good foods. Live plants and light-colored woods can complement green. Although it can be refreshing in moderate doses, green should not be overused because its reflective nature negatively affects the appearance of skin tones and some foods.

YELLOW

Yellow suggests radiant sunlight, expansiveness, and high spirits. In small doses, it can evoke cheerful, exuberant feelings, and it is particularly appropriate in breakfast areas. Yellow commands attention and can be used effectively as a color accent or an architectural symbol, as in the McDonald's arch. Green-cast yellows, however, have a disturbing effect.

GOLD

Like yellow, gold has a warming influence. It can help offset cold materials (like stone) and brighten dark materials (like dark wood). Gold is associated with wealth and power, and it tends to invoke a timeless feeling because of its historical overtones.

BLUE

Blue is stark, cool, and refreshing. It can visually expand a room, but it does not complement most foods and so should be avoided on the tabletop. Blue goes particularly well with warm colors and materials and is complemented by bleached or light woods. It is said to have a calming effect.

NEUTRALS

Darker browns suggest masculinity, and lighter terra cottas suggest warmth and femininity. A rosy hue complements food and people. Neutrals are excellent for the tabletop because they tend to enhance the colors of food. Another advantage of neutrals is that they provide an excellent backdrop and an effective canvas for a variety of color effects. A neutral backdrop also allows for flexibility, because the mood of a room can be changed just by changing the color accents.

WHITE

White is extremely effective when it is harmonized with other colors. It works well as a background or as a statement in its own right, but it is not ideal for walls because its brightness produces glare that can lead to eyestrain. However, in a quick-service environment, where contact time is minimal, white walls can encourage turnover and are in keeping with the bright, clean atmosphere. Although white is traditionally associated with tabletops, it is not always the best choice because white tends to neutralize the color of the food and the tabletop pieces. White tabletops can also contribute to glare in sun-filled restaurants.

BLACK

Black has negative sociological connotations. It is associated with depression and mourning, but it can be stylish and it works well as an accent with all other colors. Black goes especially well with white—its opposite—creating a classic statement. It does not usually work well as a background color, with the exception of nightclub environments or in conjunction with colored lighting.

SAFETY AND HEALTH

Walk into a darkened room and then into a well-lit room. Invariably, you feel safer or more comfortable in the well-lit room. The darkened room represents the unknown, and for many, that generates a feeling of fear or discomfort. The darkness can also create a feeling that you cannot get out. In the case of someone with claustrophobia, the feeling of being trapped can trigger a severe panic attack.

Strong downlighting that creates bright-dark-bright-dark areas as one walks down a long corridor can trigger unrest. The bright light closes the pupil, making it that much more difficult to see when stepping into a dark area. This condition happens in restaurants when guests arrive at a westerly facing restaurant at 5:00 PM. Pupils will contract due to the sun, and a long walk from where the car is parked in bright sun will exacerbate the problem. When the guest walks into a softly lit entryway, they will effectively be blinded. This is the first impression that they get of a restaurant's interior. The physical experience could create a subliminal memory that could prevent a guest from returning.

Slippery walkways, wet interior floors, or tripping over a worn piece of carpeting could create additional fears about safety. On an outdoor deck, inexpensive "plastic" chairs degrade under the sun's ultraviolet rays, which weakens the chairs and makes them feel flimsy. In extreme cases, a chair can break even when someone who is not oversized sits on it.

Health issues also have a psychological effect on customers. If a customer sees the waiter drop a roll and then pop it back in the basket and take it to a table, they begin to wonder how the food that they will eat is being handled. Similarly, when one walks into a bar that smells of stale beer, one has to wonder if the smell is caused by beer that has spilled or draft beer lines and tap head that have not been properly cleaned.

Perhaps one of the greatest design challenges comes when cooks work in a display kitchen. While the setting keeps them honest, the need to be assiduously clean is paramount. Ensuring that there are sufficient hand sinks near every work station is an essential design concern. Also, cooking surfaces need to appear clean. For example, a chrome-topped griddle will continue to shine, whereas a rolled-steel griddle will darken with use and appear as though food might be stuck to it. Comfortable employee uniforms that won't stain easily and that don't lead to excessive sweating and body odor are another design element that impacts a customer's perception of health concerns.

SUMMARY

All design applications in the restaurant engage and manipulate the senses. Today, design elements are looked at separately and analyzed for their psychological contribution to the whole. Whether or not intentionally, almost every design element and environmental condition in the restaurant works as a psychological tool. Optimally, the interactions of the various stimuli in the room will work together synergistically. From lighting to color, to texture and temperature, the nuances that influence people's feelings and behavior number in the hundreds. Design choices, therefore, should reflect careful consideration of their psychological impact. Customers can be encouraged to leave or to linger, feel exuberant or mellow, feel like part of the action or secure in an intimate enclave—all as a result of design applications. Such attention to the psychological impact of design can have a marked effect on the diner and, hence, on the operation's profitability.

CHAPTER 4

DESIGN IMPLEMENTATION: FRONT TO BACK THROUGH THE CUSTOMERS' EYES

Successful restaurant design is based, in part, on the management team and their ability to generate a profit. However, sales need to be generated to produce profit, and it is the customer's perceptions of a restaurant that generates those sales. A customer's perception is based on a complex set of factors unique to each restaurant and to each individual. One person may hear about the restaurant from a friend, read an advertisement, or watch the construction of the building that will house the restaurant. Others develop their perceptions based on the fact that the restaurant parking lot is nearly full every evening when they drive past. Others read the food section in their local newspaper and hit each new restaurant when it opens. For these potential customers, the data that makes up their perception comes together as a "go" or "no go" decision to visit the restaurant for the first time. However, it is during their first experience when most customers will determine whether to return for another meal. During that initial meal, they experience the three legs of a successful restaurant: food, service, and design that must work together seamlessly.

This chapter addresses the ways in which front-of-the-house design affects customers, from their first glimpse of the signage and façade to the end of the meal, to their walk across the parking lot to their cars. It follows the progression of spaces as the patron perceives them, starting with the exterior and moving on to the entryway area, the dining room, the bar/lounge, and the restroom. It covers the basic principles of design decision making for such areas as signage and graphics; seating; tabletop elements; lighting; color; floor, wall, window, and ceiling treatments; and acoustics.

The "dining" experience, regardless of restaurant type, involves the sequence of destination, progression, and arrival discussed herein. In an effective design, this sequence is a harmonious flow, a spatial organization that helps create a memorable restaurant experience. Once the customer enters the doors of the restaurant, the design should continue as an integrated sensory and operational experience that reinforces the decision to visit and drives the decision to return again.

EXTERIOR IMAGE

The exterior image of a restaurant influences customers in many ways (Figure 4.1). Obviously, location plays an important role in determining an appropriate architectural style. A restaurant nestled in the backcountry of Alaska might be an A-frame structure supported by lodge-pole pine logs that reflect the wooded environment. A restaurant sitting adjacent to the atrium of the newest high-rise office building in New York might be decorated with marble and stainless-steel accents that relate to the sleek architectural style of the building. In both of these cases, the customer

Figure 4.1
The inviting entrance of Bar Americain, with its brass-trimmed revolving doors and burgundy awnings, foretells a luxe experience at this New York City restaurant that is part of the Bobby Flay restaurant group.
(Photo by Joseph Durocher)

is conditioned by the restaurant's surroundings to expect a certain type of establishment.

Similarly, the restaurant architecture found along the miracle miles located on the outskirts of many cities and towns portend a certain type of restaurant image. People are conditioned to expect greasy-spoon diners, quick-service restaurants, and chain family restaurants on these stretches of highway—other types of restaurants might seem incongruous.

Sometimes, conditioned expectations can be overcome by exterior design. For example, the image of noncommercial cafeterias suffers from expectations of sterile, uncomfortable, noisy environments due to conditions in other parts of the building. Today, many institutions have upgraded their exterior, signage, and entry areas to beckon patrons inside the cafeteria—where guests find that their recollections of the boring, straight-line cafeterias of yesteryear do not match the restaurant-style atmosphere.

FAÇADE

To succeed in a cluttered visual environment, a restaurant's facade must stand out from the rest of the pack. This is particularly important for restaurants on roadways, but the façade should be considered, even when there is little competition. The same problem faces advertisers in magazines and on television. Today, with so many color ads, advertisers have employed black-and-white images in an effort to stand out. The key is to be distinctive. With respect to restaurant design, the façade of the building itself can help differentiate it from the competition and create memorable images in the minds of customers (Figure 4.2).

The exteriors of chain restaurants are sometimes quite imaginative. The façade of Bugaboo Creek, for example, with its rough wood exterior, front porch, other backwoods elements, and distinctive signage, clearly sets the restaurant

Figure 4.2
A distinctive façade, as seen here at the Weber Grill in Chicago, attracts customers and differentiates it from neighboring restaurants.
(Photo by Joseph Durocher)

apart. Eatertainment chains engage potential diners with interactive or highly dramatic exterior elements (Figure 4.3).

In other chain designs, recognizable architectural elements, such as the red roof of Pizza Hut and the golden arches of McDonald's, integrated into the sides of some of their restaurants communicate instantly to the customer without reading the actual sign. Historically, quick-service exteriors relied on vernacular imagery to impart the idea of the restaurant. A gigantic doughnut sitting on a roof or a hot-dog-on-a-bun-shaped walkup stand left no questions about the type of food being sold within. However, reliance on architectural imagery can restrict the flexibility of the building for future occupants. It can also, if not properly protected, be easily copied. Combined, all of the exterior elements form—along with the interior layout, design, and menu—the trade dress of a restaurant and are protected, much like a copyright, under Section 43(a) of the Landham Act. Many copycat

chains have used the gambrel roof developed as a Dairy Queen symbol, for example. When those chains feature soft-serve ice cream, the shape of the roof could lead customers to believe that it could be a Dairy Queen spin-off.

Other building exteriors can communicate to potential customers the type of experience they can expect inside the doors. Such is the case with the whimsical bowl and chopsticks affixed to the façade at one of the Big Bowl restaurants in Chicago, which foretells a casual Asian restaurant (Figure 4.4).

However, big storefront windows or a series of open French doors that offer clear views of the interior give a more personal sense of the type of experience inside. The façades of bistros and large gathering places, for instance, often have windowed walls totally open to the street.

Restaurateur Michael Weinstein pioneered the wide-open gathering place in New York back in the early 1980s

Figure 4.3
The thematic exteriors of the Rainforest Cafe—this one being in Chicago—are attention grabbers for all who pass. While the oversized tree frog does catch the eye, less flamboyant but distinct exteriors can also be effective.
(Photo by Joseph Durocher)

with America, which allowed pedestrians unobstructed views of the lively scenes inside, and vice versa. Today, Weinstein's Ark Restaurant Group continues that openness with restaurants like Center Café in Washington, D.C., which is a raised platform restaurant catering to travelers and commuters passing through the grand hall of Union Station and the D.C. and Las Vegas restaurants, America. We still see this treatment in urban restaurants across the country. Customers may browse for a restaurant in much the same way they look for a book. If they like the cover, chances are good that they will look inside.

SIGNAGE

Signage is such an important component of exterior building design that it merits its own discussion. Often, it is the

most recognizable element of the façade, one that arrests people's attention and remains in their minds as a symbol of the restaurant. Especially in a shopping mall or on a highway, signage can be an extremely effective attention grabber. Different feelings are created by a big, comfortable logo versus an understated sign whose only identification is a street address.

Easy-to-read signs are essential when potential customers have but a few seconds to notice and react as they speed by. The ubiquitous roadside sign with McDonald's golden arches or the burger bun filled with the words Burger King are examples of signs that have almost become ideograms in today's culture.

Less well known but still well recognized in its venue is the seven-story-high cactus emblazoned with the name of the Hilltop Steak House in Saugus, Massachusetts. The name, in red neon, can be seen from both sides of the

Figure 4.4
The tilting bowl and chopsticks of this Big Bowl restaurant, one of several operated by the Chicago-based Lettuce Entertain You group, is clearly an ideogram that passersby recognize without reading the name of the restaurant.
(Photo by Joseph Durocher)

highway—a mile away (Figure 4.5). Add to this a herd of inanimate cattle grazing on the front lawn, and passing motorists know for sure that steaks are being cooked inside the barnlike structure.

Graphic designers create effective signage—with type, color, form, and light—that carry strong and clear visual messages. The typeface should echo the style of the restaurant, thus giving people another clue about what they're going to encounter inside. No matter what type of establishment, a readable typeface is essential.

At times, signage becomes an integral component of the architectural design; in other instances, it is a separate element. Even when it is freestanding, however, sign design should mesh with architectural design.

Whether mounted on signposts high above the highway or integrated into façades, a well-conceived and -designed

sign can become a recognizable ideogram (Figure 4.6) that symbolizes the restaurant or club. Used as a logo throughout the space, such an ideogram creates a lasting impression.

Ideogram signs can also be integrated with advertising programs, which play an important part in developing the first impression of a restaurant. While advertising is not an integral part of the design program, it should work in conjunction with the design to express a coordinated message. Care should be given to how the colors, shape, and typeface of the sign will read in any form of advertising medium. For example, a color rendering in print media will show more accurately than the color on a web page when viewed from a computer. Depending on the resolution setting of the computer screen, some elements—lines, for example—in the image may be illegible.

Figure 4.5
The seven-story Hilltop Steak House sign in Saugus, Massachusetts, is a well-recognized symbol of this landmark restaurant.
(Photo by Joseph Durocher)

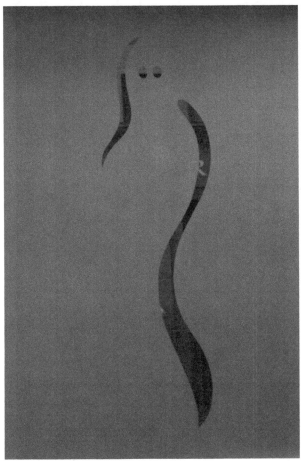

Figure 4.6
This ethereal etching on the exterior of Ghost—a popular Chicago club—is an example of an ideogram that informs customers without using text.
(Photo by Joseph Durocher)

LANDSCAPING

Patrons driving or walking past a freestanding restaurant notice not only the building itself but its natural surroundings. In fact, landscaping helps form people's first impression of the restaurant. Like the façade and the signage, landscaping gives cues about what type of dining experience awaits inside. Formal landscaping, such as an eight-foot manicured hedge flanking an iron-gated driveway entrance, prepares the customer for a formal dining experience in which multiple courses are served by a large service staff.

Informal landscaping, such as those with randomly planted gardens or free-flowing bushes and trees, prepares the customer for a more casual experience. This type of landscaping is appropriate for moderately priced restaurants with friendly interior settings that don't impose a suit-and-tie-only feeling.

Restaurants that promote a green image will invariably opt for minimal landscaping or landscaping that is sustainable with minimal water, fertilizer, or pest control. Some green restaurants have incorporated herb gardens that are harvested by chefs for the day's offerings.

Sometimes landscape design works in concert with architectural design to create a dramatic first impression. The obvious example is the restaurant located on the edge of a national forest that uses log cabin architecture. Alternatively, a restaurant's architecture could relate to the rock formations found in a desert mesa area. In both cases, the relationship between the surroundings and the architecture feels appropriate.

Landscaping is a critical concern when parking areas are situated on the restaurant property. A sea of asphalt can be hidden from the view of diners with artfully placed trees or shrubs or a tiered herb garden. Landscaping can be used to conceal unsightly neighboring buildings or dumpsters as well. However, tall bushes adjacent to the exit where cars enter the roadway can create a hazard for the departing guest. Inappropriate placement of hedges can also create dangerous conditions in locales where muggings have been a concern.

The placement of the restaurant on the property can affect its streetside appearance. For example, consider a three-acre lot comprising two acres of parking and one acre of restaurant and gardens. If the restaurant sits at the back of the lot with parking in the front, its streetside appearance will be quite different from the same restaurant placed at the front end of the lot with parking in the back (Figure 4.7).

ENTRY

As noted above, the exterior image creates first impressions and heightens expectations about what will be found inside the restaurant. The next impression is created at the arrival area, where guests step through the front door and into the entry area (Figures 4.8a and b).

It's important that the arrival experience flows smoothly and creates an appropriate aesthetic impact. Spatial progression comes into play here as well, especially in upscale restaurants, where the design team wants to provide guests

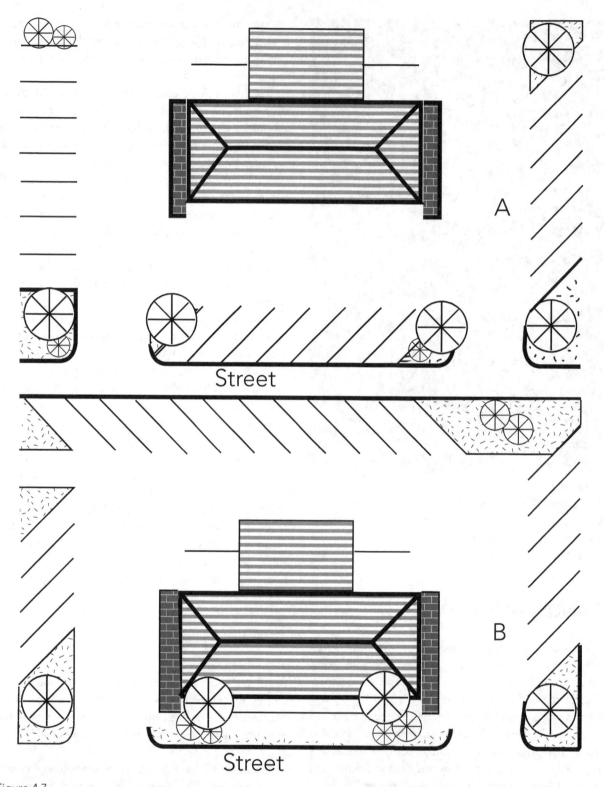

Figure 4.7
The placement of a restaurant on a lot will have a marked impact on customers. In an urban setting, a restaurant set back from the road (a) can get lost between buildings that are built at the front property line.

a.

b.

Figure 4.8
At Eleven Madison Park (a), the sign over the revolving door clearly verifies that this is not a bank, whereas at Gallagher's, the streetside view of the aging refrigerator clearly informs that yes, this is a serious steakhouse (b).
(Photos by Joseph Durocher)

time to shift gears from the outside world. In these situations, small vestibules between door and reception give patrons a brief pause before they enter the restaurant proper. However, too many restaurants have such a small entry that guests must wait for their table outdoors no matter the weather conditions. While a larger entry area takes away salable floor space, waiting in the rain or a blustery snowstorm can quickly send would-be customers to the competition.

The means by which the outside is separated from the inside must be matched to both the type of restaurant and its location. In Hawaii, the problem is easily resolved; the weather allows restaurant entrances to be without physical doors. In most places, however, a door is necessary, and its form affects the customer's perception of the restaurant. A glass door allows customers to see into the restaurant, while a solid wood door creates a feeling of anticipation. In some instances, the anticipation may be deliberate and desired, but in others, it may be intimidating enough to turn a potential guest away. The shape, size, and weight of the door, along with the handle, send subtle psychological messages and must be carefully considered.

As a general guideline, the portal to a restaurant should be as unencumbered as possible. In addition to evoking the theme of the restaurant, it should be easy to use. A heavy oak door with a cast-iron ring handle may give the feeling of entering a castle but, if not carefully balanced, it may be too hard for people to open (Figure 4.9). Glass doors or doors with windows invite guests to preview the interior and, in some cases, allow diners to look out on the show outside. Particularly in cold climates, double sets of door minimize the blast of cold air that enters when the outer doors are opened. In some settings, energy-efficient revolving doors may be appropriate. Air curtains are used in some locations, but never in formal settings, where they might disturb a guest's hair. Air curtains help with climate control and prevent flying insects from entering a restaurant.

RECEPTION

The reception area or landing area serves as a conduit from the exterior to one of the destination spaces. In a quick-service operation, the landing area should lead directly to the

Figure 4.9
The heavy wood doors at Buddha Bar in New York City prevent arriving customers from seeing inside the bar, which helps to build a sense of anticipation.
(Photo by Joseph Durocher)

order counter. If the pickup counter is not immediately visible, customers can become disoriented because they expect to find it as soon as they enter the restaurant. A similar phenomenon exists in tableservice restaurants. In France, people are often drawn well into a restaurant before they are guided by the maître d' to their destination. However, in most other countries, customers expect to be greeted and guided to the dining room as soon as they step through the entry door.

The reception area of a cafeteria plays an important role because it is here that customers stop to think about their options (Figure 4.10). It should include a tray dispenser, information about specials, and a vantage point for customers to view the servery. Customers gain an overview of the servery food stations and begin to develop a sense of where they will be going and what they will buy. The design of this space is particularly important in a cafeteria because, unlike the tableservice restaurant, with a maître d', or the quick-service operation, with its pickup counter, customers must make decisions about which areas of the servery they should approach, and in which order. Utensils and napkins should be dispensed near the exit end of the servery.

If people can clearly see each of the stations in the servery, even as they stop to pick up their tray, they can calculate whether they want to wait in line for hot entrées, grilled burgers, or individually prepared sandwiches or perhaps to make their own salad at the salad bar. Further, they must figure how many stations they will approach. Customers must be moved quickly through this reception area. Any delay can cause them to decide to skip lunch, jump in a car for a trip to the local quick-service eatery, or bring a brown-bag meal in the future.

This area is particularly important in college and university feeding. While many schools post their menu items on the Web, most student stop in the reception area to make a decision about which food stations they will visit on any given day. Large, wall-mounted screens that display the daily specials available at each station can inform their decision while students are still in the reception area. In operations where biometric handprint scanning is employed to control access, wall-mounted hand sanitizer pumps should be installed.

COATROOM

The coatroom should be included in the entry area so guests can store items they do not wish to carry to the table. Coatrooms are typically found in full-service restaurants and may have an attendant or be self-service. If a member

Figure 4.10
When patrons step into the entryway of the Philbrook cafeteria on the campus of the University of New Hampshire, they can quickly scan all of the food stations from a single point. Such a layout is particularly useful where transient diners are expected, because scramble layouts with stations that cannot be seen from the entry area force patrons to wander through the entire servery, which can create excess congestion.
(Photo by Joseph Durocher)

of the staff does not control them, they should be designed so that several guests can use the space at one time. Further, some effort should be made to ensure that the maître d' can watch the space to limit the potential for theft. In upscale restaurants, care must be taken when guests arrive in furs and other expensive coats. A separate storage space for this outerwear should be considered as well as for briefcases and laptops, which, when carried to the table, can get in the way of servers and other guests as they pass a table.

Although coatrooms are common in full-service restaurants, they are frequently overlooked in other types of establishments. In a university cafeteria, a coatroom, lockers, or storage cubbies at the entryway is a welcome design addition for storing books and coats. (Video surveillance should be installed in open storage areas to aid in the recovery of personal items that are removed by other than the rightful owner of a coat or backpack.) Students may make additional purchases when their trays are not crowded with books—purchases that otherwise might not be made. The number of students that can be seated at one time will increase because chairs will not be filled with backpacks and coats.

In malls, shoppers are frequently burdened with packages when they drop into the food court; this may limit their food purchases because their arms are full. A bank of keyed self-service lockers could alleviate their burden and increase sales. The lockers should have see-thru doors so that security officers can view the contents of the lockers from outside.

Without coat and package storage space, problems can arise in any type of dining area. In casual restaurants that do not have coatrooms, hat and coat racks should be provided in the dining area—although this does not solve the problem of people setting their belongings on empty chairs at neighboring tables. If no provision is made for garments, people will drape their coats over the backs of chairs or over the drink rails in bars, thus destroying the look of even the most carefully developed design and creating a hazard for both servers and guests.

WAITING AREA

In most full-service restaurants, guests—even those with a reservation—will be asked to wait for their table. Space should be allocated to allow guests to wait comfortably. However, a thoughtfully designed area can provide needed waiting space plus potential for sales. Some restaurants earn

a substantial portion of their revenue from the sale of clothing or food items available in a restaurant gift shop or store that is actually a part of the waiting area.

An example is the seafood restaurant where guests mill around looking at the tanks filled with lobsters or iced seafood that can be purchased for takeout at the end of the meal. The appearance of the fresh seafood tells people about the experience to come. The same is true of a steakhouse, such as the landmark Gallagher's in New York, where tons of aging strip loins are visible through the glass sidewall of a walkway that flanks the exterior and entryway.

MERCHANDISING

Waiting areas have the potential of significant incremental sales for a restaurant. For example, on Sunday mornings in most coffee shops or diners, inadequate waiting areas force guests to stand in a cramped entryway. With just a little additional space, a self-service coffee bar and takeout station could be added to the waiting area. This could provide a carry-out continental breakfast option for customers who would rather not wait for a seat, and a welcome cup of coffee for guests who do choose to wait. The additional business generated through coffee and takeout sales, as well as customer goodwill, would justify a bit of extra footage.

Merchandising opportunities in the waiting area are unlimited. Operators can display and sell fresh-baked goods, house salad dressings or sauces, custom-printed clothing that will boost sales, and so on. Such chains as the Rainforest Cafe and the Hard Rock Cafe take full advantage of nonfood sales areas. In independent restaurants as well as chains, a retail store is sometimes part of the waiting area (Figures 4.11).

In full-service restaurants, the waiting area can incorporate design elements that serve as menu merchandising devices. Posting a menu or menu board with the specials of the evening markets the meal before the guest arrives at the table. This may speed up the ordering process because guests preview the menu during the waiting period, thus leading to faster turnover at the tables.

New technology makes it possible for guests to make menu selections while waiting. The orders are sent automatically to the kitchen and are ready to be filled as soon as the guest is seated. Kiosk-mounted or portable devices can be used to preview menu offerings, print out discount coupons for future visits, and order meals. Such high-tech devices can keep patrons occupied while they are waiting,

Figure 4.11
Retail stores are integrated into the entry area of many restaurants, as seen here in the Chicago Hard Rock Cafe and Rainforest Cafe restaurants. Sales of soft goods and specialty foods related to the restaurant can significantly bolster overall revenue.

(Photos by Joseph Durocher)

ensure speedy service when they are seated, and help increase table turns (Figure 4.12).

Another menu merchandising technique that depends on design is the addition of a dessert cart or espresso station adjacent to the waiting area. Both of these elements condition guests to make purchases after the meal. While a dessert cart or wine rack can be added to the waiting area as an afterthought, they are most effective as merchandising tools when incorporated with the original design. A display area where plates of the day's specials can be highlighted (along with a description of the dishes) is another consideration. Similarly, a view of an antipasto station in an Italian restaurant predisposes waiting guests to put in an appetizer order as soon as they are seated.

A successful waiting area previews the design as well as the menu. Glimpses into the dining area hint at the type of service, customers, food, and decor to come. However, the design should respect already seated diners by ensuring that they are not distracted by the movement invariably associated with the waiting area.

ENVIRONMENTAL CONCERNS

Three environmental conditions make an enormous difference to customer comfort in the waiting area: light,

Figure 4.12
An order-entry kiosk in the entry area affords waiting guests an opportunity to view the menu before being seated. Some systems even allow guests to preorder their meal, which will be automatically entered when the party is seated. Such kiosks can also display information about local attractions.
(Photo by Joseph Durocher)

temperature, and sound levels. Lighting levels must be controlled to provide a painless transition from outside space to interior space. Entering the waiting area of a restaurant with an entrance facing west can be an ocular assault, for example, because going from bright daylight into a dim room is temporarily blinding. This is a particular problem for older people, whose eyes take longer to adjust to rapid change in light levels. In all circumstances, both entry and waiting area lighting should be dimmer controlled to relate and react to exterior lighting levels.

Temperature control in entry and waiting areas is a vital matter. As mentioned earlier, double sets of entry doors or revolving doors can prevent a blast of air entering the waiting area each time a customer enters. Heating, ventilating, and air conditioning (HVAC) systems should be designed so that an extra blast of heat warms guests coming in from the cold. In southern locations, an air screen can be used to limit the mixing of outside and inside air. In general, the design team must always be aware of the infiltration of outside air and program the space for maximum temperature comfort.

Sound levels must also be controlled in the waiting area, which often holds more people per square foot than any other part of the restaurant. So it is here in the entry that the most effective sound-absorbing materials are needed on ceilings and walls.

PAGING SYSTEMS

Picture this: a couple arrives at a restaurant only to be faced with a waiting area filled with customers. The question: "Should we fight our way through the crowd to find out how long we'll have to wait, or should we go somewhere else?"

If they choose the latter, the design has cost the operation important revenue potential. One reason waiting areas are frequently overcrowded is that customers fear they will not hear the page for their table when it is called, so they do not move into the bar, where the restaurateur could accrue additional revenues.

An important solution, and one that must be considered during the design phase, is to integrate a paging system that works with the overall layout of the restaurant. Prior to the mid-1990s, paging systems consisted of loudspeakers or hostesses who yelled out the name of the next party. Today, vibrating pocket pagers or lighted pagers do the job. A recently developed paging system integrates lights, an audible alarm, and a customizable audible page message. These high-tech pagers allow people to shop in the restaurant store, stand outside, sit comfortably in the bar, or even

head for the rest room, knowing that they will not miss their page. Pagers that display projected wait time offer an extra level of service—and potential revenue for the operation. Guests may decide to purchase that extra drink if they know their table won't be ready for another 20 minutes.

DESTINATION DRINKING

Customers progress to the bar for many reasons, depending on their needs and on the type of restaurant. The bar may be the patron's sole destination, as a place to socialize. At other times, it acts as the waiting area where customers sip a drink while waiting for their tables. In still other situations, people drift to the bar for an after-dinner drink. When foodservice is offered at the bar, single diners, in particular, may prefer to eat there rather than at a table.

Drinking spaces can be divided into three distinct areas:

1. Beverage production and storage areas
2. The service area immediately in front of the bar
3. Cocktail seating

In gathering places or theatrical restaurants, the bar is an important operational component that serves large numbers of people and generates a high profit margin. In serious gourmet restaurants, where food is the raison d'être, the bar may consist of no more than a few token stools. Bars are most often located at the front of restaurants, so that customers don't have to wend their way past diners to get there.

Often, a view of the bar, with its throngs of patrons and bustling conviviality, helps merchandise the restaurant to passersby. This technique works especially well on urban streets and inside hotels, where the most successful bars are open to the street or lobbies and corridors of a hotel. But every rule has exceptions and, in some restaurants, unusual bar placement—at the back of the room or up a flight of stairs—works to the operation's advantage. Such is the case at the Four Seasons hotel in New York. The TY Lounge—which offers patrons high tea, hors d'oeuvres with premium beverages in a setting designed for people watching, and sybaritic relaxation—sits up a flight of steps adjacent to the registration area. The bar is located over 200 feet from the front of the hotel and up yet another flight of steps. However, this space, with its high ceilings and stylish clientele, is a destination bar for patrons from around the city. The bar location decision depends on many factors, but circulation paths should always be considered.

Designing a bar operation is every bit as complex as designing a restaurant. The same 10 factors outlined on pages 1–2 should be considered. When a bar is affiliated with a restaurant, it must meld with the restaurant design concept to make the spaces mutually supportive. The selection of equipment and decor items should begin only after the nature of the bar and a managerial philosophy about the bar is established.

In the past, many operators aimed at a sales mix of 60 percent food sales and 40 percent liquor sales. The high profitability of liquor led to many promotions (happy hours, two-for-one specials, etc.) that increased beverage traffic. Today, however, there is a lot of pressure to reduce excessive alcohol consumption and concern about the legal issues of liquor liability. Even gathering places and theatrical restaurants with deliberately big bar scenes have shifted the sales mix. As long ago as the mid-1980s, New York's America, for example, reduced an initial sales mix of 40 percent beverage sales to 30 percent because management did not want to promote the establishment as a drinking place. America maintained its profitability and its reputation as a restaurant, which spawned cousins in Washington, D.C., and Las Vegas.

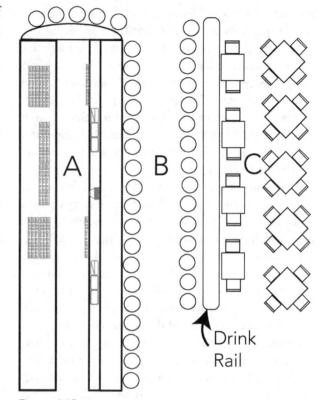

Figure 4.13
A bar is typically divided into three areas: (a) Production and storage, (b) Service area, (c) Cocktail seating. Drink rails help divide the scene into a more active service area on one side of the rail, and a quieter lounge area filled with tables and chairs on the other side.

BEVERAGE PRODUCTION AND STORAGE

A well-designed bar can help to control beverage consumption and increase beverage sales. The design of the bar's backside and service side can add to the bottom line through increased customer counts and decreased operating costs. Properly displayed call brands can increase the sale of these higher-priced beverages.

Drinking spaces can be divided into three areas (Figure 4.13):

1. Beverage production and storage areas
2. The service area located in front of the bar, including bar stools
3. Cocktail seating

As mentioned above, the type of equipment installed at a bar is a function of the type of operation. The low-volume neighborhood tavern may elect to serve bottled beer because the volume of draws does not warrant installing a draft system. However, brewers have added "sixth barrels" (5 gallons) and "pony kegs" (7.5 gallons), which are smaller than the standard half-barrel (15.5 gallons) in an effort to drive their draft offerings into smaller-scale bars. A large-volume gathering place—where the potential for selling draft beer is apparent—may opt to sell both draft and bottled beer to increase their number of offerings. In operations where a large volume of beer sales is expected, dozens of beers can be served from a draft system (Figure 4.14).

Here are the most important questions to ask when considering bar equipment:

Figure 4.14
Compact beer heads can save space at a busy bar while offering guests a choice of many different brews.
(Photo by Joseph Durocher)

1. Will wine be served by the glass?

The least expensive solution is to place open bottles in a reach-in refrigerator. The optimal solution is to place reds and whites in temperature-controlled, glass-fronted dispenser cabinets where customers can clearly view the bottles from the front of the bar. The system automatically injects inert nitrogen gas to maximize the shelf life of the open bottle.

2. Will frozen drinks be prepared individually or in bulk?

Blender-prepared frozen drinks—from margaritas to frozen daiquiris—require that the bartender prepare them one to four at a time. However, the bartender can use the same piece of equipment to prepare any type of frozen drink. There are several frozen drink dispensers that enable bartenders to serve frozen drinks in a matter of seconds because the drink ingredients are mixed in advance of serving times. However, the dispenser can hold and dispense only one type of drink at a time. One type of dispenser holds the chilled blend in 2- to 3-quart see-through tanks that help to merchandise the drinks. An alternative is a stainless dispenser that looks like a soft-serve ice cream machine. Such models come with one or two heads, each with its own freezer cylinder and up to 20-quart mix hopper.

3. How will liquor be poured?

If liquors are poured directly from the bottle, each bottle needs to be within easy reach of each bartender workstation. If liquors are dispensed with a gun or dispenser tower, less display space for bottles is needed on the back bar and in the well. However, a separate storage space where the open bottles are stored and linked into the dispenser system is required.

4. Will a point-of-sale (POS) system be integrated with the beverage dispensing process?

When a POS is integrated with a beverage dispensing system, only those drinks that have been ordered through a POS should be made by the bartender. In some setups, servers enter the drink orders at a remote order-entry station; the order is printed out at the bar, indicating to the bartender that the drink has been charged to a guest check. In automated dispensing systems, the beverages can be delivered only after the drinks are entered into a POS.

5. Will draft beer kegs be tapped centrally or undercounter?

When kegs are stored in a central refrigerated space, the brew can be directed to draft towers located on separate floors or at separate stations in a large bar. If, however, kegs are to be held in undercounter refrigeration at the bar, sufficient space is needed to manipulate the kegs to and from the bar.

Central storage doesn't disrupt customers as much as undercounter keg storage. However, the proximity of the refrigerated walk-in to the dispenser heads is important.

The lines must not run too long and must be refrigerated along their entire length. This is an important element to incorporate during the design phase of the project.

Important questions to ask when considering what bar equipment to choose include:

• Will wine be served by the glass?

• Will frozen drinks be prepared individually or in bulk?

• How will liquor be poured?

• Will a POS be integrated in the beverage dispensing process?

• Will draft beer kegs be tapped centrally or undercounter?

• How will the glassware be washed?

• Will glasses be prechilled?

• Will mixers be held in containers or be dispensed from a gun?

---

6. How will the glassware be washed?

A three-compartment sink with brushes is the least expensive glass-cleaning option. However, the time that bartenders spend washing glasses takes away from the time they spend mixing drinks and serving customers. An alternative is to install a glass washer at the bar, allowing bartenders to load the glasses at one end and remove them at the other. A third option is to place bus buckets at the bar for dirty glasses, which are transferred to the kitchen for washing. Obviously, each of these options affects bar design and layout.

7. Will glasses be chilled?

While not essential, chilled glassware can have a special appeal. Will all glassware be chilled or only the beer mugs and martini glasses? Will a clean, chilled glass be used for refills? Answers to these questions will determine the size, number, and placement of the chillers.

8. Will mixers be held in containers or dispensed from a gun?

Mixers poured from bottles of other containers typically need refrigerated or iced storage to remain chilled. Gun dispensers require a separate storage area to hold the bulk syrup that is pumped to and mixed with chilled water in the head of the gun or dispenser tower. Because these functional aspects of bar design are usually far less successfully realized than the aesthetic aspects, a detailed discussion follows.

LAYOUT CONSIDERATIONS

A typical double-sided bar workstation includes the back bar, where bottled beer, call liquors, and specialty glasses are stored, and the front workstation, where most of the mixing action takes place (Figure 4.15). At the center of all workstations is the ice bin, and every other piece of equipment should be placed around this focal point. Following the assumption that most bartenders are right-handed, the undercounter glass storage is usually placed to the left of the ice bin and the mixers to the right. Frequently used liquors should go in the speed rail that fits between the ice bin and the bartender.

A bar layout involving more than one station (and more than one bartender) (Figure 4.16) is a bit more complex. As

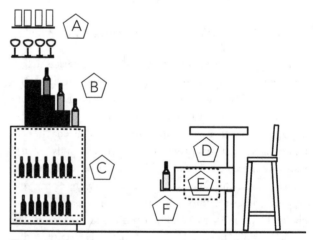

Figure 4.15

This sectional drawing shows the various components of a sample bar work station (a) specialty glass storage; (b) call liquors on display; (c) bottled beer cooler; (d) underbar, where common glassware is stored along with utensils and mixing equipment; (e) ice bin, waste, and wash sink; and (f) speed rails where inexpensive commonly used liquor is stored.

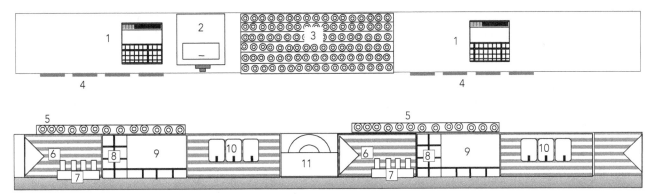

Figure 4.16
A typical double bar incorporates: (1) POS unit, (2) frozen drink machine, (3) back-bar liquor display, (4) undercounter refrigeration, (5) speed rail, (6) glass drainage and storage, (7) beer- and soda-dispensing heads, (8) mixer storage, (9) ice bin, (10) wash sink and dump station, and (11) glasswasher.

can be seen, the glass washer is often placed between the two stations. The placement is more convenient for the bartender located to its right because she or he can easily take clean glasses from the washer and set them on the drain board to await service. The other bartender has a harder time because the glasses must be carried several steps to be set on a drain board. As an alternative, a manual washing system, with separate sinks in each station, could be installed.

Sales control systems must be part of every beverage station. These can be simple cash drawers but, increasingly, they are complex POS systems integrated with beverage dispensing equipment. In one of the most elaborate systems, the bartender need only enter into the POS the desired drink and place the appropriately iced glass under the beverage head; in seconds, the glass is filled with the requested beverage. Such a system requires only three running feet of bar space and contains the POS plus a beverage service head that can dispense 71 different products.

Fully integrated cash and beverage dispensing systems are usually installed in large-volume restaurants or operations where management is not available constantly to supervise the bartenders. The commonly used liquors and mixes are frequently stored in a central location and piped to the workstations. One storage area can be used to supply several workstations at a single bar or at multiple bars. An advantage of such centralization is that pilferage is minimized because no bottles—or just the call liquors—are issued to the bartenders and most liquors come out of the beverage dispensing head. No drinks can be ordered unless they are rung into the POS.

Further savings accrue because liquors can be purchased in half-gallon containers rather than liter bottles. Draft beer can also be tied into the POS system. In general, one of the greatest advantages of a centralized storage and control system is that the amount of space required on the back bar is significantly decreased. Of course, the overriding question is whether the cost of the control system is less than the potential losses due to lack of controls. Of course, there is also the panache of free-pouring drinks. While customers might like free pouring, even the best bartender cannot consistently pour equal portions, which could easily lead to overpouring and the potential for a Dram Shop liability lawsuit.

Storage procedures for alcoholic beverages must be even more stringent than for food products. Alcoholic beverages are common targets for theft and therefore must be secured, both before and after issuing. In storerooms, this is accomplished via locked spaces kept separate from food storage areas. At the bar itself, a means of securing the liquor and dispensing equipment is imperative.

In bars where bottles are stored at the bar, well brands—the liquors used for most mixed drinks—are stored in speed rails, which run along the face of the underbar. For call brands—brands that are specifically requested—storage is generally on top of the back bar, with backup storage in cabinets. Tiered shelving, sometimes with bottom lighting, helps merchandise call brands while making them more accessible to the bartender. In some restaurants, call brands are stored in Plexiglas™ cabinetry above the front bar, which is another way to merchandise these higher-priced spirits.

Bottles of beer can be stored in back-bar refrigeration, in ice-filled Plexiglas bins set on the front bar, or in under-counter bottle coolers, which are convenient for high-volume operations because they give more storage capacity than back-bar refrigeration in the same amount of floor space.

Glass frosters and chillers, designed to lower the temperature of glasses before a drink is poured into them, are also included in many bar workstations. At draft beer stations, glass chillers bring the temperature of mugs and other glassware down to as low as zero degrees Fahrenheit, which helps keep drawn beer cold. However, the cold limits the head that forms in the glass, thus decreasing profits. Outside the United States, beer is consumed at higher temperatures, which is important to consider if the bar is to appeal to an international crowd or if international brews are served.

Workboards are important elements of any bartender's workstation. The workboard should include a counter with a sink and a waste disposal area. The sink is used for cleaning hands, drawing water, and draining glassware. A dump station for straws, napkins, and waste fruit is also needed to keep the workstation clean.

OPERATIONAL CONSIDERATIONS

Straight-line bars are the most common and economical type to build and service. However, free-form bars have become popular in many new restaurants. While equipment manufacturers will gladly construct high-priced customized bars, modular units can generally be installed at a much lower price and still function well. A recent development from the Perlick Corporation, the largest manufacturer of bar equipment, is a prefabricated cantilevered bar unit that hangs workstation equipment from the front frame of the bar. To speed installation, the bartop and front panels lift out of place to enable plumbers, electricians, and other installers to hook up each piece of equipment easily (Figure 4.17).

One of the most important concerns when laying out a bar is the appearance of the underbar area. The clean lines of the back-bar liquor and refrigeration systems in a straight-line bar are aesthetically appealing. However, L-shaped or curved bars give customers a view of the underside of the front bar, an area that is often a jumble of ingredients, glassware, and cleaning materials.

In this situation, a glass washing machine is a good choice because glasses are taken from the bartop and placed directly in the glass washer, where they are out of sight of the guests. As glasses emerge from the clean side of the machine, they can be loaded into a glass froster or chiller, where again they are out of sight, or placed on back-bar storage shelves. Pipes, wires, and tubing must be carefully concealed where the underbar is exposed so that their appearance does not detract from the aesthetic of the bar. Other equipment needed in most bars includes blenders, frozen drink dispensers, and bottled wine storage or bulk wine dispensers. The bar can require as much planning as the rest of the restaurant if it is to operate at top efficiency.

Figure 4.17
Perlick's modular bar configuration speeds installation. Workstation units are held above the floor to facilitate cleaning behind the bar.
(© 2007 Perlick Corporation)

BAR SERVICE AREA

The bar service area includes the barstools and the standing area immediately behind the stools. Typically, one stool can be added for each 18 inches of bar length. At a bar 20 feet long, 11 guests can be comfortably seated at stools. While seating is important at a bar, the real profits come from the guests who are standing behind the bar stools. The standing area can hold enough guests to triple the total number of clients at the bar. When a large number of standees is expected, additional workstations may be needed. The profitability of the bar will be adversely affected if the standees—or, for that matter, any bar customer—must wait for an extended time before bartenders get to their order.

If standees are expected at a bar, drink rails should be installed to separate standees from guests seated at cocktail or dining tables (Figure 4.18). Too often, this separation is omitted, and dinner guests end up being bumped against while dining.

Careful thought must be given to the section of the bar that services the dining room. Several operational decisions have a marked impact on the layout of this important space. Consider the following questions:

- Will a POS unit be incorporated with the station?
- Will the servers set up the glasses from glass storage on their side of the service bar?
- Will the servers add ice, mixers, and garnish their own drinks?
- Will soiled glassware be returned to the kitchen or the bar for washing?
- Where will bottles of wine be stored and who will have access to the area?

When bartenders need only portion liquor, draw drafts, and hand out bottles of beer, they have more time to attend to customers at the bar. If the service bar serves a large dining room, then sufficient space should be provided to allow several servers to access the bar at one time.

Hard, smooth-surfaced floors should be installed under bar stools and in standing areas. The smooth surfaces make it easier for people to get off and on bar stools and are not easily damaged. Hard materials such as wood, brass, and tile are typically specified in bar areas. These materials are usually easy to maintain, and their sound reflecting

qualities are assets if operators want to create a high-energy atmosphere.

Ventilation is vital in bar areas; in restaurants that allow smoking, people light up cigarettes more frequently here than in dining rooms. While custom ventilation systems are optimal, several ceiling-mounted smoke-filtering units can keep the air in a bar surprisingly smoke free. As in the dining area, a well-designed ventilation system ensures that both smokers and nonsmokers can be accommodated. To minimize smoke carry-over to the dining room, a negative air pressure should be maintained in the bar so that dining room air flows into the bar rather than bar air flowing into the dining room.

Illumination sets the mood in the bar just as it does in dining areas, and in recent years the typical bar atmosphere

Figure 4.18

Drink rails or railings can also prevent bar goers from getting injured or interfering with traffic flow to other areas of a restaurant.

(Photo by Joseph Durocher)

has gone from dim to brightly lit. Bar lighting has played an important role in transforming a dark hideaway into an animated meeting place.

Music and video systems have become increasingly important components of bars because they contribute to the kind of entertainment milieu that today's patrons look for when they go out to socialize. Like other design elements, these systems should be integrated with the bar design from the start of the project, taking into account such issues as speaker quality and placement, and choice and placement of video projection screens or TV monitors. A sound consultant can help optimize the system in the bar and can help minimize sound carry-over to the dining room.

Equipment like pool tables, dartboards, and video games must be planned for early in the design process. When equipment is added as an afterthought, it can have a negative impact on customers who are not playing the games.

In sports bars, TV monitors or video projection systems play an important role. Designers should ensure that every customer can see at least one screen. In many sports bars, diners are separated from drinkers by balconies or raised seating areas.

LOUNGE AREAS

Table seating in lounge areas plays an important role in many restaurants, especially when the lounge serves as a waiting area for diners. Table seating requires more floor space per drink served, but it creates a mood and draws a crowd that might not be captured with bar seating alone.

Lounge areas are popular before meals, but they can also encourage diners to linger after they eat, particularly if after-dinner drinks and coffees are promoted on the menu. Low cocktail seating is most commonly found in quiet lounge areas, while highboy tables and stools tend to be used in higher-energy bars. A growing number of restaurants are adding dance floors or areas for entertainers to perform in cocktail lounges. Dancing or entertainment can entice diners who might otherwise leave the restaurant to stay for an after-dinner drink.

FOODSERVICE IN BARS

Foodservice in bars has become an increasingly popular option for many types of restaurants, particularly for single diners. Because many customers have cut back on the numbers of drinks they consume, the sale of appetizers and hors d'oeuvres is increasingly important to the restaurant's bottom line. In addition to increasing bar revenues, appetizer sales in the bar area can decrease the time guests spend at dinner tables, thus increasing table turns.

In restaurants such as tapas bars, food and beverage sales at the bar go hand in hand. In this situation, it is advisable to locate the bar close to the kitchen. Bar-friendly food production equipment should be considered when the kitchen is distant from the bar or when food is offered after the kitchen is closed. Compact automated fryers that can be installed without ventilation hoods in some jurisdictions enable bartenders to offer items like poppers and chicken wings at any time. High-speed compact ovens (Figure 4.19) that

Figure 4.19
This combination oven is fast and flexible. It can function as a convection oven, a convection steamer, or in combined mode as an oven with steam. Its small footprint makes it ideal for heating foods at a compact bar.
(Photo by Joseph Durocher)

use microwaves, light, impingement air, or a combination of these cooking methods can produce pizzas, quesadillas, and other snack foods in minutes. In addition, a reach-in or chest-style freezer is usually needed to support cooking equipment at a bar.

SECURITY AND SAFETY

The choice of beverage-dispensing equipment and the spatial design of the bar have an effect on safety and security. Management needs to determine how closely they need to control their bar offerings. For example, in bars where mixed drinks cost $6 each, tighter portion control is needed than in an operation where that same drink is sold for $16. Free pouring in high-end bars is an important part of the panache of those facilities. However, in midscale chain restaurants where careful portioning is the only way to ensure a profitable liquor operation, dispensing equipment is essential, as is sophisticated POS software that links each drink order with the dispensing equipment. While not a design issue, free pouring can lead to overpouring, which could lead to an expensive Dram Shop liability lawsuit.

The business end of bars can quickly get soaked with spilled drinks, ice, and spent orange slices, so flooring that maximizes traction is important for employee safety. That said, flooring such as roll-up perforated rubber mats can significantly reduce injuries due to wet floors.

Staff—be they bartenders or servers—must always add ice to a glass with a scoop and not their hands. Ice should never be scooped up with a glass; if the glass breaks, shards could get mixed in with ice in the bin, which then needs to be completely dumped before service can continue.

DESIGN DECISIONS

The following points should always be taken into consideration when planning a bar design:

- A high-visibility bar can help draw patrons into the restaurant.
- The choice of partial, full, or no barriers between bar and dining room depends on the type of restaurant and the desired ambience. Some form of sound control from bar to restaurant is almost always desirable.

- If food is offered, the bar should be accessible to the kitchen unless cooking equipment will be installed at the bar itself.
- In restaurants where the bar provides beverage service to the dining room, the servers' pathway between the two areas should be short and simple. In large operations where a separate service bar is located in the kitchen, the bar can be located farther from the dining areas.
- Sound and video systems should be integrated with the design scheme and not slapped on as an afterthought.
- If live entertainment or dancing is planned for a lounge area, extra floor space must be allocated.
- Light, noise, and hard materials help create the animated, high-energy environments typical of today's gathering places.
- The type of restaurant should dictate the type of bar it contains.

DESTINATION DINING

The elements of design must come together seamlessly in the front of the house. It is here that customers react to the environment and form opinions that will lead them to return or to avoid the restaurant in the future. The front of the house is the milieu in which guests fulfill the main purpose of going out to dine: the food. They are also influenced by service, which can be facilitated or compromised by the layout and design. Thus, it is important to consider how design elements work together to form the dining experience for the guest.

Numerous questions must be resolved before the design process begins:

1. What is the demographic and psychographic profile of the intended market?

Age and education are useful bits of demographic information, but psychographic information, such as knowing whether the target market prefers beer, wine, or spirits, can be even more important.

2. How should the restaurant stand out from the competition?

3. What type of cuisine will be featured?

4. What style(s) of service will be employed?

The style of service will impact floor space needs per seat, placement of POS systems, and, in some cases, the ventilation configuration.

5. How long will the average party spend at the table?

Turnover impacts the total number of persons to be served, which affects the amount of space needed for side station reset tableware.

6. What type of seating (booth, banquette, freestanding) is optimal?

There are numerous seating considerations. Hard seats will speed turnaround, whereas soft cushioned seating will invite guests to linger. Banquette seating gives flexibility for different-sized dining parties, while booth seating fosters intimacy.

7. What feeling should the design elements evoke in the space?

The atmosphere is the amalgamation of all of the elements into a coherent sensory experience.

With answers to these questions as a starting point, it is time to consider the individual elements.

SEATING

The first element that patrons come into direct body contact with is their chair, banquette, or booth. Seating immediately affects how people perceive a space and how long they stay in the space. The surface and shape of the seat, its height and width, its position relative to the table (both distance from the table and the level of the occupied seat in relationship to the top of the table), its spatial relationship to other seats, and its visual relationship to other parts of the room design all influence the customer's perception (Figure 4.20).

Obviously, different types of seating make different types of impressions. The ubiquitous bentwood café chair often signals casual dining, an upholstered armchair tells patrons that the food will be serious, and booth seating signals an intimate dining experience.

TYPE OF SEATING

The hard surface and relatively small seat of a bentwood chair speeds diners along. It can be a comfortable seat for people with a small to average physique, but not for larger folks. Other wooden chairs are made more comfortable by increasing the size of the seat itself, by contouring its shape, and adding arms.

Armchairs are the most comfortable type of seating; they especially appeal to older diners, who use the arms to

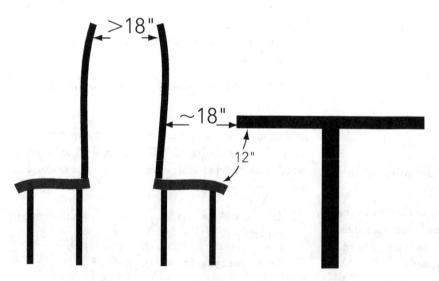

Figure 4.20
At least 18 inches of space should be planned between chairs to prevent customers from getting bumped as servers and guests pass by. The same distance from the chair back to the table edge serves as a guideline. The seat cushion should sit 12 inches below the tabletop. The same rules apply to booth and banquette seating.

push themselves up and out of the chair. However, if the fill and webbing in the chair is not high quality, the seat height may drop to an uncomfortable point.

Banquettes on one side of a table typically are paired with freestanding chairs on the other side. Banquettes afford flexible seating, particularly in a room that also has deuce and four-top tables. Multiple banquette tables can be moved together to accommodate larger parties. As with cushioned seating, the construction of the seat padding is important. Lower-quality foam filling will quickly compress and change the relationship between the diner and the tabletop: The padding can compress to a point where diners feel the top edge of the banquette seat-face under their legs.

Booths offer an intimate experience, particularly when the backs prevent diners from seeing the action at the next booth. The spatial relationship between the booth seat and the table edge is crucial because booths cannot be pushed back to accommodate stout diners (Figure 4.21). The same cautions associated with the construction of banquette seating apply to booth seats. For any type of seating, designers can specify extra layers of upholstery material or padding to ensure comfort. Seating can also be chosen to evoke a theme. High-styled chairs evoke a hip, chic setting, while a traditional captain's chair hints of a seafood theme. When booth seating is used for a chef's table, a wraparound booth maximizes seating, and prevents guests or employees from tripping over chairs in a busy kitchen environment (Figure 4.22).

SEATING MATERIAL

Chairs with wood seats are easy to maintain and are usually lightweight so that they can be moved easily. They have a clean, attractive look and, as noted earlier, can help turn tables because they typically don't remain comfortable for long. However, the discomfort is often not appropriate to the overall setting. To elicit a feeling similar to that of an all-wood chair, consider a wooden chair with thin seat and back pads.

Upholstery offers an opportunity to match the colors, textures, and patterns of the overall design with the seating. Nylon upholstery holds up extremely well and, for a more luxurious look, can be blended with wool or wool and silk. Even in high-ticket establishments, maintenance is a key consideration when choosing upholstery-covered seating because the finest silk won't impress a customer if it is stained or worn. In general, it makes sense to use delicate materials on seat backs rather than on seat bottoms, as bottoms get more wear and tear. Choose commercial-grade upholstery that has been treated with spot-resisting chemicals to maximize the useful life of the seating. Wherever possible, avoid crevasses and button tufting, where crumbs tend to lodge.

Vinyl seat coverings come in a variety of colors and patterns and can have a leather-like texture. Commercial-grade vinyl seat coverings are highly durable, spill resistant, easy to clean, and will not crack when fitted over high-quality padding that does not cause the coverings to bend and stretch excessively. But vinyl becomes hot and uncomfortable when sat on for extended periods, so it is best suited for short- to medium-length dining experiences.

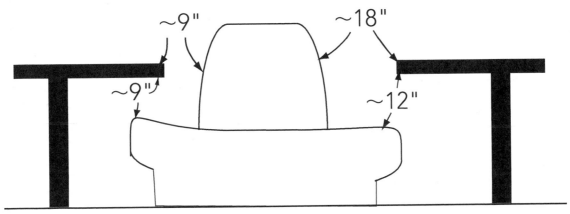

Figure 4.21
When the distance between the booth back and the tabletop is too narrow (left), customers feel cramped. Inexpensive construction used in booth seats means the back edge of the seat compresses while the front edge rises to make an uncomfortable seating arrangement.

Figure 4.22
The chef's table at Bucca di Beppo's in Chicago is directly across from the busy hot foods pickup station. The table and booth are elevated slightly above the kitchen floor, which affords a better view for diners and helps keep the floor under the table from getting soiled should spills occur.
(Photo by Joseph Durocher)

Leather gives a feeling of elegance and is both highly durable and easy to clean.

Resin chairs and tables are most often used in outdoor dining spaces. Look for commercial resin furniture that has been certified for nonresidential outdoor use. Such seating is more rigid than less expensive seating and has extra material in stress areas where hairline fractures can develop. Most important, look for tables and chairs that are ultraviolet (UV) resistant. UV sunlight can weaken some resin chairs to a point where they bend easily or break under the weight of a guest. UV protection is not as important if acrylic or other resins are used for interior seating. Such

seating comes in a wide array of rich colors with inviting contours that offer surprising comfort.

Wrought-iron furniture was once the only choice for outdoor seating and tables, and it is still a good choice. Wrought-iron furniture is highly durable and, because it is available in a wide variety of painted colors, it can blend in with any decor. With the addition of seat and back pads, wrought-iron seating can be quite comfortable.

STRUCTURE

In addition to the covering of the seat, its size and pitch (both back and seat) affect the guest's comfort. A slight forward pitch of a molded plastic seat in a quick-service restaurant makes customers feel as if they are slipping off the seat. Such seating can speed turnover rates. Conversely, deeply padded armchairs cause diners to linger at their table.

For optimal comfort levels, seats must be matched to their intended use. In cocktail lounges, seating is typically lower and deeper than at dining tables. Dining chairs, however, must be matched closely to the height of the dining table. Although tables and chairs come in standard sizes (tables from 26 to 30 inches high and chairs, with seats, from 16 to 18 inches high), the designer should always double-check that the table and seat height are matched for comfort. All too often, chairs are too low or too high. This problem seems especially prevalent with custom-designed banquettes, where seats sometimes sink so low that not only is eating difficult, but getting in and out of the seat requires a dancer's flexibility. Adding casters to the legs of a chair can make it too high to match a table.

The structural integrity of the chair is a crucial consideration. A good chair should be able to withstand the weight of even the most portly individual. In the restaurant environment, wear and tear take their toll so quickly that seating made for residential use generally won't hold up more than a few months. Antique seating should be avoided. If antique styling is needed, custom chairs can be produced based on an antique sample.

Commercial seating is built with extra structural reinforcements in order to withstand heavy use. A retail version would look exactly the same to the customer—but not for long because it would soon begin falling apart at the stress points.

SPECIAL FEATURES

The weight of movable seating contributes to the overall image of a restaurant but also has operational implications.

Lightweight chairs are easy for customers to move toward and away from a table. More substantial chairs are harder to move and, as they are moved in and out from the table, they can damage the floor surface (Figure 4.23). However, heavy seating gives an elegant or regal feeling that is appropriate in some settings, although the weight of cast-iron furniture can make it difficult for guests to move, particularly when "floor" surfaces are uneven.

Casters aid in moving chairs to and from the table; the type of caster must be matched to the type of flooring. Casters are particularly appropriate when installed on heavy chairs. However, they can cause a chair to slip out from under diners as they sit down or stand up, particularly when set on a hard-surfaced floor.

Booster seats and high chairs are essential for restaurants that cater to families. Space should be set aside to store these seats when not in use. Most high chairs have a larger footprint than many restaurant chairs, so adjacent tables may have to be moved to accommodate families with a child or children in high chairs.

In fast feeders, cafeterias, and other restaurants that depend on high turnover, the seat itself can play an integral part in moving people through the space. For over 40 years, molded plastic, fixed seating was the standard in high-turnover restaurants. Recently, however, in an effort to expand market share and make the space more conducive to dining, the variety of seating has greatly expanded to include wooden benches or café chairs, fashionably styled metal chairs in a spectrum of colors, and even upholstered chairs. Such seating choices create a totally different impression from the old institutional-looking furniture, but consideration must always be given to the desired turnover time. When a restaurant depends on 30-minute turnover, chair design should not encourage patrons to linger for two hours.

SEATING LAYOUT

Seating can create a feeling of intimacy. Booth seating, curved banquette seating, and high-backed chairs engender a private feeling, for example, because they restrict sight lines and the seating wraps around the guests.

The atmosphere is also affected by the relative position of seats and tables. The crowded feeling of a French bistro depends on tightly packed seating at small tables; in a fine-dining operation, generous spacing between tables—usually in excess of 15 square feet of floor space per seat—gives a feeling of elegance. While square foot guidelines exist, they should be viewed solely as guidelines (Table 4.1).

Although part of the goal of good design is to carefully match the mix of deuces, four-tops, and so on with the size of parties that frequent the restaurant, it should be noted

Figure 4.23
This image of Metro Nine in Framingham, Massachusetts, designed by Judd Brown Designs, shows heavy leather chairs at one table and commercial dining chairs at other tables. The commercial chairs are easy for guests to move in and out from the table. The heavy chairs, while difficult to move, convey the steakhouse atmosphere.
(Photography by Warren Jagger Photography, Inc.)

TABLE 4.1 FRONT-OF-THE-HOUSE SQUARE FOOTAGE ESTIMATES	
Type of Service	**Square Footage per Seat**
À la carte	8–16
Full-service	16–20
Quick service	10–14
Banquet	10–16
Family style	13–16
Buffet	12–18
Cafeteria	12–15

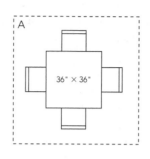

7' 6" X 7' 6" ~ 56 ☐ per 4-top

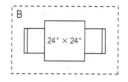

6' 6" × 3' 6" ~23 ☐ per 2-top

Circulation in drawings A, B, and C allows for 18" clearance on all sides of tables and chairs

that a mix of table sizes and seating configurations creates more visual interest than a single type of table. Seating variety offers patrons the choice of more intimate or more open seating, depending on their mood. In addition, the table and seating selection also affects the numbers of seats that can be accommodated in a given space (Figure 4.24).

TABLES AND TABLETOPS

Every guest wants the best table in the house. Ideally, every table should be perceived as "the best table," but that's not possible. Every seat, of course, isn't a window seat. There is only one natural prime spot—a table that is the visual focal point of the restaurant, one from which the entire dining room can be viewed. And there are times that the seats preferred by celebrities, not the design, define the prime seats.

Designers can employ a variety of techniques to ensure that every table is indeed desirable, even if not "the best." Terracing backward and upward from a wall of windows, for example, allows patrons in the back of the room a view similar to that seen by guests in the front of the room.

Sight lines and flow patterns of both guests and employees are crucial considerations when laying out the tables in a restaurant. Customers disdain a view of the restroom, the smell of the garbage room, and the clanging from the pot sink. In the past, they shunned a view of the kitchen, and still do if it is seen through a set of swinging doors. But well-designed display kitchens can turn the table closest to the kitchen into a prime table. The secret is to take what could be a bad situation and make it something special. A nook adjacent to the wine cellar can become a special party space because it overlooks the wine display. A large antique table positioned in the center of the dining room can become a captain's table for single diners. Deuces

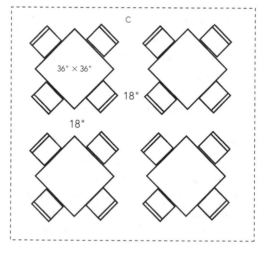

11' 6" × 11' 6" ~ 133 ☐   per 16 seats

Figure 4.24
The layout of seating and tables affects the square footage requirement per seat. In (A), 14 square feet is required per seat. (B) requires 11½ square feet per seat. In (C), the most efficient layout, only 8⅔ square feet is required per seat.

elevated on a sidewall highlight those seats and put those diners on display.

The shapes of tables and the number of seats at tables are important considerations, again depending on the type of restaurant as well as the dining habits of typical customers. An average place setting is 24 inches wide, but more room is needed to serve a formal meal and space can be tightened for banquet-style service. In cafeterias, the size and shape of the trays must be considered when specifying table size. Theatrical restaurants feature more large tables than do small full-service establishments where the emphasis is on food. This is because more families and

When matching the tabletop with seating, consider the following:

- Will the table look overcrowded with a full assortment of plates, flatware, and glassware?

- Should four-tops be square or rectangular?

- Will there be a need to convert a four-top into a round that seats six?

- Will there be a need to convert a six-top into an eight-top?

- Will space be needed on the tabletop to accommodate a laptop along with tableware?

groups tend to frequent theatrical restaurants, while more single couples tend to frequent traditional restaurants that emphasize the food.

The tabletop provides the most immediate and personal experience in the restaurant because diners come in direct contact with their plates, food, glasses, flatware, and napery. The texture, temperature, color, and balance of each element—separately and in concert—should all be taken into consideration during the design process. An entire book could be written on the selection of tabletop elements, but basic principles can guide the development of an effective tabletop design.

THE TABLE ITSELF

Size, shape, position, and surface materials are critical components to consider when selecting tables for a restaurant. For example, a series of deuces along a banquette can be moved together to accommodate larger parties. A 36-inch square table can accommodate four diners, whereas that same 36-inch table with flip-up leaves can become a round table that accommodates five.

In most cases, a mix of table sizes makes it possible to deal with any number of guests in a party. Size should also relate to the amount of hardware that will be placed on the table and the size of the plates that will come from the kitchen. Family-style service requires the largest amount of table surface per diner as the platters of food need space on the table along with each place setting. Extra space must also be considered for banquet or full-service restaurants where a full setting of flatware and glassware are preset for each guest.

A mix of table shapes also adds visual interest to the room and helps the operation accommodate a range of diners. Restaurants typically incorporate at least round and square tables. Oval tables work well with curved banquet seating. Long rectangular tables have become fashionable for group dining or for single diners who wish to not dine alone. In some operations such tables are raised above the level of the rest of the tables and matched with stool-high seating.

The base must relate to the tabletop, how the table will be used, and the type of flooring on which the table will be set. The basic choice is between a pedestal base and four legs. The pedestal is handy because it does not get in the way of chairs when they are pushed under the table, nor do guests hit against it when they are seated. However, if large-diameter tables are used, a guest pushing down on one side of the table could cause water glasses on the other side to spill.

Table bases should always be substantial enough to support the table's size and weight and to convey a secure and stable feeling to the customer. When tables are set on uneven floors, the bases must be equipped with levelers that keep the table from wobbling. Wobbling is also a problem when the table supports are not well constructed. Inexpensive bases are fashioned from lightweight materials not intended for the rigors of a restaurant environment.

When tables are covered with a cloth, little thought is given to the appearance of the pedestals or legs, but when there is no cloth, the base should either add to the appeal of the room or be innocuous.

It's important to match the size of the tabletop with the overall dining experience. Consider the following:

- Will the table look overcrowded with a full assortment of plates, flatware, and glassware?

- Should the four-top be square or rectangular?

- Will there be a need to convert a four-top into a round that seats six?

- Will there be a need to convert a six-top into an eight-top?

- Will space be needed on the tabletop to accommodate a laptop computer along with tableware?

TABLETOP SURFACE

The actual tabletop material itself is most important when it is visible to the guest. Tabletop materials of marble, glass, Formica™, and other hard materials give a different feeling than the warmth of wood tabletops and the fine dining image of linen. The choice should be visually compatible with the overall design. Colorful resin tabletops or hard materials such as marble-like compressed stone or polished granite are often specified for non-table-linen tabletops.

Both durability and cleaning should be considered when selecting a tabletop material. For tops that will not be covered with a cloth, surfaces that can be wiped clean with a few strokes are essential. Stone tabletops, for example, are highly durable but not easy to clean; they can stain or discolor when grease is spilled on them.

When dealing with cloth-covered tables, remember that while the tabletop material is invisible to the guest 90 percent of the time, it flashes into view when the linen is changed. In casual operations, an inexpensive plywood top may be acceptable, but elegant, high-ticket establishments should carry through the high-end aesthetic by adding a table pad, even though guests may view the tabletop for only a few seconds.

TABLE BASE

Single pedestal, wall-mounted, and four-leg configuration table bases offer different advantages and challenges. The single pedestal keeps the table support away from the edges, which offers unobstructed seating. Large tables with a center pedestal can accommodate varying party sizes. Wall-mounted tables are the most stable, yet cannot be used in the center of a room unless they are attached to pillars. Four-legged tables can obstruct the knee space under the tabletop. Pedestal and four-legged tables need to have height adjusters installed on their bases to ensure that the table will not wobble.

NAPERY

The color and design of tablecloths and napkins should be integrated with the overall design scheme. Napery design forms such a strong image in the restaurant that, at times, a change of tablecloths and napkins can create a fresh new look for the interior. Yellow-accented napery at breakfast, rose colors at lunch, and burgundy tones in the evening evoke entirely different feelings.

When specifying linen, attention should be given to flame resistance, stain resistance, and texture. Polyester, cotton, or cotton-polyester blend napkins each have their own feel and usability characteristics. Generally speaking, the following should be considered when purchasing linens:

- Absorbency
- Color (availability and fastness)

- Folding and starchability
- Wearability
- Shrinkage
- Stain resistance

From a design perspective, the most important issues are color availability and fastness. Polyester fabrics come in a wider variety of colors than do pure cotton fabrics, and they do not fade as quickly.

It may be advisable to select one type of material for the tablecloth and another material for the napkin. A blended tablecloth can work quite well with cotton napkins. In any event, it is important to remember that guests touch table linens, and the feel leaves a lasting impression.

Banquet chair slipcovers and table skirts round out the linens found in most restaurants. Both of these types of linen should be fashioned from highly durable and stain-resistant material. Table skirts—commonly used in buffet setups—come in a variety of colors and patterns. Chair drapes can be permanently affixed to chairs, or they can be added to create a luxurious feeling for special events.

FLATWARE

Guests handle flatware more than any other item on the tabletop. Its pattern, heft, shape, cleanliness, and material all affect the perception of the meal. Stainless steel is the most common material for restaurant flatware, but a wide spectrum of grades of stainless give varying appearances after even limited use. Some inexpensive flatware shows scratches and a dull finish after only a month. Better (more expensive) grades take on a shine that lights up the tabletop. A stainless-steel mix with 18 percent chrome and 8 percent nickel—referred to as 18/8 stainless—yields the best results in terms of both corrosion resistance and luster.

Silver-plated flatware is appropriate for high-ticket establishments, but it places additional responsibility on the operator. Several grades—which reflect the quality of the silver, the number of platings, and the weight of the blanks that form the individual pieces—determine the durability of silver-plated flatware. Some manufacturers plate more silver on the back of the pieces because the touch points—those areas that come in contact with the table or dishware—are thus better protected.

One popular choice is silver-plated flatware made from a stainless-steel base. However, the silver coating tarnishes quickly and needs to be burnished or polished periodically. This can be done with a machine, in soaking bins, or by hand; the need to polish must be recognized and incorporated with the overall design of the warewashing area. Sterling silver is rarely used in restaurants, not only because of its expense but also because it requires even more care than silver plate.

When considering shape, heft, and balance, it is important to beware of forks that are thin near the shank (the part of the handle that attaches to the shoulder of the tines). When too thin, it is difficult to hold the fork without having it roll in the hand and all but impossible to use for cutting. Forks with a thin shank are also prone to bending (Figure 4.25).

Knives pose a special problem because the blade, if not made of high-quality stainless steel, will show scratches and mar the appearance of even the most beautiful tabletop. Adequate metal at stress and touch points, and proper grading or thickness, yields a sturdy and well-balanced piece of flatware. Knives can also be purchased with solid or hollow handles, each of which has a different weight and feel when people use them.

For those operations specializing in steaks and chops, serrated knives should be a part of the tabletop hardware. Some flatware patterns offer steak knives, while others do not. When seafood is served, fish knives should be included as an added tabletop feature, and in some operations a flat sauce spoon adds an air of elegance.

Obviously, the flatware pattern must work with the other tabletop items and the overall design. Several other issues must also be considered:

- *Pattern lifespan.* How long will the pattern be available? While a new pattern may make an exciting design

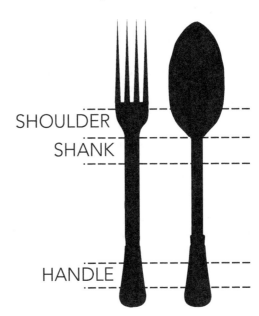

Figure 4.25
Spoons and forks are particularly prone to bending where the shoulder joins the shank. Some manufacturers add reinforcements to prevent bending.

statement, it may be discontinued by the manufacturer if it does not sell well.

- *Variety of pieces.* Some patterns are produced with two dozen or more different pieces of flatware from which to choose for a tabletop. Others are available with a knife, fork, teaspoon, and soup spoon only. How many different pieces are needed? It's important to determine the variety of pieces needed for the menu (Figure 4.26).

Figure 4.26
Quality flatware manufacturers offer a wide variety of patterns and pieces. Some patterns have a limited range of pieces, while others have a wide range of pieces to suit the flatware needs of any menu item.
(Photo by Joseph Durocher)

Generally, the number of pieces per pattern ranges from 10 to 17.

- *Availability*. Are replacements readily available? Some patterns may not be in stock at all times, so purchasing a resupply may be problematic. Check the lead time for delivery of any flatware pattern before making a final choice.

- *Special care*. Will the flatware need special maintenance? A burnisher not only removes discolorations but also smooths out scratches that appear on flatware; it can actually help extend the usable life of silver-plated flatware if used twice monthly.

- *Flatware sorters*. Does automated flatware sorting make sense? The volume of flatware used in some facilities justifies the space and expense of an automated flatware sorter. The sorters minimize hand contact with flatware and the amount of labor needed to sort it.

DINNERWARE

Along with the flatware and holloware, the plates, bowls, and other elements that hold food and beverages play an important role in the customer's perception of the food. The plate's size and heft should reflect the foods being served on it. Dinnerware can also anchor the aesthetics of the tabletop design.

Many restaurateurs use heavy plates that give the perception of holding a lot of food. Other restaurateurs choose oversized plates to create a canvas on which to arrange food artfully. While these plates help showcase and frame the food presentation, they must be carefully matched to the tabletop so as not to overwhelm the space. Oversize plates can make portions look small, which, in the long run, could lead to customer dissatisfaction. Heavy, oversized plates may not fit in standard-size plate storage cabinets and require more storage space than conventional serving vessels.

Restaurant plates decorated with or fired with color are the most commonly found dinnerware in the restaurant industry. Heavily patterned plates that make strong design statements can serve as excellent base plates—those plates already set on the table when guests arrive—but they should never be chosen for serving food.

While some patterns look attractive on their own, they can actually detract from the appearance of foods. Other base-plate designs, such as one with a band of color one-fourth- to one-half-inch wide around the rim of the dish, can make a striking statement in the dining room and also be suitable for serving food. All too often, however, the colored rims are marred with fingerprints from careless service personnel. Plate selection must always recognize the visual limitations and operational considerations involved with the choice.

Equal care should be taken with the selection of other dinnerware items. Consider the handle design of cups, for instance. Some handles will withstand the wear and tear of brutish bus staff, while others break with a simple tap. Then there is the actual feeling of the handle. The heavy, large handle of a commercial coffee mug, while not suited to a fine dining operation, is easy to grasp. In contrast, the dainty handle of a bone dinnerware teacup is fine for sipping afternoon tea in a leisurely fashion but impossible for all but the most slender individuals to easily put a finger through.

Shape, size, material, design, and the manufacturing process affect the life span of dinnerware. The thickness of a piece of dinnerware does not necessarily foretell its life span. Commercial-grade dinnerware, produced to withstand the rigors of the restaurant environment, is designed with strength and resistance to breaking and chipping as important characteristics. In addition, commercial dinnerware manufacturers tend to recognize the importance of a design suitable for storage and commercial warewashing.

The following are important considerations for dinnerware specifications.

SHAPE

Nine-inch plates are not all created equal. The size of the well—that is, the actual area on which food is set—varies. The shoulder and rim of each style has a different width, and the angle of the rim also changes from plate to plate. The shape of dinnerware affects its durability. A rolled edge (reinforced) adds strength at a point that is most prone to chipping.

Specialty shapes, like fish and octagons, and plates with dividers can be used to create a whimsical presentation or to keep entrée items separated. The shape of a plate can relate to the products that will be served on it. For example, an oval plate is a better choice than a round plate for serving baked burritos.

SIZE

Size is important because it impacts the appearance of food on the plate and the apparent portion size. A 12-ounce steak served on a 9-inch plate appears much larger than if the same steak is served on a 12-inch plate. The size of the well also affects the appearance of the portion. When selecting a dinnerware pattern, it's important to review all of the sizes available for each pattern. If, at a later time, it becomes necessary to choose a smaller size, the change can be made without having to purchase plates that do not match.

MATERIAL

Dinnerware is fashioned from clay containing additives that improve its hardness or porosity. An alumina body increases the strength of a piece of dinnerware, makes it lighter, helps keep foods warm longer, and can be placed under a broiler. Glass is frequently used for salad plates and in some operations for other dinnerware. However, dinner plates made from glass do not maintain heat as long as a china dish will. A third option, one that is ideal for serving sizzling servings, is metal such as cast iron, stainless, aluminum, or pewter. Each material has its own unique qualities. And each matches different types of operation.

DESIGN

The means by which designs are applied to dinnerware affect its price. The least costly method is a printed design. Decals are a bit more expensive but can give greater detail than printed designs. Hand-painted dinnerware is the most expensive, and adding gold or silver rim lines further increases the cost. Custom-designed plates—whether the design is hand painted or applied by decal—create a signature design element and may not be that much more expensive than stock tableware.

MANUFACTURING PROCESS

The process begins with the choice of the basic material. Dinnerware that is not lead free can pose a health risk if the glazing is cracked. Some manufacturers use a pure white base clay, while others use an off-white clay. The vitrification process fuses the components of the clay body into a glasslike substance in high-heat kilns. Some dinnerware is fired in a kiln to form a bisque; then the decoration and glaze is applied and the dinnerware fired a second time. Once-fired dinnerware—dinnerware that is fired only one time—has the decorations and glaze added prior to firing. The quality of the glaze and the temperature at which it is fired affect the durability of dinnerware. Gold-rimmed plates, while they look good, are prone to premature wear because they are fired at relatively low temperatures that leave a less resilient finish than high-temperature firing. Once-fired dinnerware has a dry foot, which means no glaze is applied to the bottom. The exposed base of such dinnerware can abrade the surface of any glazed plate on which it is set.

Residential dinnerware, like residential furniture, won't last long in the restaurant environment. Another advantage of commercial dinnerware is that stock patterns are maintained for quick delivery from the manufacturer. For a minimal additional investment, custom-designed plates can be created to coordinate with a restaurant's graphics program. These signature plates can create a sense of identity for a restaurant. However, it is important to verify the number of pieces that must be purchased when reordering. As a rule of thumb, expect to order at least 15 dozen of each item for each reorder.

The lead time needed to order and reorder is important when considering custom-designed dinnerware. Producing dinnerware with a simple line treatment can take a month and a half, with a crest and line up to two months, and with a more complex pattern up to three months. Developing a custom design can take the manufacturer up to four additional weeks.

In recent years, increasing attention has being paid to the aesthetics of the tabletop (Figure 4.27). No longer do ornately designed plates compete with the chef's art. Today, the shape and form of the plate serve to highlight cuisine.

In the case of full-service restaurants, the design team should remember that there are numerous courses to each meal and many variables to each course. Traditionally, a meal includes an appetizer, main course, salad, dessert, and beverages. But the appetizer selection alone might include a dozen or more items, each of which comes with its own garnish, serving plate, underliner, eating utensils, and condiments. The same may be true for other courses.

According to experts, the average piece of dinnerware will be used about 7,000 times and will endure approximately three years of typical restaurant use, if handled properly. Some dinnerware manufacturers estimate that 25 percent of a restaurant's dinnerware will be broken each year. Needless to say, replacement costs can be astronomical. It is essential, therefore, that the design team not only specify well-constructed items but also make sure that all of the back- and front-of-the-house support stations be adequately designed for storage (Figure 4.28). The greater the variety of tabletop elements, the greater the need for storage in the kitchen, dishroom, and at the front-of-the-house server stations.

Figure 4.27
The simplicity of this table setting creates a strong visual image in keeping with the room's modern design.
(Photo by Joseph Durocher)

Figure 4.28
Service stations must be designed to hold the full variety of table elements in backup storage space, along with order-entry equipment. Built-in units can be designed to blend into the overall decor.
(Photo by Joseph Durocher)

GLASSWARE

A fine Bordeaux is best appreciated in a high-quality, thin-walled, clear wineglass. While most restaurants choose stemware for wine service, a growing number have shifted to stemless wine glasses available from a variety of manufacturers. Stemless glassware requires less storage space, is less prone to tipping over (and breakage), and is available for serving beverages as diverse as martinis, draft beer, and full-bodied wines. If a different glass is specified for each type of drink, the bartender may have to stock 25 or more types of glasses. The use of a single glass goblet for all beverages—wine, beer, soda, champagne, and mixed drinks—is not the most aesthetic approach but, from an operational perspective, it is certainly the easiest.

The size and shape of glassware, along with the manufacturing process, will affect its breakability. For example, heat-tempered glassware helps protect the lip of the glass from breakage. So, too, will the shape of the glassware, as shown in Figure 4.29. Today, machine-blown glassware can be purchased at roughly half the cost of hand-blown glassware.

While the variety of glasses used for beverage service is usually determined by management, the designers—both back and front of the house—must be cognizant of this decision because it affects the amount of storage space needed. With more types of glassware, additional storage space is needed in the clean dish storage areas as well as at the bar itself. A variety of glassware may also affect the requirements for storage at the server stations.

Figure 4.29
Stemware is particularly prone to breakage. One option is to choose a glass with a short stem. Breakage at the lip of a glass is another problem. While tempering or building up the lip helps, a bowl that is wider than the lip also minimizes breakage when a glass falls over.

HOLLOWARE

The selection of holloware—tabletop elements such as salt and pepper shakers, candlesticks, and sugar and creamer sets—must be coordinated with flatware, dinnerware, glassware, and the overall design of the restaurant. In simple terms, a restaurant where fine linen and silver-plated flatware are used needs holloware that is either silver plated or high-quality stainless steel. By the same token, the 1950s diner calls for pour-top sugar dispensers, plastic water pitchers, and squeeze bottles for ketchup and mustard.

In addition, the designer must consider all flatware and holloware items necessary for each menu item to ensure that the overall look is integrated. Manufacturers don't always offer a total set of holloware in the same design pattern as flatware, so it is important to select visually compatible patterns.

In addition to matching the overall decor, holloware should be chosen to support the operation. For example, hinge-top holloware takes a great deal of abuse and, if the hinge is not strong enough, the tops will soon fall off. Holloware fitted with tops that swing back 180 degrees are easy to clean in a dish machine and are less likely to have their hinges broken.

Coffee servers are an example of holloware that must be considered in any full-service restaurant. For most full-service restaurants, clear glass "pots" are used for coffee service. However, to upscale the experience slightly, silver-plated or well-designed stainless-steel or porcelain pots should be considered.

Silver-plated flatware, holloware, and items like chafing dishes require a secure area in which they can be stored. Such storage areas should be planned for during the design phase of the project and not as an afterthought. Burnishing equipment and polishing supplies are often kept in these areas as well.

LIGHTING

As noted in Chapter 3, lighting influences diners in many ways, from the rosy glow it can impart to people's complexions to the mysterious patterns it can throw on wall surfaces. Lighting that is too bright or too dim may lead to serious eyestrain. Lighting that is too uniform makes the atmosphere seem dull. Lighting that is too harsh can cause food to look unappetizing. Light can totally change the perception of colored surfaces.

Lighting that is too uniform makes the atmosphere seem dull. Lighting that is too harsh can cause food to look unappetizing.

The design team of Aumiller Youngquist stresses the importance of choosing lighting to enhance every phase of a customer's experience. "Some designers only think about the wow factor when customers arrive and fail to consider the impact of the lighting in the parking lot when customers leave," they say. Lighting the variety of spaces in a restaurant is an art in itself, and in complex or big-budget projects, a lighting designer is often enlisted to help develop an illumination scheme.

In other instances, well-informed architects or interior designers implement the lighting program, which defines the type of fixtures and bulbs (lamps) along with any control equipment. Both operational and aesthetic issues must be considered when selecting light sources and control equipment. Operators should be educated about the basic elements and the control equipment so that they can communicate the proper operational information to staff and to maintenance people about relamping and focus adjustment.

THE LIGHTING PLAN

One of the reasons that restaurant lighting is so complicated is that it involves not only the selection of light sources but also the programming of light levels that respond both to various time periods and various places in the room. In order to be effective, light levels, light sources, and quality of light must interact consistently with other design elements in the restaurant.

When establishing lighting plans for interiors, the design team should consider the following classifications.

MOOD/DECOR/ART LIGHTING

This category of lighting can create the most dramatic illumination in a restaurant. It really begins outside with signage and architectural lighting, and carries forward to the interior, where objects or surfaces are spotlighted with overlays of direct or indirect lighting. Artwork is frequently lit with carefully focused track lights manipulated to avoid glare yet allow the images to be clearly viewed. Plantings and wall surfaces are often uplit so that they glow and their texture is emphasized. Generally, objects can be spotlit with direct light for the most powerful effect, but some lighting designers caution against juxtaposing brightly spotlit objects with a dark backdrop because the contrast can cause discomfort.

PEOPLE/FOOD LIGHTING

Effectively illuminating people and food involves delicate manipulation of light sources and light levels. The color temperature of the lamp (CCT) and the color rendering index (CRI) should both be considered when selecting lamps for restaurants. Lamps with a low CCT—2,000 to 3,000K—are referred to as warm light because they produce light high in the red, orange, and yellow range of the spectrum. Lamps with high CCT—greater than 4,000K—produce more blue and are referred to as cool light. Lamps with a high CRI rating make colors look natural and vibrant. Lamps with a low CRI rating make colors look washed out or of a different hue.

For reference, conventional incandescent bulbs have a 2,700 CCT rating and a CRI of 95, and halogen lamps have a 3,000 CCT rating and a 95 CRI. The typical fluorescent bulb produces a CCT of approximately 5,000K and a CRI of 90. In simple terms, these three bulbs will give relatively the same color rendition, but the fluorescent will make blue colors stand out more.

Obviously, the goal is for both people and food to look as attractive as possible. Designers have different theories about the best way to achieve this goal. Without question, people and food look best under incandescent or halogen light, but improvements in some fluorescent lamps make them acceptable in certain restaurant settings. Many designers say that the space should be lit in such a way that the tables and diners become the focus of the room. However, highly focused spotlights directed at the center of a table can create glare, detract from the appearance of guests, and cause uncomfortable dark shadows. Indirect light that softly illuminates people's faces is ideal. Tabletop candle lamps can provide soft illumination when general indirect lighting is not appropriate.

Many designers say that the space should be lit in such a way that the tables and diners become the focus of the room.

Increasingly, designers must react to an aging Baby Boomer population when designing a lighting plan. Gone are the days when Boomers could read 9-point brown type on a rough-textured, cream-colored menu card. Higher light levels are needed to create the contrast necessary for aging eyes to read menus. Greater contrast between the print ink and the paper stock, along with an increase in type size and typeface, can also help.

MOTIVATIONAL/TASK LIGHTING

This type of lighting is most important for the employees of a restaurant. Correct light levels—bright, but not blinding—will help them perform their assigned tasks and, in some instances, can drastically affect productivity. Task lighting is all too often overlooked in the front of the house. The bartender needs good task lighting when mixing drinks, the service staff when filling out guest checks, and the flambé chef while preparing duck à l'orange. Task lighting is essential at POS stations, particularly those that use a keyboard or touchpad for input or include a cash drawer. When touch screens are used, light levels should be low enough to prevent glare on the screen.

SAFETY AND SECURITY LIGHTING

This lighting is essential for the well-being of guests, employees, and management and in many cases is required by law. This includes exit lights inside the restaurant, emergency lighting in case of power outages, parking lot and other exterior lighting, and lighting bright enough in the back of the house so employees can work safely. With strategic planning, none of these light sources need be offensive to look at. Emergency lights, for example, can be totally recessed into the ceiling, although emergency exit signs must always be in clear view.

All of the issues noted here, and much more, go into a good restaurant lighting plan. Most experts recommend that a variety of concealed and decorative fixtures are desirable to achieve successful results. To recap, the following factors must be considered before final decisions are made.

LOCATION AND ORIENTATION

Precisely which space will be lit affects all other factors. Exterior light, be it natural or artificial, can affect the interior lighting plan if there is an expanse of exterior glass. The angle of light fixtures must be incorporated into the plan. The direction of the lighting (up or down) should also be noted. Most restaurant lighting plans incorporate a mix of uplighting, downlighting, and direct and indirect lighting.

TYPES OF LIGHTING

Will a single type of lamp (bulb) be used or a mix of lamps? Will a single type of luminaire (fixture) or a mix be used? Each luminaire coupled with a given lamp outputs a given amount of light. Change the structure of the luminaire and the light output changes.

DISTANCE

The distance of each luminaire from objects that are to be lit affects the plan. A room with a 10-foot-high ceiling needs far fewer fixtures and lamps than does a room with a 20-foot high ceiling if the tabletops are to be lit to the same level of foot-candles. Beam spread should also be considered when planning the distance between a luminaire and a surface to be lighted.

LIGHT QUALITY

What are the spectral characteristics of the light and how will these characteristics affect the people using the space and the appearance of colors in the space? If more than one light source is used, how will the quality of light be affected by the mix, both overall and in specific areas?

QUANTITY OF LIGHT

How much light is needed? What is the optimal foot-candle level for each space? Must some points be illuminated more than other points? The type of luminaire, lamp, distance, and number of fixtures all affect the quantity of light. Lighting guidelines for restaurants appear in Table 4.2.

ENERGY UTILIZATION

Total energy consumption, total energy cost, and the coefficient of utilization (CU) of the lamps must be considered. Incandescent lamps, while producing a high quality of light, use much of the wattage they consume to generate heat rather than light. Fluorescents are far more energy efficient, and sodium and mercury vapor lamps even more so (Table 4.3), though they are not appropriate for most restaurant interiors. LED lights, first introduced in 1962 as a red light, can now be purchased as white light; however, the cost for the diodes that produce white light are roughly 10 times the cost of diodes that produce other colors (red, yellow, and green).

MAINTENANCE

How often must the lamps be replaced? Can the fixtures be cleaned, and how? The relamping program is an important consideration that influences maintenance as well as luminaire and lamp selection. Must a lamp be replaced whenever it burns out? Will lamps be replaced when a certain percentage of the lamps burn out? Will all of the lamps be replaced when the first or a percentage of the lamps burn out? Obviously, the relamping plan will affect operating

TABLE 4.2 LIGHTING LEVELS IN FOOT-CANDLES BY AREA

Restaurant Area	Minimum Foot-Candles
Receiving	25– 45
Storage	15– 20
Pre-preparation	20– 30
Preparation/Production	30– 50
Warewashing	70–100
POS/Cashier	35– 50
Intimate dining	5– 15
Fast-food dining	75–100
Dining room cleaning	30– 50

TABLE 4.3 TYPICAL LIFE AND LUMENS/WATT FOR SAMPLE LAMPS

Lamp Type	Life in Hours	Lumens/Watt
Incandescent	750–2,500	5–15
Halogen	3,000	15–20
Linear fluorescent	10,000–20,000	80–90
Low-watt compact fluorescent	10,000	30
High-watt compact fluorescent	10,000	70
High-intensity discharge (mercury vapor, metal halide, sodium)	10,000–20,000	30–140
Light-emitting diode (LED)	10,000+	Up to 150

costs and light levels. Some lamps are designed for a specific installation orientation—that is, some are designed for straight-down installation and others for horizontal installation. Incorrectly installed fixtures and lamps can significantly decrease the life span of the lamp.

Beware of luminaires in difficult-to-reach places. One Boston restaurant designer specified lighting fixtures for a ceiling so high that a scissor lift was needed to reach it. This was not a problem during the initial installation, but the designers learned after opening that a scissor lift did not fit in the small personal elevator that goes to this dining floor. Consequently, the bulbs in the ceiling fixtures were not replaced as they "burned out" and wall sconces were installed instead.

Today, few restaurants use the 2- by 4-foot fluorescent fixtures commonly found in office buildings, with the exception of some corporate and other noncommercial cafeterias. Instead, many restaurant designers specify recessed lighting, track lighting, or indirect lighting coves as part of the ceiling design. These treatments increase the complexity of the ceiling structure but also improve the quality of lighting in the space. In some cases, skylights, either real or simulated, become a light source and a ceiling element. When cove lighting is used, the ceiling reflects light into the dining space and conceals the luminaires.

NATURAL VERSUS ARTIFICIAL LIGHT

When a restaurant is entirely interior (with no outside source of light), controlling lighting levels throughout the day is relatively easy. However, when sunlight (natural) or other external lighting sources (hallways, streetlamps, etc.) enter the restaurant, establishing a lighting scheme is more difficult. The location of windows can influence the impact of sunlight because indirect light entering a restaurant is different than the glaring direct rays of the sun.

In new construction, the architect can plan north-facing windows or windows that do not face the sun during service hours, roof overhangs, or tinted glass to help alleviate the problems associated with glare. In existing buildings, exterior plantings and window-shading elements such as curtains, drapes, and blinds can minimize the impact of the sun on interior lighting levels.

The main dining room of New York's Tavern on the Green is a classic example of good natural light control. The south-facing Crystal Room has a long wall of windows that, during the summer, is partially shaded by trees, with just enough light filtering into the room to create a bright and cheery atmosphere. In the winter, the leafless trees allow the sun, low on the horizon, to pour all of its warming rays into the room. During evenings throughout the year, thousands of miniature lights festooned on tree branches outside the windows allow guests to dine by sparkling urban starlight. The 45 chandeliers with some 15,000 crystals and over 50 mirrors that adorn the walls throughout the facility add further sparkle to its baroque décor.

The use of greenhouse units in quick-service and family dining restaurants should be approached with caution because of the challenges they present. While natural light enlivens the dining areas, the glare and heat load in greenhouse units can be excessive. At night, lighting from mercury or sodium vapor parking lot fixtures will make complexions and food look pasty and unappealing if allowed to pour in through uncovered greenhouse windows.

LIGHTING LEVELS

As noted earlier, lighting levels should be carefully monitored throughout the restaurant, and a light transition zone at the entry area is essential. A dimly lit dining alcove can help create an intimate milieu, but lighting levels that are too low cause problems for diners. Even the most artful plate presentation cannot be appreciated in the dark. Further, a single light level in the restaurant can cause the environment to feel monotonous.

A typical programmed dimmer system has set lighting levels for different times of day keyed to various sections of a restaurant. The restaurant manager simply pushes a number that relates to an outside brightness condition ranging from intense sunlight to total darkness, and the light level dims accordingly. Albeit more expensive than a manual system, such automatic dimming control is the superior choice because once the levels have been worked out and programmed into the system, they remain in the unit's memory forever. Management doesn't have to fool around trying to find the right light levels, and patrons don't have to experience the discomfort of a room going from bright to dim to dark to bright, as operators fiddle around for the right level.

DIRECT VERSUS INDIRECT LIGHTING

As discussed briefly in Chapter 3, a mix of direct and indirect lighting is usually the best choice for the restaurant environment (Figure 4.30). Indirect lighting—where the lamps cannot be seen—minimizes shadows that make people look unattractive and gives an overall glow to the space. These concealed sources can create what is called the ambient light level, filling the nooks and crannies with even, diffuse illumination. They can also help achieve different light levels and, as is often the case with wall sconces, cast soft patterns of light on the walls that integrate with the design. Some designers like to use indirect lighting almost exclusively in a restaurant.

To add the sparkle that enlivens a space, direct lighting should be applied in a controlled manner. Direct lighting usually involves some sort of visible bulb, such as exposed bare-filament lamps or chandeliers. The direction of the light path, the spread of the beam emitted from the lamp or luminaire, and the glare from the lamp must always be considered. Another direct lighting application frequently used in restaurants involves high-intensity lamps that provide a pinpoint of light on tabletops. As mentioned earlier,

Figure 4.30
Direct downlighting (top) can create glare and harsh shadows. Indirect lighting, on the other hand, creates soft overall light and soft shadows. The optimal design exploits these and other lighting techniques.

these lights can be used to highlight the tabletop and the food placed on it, but the effect can backfire if the light is too bright or improperly angled. In any scenario, direct and indirect illumination must work in concert to create a lighting mix that matches the overall design image of the restaurant (Figure 4.31).

SPECIAL EFFECTS

Special-effects lighting is used not so much to illuminate the room as to dramatize it. Neon, in many colors and configurations, is one light source to consider. Most effective when used in moderation, it is often specified for signage—as restaurant logo outside and inside, or to identify a space in the restaurant, such as a raw bar or salad bar.

Figure 4.31
The blend of wall sconces, shaded chandeliers, and ceiling uplighting creates a warm glow of illumination throughout the dining area of Eleven Madison Park restaurant.

(Photo by Joseph Durocher)

Neon can also be an effective directional signal. However, the impact of the neon light must be considered. On an elaborate scale, the neon lamps—nestled in a cove—that ring the rim of the vaulted ceiling at the N9NE Steakhouse in Chicago create an ever-changing color glow on the ceiling. The changing hues do not affect the appearance of food or people in the areas below, as much of the ambient lighting is provided by other lamps (Figure 4.32).

Often, theatrical fixtures are used in much the same fashion as they are on stage—to highlight interesting details. Theatrical framing projectors can be used to cast varied patterns (gobos) on floors, walls, or ceiling. These devices use a template to give a variety of effects. A good alternative to the more expensive fixtures made for theaters are scaled-down versions offered by commercial lighting manufacturers, which are better suited to the restaurant environment. In either case, light can transform a monochromatic backdrop into a fascinating design of color and pattern, depending on the template design. Theatrical light projections can communicate virtually any image, including corporate logos, directional arrows, and starbursts.

The direct light of chandeliers, especially sparkling off glass and crystal, is a staple of banquet lighting. Typically used in large, open spaces, chandeliers also find their way—in highly stylized formats—into restaurants. These ceiling luminaires can provide both direct and indirect lighting to a restaurant interior. The chandelier can also be used as a focal point in a stairwell that connects multifloor restaurants. One of the most compelling chandelier installations was in Farallon in San Francisco, where oversized jellyfish with glowing bodies and streaming tendrils cast a soft glow on the tables and guests below while being highly attractive design elements.

OPERATIONAL CONCERNS

From an operational perspective, the design team should be aware of several lighting concerns. As mentioned earlier, relamping policies must be considered when selecting light sources. Easy relamping should be a goal of every restaurant lighting scheme, but the job can become difficult when many lamp types are used. One trick that can make the operator's life easier is to specify higher-wattage lamps than the space requires, then keep them dimmed down. A 150-watt lamp run at full capacity burns out quickly, but if it is never turned up to more than 50 percent of capacity, its life increases substantially. However, not all lamps can be dimmed. Some lamps can be dimmed, while those from

Figure 4.32
At N9NE Steakhouse, a popular Chicago eatery, a mix of direct downlighting with an ever-changing uplit glow of neon tubes hidden in a ceiling soffit creates a hip atmosphere.
(Photo by Joseph Durocher)

another manufacturer cannot be dimmed, so always check the specifications.

Another concern is the need for additional light during cleaning periods. A separate set of lights or a dimming system that can be turned up helps with this issue. A dimming system not only allows light levels to be turned up enough for the cleaning crew but also, on slow nights in large restaurants, it enables management to leave unused sections darkened.

ENERGY EFFICIENCY

Energy-efficient lighting is important in any type of restaurant operation. Quick-service operations use a little more than a quarter of their total energy consumption, and full-service restaurants use less than a tenth of their total for lighting. Energy conservation pertains both to the energy used by lamps for illumination and the energy that lamps convert to heat. Certain lighting plans may actually necessitate increased ventilation capacity to prevent the dining areas from overheating.

The better the lighting plan, the less aware the customer is that there is such a plan.

Energy efficiency will be affected by the choice of luminaire and lamp. One option might include a low initial installation cost for the luminaire, moderate energy consumption, and high replacement frequency. Another option might entail high initial installation costs, low energy consumption, and low replacement frequency. The second option seems to be the obvious choice, yet with lighting packages costing at least $8 to $10 per square foot, a financially strapped restaurateur may choose the first option, hoping to retrofit the lighting scheme after the restaurant becomes profitable.

These and other factors must be considered when planning an illumination scheme. In the end, it all comes together as a subliminal experience for patrons. The better the lighting plan, the less aware the customer is that there is such a plan. Instead, diners bask in an atmosphere that is both comfortable and exciting, bathed in flattering light.

COLOR

Color is linked closely with light because, without light, there is no perception of color. With certain types of light, colors can appear more vibrant, but other types of light make the same colors look dull and gray. This is the basic principle of light reflection and is essential to the selection of color and lighting in restaurants.

When white light—light that is composed of equal color components (violet, indigo, blue, green, yellow, orange, and red)—strikes a surface that is painted red, more red is reflected from the surface than any other components of

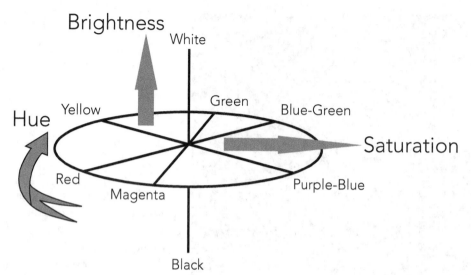

Figure 4.33
Munsell color wheel.

the light and the surface appears red. The same is true when light passes through a red glass or gel; the red component of the light is transmitted, while the other components are filtered out of the resulting beam.

There are many classifications of color. The Munsell system includes three important means of classifying a given color: hue (shade of a given color), value (brilliance of the color), and chroma (the saturation or purity of the color) (Figure 4.33). Colors appearing on opposing sides of the color wheel are complementary colors. If a wall painted red is illuminated with a blue-green light source, it appears gray. In effect, the light reduces the apparent chroma level of the wall. Chroma levels are also affected by intensity of lighting. A peach-colored tabletop that looks good under indirect sunlight may look washed out under direct sunlight. Thus, it is important to use paints that are heavily saturated (with high chroma levels) in operations with high light levels. Pastels in brightly lit rooms can appear faded.

A peach-colored tabletop that looks good under indirect sunlight may look washed out under direct sunlight.

FLOORS

Restaurant flooring means more to patrons than just a surface to walk on. Flooring can act as a directional signal, yield a soft, cushy feeling of elegance, and either absorb or reflect sound. Selecting a floor material seems easy; it should last forever, be easy to clean, be available in colors that complement other colors in the space, deaden or heighten noise as needed, and be priced to match other design elements. As with lighting systems, a careful analysis of the advantages and disadvantages of floor covering plans is important.

By most standards, vinyl is the least expensive floor covering to purchase and install, and terrazzo is among the most expensive. In fact, the installed cost of terrazzo is approximately six times greater than vinyl. Again, the owner short on cash may opt for the inexpensive floor solution—but added to the installation cost should be the expense of maintaining the floor, its usable life span, and its replacement cost. These additional factors yield a total cost per square foot of flooring over time.

Vinyl flooring, for example, must be replaced after 8 to 15 years, whereas terrazzo has a much longer usable life span (over 40 years, the total cost per square foot of terrazzo is only 12 percent higher than vinyl). Unglazed ceramic tiles, if properly maintained by mopping and occasional sealing, can hold up almost indefinitely, but the finish on glazed ceramic tile wears quickly.

Wood floors, often chosen for their warmth and eye appeal, have to be refinished approximately every nine months. Laminated wood flooring is easy to install and holds up well in abusive restaurant environments. Environmentally friendly alternatives that have recently been used for restaurant flooring include bamboo, which is more than 25 percent harder than red oak. Another eco-friendly option is tongue-and-groove flooring squares made out of 78 percent recycled vinyl and carpet. These panels are available in a variety of colors and designs and are adhesive free. They measure almost 24 inches square, so they install quickly over any smooth subflooring and earn Leadership in Energy and Environmental Design (LEED) credits. Cork and cork/rubber flooring are two additional eco-friendly flooring options to consider.

Carpeting is the floor covering of choice for acoustic control. The thicker the carpet and padding, the more noise it absorbs. Nylon or a nylon-wool blend is a practical choice because it is flame retardant and stain resistant. Note that a solid color shows dirt, stains, and spills far more than a patterned carpet.

Marble can take a great deal of abuse, but alcohol spills will soak in and leave stains. Granite, a less porous material, withstands abuse even better than marble.

Composite stone flooring, made of small, compressed bits, has become a popular, easy-maintenance option. Poured resin floors are easy to install, are impervious to moisture, clean up quickly, and are slip resistant.

Concrete floors are among the most durable of floors, but left unadorned they look very institutional. That's where acid-stained or stamped concrete can really help. Acid-stained concrete can mimic surfaces ranging from stained wood to polished marble. Reactive stains contain salts that react with the concrete itself to permanently stain the surface. Nonreactive stains are similar to those that are used on wood. They come in a wide range of colors and can be used to create intricate designs on floors, countertops, and walls. Unlike the reactive stains, the color of these stained areas will be uniform.

A clear sealer applied to exterior areas or wax on indoor areas will prolong the life of acid-washed floors, enhance the appearance of any designs, and provide a sheen.

Building codes and safety issues must always be considered when choosing floor materials for a restaurant. Certain types of flooring may be excluded because of local building or health codes.

In the front of the house, it is appropriate for the designers to specify flooring for its aesthetic appeal. A mix of floor surfaces can give various sensations to the customers. For example, people can promenade down a marble runner and then settle in at their seats with warm carpeting below their feet. However, different flooring materials require different cleaning techniques, which means various cleaning chemicals (and polishes, where necessary), equipment, and staff training for cleaning each surface.

Flooring materials perform various functional roles. In one restaurant, for example, the bar floor might be covered with gray ground concrete that is well suited to the beating taken from spilled drinks, snuffed-out cigarettes, and dripping umbrellas as people wait for a dinner table. When guests reach the dining room, they might encounter an island of sound-absorbing carpet surrounded by a boardwalk of wood flooring for visual interest.

In the quick-service environment, a practical flooring material can take on new meaning if cleverly applied. For instance, unglazed ceramic tile in a custom-designed pattern resembling a needlepoint rug dresses up a quick-service eatery with a Victorian motif, and is easy to maintain. Arranged differently, such tiles could also create stylized arrows to guide customers through the various stations.

Entry floors, because of the high wear and tear resulting from off-street dirt, should be covered in highly resilient materials. The designer should be aware that polished stone flooring becomes slippery when wet, so if specified in entry areas where rain and snow could be tracked in, they should be covered with runners.

Entry floors, because of the high wear and tear resulting from off-street dirt, should be covered in highly resilient materials.

Relaxed dining settings benefit from carpeting, which deadens noise and gives a warm feeling to the space. However, restaurant dining areas that depend on high noise levels to generate excitement often rely on hard flooring surfaces that reflect noise, can take abuse, and are easy to clean.

For any floor material subject to the rigors of restaurant traffic, the following points should be considered in concert with the aesthetics of the materials:

- *Flammability.* This is particularly important in display kitchens or dining rooms where tableside cooking is offered.
- *Color/light fastness.* An important consideration with carpeting, fading can also be a problem with wood flooring.
- *Flooring adhesive.* For conventional wood flooring, conventional nails may be a sufficient adhesive, but in some cases box-coated nails will reduce squeaking. Box-coated nails plus glue ensure a squeak-free wooden floor. Some manufactured wood floors require a glue-down installation. For carpeting, proper adhesion prevents carpet slippage and

premature wear and wrinkling. Adhesives for vinyl, rubber sheeting, and tiles (along with the subfloor) play an important role in the life span of the surface. While the best adhesives are significantly more expensive, they usually pay back the investment in extended trouble-free usage.

Increased emphasis on the environment has led many flooring manufacturers to create flooring that does not need adhesives, comes from renewable sources, or uses recycled materials. Volatile organic compounds (VOC) used in many materials and finishes have been identified as being harmful to the environment, particularly indoor environments. VOCs have been blamed for allergic reactions and other health problems as well as being a contributor to air pollution.

The wearability of the finished floor depends a great deal on the subfloor. If the subfloor cracks and splits or does not take well to an adhesive, the finished floor won't last long under normal restaurant conditions.

WALLS

Walls enclose patrons, provide surfaces for points of interest such as artwork and lighting sconces, and open vistas to the outside world. Windows are important parts of walls in many establishments, particularly in freestanding restaurants and large urban gathering places, and should be selected with energy conservation and lighting concerns in mind. The glazing itself has great impact on energy conservation. Single-pane windows are the least energy efficient option. Thermopane (insulated glass) units are the most efficient insulators, particularly when built with three panes of glass and coated with a metal coating that gives them a low-E rating. Window coverings such as shades, blinds, screens, and exterior awnings can improve energy usage. To minimize thermal loading, select low-E glass that is coated on the outside. Also, consider windows with argon or krypton gas in between the layers. Both gases will further limit the flow of heat through the window, although the cost and spacing between panes of glass differ for each.

Walls and their coverings play an important role in the overall design of a restaurant. The shapes of walls, the materials they are made of, and the finishes placed on them can range from simple painted sheetrock on flat walls to elaborately curved walls trimmed with polished metal and marble. Wall treatments perform a number of aesthetic and practical roles. Hard-surfaced walls tend to increase sound levels, which can be countered by applying sound-absorbing materials.

The intricacy of the design and the quality of the wall coverings can drastically influence the cost and durability of a wall. Like floors, walls take a great deal of beating in the restaurant environment. Painted surfaces are the least resilient and should be used only in areas not prone to wear. Longer-lasting, wear-resistant materials such as vinyl wall covering in medium-impact areas can keep maintenance costs low and wall surfaces looking like new. Installing chair rails, a wooden wainscoting, or even more resilient stone or metal material on a wall can eliminate scuffmarks made by the backs of chairs. Sound-absorbing panels positioned high on a wall in a checkerboard pattern that maximizes the sound-absorbing capacity of the panels can significantly decrease noise levels.

Much artistry can be used in the selection and application of wall materials. The rough brick, plaster, and concrete of the patched-up walls at some restaurants create a fascinating textural milieu. In fashionable and formal restaurants, cherry, bird's-eye maple, or other rare wood panels are reminiscent of high-powered boardrooms and add to the upscale atmosphere of a space. In most quick-service environments, wall elements are fashioned from plastic materials and slapped on as an overlay. Such treatments don't trick customers for long. Walls offer one of the most accepting palettes for interior design and art elements, but these should always be thoughtfully applied. Just because a wall exists doesn't mean it must be decoratively covered.

Just because a wall exists doesn't mean it must be decoratively covered.

From an operational perspective, walls and their coverings should be easy to clean and resistant to wear and tear. In high-impact areas, wood, metal, plastic, or other hard materials should be used due to their durability. While some finishes may detract from an otherwise seamless design, a scuff mark or hole punched through a sheetrock wall can be even more distracting to the customer.

CEILINGS

Too often neglected in the restaurant design scheme, the ceiling is always noticed by customers. As with walls, hard sheetrock surfaces tend to reflect sound and light. The designer Sarah Tomerlin Lee once said that in an otherwise simple room, a special ceiling treatment could work like a woman's hat; the ceiling can dress a plain room in the same way that the hat can transform a simple sheath into a fashionable outfit. Imagine, for example, a vaulted ceiling covered with stretched Lycra sails. To accentuate the ceiling even more, ceiling lights set above the sails will create a warm overall glow in the space.

Technically, the ceiling usually consists of several elements: the basic ceiling structure, luminaires, acoustical treatments, and ventilation grillwork. The basic ceiling structure may be the framework to which the other elements are attached. Painted sheetrock is often the material of choice on fixed ceilings. Structural elements are sometimes deliberately left exposed, along with the lighting; plumbing; and heating, ventilating, and air conditioning (HVAC) mechanicals, to achieve a high-tech look.

Acoustic ceiling treatments are the most effective way to control sound in a restaurant. Acoustic ceiling tiles, insulation, and other sound-absorbing materials applied to ceilings minimize reverberation and absorb sound. Ceiling alcoves, such as lighting alcoves or simply dead airspace above a perforated ceiling, also serve to trap and limit reverberation. Fiberglass panels wrapped with fabric; banners; and color-coordinated, vinyl-coated acoustical drywall panels are also popular choices for ceiling treatments. Many good designs combine a number of these treatments. Ceiling tiles with imprinted images are a recently introduced product that can dress up a ceiling. When the designs are installed on backlit light lenses, they can offer a simulated skylight filled with large puffy clouds or a forest of trees arching overhead.

AIR CONTROL

One of the goals of air control in dining spaces is to deliver heating and cooling unobtrusively—meaning no drafts and no hot and cool spots. It also means controlling smoke and preventing other smells from carrying into the dining room. The distribution of fresh air and removal of stale air is usually integrated with the ceiling treatment. Care must be taken to ensure that adequate air is supplied to all areas of the dining room without creating a draft in any one spot. This is best accomplished by installing oversized ventilation grills, but the appearance of the grills usually detracts from the appearance of the ceiling. In some cases, makeup air can be piped into the dining room via coffered ceiling spaces, thus providing indirect ventilation that limits the chance of drafts.

HEATING AND COOLING

Air-handling units are the most efficient way to control temperature and air quality in a restaurant. Such units, when properly chosen, installed, and balanced, can address all of the heating and cooling needs in various dining spaces.

However, are mechanical means of heating and cooling necessary in all restaurants? Clearly, the answer is no. Anyone who has ever sat in an open-air oceanfront dining space in Hawaii or the Caribbean knows that tropical breezes can eliminate the need for mechanical cooling. In northern climates, heat can be effectively supplied via baseboard hot water units, fresh air via open windows, and cooling via through-wall air conditioners. No matter the setting, the goal is the same: temperature and air quality should not detract from the dining experience.

For restaurants without operable windows or where dining spaces are 50 feet or more from an outside wall, air-handling units are probably the optimal means of controlling air quality. Often, air-handling units are tied into a single thermostat. This can pose a significant problem, as some areas in the dining room are hotter or colder than others. If the air handlers have a single zone, they cannot react to such temperature variances.

The solution is an HVAC unit that delivers cool air to one area and heated air to another. These units often rely on boilers for heating and chilled-water units for cooling. If, however, the system allows only heating or cooling to operate at one time, its usefulness is limited.

SMOKE CONTROL

A positive pressure must be maintained in the dining room to ensure that smoke and airborne grease do not enter from the kitchen. What this often translates to is a system where all air sweeps across the dining room, through the kitchen doors, and out the exhaust hood in the kitchen. Negative air pressure in the kitchen ensures that the smoke and grease-laden air produced is exhausted to the outdoors rather than flowing into the dining room.

However, smoke control can become more complex in restaurants where customers are allowed to smoke in interior areas (Figure 4.34). The challenge facing restaurateurs in jurisdictions that still allow smoking in public spaces is how to accommodate both smokers and nonsmokers.

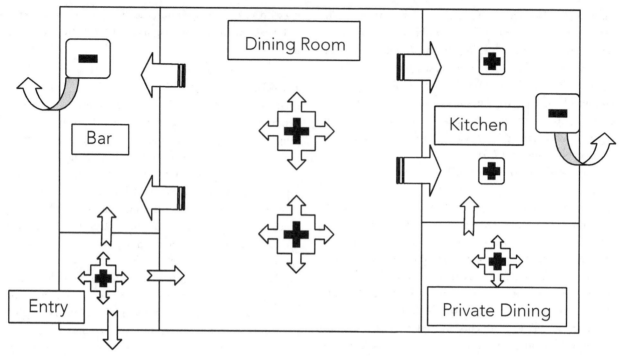

Figure 4.34
Controlling smoke and dust is no easy task in a restaurant. Here, a positive pressure is maintained in the entry to prevent street dust from entering. A negative pressure is maintained in the bar to contain smoke within that area. A positive pressure is maintained in the dining room to keep cigarette smoke in the bar and kitchen smoke in the kitchen. While makeup air is added to the kitchen, the overall design promotes a negative pressure that keeps kitchen air pollution from reaching the dining room.

If smoking is allowed in the bar areas, a negative pressure must be maintained in that space. However, the containment is only part of the solution. Filtration helps to prevent carryover of smoke-laden air to the dining room, and it improves the air quality in those spaces where smoking is allowed. It also means fully exhausting the air from those spaces where smoking is allowed rather than mixing an amount of the air with fresh makeup air. Wherever smoking is allowed, air-filtration units should be installed. The air filters improve the environment for smokers, non-smokers, and servers alike.

CUSTOMER ALLERGIES

High-efficiency particulate arresting (HEPA) air filtering systems can significantly diminish interior air pollutants that could cause customers to have allergic reactions. Ionizers will change the electric charge on dust particles, which further purifies the air and minimizes allergic reactions.

One of the newest branding efforts engages the sense of smell by using scents that customers will associate with positive emotions or perhaps a chain of restaurants. Scents should be used judiciously. While the chemicals used to produce these scents might not trigger an allergic reaction, the scent could possibly cause a psychosomatic reaction.

Nut and seafood allergies are probably the most common and potentially dangerous allergies. While removing these ingredients from menus is impossible, a well-designed air-handling system could potentially minimize reactions by highly sensitive guests to foods served at adjacent tables.

DESTINATION RESTROOMS

A visit to the restroom is a common part of the restaurant experience for most patrons, yet restroom design is all too often neglected. When faced with budget overruns, ownership tends to pull back funding for restroom decor. In the worst scenario, impractical design contributes to a messy, dirty environment—which may lead customers to believe that the kitchen is dirty, too. However, an attractive, clean restroom—one that carries through the design scheme of the restaurant—speaks volumes about the caring attitude of management. If used by smokers, restrooms should contain wall-mounted ashtrays to keep the floor clean and prevent the disposal of cigarettes in a way that may lead to a fire.

Local building and sanitation codes mandate the size and number of water closets (and urinals) required in restaurant restrooms. As mentioned earlier, care must be taken to ensure that restrooms comply with the Americans with Disabilities Act (ADA). However, the architectural manuals do not emphasize the importance of restrooms to the overall success of the restaurant, nor do they discuss the ramifications of design and decor.

Privacy of both sight and sound is an important consideration for any restaurant restroom. Vanity screens or some sort of labyrinth must be installed to ensure that sight lines into the restrooms are limited from exterior view. Mirrors must be carefully placed so as not to interfere with people's privacy.

Adequate ventilation is another absolute requirement. Exhaust fans in restrooms should be strong enough to create a negative pressure that will draw air in from the dining room, through the restroom, and out the vent. Some restaurateurs may opt for air-freshening units, but these can't surpass the effectiveness of plain old fresh air and frequent cleaning.

Cleanability and sanitation should be core design concerns. While high-designed sinks offer great visual appeal, they may have nooks that are hard to clean and will in a short time collect dirt that mars their appearance. All too often, the spout of a soap dispenser rests over the counter and leaves trailings of soap that must be wiped up frequently if a clean appearance is to be maintained. Also, trash cans are frequently undersized and end up overfilled with crumpled towels hours before the next scheduled restroom cleaning.

Spotless restrooms are comforting to restaurant guests, as they imply that the rest of the restaurant is also clean. Nonporous, easily cleanable materials are an excellent way of ensuring that a trip to the restroom is not a turn-off. Tiles, vinyl wall coverings, and other practical materials can help the restaurateur maintain a spotless restroom with

minimal effort. These applications don't have to look institutional, either; manufacturers offer textures, colors, and designs that carry through a fashionable look.

Tiles, vinyl wall coverings, and other practical materials can help the restaurateur maintain a spotless restroom with minimal effort.

To address issues of personal sanitation, include hands-off hardware wherever possible. That means sensors that pump soap and dispense water and paper towels as needed without guests having to come in contact with potentially contaminated surfaces. Proper sizing and placement of trash receptacles will also prevent towels from being dropped on the floor. High-velocity hand dryers that will dry hands in a matter of seconds can be used as an alternative or backup to towels. A welcome addition for many is an automated hand sanitizer dispenser. Sanitizer dispensers are particularly welcome near baby changing stations.

Lighting plays an important role in restroom design. In quick-service and other foodservice environments that use fluorescent lighting in the front of the house, fluorescent lighting is acceptable. However, in a softly lit full-service restaurant, where incandescent lighting provides a flattering glow, the blue-hued glare of traditional fluorescent tubes in the restroom can be shocking when guests look in the mirror before returning to the dining room.

The addition of candles adds a calming mood in restrooms along with the touch of light. Video monitors strategically placed in restrooms offer a point of interest that can create a buzz that brings in customers (Figure 4.35).

WOMEN'S RESTROOMS

As reported by the National Restaurant Association, the average woman takes 8 to 10 minutes on a trip to the restroom. Men take an average of 4 minutes. The time difference points to some important design considerations. Men generally use restrooms for totally utilitarian purposes. Women, however, use restrooms to perform many activities, including retouching makeup, fixing hair, perfuming, adjusting clothes, and talking with friends. All these activities require extra space and specialized elements. A makeup table or cosmetics shelf across from the sinks is an inexpensive yet helpful addition to the women's room.

Figure 4.35
Monitors over urinals or behind stall doors that play sporting or other broadcast video are unexpected—and give customers something to talk about when they return to the table.
(Photo by Joseph Durocher)

Mirrors over the sink and over the makeup area should be high quality, distortion free, and polished. Wherever possible, a full-length mirror placed by the exit door is a welcome addition.

A final inclusion, particularly important in restaurants that cater to singles, is a place for women to talk within the restroom. This may be one and the same with the makeup area or separate from it. Regardless, it should be large enough so that several conversations can be conducted. When separated from the water closet and sink areas, these spaces can have a much more residential feeling, with touches such as a carpeted floor to diminish sound levels.

MEN'S RESTROOMS

As mentioned earlier, men take a more utilitarian approach to restrooms. However, such added amenities as a shoeshine are appropriate in certain settings. A hanger in the water closet is appreciated for hanging suit jackets. In quick-service restaurants or diners where laborers often eat lunch, two soap dispensers—one with mild soap and one with abrasive soap for deep cleaning—should be considered.

Vanity screens are sometimes placed between urinals. If they are to be wall mounted, they must be firmly secured or else, within a short time, they will loosen, fall from their place, and leave unsightly holes in the wall. All too often, when urinals are separated with vanity screens, they are placed too closely together, and oversized men inadvertently loosen the screens as they push past them. Another disadvantage of the screens is that they are frequently splashed and rust quickly.

CUSTOMIZED RESTROOMS

The same attention to design detailing in the dining room can be carried into the restroom for a pleasing effect. In a seafood restaurant, faux portholes can filter light into the space.

In upscale restaurants with contemporary design, the standard vitrified dinnerware sinks can be replaced with stainless steel. The addition of a floral display in the restroom adds a residential touch that can downplay institutional elements.

This customization can go beyond the standard applications to little elements that are peculiar to a specific type of restaurant (Figure 4.36). Consider a barbecue ribs restaurant. A toothpick dispenser and hot towel dispenser in the restrooms become conversation points and are helpful to guests. An area map and distance chart on the restroom walls in roadside restaurants is useful to travelers. In many restrooms, vending machines can generate revenues for the owners and are helpful to the guests.

Figure 4.36
This unisex restroom at Blowfish restaurant in Toronto has separate cubicles accessible to males or females and a central wash sink between the cubicles.
(Photography by Volker Seding)

As mentioned earlier, restrooms should be seen as an integral part of the design scheme. When well designed, they are a positive addition. When dealt with as an afterthought, they can appear incongruous and may be a reason not to return to the restaurant.

SUMMARY

Front-of-the-house design involves a delicate orchestration of spaces that works to create a total experience. From the moment customers set sight on the building to the moment when they step back outside after a meal, design should be part of an integrated plan. Each design decision should reflect thoughtful problem solving that is sensitive both to the needs of the operation and to the design concept. Once the design team understands the basic principles discussed above, they can begin to make specific decisions.

CHAPTER 5

DESIGN IMPLEMENTATION: BACK TO FRONT THROUGH MANAGEMENT'S EYES

In a process-oriented approach to restaurant design, solutions come from analyzing the functional needs of a given operation. That analysis begins with the menu and then continues on to the areas within the kitchen that support that menu. We touched on these subsystems in Chapter 1, where we outlined the general function of each subsystem. In this chapter we will look at the back of the house in greater detail.

To understand the principles of kitchen design, therefore, we systematically move through the back of the house from an operational point of view, starting with the receiving of unprocessed food and ending with the plating of prepared food for service. This technique enables the designer to fill in the floorplan with appropriate workstations and equipment, because each space or functional area in the back of the house has certain operating characteristics that translate into design features. While these areas are discussed individually, it is important to remember that, in the final design, they must be integrated as a whole.

KITCHEN SUPPORT AREAS

Kitchen support areas are those spaces not primarily designated for food preparation or service—that is, receiving, storage, and office space. All too often, the back-of-the-house design process centers on the production area but overlooks the importance of support spaces. For example, if office space is not included, managers may not be able to secure important documents. While some kitchens incorporate a shelf with a computer in the kitchen for managers, the lack of privacy in such areas limits management's ability to update personnel files that, by law, must be kept confidential. If storage space is inadequate, more frequent deliveries—with an attendant upcharge from the supplier—will be required. These areas are not glamorous, but they are the backbone of the kitchen.

RECEIVING

The receiving area should be accessible to the loading dock and the storerooms wherever possible to facilitate a smooth flow of food from delivery to receiving to storage. Ideally, the loading dock leads directly to the receiving area, which is adjacent to the various storage areas. In some restaurants, the purchasing agent's office is located near the receiving area, but for reasons of internal control, the purchasing function is frequently handled from an office separate from the receiving area.

It is in this area that the onsite Hazard Analysis Critical Control Point (HACCP) procedures begin. Refrigerated or frozen foods must move through this space as quickly as possible to ensure that foods do not warm up. Also, quick transit of crates of fresh produce is essential lest they become infested with bugs or other contaminants. The Food and Drug Administration's HAACP Backgrounder outlines control points that could be impacted by design:

Any action or activity that can be used to prevent, eliminate or reduce a significant hazard.
Any step at which biological, chemical, or physical factors can be controlled.

Receiving area floors must be smooth so that hand trucks, pallet lifts, or carts can be moved about easily. Smooth surfaces are also easy to clean, which helps to minimize buildup of dirt and grime. All foods must be carefully inspected when they arrive, so the area should be well lit. The optimum light scheme supplies overall lighting with fluorescent tubes and task lighting with fluorescent, halogen, or light-emitting diode (LED) spotlighting luminaires.

Scales are most important in this area, as many foods are purchased by weight. In operations where large quantities of meats are purchased, built-in floor scales are ideal; pallets loaded with boxes of meat can be rolled onto the floor scale and easily weighed. Individual boxes of meat or other items purchased by weight can be weighed with a freestanding floor scale or table scale. The chosen scale must match the operation's

receiving needs. Large hotels and institutional operations are most likely to need a built-in floor scale capable of holding pallets of food weighing a ton or more.

However, the majority of operations purchase foods in batches smaller than 300 pounds, so a portable platform scale is called for. For ease of use, nothing beats a scale with a digital readout (Figure 5.1). Portable platform scales are frequently fashioned from stainless steel and have a platform that can hold 300-lb. cases. Some come with a display powered by a long-life battery that allows the scale to be placed wherever needed. A display pad that extends two and one-half feet above the floor makes for easy reading.

One vital aspect of platform scales is the tare feature, which enables the receiving clerk to program in the weight of the packaging and automatically subtract it from the gross weight to yield the net weight of the case contents. This feature makes it faster and more accurate to weigh in a large delivery. Some platform scales can be programmed for over/under checks; this is particularly useful for weighing in portion-controlled foods. A helpful addition to a platform scale is a thermal printer that delivers a permanent record of delivery weights. This information can be attached to receiving invoices.

While trash is frequently removed through the receiving area, the building and health codes of many locales mandate a separate area to handle trash. Ideally, fresh foods should not

HAZARD ANALYSIS CRITICAL CONTROL POINT

Hazard Analysis Critical Control Point (HACCP) is a system of controls and documentation designed to minimize the potential for food-borne illness due to pathogens or physical or chemical contamination. HACCP programs are used worldwide because they identify unsafe links in the food chain. Once identified, the links can be eliminated.

Restaurant design and the choice of equipment play an important role in an HACCP program. Proper refrigeration helps keep foods at temperatures where bacterial growth is minimized. Easy-to-clean food processing equipment helps to ensure that employees clean such

equipment as slicers, soft-serve machines, and hand tools to minimize the chances of bacterial growth or cross-contamination. Open kitchens in full view of customers also decrease the chances that personnel will employ practices that could lead to contamination.

Hand sinks play an important role in an HACCP program. Foot- or elbow-operated faucets ensure that employees do not cross-contaminate their hands when they shut the water off. Another option is an automated hand washer, which directs cleaning solution and rinse water onto an employee's hands when they are slipped into the two tubes on top of the device. Paper towels and hand soap need to be accessible at each hand sink, and every workstation should ideally have its own hand sink.

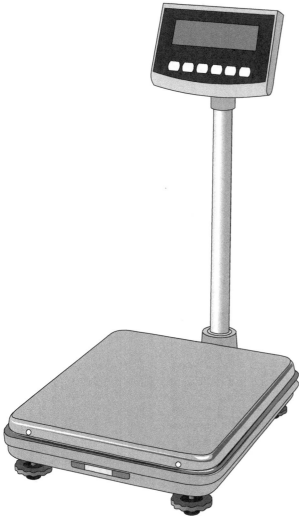

Figure 5.1
The platform scale ensures an easy means to check in products sold by weight. The tower makes the digital readout easy to use. Although the scale has a footprint of less than four square feet, sufficient space must be planned for its use.
(Courtesy of Hobart)

travel through the same spaces as trash, nor should they be stored in the same area. A refrigerated space may be needed to store wet garbage from the kitchen. Refrigerating garbage, particularly in hot climates, eliminates the chance of customers being greeted with unpleasant smells as they arrive.

In a restaurant that is committed to sustainability, space for dumpsters used to hold recyclables must be included. If the restaurant plans to use waste food for composting, a waterproof dumpster is another essential.

STORAGE

The storage areas should be located so that they are easily accessible from both the loading dock and the production areas. If they cannot be placed conveniently between these two areas, it makes sense to place them closer to production, because this proximity will save labor time. Generally, food is received in large quantities and placed on rolling stock for transport to the storage areas. On a given day, a typical restaurant may receive 3 to 10 deliveries. The production personnel, however, may have to draw goods from the dry, refrigerated, or frozen foods storage areas as many as 100 to 300 times each day. In a complex food operation involving more than one kitchen, the storage areas should be placed near the most active kitchen (Figure 5.2).

Proper shelving systems are needed in every storage area to make them effective. Fixed shelving units are the industry standard, along with dunnage racks for storing large or bulky items. Good shelving should be flexible, which means that the height of each shelf should be adjustable. Under ideal conditions, shelving minimizes the need for costly aisle space. This is accomplished by placing the shelves on wheels—an especially useful feature in refrigerated or frozen food storage areas. Manufacturers claim that up to 36 percent more storage can be installed in a high-density storage area. Shelf depth and overall height should match the products to be stored and the height of the people who will be drawing goods from the shelves.

The ratio of shelving in dry or refrigerated space is a function of the menu, the frequency of delivery, the state of the foods as they are purchased, and the number of meals to be served. Frozen foods that are ready for cooking require the least amount of storage per customer served. Fresh food requires greater storage space. Total storage per cover can range anywhere from one to two and one-half cubic feet, with the mix between dry and refrigerated/frozen storage being a function of the menu and management policy.

Lighting and ventilation in storage areas is typically poor. However, high temperatures can shorten the shelf life of certain foods, and poor lighting levels can lead to inadequate cleaning and poor product management. Incandescent lights, which can be turned on and off without decreasing bulb life, should be used in all storage areas. To ensure that lights are extinguished, a motion sensor that automatically turns the lights off can pay for itself in a matter of months.

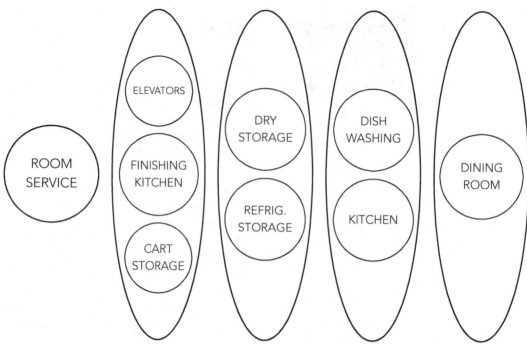

Figure 5.2

This bubble diagram for a hotel restaurant kitchen shows how storage areas can be placed between production areas to minimize distances that must be traveled from both the main and room-service kitchens to storage areas.

As indicated earlier, storage is generally divided into three major areas: dry goods, refrigerated, and frozen. The size and location of each area are greatly affected by the menu, limitations of the architecture, and purchasing and receiving procedures. Following is a discussion of the design principles for each.

DRY GOODS

Dry goods are frequently broken into four categories:

1. Dry and canned foods
2. Disposable paper goods and other nonchemical supplies
3. Cleaning and chemical supplies
4. Spirited beverages

Ideally, each of these categories of dry goods will be stored in its own storage space. Dry and canned foods need shelving and dunnage racks. Paper supplies arrive in large cases, so the shelves that hold them are often far apart. Styrofoam containers take up the largest amount of space, but their light weight makes it possible to store them in taller piles than other dry goods.

While paper goods can be stored with dry and canned goods, a separate space is essential for cleaning and chemical supplies. Many cleaning agents outgas odors that can be absorbed by dry goods like flour and pasta. For security reasons, spirited beverages must also be stored in their own space. At times, spirits are kept in a locked cage within the confines of the dry foods storage area, but, most frequently, they are kept in their own area under the supervision of the beverage manager. Special humidity- and temperature-controlled spaces are needed to store fine wines, and draft beer requires refrigerated storage.

In addition to these long-term storage spaces, breakout pantries adjacent to production areas are frequently stocked with a par inventory of commonly used foods. The well-designed kitchen has par stock areas of dry goods and paper goods for each production section. To ensure maximum efficiency in a bar operation, the par stock of spirits should be enough to supply a busy evening of drink orders.

REFRIGERATION

Refrigerated storage units come in many different sizes and must be matched carefully to the operation. Generally, a mix of walk-in, reach-in, and undercounter refrigeration is used in restaurant kitchens. Three overlying issues must be considered when choosing refrigerated equipment: labor costs, food costs, and food safety.

LABOR COSTS

One of the most effective ways to control labor costs is to design self-sufficient workstations in the kitchen. That means that each employee has work and storage space that's immediately accessible. In the cold-food station, for example, reach-in refrigeration is effective. One section of the reach-in is used to hold unprocessed foods, while prepared or plated foods are held in another.

The placement of the reach-in can improve or inhibit efficiency. For example, if plated salads are stored in a back line reach-in, the production staff must physically transfer a salad to servers each time a request is made. Alternatively, two-sided reach-ins, whether floor units or overcounter units, could be placed between the preparation and pickup sides of the cold-food station. Preparation staff store the ready-to-be-dressed salads on trays. Servers access the salads from the front of the line, dress them, and get back on the floor as quickly as possible. This practice saves time for production personnel and speeds service.

In the hot-food section, it's important to consider how far each of the chefs must travel to reach refrigerated space. Traditionally, a pair of reach-ins was installed near each end of a hot-food cooking battery. Today, those reach-ins are often replaced with undercounter refrigerated drawers below each cooking station to give cooks all the refrigerated or frozen food they need within arm's reach (Figure 5.3).

FOOD COSTS

Well-chosen and well-positioned refrigeration can help prevent food spoilage. If too much heat is added to the inside of a refrigerator—due to excessive door openings or the addition of a large pot of steaming hot soup, for example—the mechanical system cannot remove the heat effectively and foods might spoil.

Lettuce will grow limp and milk will sour prematurely if they are stored under refrigeration where the temperature is not maintained consistently below 40 degrees Fahrenheit. Reach-ins can maintain milk at serving temperature for a couple of days, but if a milk delivery is intended for use over four to five days, it should be stored in a walk-in, where there is less temperature fluctuation.

FOOD SAFETY

If refrigerated spaces are not within easy reach of kitchen workers, their tendency is to allow protein foods to sit out on a counter for too long. This scenario increases the potential for food poisoning, as does food left too long on a loading dock before being placed under refrigeration. Shelving in walk-ins should allow for sufficient air circulation around all stored foods. A key food safety issue is to minimize the time that food temperatures remain in the danger zone (40–140 degrees Fahrenheit). A stock chiller that can chill up to five gallons of stock or soup from 190 to 40 degrees Fahrenheit in just six minutes decreases the chances of foodborne illness. Pots of stock or soup that are chilled in a walk-in can cause the temperature of other items in the walk-in to rise to unsafe levels.

Figure 5.3
This four-drawer undercounter refrigeration unit keeps food refrigerated, minimizes traffic in a busy production line, and improves efficiency.
(Photo by Joseph Durocher)

WALK-INS

Walk-in refrigerators should be utilized for extended-term storage of bulk foods and for short-term storage of batch-prepared foods or plated foods for banquets. Such refrigeration systems are expensive and take up a great deal of space in the operation. Walk-ins, with a weather cap, can be installed outdoors to save space inside a restaurant. In some instances, the walk-in is placed adjacent to the building so that its access door opens through an exterior wall of the kitchen. This practice gains valuable space inside a kitchen and eliminates the weather problem that occurs when employees have to go outside to access a walk-in. Also, with an interior door, there's little chance that an employee can steal.

Walk-in refrigerators should be utilized for extended-term storage of bulk foods and for short-term storage of batch-prepared foods or plated foods for banquets.

Today's walk-ins are highly engineered units that come in myriad sizes and configurations. The walls, floor, and ceilings are fashioned from sandwiched insulated panels that can be snapped together on site. To maximize the efficiency of a walk-in, it is advisable to insulate its floor. In new construction, insulation can be installed under the tile floor; in a retrofit, insulation can be installed over the existing floor. However, a ramp, whether inside or outside the walk-in, must be provided so that staff can easily roll carts in and out of the refrigerator.

Here are questions that must be addressed before choosing a walk-in:

1. How many walk-ins are needed?

As with dry goods, it often makes sense to put refrigerated items in separate spaces. Beer in kegs must be kept under refrigeration at all times. While canned and bottled beer can be stored in ambient temperatures, chilling them before they head for the bar ensures correct serving temperatures. Dairy products frequently have their own storage space, particularly when strong-smelling cheeses are on the menu. Vegetables and fruits that easily pick up odors should be stored away from dairy products or other foods that give off strong smells. In some cases, a walk-in is needed to age wholesale cuts of beef or to keep beef and other protein items separate from produce and dairy. In high-volume restaurants, fresh seafood can be kept in a separate walk-in, but most often is stored in a fish file (refrigerated drawers typically installed at the end of the hot-food line) that is restocked daily.

2. Is a remote compressor possible?

Walk-ins require a good deal of mechanical refrigeration to keep their contents cool. The refrigeration system releases a lot of heat, and the condensor fan can be noisy, so a remote compressor is often advisable. The remote compressor ensures that waste heat from the refrigeration cycle is dumped outside the restaurant rather than in the kitchen.

3. Where will the walk-ins be located?

Walk-ins are frequently ganged together into one space. However, a walk-in used to store kegs of beer should be as close to the dispensing point as possible. The longer the run from the walk-in to the draft head, the higher the cost of refrigerating and maintaining the supply line.

REACH-INS

Reach-in refrigerators are available in many configurations. They can be cooled by built-in or remote compressors. Single- or multiple-section units equipped with half or full doors, reach-in or pass-through, solid or see-through doors, locking doors, interior lights, externally displayed temperature readouts, and HACCP alarms and recording units are among the configuration options. As with walk-ins, several questions must be addressed before a purchasing decision is made:

1. On which side of the door will the hinges be installed?

The directional flow of materials to and from the workstation should influence this decision. Some manufacturers offer walk-ins with door swings that can be adjusted in the field.

2. What is the optimal door configuration for the reach-ins?

This usually comes down to choosing between convenience and energy savings. Single doors can support roll-in shelving and allow the user to view the contents of the entire refrigerator by opening just one door. However, while that door is held open, more heat infiltrates the unit than with a half-door reach-in. See-through doors make it possible to view the contents without opening the door, but solid doors offer more insulation.

3. Are pass-through reach-ins appropriate?

The extra cost is warranted only when the reach-ins will be accessed from both sides. In a layout where salads are plated but not dressed by the cold-food station staff, reach-ins are a wise investment. Servers pull the salads from the service side of the reach-in, dress them, and quickly return to the dining room. Pass-through reach-ins are also appropriate for cafeteria lines where foods are loaded on the kitchen side and removed by counter staff on the service side.

SPECIALTY REFRIGERATION

Refrigerated drawers are often used near grill areas for holding meats and toppings, or installed near a broiler station for holding fresh seafood. They are either integrated with a standard reach-in unit or specified as freestanding units.

Undercounter refrigerators are typically part of sandwich stations or are placed under grill or broiler units. For installation under a countertop broiler or fryer, refrigerated drawers are the best configuration. When placed under a sandwich unit where tall containers of condiments and backup pans of fillings are held, reach-in units are a better choice.

FROZEN STORAGE

The configurations of frozen food storage units are similar to refrigerated units, except for the addition of chest storage, which is generally reserved for ice cream. Unlike walk-in refrigerators, walk-in freezers must have insulated floors. In addition, unless insulation is inlaid in the floor slab, a ramp must also be provided. Wherever possible, the door of the walk-in freezer should open into a walk-in refrigerator. This will improve operating efficiency of both the refrigerator and the freezer. A heater strip is an excellent addition around the doors of any type of freezer, as it prevents the buildup of frozen condensate around the door. Undercounter freezers equipped with drawers are well suited to quick-service operations where frozen French fries and prebreaded foods need to be in close proximity to the fryers. Chest-type freezers are perfectly suited to ice

cream storage because their minimal temperature variations lengthen product life.

ADDITIONAL CONSIDERATIONS

Locking systems are imperative for refrigeration in complex operations. Doors that accommodate hasp locks make it possible to change locks periodically for security reasons. However, doors with built-in key-locks offer enough security in most restaurant settings.

The refrigerator's exterior finish must also be considered. A stainless-steel surface looks great when first installed, but cleaning and maintaining that high sheen can become problematic. An alternative is to choose refrigeration with an enamel surface that is easier to clean.

The addition of a recording thermometer provides a permanent log of the refrigerator's internal temperature and is an integral part of an HACCP program. The log helps monitor temperatures overnight when the kitchen is unattended. The thermometer can be linked to an automated calling system that sends out an alert message when the temperature of a refrigerator exceeds a safe limit.

In locations where frequent power outages occur, a backup power generator sufficient to keep foods from spoiling should be considered during the design phase. A generator sufficient to supply all of the electric needs of the operation will require a different wiring configuration than if one is used solely for selected pieces of equipment or areas of the restaurant.

In locations where frequent power outages occur, a backup power generator sufficient to keep foods from spoiling should be considered during the design phase.

Roll-in freezers and refrigerators are particularly helpful in banquet preparation areas, where roll-in carts containing preportioned desserts or salads can be held for service.

OFFICE AND EMPLOYEE SUPPORT AREAS

Restaurant offices are more functional than decorative. Space and equipment are needed to complete paperwork and to store records, product information, and reference books. Sufficient lighting, along with an adequate supply of electrical outlets, is necessary. To accommodate computers, a separate electrical supply—including an uninterrupted power supply (UPS)—and an Internet connection should be provided.

LOCKER ROOMS

Back-of-the-house restrooms and locker rooms are typically underdesigned and poorly maintained—and frequently nonexistent. Employee morale can be improved if the locker areas are well maintained and the lockers are large enough to secure street clothes and other personal belongings.

An appropriate number of urinals and toilets should be provided, with enough toilet facilities for women. (Wherever possible, employees should not use the same restrooms as guests.) In addition, there should be enough space adjacent to the hand sinks for staff members to place personal toiletry items. For a clean, efficient operation, it helps to provide air dryers as a backup to paper towels.

Tile flooring with a floor drain is ideal for restrooms. This treatment facilitates easy cleanup if a backup occurs or if the area needs to be sanitized. Glazed tile or paneling with a moisture-resistant coating is the preferred covering for walls because they hold up better than painted, metal, or sheetrock surfaces—and will not develop mold. Adequate ventilation and lighting are essential.

EMPLOYEE DINING

Some restaurants provide an employee dining area. In such cases, durability is a key factor in the design. This area should receive aesthetic attention because employee morale will be greatly boosted by a comfortable, attractive dining area that reflects caring management. Such areas are typically found in large institutional or lodging operations.

KITCHEN

A well-designed kitchen integrates all of the necessary subsystems discussed in Chapter 1. Within the preparation subsystem there may be several areas, each driven by the menu and designed for the preparation and service of different items. Each must function individually, yet work in concert with other kitchen spaces.

DESIGN ESSENTIALS

Kitchen design begins with an analysis of the individual tasks that must be performed in each area. This task analysis becomes the basis for designing the kitchen and for developing training programs for employees. In some cases, for example, two people who perform similar tasks will share a given piece of equipment, so the equipment must be positioned centrally to both employees. In other cases, a 360-degree workstation is self-contained.

The next step is to develop workstations that are combined into work sections and, eventually, into the areas that make up the kitchen.

After a task analysis, the next step is to develop workstations that are combined into work sections and, eventually, into the areas that make up the kitchen.

A useful step, at this point, is to create a bubble diagram (Figure 5.4) that depicts the major areas in the back of the house. In most cases, this diagram will show the relationship to the front of the house and will include:

- Hot foods
- Cold foods
- Beverage
- Service
- Warewashing
- Storage and receiving
- Offices

The size and relative position of each bubble is a function of the type of restaurant. For example, in a quick-service restaurant that relies on disposables, the warewashing bubble will be quite small (Figure 5.5) because warewashing is limited to cleaning kitchen utensils and equipment. It can be positioned at any point in the kitchen. However, the placement of the warewashing area is more important in a banquet kitchen (Figure 5.6), and the cooking areas are much larger.

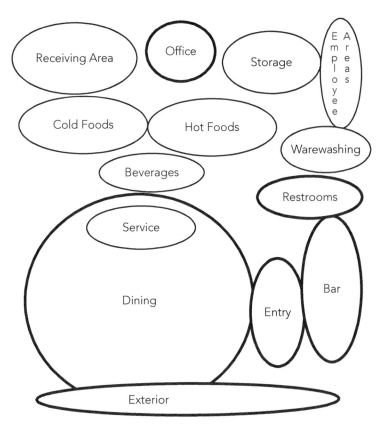

Figure 5.4
A bubble diagram quickly shows the spatial relationships among major areas of the restaurant.

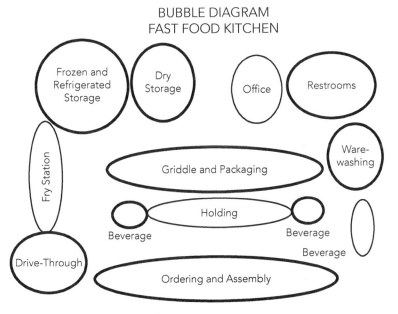

Figure 5.5
The quick-service bubble diagram shows the spaces needed to support this type of service system, such as multiple beverage areas.

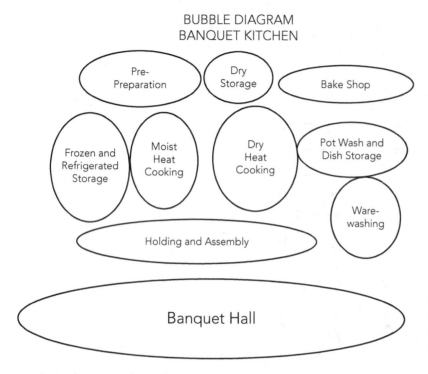

BUBBLE DIAGRAM
BANQUET KITCHEN

Figure 5.6
A banquet kitchen bubble diagram shows how this type of service system depends on warewashing and on volume production equipment.

WORKSTATIONS

Workstations are the building blocks of a kitchen design. A workstation is the space—flooring, work counters, production equipment, storage equipment, utilities—where a particular set of tasks is completed. Generally, the station is designed for one worker.

To understand the process of designing a successful workstation, first identify the task or tasks that need to be performed in the station. Figure 5.7a diagrams a single-sided workstation where a sauté cook stands at the range and sautés food to order. In real life, however, no workstation is as simple as this design. One essential component, for example, is refrigeration to hold the uncooked portions of meat. To resolve this, as shown in Figure 5.7b, a mobile refrigerator was added to the station.

But the station is still inadequate. Go further and think of it as a circle, with multidirectional characteristics (Figure 5.7c). The cook sautés meat on the range, reaches around to pick up a serving plate, places the portion on the plate, then turns to finish off the plate with vegetables and a garnish from the steam table.

In Figure 5.7d, the back half of the workstation appears in elevation from the worker's perspective, showing the range with an overshelf where plates can be held, plus an undercounter refrigerator. Note that the overshelf eliminates the cook's need to turn around for plates, and the undercounter refrigerator does not block the aisle.

The complete station is most easily understood when it is thought of in three dimensions. The sauté cook can easily reach the meat in the undercounter refrigerator. After the meat is prepared, the plates are within easy reach on the overshelf, and the vegetables are ready for service on the steam table. This is not to say that this is the ideal sauté station for every restaurant. Rather, it is a station designed for a specific purpose at a specific location. The key is that the station design is based on a single worker's performing a defined set of tasks.

SECTIONS

Continuing with a hypothetical kitchen design, imagine that a broiler station will be installed to the right of the sauté station, with an open-grate gas broiler for broiling steaks and chops.

A fry station will be installed to the right of the broiler station. Two deep-fat fryers will be specified, for frying breaded seafood and French fries. Storage space for plates, a steam

WORK STATION DESIGN

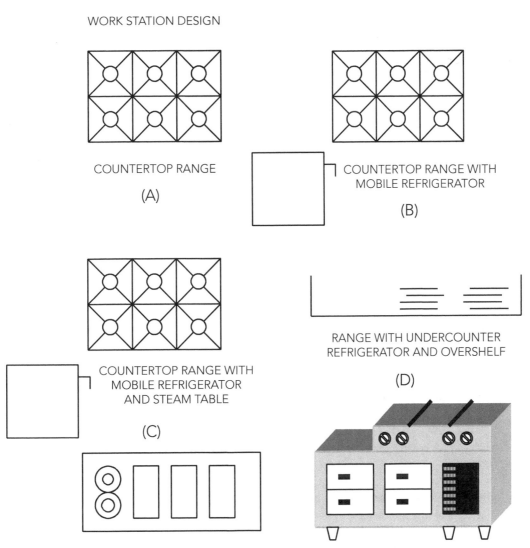

COUNTERTOP RANGE

(A)

COUNTERTOP RANGE WITH
MOBILE REFRIGERATOR

(B)

COUNTERTOP RANGE WITH
MOBILE REFRIGERATOR
AND STEAM TABLE

(C)

RANGE WITH UNDERCOUNTER
REFRIGERATOR AND OVERSHELF

(D)

Figure 5.7
Building a workstation begins with a basic piece of equipment, to which other pieces are added. For example, start with the basic range (a) and add a rolling refrigerator to the left of the station. (b) Next, a steam table and plate lowerator (c) are added to make use of the full circle around the worker. In (d), the elevation shows how the refrigerator could actually be placed under a countertop range to save floor space and improve flow.

table to hold vegetables, and a freezer to hold the seafood and fries are all necessary components for these stations.

Together, these three workstations comprise the cooking side of a hot-food à la carte section. However, were they not grouped together, each would have to have its own steam table and refrigerator, and the end design would be unwieldy and costly. One solution, as seen in Figure 5.8, is to place the refrigeration unit so that it is accessible to the range and the broiler stations, and to place a freezer under

the fryers. The drawers of the undercounter refrigerator and freezer make them easier for the cooks to use than if they were equipped with hinged doors. On the front side of the section, a single steam table with plate lowerators on either end is added. Between the range and the fry station, a spreader plate is installed for safety; it also functions as a work surface.

Of course, compromises are always necessary. The cooks have to lean over to take food out of the refrigerated and

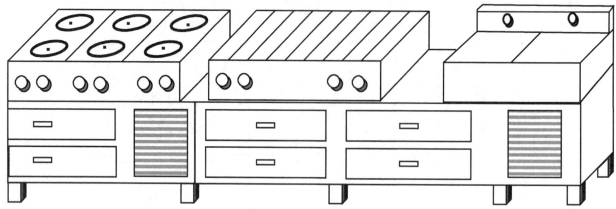

Figure 5.8
This hot-food à la carte section is composed of three workstations: range, broiler, and fryer. The position of each station depends on the menu, the type of equipment in the station, the interaction of each of the stations, and safety requirements.

frozen drawers, but the section can be easily worked by three people or, during slower periods, by one or two cooks. Task-oriented designs like this are wise financial investments because they contribute to efficient job performance.

AREAS

As the kitchen design progresses, sections are melded together to form areas of the kitchen. For example, the hot-food area may include an à la carte section, a long-term roasting section, and a steam-cooking section.

Relative positioning of the various sections will affect the efficiency of the kitchen. Designers need to study the overall plan to determine the best location for the various sections in relation to each other within each area. In turn, the relationship between areas in terms of production and their interaction with the front of the house must be considered.

The bubble diagram shown in Figure 5.9A, an à la carte kitchen where the servers must make several trips to the kitchen to service each table, has three glaring errors in its design:

1. The dish machine should be placed where the bakeshop is located.

2. The beverage station should be located where the walk-in refrigerator is located.

3. The cold-food station should be located where the dry goods storage area is located.

The corrected design appears in Figure 5.9B. While the solutions may seem obvious, inefficient designs are often developed because care is not taken to think through the floorplan from an operational perspective.

The placement of workstations, sections, and areas becomes even more important in complex foodservice systems where many dining areas are serviced from a single kitchen. Careful attention must be paid to the service systems in each dining area. If a tableservice dining room and banquet room are to be serviced out of one kitchen, for instance, it generally makes sense to place the dish machine closer to the dining room than to the banquet space. This is because the service staff will take more individual trips to the dish machine from the dining room than from the banquet space. Similarly, the hot-food station is usually situated closer to the dining room because staff travels back and forth from the hot-food station to the dining room more often than they do to the banquet space.

Careful thought must be given to each station, section, and area that make up the final design. In the worst scenario, a station is completely forgotten. This can lead to a costly kitchen renovation long before it should be necessary.

Kitchens designers must think through functions performed throughout the kitchen and pull them together into well-integrated sections, then into areas. The areas

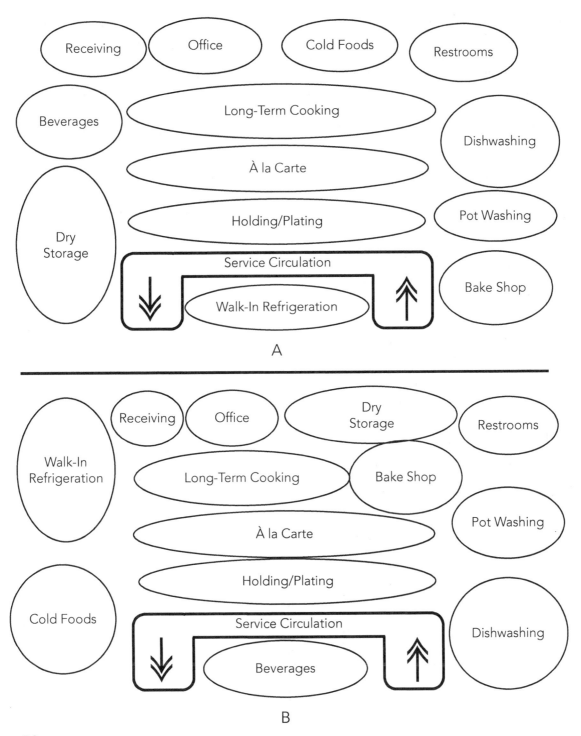

Figure 5.9
A detailed bubble diagram offers the design team a quick way to look at the interaction of various areas in a kitchen. In these bubble diagrams of an à la carte restaurant, layout A puts the cold-food, beverage, and warewashing areas too far away from the service staff. The rearranged spaces in layout B make the flow convenient for both the production and service staff.

must be considered in relationship to each other. Consider a restaurant that incorporates its own bakeshop area to be used primarily for overnight production. If the bakeshop area is located close to the hot-food area that incorporates roasting ovens, the baking and roasting could be done in one set of ovens rather than two.

Of course, bake ovens are different from roasting ovens. To cook crisp French bread, for example, a steam-injected oven is needed. However, roasts, pies, and cakes can all be cooked in a steam-injected oven if the steam is turned off. Meats roasted in an oven into which steam is injected will shrink less.

Flexibility is the key to planning both equipment and workstations. What serves as a sandwich station for lunch can double as a dessert station for dinner if the space is properly designed. The final outcome of planning stations, sections, and areas is the overall kitchen floorplan (Figure 5.10).

KITCHEN AREA GUIDELINES

Remembering the basic equipment needed for each workstation is easy: a broiler in a broiler station, a range in a sauté station, and so on. General design requirements also

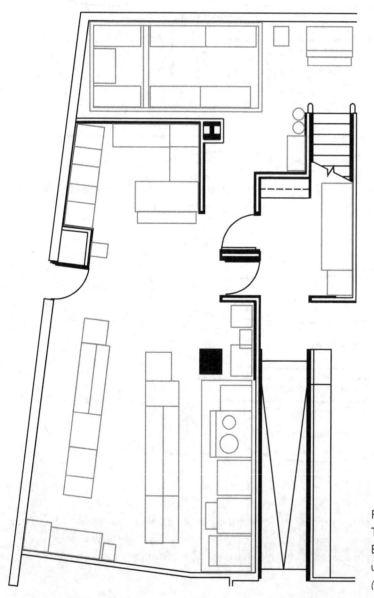

Figure 5.10
This kitchen plan of Douzo restaurant in Boston depicts all of the equipment that is used to support the operation.
(Courtesy Darlow Christ Architects)

must be integrated into each station if it is to function effectively. Here are some of the requirements:

- *Ambient and task lighting.* Task lighting prevents eyestrain and injuries in areas where detail work such as cake decorating and meat fabrication are performed. Task lighting is also useful when a portion-control scale is used to weigh a large number of individual portions. Ambient lighting under exhaust hoods should provide adequate lighting over all of the stations. The tubes or bulbs must be shielded to prevent them from breaking and dropping glass into food products.

- *Controlled and ambient temperature storage for unprepared food.* A supply of spices centrally located in a kitchen ensures that all stations can draw from one supply. However, if spices are used frequently, space is needed to store them within a workstation.

- *Disposal or trash cans.* Space to store a trash can is frequently overlooked in kitchen design. A cutout under a work counter that might otherwise contain shelves can situate a trash can within easy reach of two workstations. This simple feature saves labor and keeps workstations cleaner.

- *Ventilation.* Exhaust and makeup air must be provided in areas where heat and steam are produced.

- *Special floor elements.* Tile floors are commonly found in kitchens, and they are an effective choice. But floor drains or recessed floor areas under cooking sections are often overlooked. Such drains are particularly valuable under steam kettles and tilting braising pans.

- *Hand sanitation.* Sinks, soap, and toweling must be accessible to every station.

- *Water supply for cooking and cleaning.* A metered water faucet saves labor when filling a large steam kettle. A hose equipped with a high-pressure spray head speeds cleanup beneath the kettle.

While no two sections are exactly alike, Table 5.1 lists five common sections with the stations typically incorporated in them. In some high-volume operations, two or more of the same type of station may be needed in a given section.

The following discussion of each section can serve as a guide to kitchen planning.

Hot-Food Section

The hot-food section can be thought of in terms of a matrix (Figure 5.11). On one axis, the station can be divided into à la carte cooking and long-term cooking; on the second axis, it can be divided into moist-heat cooking and dry-heat cooking.

Dry-heat cooking areas contain ovens, ranges, griddles, broilers, tilting fry kettles, and deep fryers. Moist-heat cooking areas include steamers, steam-jacketed and trunnion kettles, and, occasionally, ranges.

In some cases, a single piece of equipment will satisfy the needs of multiple modes of cooking. An example of this is the combination oven (Figure 5.12), which is so versatile that it can fit into any quadrant of the matrix. The combination oven can dry roast à la carte items or roast large

TABLE 5.1 COMMON SECTIONS WITH TYPICAL STATION CONFIGURATION

Hot Foods

À la carte range

Broiler station

Fry station

Griddle station

Sauté station

Holding

Salad and Dessert Station

Salad preparation

Dessert preparation

Frozen dessert preparation

Bakery

Mixer station

Dough holding/proofing

Dough rolling/forming

Baking

Banquet

Steam cooking

Dry-heat cooking

Banquet holding and service

Short-Order Station

Griddle station

Fry station

Broiler station

Steam Cooking

Pressure steamers

Convection steaming

Floor-mounted steam kettles

Tilting braising pans

Countertop trunnion kettles

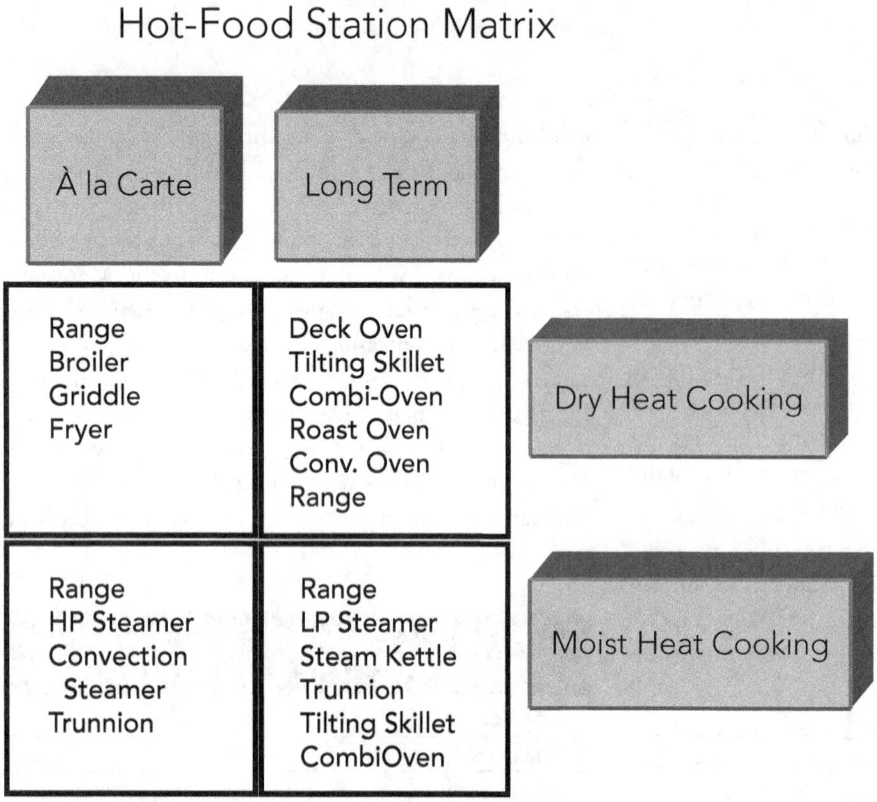

Hot-Food Station Matrix

À la Carte	Long Term	
Range Broiler Griddle Fryer	Deck Oven Tilting Skillet Combi-Oven Roast Oven Conv. Oven Range	**Dry Heat Cooking**
Range HP Steamer Convection Steamer Trunnion	Range LP Steamer Steam Kettle Trunnion Tilting Skillet CombiOven	**Moist Heat Cooking**

Figure 5.11
The kitchen's hot-food section resembles a matrix, with equipment divided by speed of cooking and type of heat.

Figure 5.12
This roll-in combination oven in the kitchen of Holloway Hall at the University of New Hampshire is capable of producing enough food to feed up to 5,000 students per meal.
(Photo by Joseph Durocher)

pieces of meat with injected steam to minimize shrinkage. The roasting feature can be shut off, and the unit converts to a convection steamer that can cook rice, a quick batch of green beans, or a serving of tortillas.

From a design perspective, grouping equipment that supports different cooking methods makes sense. Long-term dry-heat-cooked or stewed/braised foods usually need little attention save for periodic checks. Conversely, dry-heat à la carte cooking such as sautéing or frying requires continuous attention. The logical layout places à la carte equipment on the action side of the hot-food section and long-term equipment in a more remote location on the back side of the section.

The equipment on the front action side of the line is designed for quick cooking of food, often made to order. Unlike extended cooking, quick cooking requires precision timing. If deep-fried scallops cook just 30 seconds too long, they will be overdone. A broiled strip steak cannot be left alone. It must be turned and cared for not only because of flare-ups when fat drips into the broiler but also because the windows of time when a steak is cooked to rare, medium, or well done are narrow.

Practical as well as aesthetic considerations pertain to the relative positioning of each of these pieces of equipment. In Figure 5.13, the layout looks logical in the plan view. The rangetop is on the left, and the broiler and fryers are grouped together (separated by a spreader plate that functions as a work surface) because fried and broiled foods often go together. However, the elevation drawing reveals that the placement of the upright broiler visually separates the range from the fryers and, when the broiler racks are in the out position, the range cook is blocked from the rest of the station.

Figure 5.14, however, places the two high-rise pieces of equipment at the ends of the workstation. The broiler and fry stations are still close, but the sight lines along the entire station are not interrupted. Placing the high-rise equipment on the outside ends of the station also improves the efficiency of the exhaust equipment.

STATION OPTIONS

SPECIALTY EQUIPMENT

Microwave ovens have been around since the 1950s. However, recent innovations have melded microwave

À LA CARTE PLAN AND ELEVATION
OPTION 1

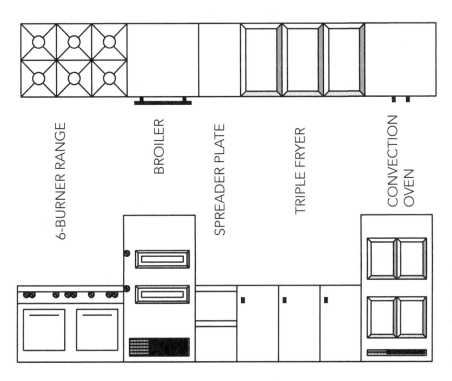

6-BURNER RANGE
BROILER
SPREADER PLATE
TRIPLE FRYER
CONVECTION OVEN

Figure 5.13
The plan view of these four pieces of equipment for an à la carte kitchen appears to be functional. However, the elevation drawing shows a problem with the placement of the broiler.

À LA CARTE PLAN AND ELEVATION
OPTION 2

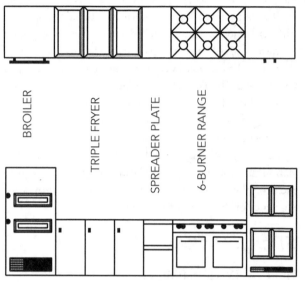

Figure 5.14
This drawing includes the same pieces of equipment shown in Figure 5.13, but with improved sight lines and flow patterns.

(moist-heat cooking) and dry-heat convection (dry-heat cooking) to shorten cooking times and to ensure a well-browned surface.

The selection of hot-food equipment depends on the menu items and their style of preparation; however, in many instances the menu has not been finalized when the layout is agreed to. Flexibility is important, but a completely flexible kitchen (one layout fits all) will be problematic for the production staff. Following is a brief guide to the generic needs of each hot-food station.

BROILER STATION OPTIONS

In this station, several pieces of equipment are referred to as broilers. Each yields a different product, so it is important to understand their advantages and disadvantages. Gas, electric, and charcoal are the major heat sources from which to choose; hardwood is used in some instances. Each heat source and broiler configuration has specific cooking characteristics.

A major differentiating characteristic of broilers is the location of the heat source. Top-heat broilers—which can be double-stacked—can broil steaks and vegetables, and

color the tops of casseroles. These broilers are heated with gas or electricity. Bottom-heat charcoal broilers are high heat and high smoke and need careful attention during the cooking process. They can create so much smoke that the ventilation system may require upgrading. Gas and electric bottom-heat broilers are available and are easier to use than their charcoal counterparts.

ROTISSERIE OPTIONS

In rotisserie cooking, the heat source is usually vertical rather than horizontal. Gas, electric, or charcoal is used to heat a rotisserie. An important design concern is the amount of radiated heat that emanates from a rotisserie, particularly when it is not fully loaded.

Rotisseries cook with dry heat, but the continual rotation of foods as they cook helps maintain their natural juices. Chickens are the most frequently cooked rotisserie items; lamb, pork, and beef dishes can also be prepared on this equipment. Some rotisseries can be fitted with baskets so whole fish or large pieces of vegetable can be cooked.

Rotisseries are often placed in display kitchens where the rotating motion of foods is a merchandising tool. Cooking with hardwood charcoal adds merchandising appeal, but without careful attention, the benefits may not justify the costs of maintaining the fire.

FRY STATION OPTIONS

Both gas and electric fry units are available. One major differentiating feature is the size of the fat bin, rated in pounds of fry medium. The amount of fry medium and the amount of food that can be cooked in a single batch are directly correlated. Generally, a 1:5 ratio of food to fry medium is used as a guide. If more food is placed in the fryer at one time, the temperature of the fry medium will drop excessively and the cooking time will be extended. During the extended cooking time, more fry medium is absorbed in the food. Not only does that result in a grease-laden product, but it also increases the cost of replacing the fry medium.

The heat source and distribution of heat to the frying kettle affect recovery time. Operating practices also affect the efficiency of a fryer. For example, some countertop fryers use a ribbon element that snakes across the entire bottom of the fry bin. The large surface area and full coverage of the bottom of the fry bin ensures that these fryers recover quickly and provide even cooking.

However, if freshly breaded foods are cooked in this fryer, the breading that falls off during cooking can collect around the elements. This leads to slower recovery time, premature browning of the fry medium, and increased fat breakdown. An alternative electric fryer places the heating elements around the inside wall of the fry bin, so breading that flakes off foods does not fall directly onto the heating elements. The point here is that the kitchen designer must think about how each piece of equipment will be used, then select it in the context of the overall operation and the menu.

Floor-model fryers generally have large fry bins and, therefore, the highest cooking capacity. Tabletop models that can sit on top of an undercounter refrigerator/freezer are space savers, but their smaller fat kettles translate into smaller batches.

The appropriate number of fryers rests, in part, on the number of fried foods that appear on the menu. Potatoes should be cooked in a fryer that is used for nothing else. Seafood should also be cooked in its own fryer. Items like onion rings, jalapeño poppers, and breaded mushrooms should be cooked in a third fryer.

In high-volume operations, multiple fryers are needed to cook a popular food item like French fries. For high-volume cooking of a single item with substantial mass (like breaded chicken, which is difficult to cook in a conventional fryer), a convection fryer affords the highest output, continuous filtering, and a smaller footprint than conventional fryers. The pressure and convection currents within the sealed fry bin speed cooking to the center of the product without burning the exterior.

A convection air "fryer" that produces fried foods without using fat as the heat transfer medium is suited to operations where customers are concerned about fat content. Another alternative is a robot fryer. A batch of frozen foods is placed in the load chute and, after a set time, the fully cooked foods emerge out the side of the fryer. A final type of fryer is a floor model that comes with its own hood, air filter, and fire suppression system. These are intended for seasonal operations, home meal replacement (HMR), and takeout kiosk operations, where installing an exhaust hood would be cost prohibitive. Kitchen designers should check with local building departments to determine if such fryers are allowed in the jurisdiction where the restaurant will be operating.

At the end of each shift (or day of cooking, at most), the fry medium in each fryer should be filtered. This practice is increasingly important for operators who plan to use trans-fat-free frying medium. If several fryers are ganged together, a built-in filter beneath one of the units is optimal. This minimizes cost and spills associated with portable units. Where only countertop fryers are used, or there are several fryers in separate locations, a portable filter offers the best solution. Failure to filter the fry medium frequently leads to premature breakdown of the fat, lowered smoke point, rapid darkening of the fry medium, and increased potential for fires.

If freshly breaded foods are on the menu, adequate space and equipment must be built into the design to accommodate the breading process. For low-volume restaurants, a manual three-step breading process is appropriate. This requires enough space to hold the food to be breaded, a pan of flour, a pan of egg wash, a pan of breadcrumbs, and a pan to hold the breaded foods. The amount of space is reduced if a batter-style breading is used. An alternative to hand breading is a partially or fully automated breading system.

In medium- to high-volume operations, a dump station is needed to receive foods after frying. In quick-service operations where fries are bagged, a heated area for holding the filled bags should also be planned.

GRIDDLE STATION OPTIONS

The choice of surface materials on the griddle and utility source affect heat-up time and the evenness of cooking as well as ease of cleaning. Chrome surfaces clean to a high gloss, making them appropriate in areas where guests can see the griddle surface. The downside to chrome is that foods shrink more than when cooked on other griddle surfaces. Another option is rolled steel, which (like chrome) has excellent heat transfer capabilities, yet foods shrink minimally.

The size of the cooking surface, the number of cooking zones, and the British thermal unit/kilowatt (Btu/kW) rating must also be considered as part of the process when designing griddle stations. The overall size determines the total number of items that can be cooked at a given time. Griddle surfaces are particularly important in restaurants where breakfast foods, like pancakes, make up an important part of the menu. When several types of foods will be cooked on the griddle simultaneously, it is important to have a number of temperature controls that can vary the temperature across the surface of the griddle. The recovery time—the time for the surface of the griddle to heat back up to the set temperature—will vary depending on the Btu/kW input, the thickness of the griddle surface, and the material in the griddle surface (Figure 5.15). In general, a thicker griddle surface creates a larger heat sink and, once heated, will recover faster than a thin griddle surface.

Figure 5.15
This Mongolian grill with a heavy rolled-iron surface develops a heat sink that enables the cooks to continuously prepare food without worrying about recovery time.
(Photo by Joseph Durocher)

Clamshell griddles speed cooking and minimize labor. Full-size griddles with top and bottom heat can cook burgers or chicken breasts without turning. Some clamshell tops generate steam, which keeps food from drying out while cooking. Countertop sandwich grills and panini sandwich makers are ideal for small operations. They help add menu variety without increasing the amount of raw ingredients at a sandwich station.

SAUTÉ STATION OPTIONS

Three types of ranges or cooktops, using gas or electricity, are typically used in this station:

1. The flattop sectional range usually has three sections, each of which can be heated individually. The ringtop range is a gas-fired variation.

2. The open-top range includes from two to eight open burners or elements, with grates over them in gas ranges.

3. The induction range or cooktop uses an inverter coil to create heat in ferrous pans.

FLATTOP RANGES

Flattop and ringtop ranges offer a large cooking surface on which a variety of cooking vessels can be placed. However, these solid-top ranges need heat-up time no matter what the heat source.

A nice feature of the ringtop range is that the center rings can be removed, thus allowing the range to give immediate heat through a central burner while the rest of the flat surface heats up. The sectional flattop allows the greatest flexibility in that sections can be turned on as needed.

Flattop and ringtop ranges are the equipment of choice in restaurants where the menu requires substantial sautéing. The real advantage to flat-surface ranges is that cooks have greater flexibility in the selection of pots and sauté pans.

A flattop range is ideal for breakfast operations where egg pans are used to cook eggs or omelets. The entire surface of the range can be loaded with pans—in contrast to an open-top range, where pans can be placed only on a burner or element. However, flattop ranges radiate a good deal of heat, and because they are not typically turned on and off during a shift, they tend to make the work environment less comfortable for chefs.

Open-Top Ranges

Open-top ranges have individual controls for each burner or element. In the case of gas, heat is immediate and, depending on the configuration, electric burners come up to temperature in a matter of seconds. The disadvantage to this type of range is that a pan must be placed directly over the heat source, limiting the number of pans to the number of burners/elements.

Wok ranges are a variant on the open-top gas range. The burners on these ranges have high Btu ratings—up to 80,000 Btu. Wok cooking is similar to sautéing and plays an important role in restaurants that offer Asian or fusion cooking. In some cases, a dual-surface wok range with raised burners in the back makes it possible to place larger-diameter woks on the range.

It should be noted that the efficiency of gas burners in both open and flattop ranges is diminished roughly 25 percent when propane, rather than natural gas, is used as a fuel. From a design perspective, this means that foods will take longer to cook, which could translate to a need for a larger number of flattops or more burners to meet the demands of the restaurant.

Induction Range

Induction cooktops use an inverter coil that generates instant heat when a ferrous cooking container is placed on top of it. In effect, the cooking container itself becomes the heating element, so little heat is lost from the cooktop. When the container is removed from the cooktop, the inverter coil immediately reverts to standby mode to save electricity.

Because induction cooktops don't get hot, they are safer than other cooking surfaces, particularly when used in guest contact areas. Induction cooktops are suited to both back-of-the-house and front-of-the-house applications.

Consider them for cooking omelets at brunch, saucing pasta on a buffet, and for primary cooking in remote catering locations. They are available with flat surfaces or with indented surfaces designed to hold a wok.

Look carefully at the kilowatt ratings for the induction models under consideration. For most restaurant applications, the extra expense of a 5-kW versus a 3-kW cooktop is a wise investment. Another point to consider is that these cooktops operate only with ferrous-based pans, like a rolled-steel egg pan. One induction cooktop can hold up to 16 pots and pans at one time—making it as flexible as a flattop range.

Kitchen designers should keep in mind that rangetops are subject to considerable wear and tear. The materials used for sectional or ringtops are usually heavy gauge and can withstand a beating. However, in some open-top ranges, the burner spiders are so lightweight that they will bend or bounce out of place when a heavy pot is set on them.

Kitchen designers should keep in mind that rangetops are subject to considerable wear and tear.

Not all ranges are created equal. A light- or medium-duty range is all that is needed to cook individual orders of eggs or pan-fry a few chicken breasts, but if large, heavy sautoirs are used to cook multiple portions, a light-duty restaurant range can't stand up to the beating. Slide a full pot across the grates of an open-top range: if the grates move, a range with heavier-duty grates is probably needed. On the electric side, a flat cooking surface is essential if heavy sautoirs or pots will be placed on the cooktop.

Several equipment options are available for the sauté station range. Frequently, the range comes with an oven situated under the rangetop, but because of its placement, it is difficult to reach and can restrict flow behind a busy à la carte range. However, numerous design modifications over the years have significantly improved the roasting and baking capabilities of the ovens found under most rangetops. Gone are the days when hot spots, slow heat-up, and uneven cooking temperatures caused most chefs to use their range ovens as storage cabinets.

Some manufacturers offer optional convection ovens or a combination of one conventional and one convection oven. Most oven interiors are lined with porcelain walls, although some are equipped with continuous clean surfaces.

Still other ranges come with refrigerated drawers under their cooktops. These refrigeration units are integral to the range and put foods within close reach of cooks.

Another range option, the salamander, is a top-mounted mini-broiler that is best used for browning the tops of casseroles and sandwiches. It is a useful choice if the kitchen has no other way to top-brown food, but it does not do the job of a full broiler. Perhaps the most useful (and inexpensive) range option is a simple overshelf where plates or sauté pans preheat from the rangetop's waste heat.

STEAM AND BRAISING PAN STATION OPTIONS

One of the most frequently used alternatives to making sauces on the rangetop is the steam-jacketed kettle or a tilting braising pan (kettle). This piece of equipment ranges from a 6-quart countertop "trunnion kettle" to a 150-gallon floor model. The steam jacketing envelops between 50 and 100 percent of the kettle. Fully jacketed kettles heat faster, but they also bake sauces onto the sides of a half-filled kettle, wasting product and making cleanup difficult.

Kettles can be heated with a built-in electric element, steam from a central supply, or steam from an undercounter steam generator typically heated with gas or electricity. A properly sized steam generator can heat several pieces of steam equipment at one time. Today, stainless steel is the preferred material for steam kettles because it never reacts negatively with food products.

A properly sized steam generator can heat several pieces of steam equipment at one time.

For large-capacity steam kettles, a swing-up electric mixing arm ensures that the contents cook evenly. With the addition of a pump and bagging station, a cook-chill program can be implemented. After cooking, most sauces and stocks are transferred to large pots and placed in a hot water bath (bain marie) or steam table for service. A cold water bath should be considered for chilling stocks and sauces if they are to go into refrigerated storage. Cook-chill foods packaged in a flexible bag are chilled in a tumble chiller, while foods stored in steam table inserts are chilled in a blast chiller.

The size and number of kettles, along with the steam source, are important design concerns. Sauce stations where kettles are used should be placed over a recessed portion of the floor or positioned so that the drain water from

the kettle flows into a drain trough in the floor. A water-metering faucet saves time filling the kettles. For cleaning purposes, a flexible spray hose should be installed. A large diameter draw-off valve will speed emptying and cleaning of large kettles.

Compartment steamers use steam as a medium to transfer heat. Low-pressure steamers are capable of producing hundreds of portions per batch, so they are typically used in banquet, catering, and institutional settings. High-pressure steamers are suited to cooking roughly 40 portions per batch and are a good choice for the à la carte line. Convection steamers are also fast cooking and can be purchased with a built-in steam generator. Unlike pressurized steamers, convection steamers can be opened at any time during the steaming cycle. Single-portion steamers are small countertop units that cook or reheat portions using a built-in steam generator. When steam kettles, trunnions, and compartment steamers are included in an à la carte layout, a single steam generator that heats all of the equipment should be considered.

Braising pans can hold anywhere from 10 to 40 gallons. The advantage that they have over steam kettles is that foods can be browned at temperatures up to 475 degrees Fahrenhent versus 235 degrees Fahrenheit in a steam kettle. The higher heat allows meats to brown as they would in a sauté pan. The large flat surfaces make the braising pan a useful supplement to a griddle for cooking home fries, burgers, or chicken breasts. With the addition of liquid, they can be used to braise or stew. They are available as countertop or floor-mounted models and can tilt to speed emptying.

HOLDING OPTIONS

Any of the previously mentioned pieces of equipment in the hot-food section can be used to hold foods. A steam table, whether dry or wet, is a common piece of equipment in most full-service kitchens. A single steam table with room for 6 to 12 inserts is usually sufficient, but the size of the steam table should always be closely matched to the menu and the expected volume of the operation. In some instances, a braising pan partially filled with water can double as a piece of holding equipment. The only other specialized pieces of equipment used for holding food are a heated holding/warming cabinet and a roll warmer. Holding cabinets are essential for banquet service. One set of carts is used to hold food before it is plated, and other carts are used to hold plated hot meals. These carts are also used to preheat plates and bowls for service.

CROSS-STATION OPTIONS

There are many pieces of equipment that can either be used across multiple stations or that are appropriate to specific menu items. Three of these categories are worthy of note:

1. *Microwave-combination ovens.* One of the biggest complaints about microwaves is that the cooking temperatures don't promote surface browning. Ovens that combine microwaves—for quick cooking—with dry-heat cooking that browns surfaces and improves the flavor of external surfaces can be a good choice. A recent innovation is a microwave-heatable grill and flatstone ceramic composite oven insert that, after being heated in a microwave, can shorten cooking times by as much as 90 percent.

2. *Impingement ovens.* Impingement ovens use forced hot air to cook, similar to convection ovens. The difference is that impingement ovens use directed air that blows on the top and bottom of foods as they move along on a conveyor. Most models are targeted at mid- to high-volume restaurants. As with convection ovens, cooking time and temperature need to be modified. Lower baking temperatures (compared to conventional ovens) of rolls lead to the same rate of surface browning. In an impingement oven, meat cooks faster and loses less moisture, and cooking large pieces of meat takes less time than in conventional ovens.

3. *Tandoor ovens.* Tandoor ovens are classically a clay pot with a charcoal heat source that is placed in the bottom of the pot. Commercial models can be fitted to heat with gas, which requires less maintenance. Skewered poultry, seafood, and vegetables are placed vertically into the oven, and the radiant heat cooks them quickly. Historically found in Indian restaurants, the use of Tandoor ovens has spread to nonethnic restaurants because of its quick-cooking, high-output capability.

These are but three examples of cooking equipment that could be used in multiple stations. Other cross-station equipment includes slicers, vertical cutter-mixers, and tabletop food choppers.

COLD-FOOD SECTION

In most restaurants, the salad, sandwich, and dessert stations are grouped into one section and must function as both preparation and service areas. However, the dessert station may be backed up with a bakery where the major production work occurs.

Salad and dessert sections vary greatly, depending on the menu offerings and styles of service in the restaurant. In an à la carte restaurant, salads and desserts may be prepared and plated as ordered. In large-volume operations, the preparation and plating will likely be done prior to the serving period and stored for server pickup. In restaurants offering banquet service, additional preparation equipment, rolling stock, and storage space are required for both the salad and the dessert station. However, some general requirements and considerations are worth noting. Figure 5.16 shows a useful storage system for holding large numbers of plated cold salads and desserts.

SALAD STATION OPTIONS

Salad greens must always be carefully washed for service. A two-compartment sink with sideboards is well suited for this job. One of the compartments can be used for cleaning greens and the second for draining washed greens. Sideboards are necessary for holding unprocessed greens and washed greens. Salad spinners, typically equipped with an electric motor, remove more of the water from greens than if they merely drain while sitting in a colander.

In many restaurant operations, reach-in refrigerators are used for holding washed salad ingredients. (For banquet service, a walk-in refrigerator is helpful.) The reach-in refrigerator must have tray slides to hold the sheet pans that typically become the shelves in a reach-in. Sheet pans are also used to rack up portioned salads when salads are plated in advance of service. If the service staff is responsible for plating salads as needed, an overshelf saladgreen refrigerator puts an evening's worth of greens within easy reach.

When the salad station does double duty as a sandwich station, slicers (Figure 5.17) are frequently incorporated to slice salad and sandwich ingredients. A vertical cutter-mixer (VCM) is also useful in this station when large amounts of tossed or chopped salads are prepared. (The VCM can also be used to prepare bread dough, pie crusts, or homogenized signature salad dressings.) Perhaps the most commonly used and versatile piece of equipment for cutting, chopping, and mixing in the salad station is the tabletop chopper with assorted attachments.

SANDWICH STATION OPTIONS

In some instances the salad and sandwich stations can be integrated together. However, a well-designed sandwich

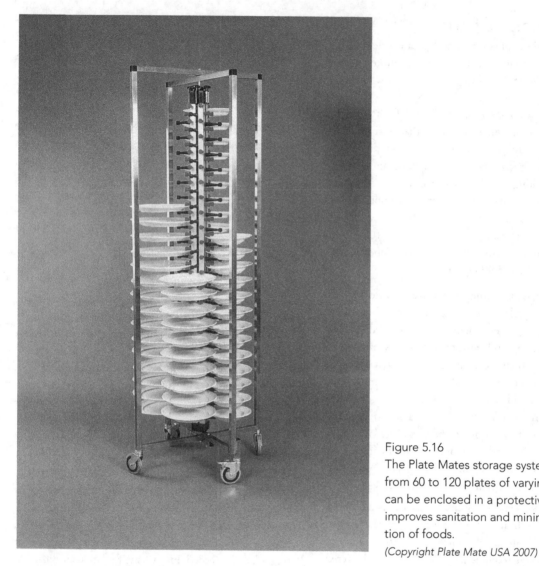

Figure 5.16
The Plate Mates storage system can hold from 60 to 120 plates of varying sizes and can be enclosed in a protective cover, which improves sanitation and minimizes dehydration of foods.
(Copyright Plate Mate USA 2007)

station improves efficiency significantly. At the heart of a sandwich station is the sandwich preparation table, with space that's large enough to hold all of the sandwich fillings and accompaniments on the menu. A swing-down lid helps keep food cold when the station is not in use, and a removable cutting board provides the assembly area. Backup supplies are stored in a refrigerated cabinet below. To ensure that sandwich fillings stay chilled, one manufacturer runs coolant through the divider bars between pans.

If meat and cheese fillings are to be sliced to order, space must be planned for the slicer. Placing the slicer on a mobile cart allows kitchen staff to use it at other stations during off hours. The cart should not obstruct traffic flow, so a

cutout in the counter large enough to hold the cart should be part of the plan. If hot sandwiches will be offered, a self-contained countertop steam table may be sufficient to keep items like brisket and pastrami at temperature. A countertop, conveyorized broiler unit may be called for to heat up meats and melt cheese piled onto rolls or bread. Clamshell sandwich griddles and panini cookers round out equipment that supports hot sandwich preparation.

DESSERT STATION

Desserts, including frozen concoctions, are often prepared in the salad and dessert section. In other kitchens, dessert preparation—except for plating—takes place in the bakeshop.

Figure 5.17
Hobart's ergonomically designed slicer incorporates numerous safety features not found in its predecessors. The easy-to-clean features of this slicer make it especially desirable for salad prep and display cooking areas.
(Courtesy of Hobart)

As with salads, desserts need plenty of refrigeration. Frozen desserts require an ice cream chest and, if preportioned, a reach-in freezer. Soft-serve machines are required where soft ice cream is served. Space to hold toppings must also be considered. A countertop mixer is needed in the dessert station, where cream or other toppings are whipped from scratch.

Work counters, shelving, and other storage areas are vital to dessert sections. Rolling stock is helpful for moving such items as trays, clean dishes, and raw materials about the kitchen. In general, flexible equipment capable of preparing a wide range of products is the key to success in salad and dessert sections, as they are often used to prepare an assortment of ever-changing offerings.

BAKERY

The bakery section may be a stand-alone section of the kitchen or shared at certain times of day with other production areas. Kitchens with a dedicated bakery will typically have six primary stations, as follows.

STORAGE AND WEIGHING STATION

Bulk ingredients such as flours and sugar, along with frequently used spices, toppings, and tools, need to be within easy reach. Because baking is a science, scales are needed to closely weigh the ingredients. Balance-beam scales are frequently used by bakers in midsize restaurants, but for large-volume production, a mobile platform scale is called for.

Storage of and ready access to raw materials is essential to efficient bakeshop design. At the heart of many bakeshops is a baker's table with overhead drawers for holding spices and sufficient clearance under the countertop to store bulk material containers. Refrigerated storage is also needed in this area to chill shortening and butter used in doughs and pastries and to hold fillings.

MIXING STATION

The mixing station includes the mixing and support equipment needed for the preparation of batters, doughs, and toppings. Support equipment includes racks to hold extra bowls, hand tools that support the mixing, and extra mixer attachments. The choice of countertop or floor-model mixers is based on the expected volume of product that will be prepared. For mixing high-gluten dough for bagels, pizza, and French bread, a spiral mixer should be considered. Extra mixing bowls and floor dollies to move large bowls filled with product should also be considered.

DOUGH HOLDING/PROOFING STATION

This is a passive station where doughs are held, generally under controlled temperatures, while they await the rolling/forming process. Yeast-raised products generally go through two proofing steps. The first step is a bulk proofing of dough as it comes from the mixing station. A second proofing is required after the dough goes through the forming station. While dough can rise at ambient room temperatures, the additional heat and moisture in a proof box will speed and improve the process. After pie pastry or puff pastry is mixed, it is usually held in refrigerated storage to improve its workability. Holding and proofing is not necessary for batter products.

DOUGH ROLLING/FORMING STATION

Bread or pastry is rolled or formed as needed, sometimes by mechanized devices and sometimes manually. Racks to hold baking pans and sheet pans used in baking should be stored in this station. Dough will typically return to the proof box after this step for a second rising. A dough sheeter is essential when a large number of pies will be prepared on a daily basis. The dough sheeter is also useful for making puff pastry dough that goes through several rolling and folding steps, which are separated by time in a refrigerator. Rolls can be portioned and shaped with the help of a dough cutter; numerous other specialty pieces of forming equipment can produce products ranging from bagels to croissants to baguettes.

BAKING STATION

The type and amount of items to be baked often determines the type of oven used for this step. For example, crusty breads require steam-injected ovens, whereas cookies do not. Deck ovens are commonly used in the bakery.

Designers should consider the various uses of the bakeshop ovens before deciding on equipment specifications.

If the bakeshop will be used in the early hours of the day for the preparation and baking of breads and pastries, and during the afternoon and evening for banquet preparation, then multipurpose ovens are needed. Their placement must be convenient to users in the bakery, banquet, and hot-food areas.

The most common oven classification is the deck oven (Figure 5.18). Deck ovens can be stacked three high for increased output per square foot of floor space and are available as roasting or baking ovens. Roasting ovens, which have greater height in the oven cavity, are similar to baking ovens but can hold large top rounds and other wholesale cuts of meat with ease. Deck ovens can be fitted with steam injectors, which help create the crusty surface on French and Italian breads.

Another option is the convection oven, which is quite effective for baking. Convection ovens can also be used for roasting, but misuse can lead to excessive meat shrinkage. Convection ovens can be double stacked for maximum output.

Combination ovens are the newest class of oven used for baking. These ovens are capable of functioning as convection ovens, convection steamers, and steam injected ovens. Their flexibility makes them best suited as a multipurpose oven used by many stations.

Cavity ovens are designed for small- or large-volume baking and roasting. The standard cavity oven—one that is placed under a rangetop—is acceptable for roasting but generally is not ideal for baking. However, the rotary oven, which holds foods on arms that rotate like a Ferris wheel inside the oven cavity, is effective as a bake or roast oven in large-volume operations. Another type of cavity oven accepts an entire proofing cart without the need to transfer product from the cart to oven shelves.

For a dedicated bakeshop, deck ovens are the best choice, with steam injection capabilities for times when crusty breads are baked. No matter what oven type is selected, sufficient rack space is needed to cool baked goods and to hold them for service.

FINISHING/DECORATING STATION

Most bread products need little more than a cooling rack after they emerge from the oven, but other baked goods need equipment for decorating, including trays, racks, mixers, and, in some cases, cooktops.

In bakeshops where special confections and toppings are made, additional stations are required. A candy station, for

Figure 5.18
This pizza oven is one of many types of deck ovens.
(Photo by Joseph Durocher)

example, will need a rangetop and, in some cases, a trunnion kettle. For a large volume of candy items—particularly if a lot of chocolate products are prepared—a separate, refrigerated room should be considered. Cakes and pastries need to be decorated, and mixers and ranges are sometimes used to make the frosting or fillings used during this phase.

BANQUET

Banquet sections are required only in restaurants where banquet service cannot be accommodated by other production stations. Meal preparation for small private parties, for instance, will not require a separate banquet station. However, when banquet business exceeds by 25 percent or more the ongoing volume of the restaurant, it makes sense to design a separate banquet section in the kitchen.

BANQUET MOIST-HEAT COOKING

Steam equipment for banquets consists of large steam-jacketed kettles—over 10 gallons—for soup, sauces, and stewed items (Figure 5.19). Tilting braising pans are a good alternative to the steam kettle. When 350-person or larger banquets are expected, large-volume low-pressure steamers should be included. As with the à la carte section, the steam equipment can use central steam or be self-contained. Due to the large volume of food cooked in this area, floor drainage is necessary for the disposal of wastewater. A floor grate or drain that runs the entire length of the section, or a recessed floor with drain holes, minimizes water spills during cleaning.

BANQUET DRY-HEAT COOKING

One or more tilting braising pans can be helpful in large banquet operations. The flexibility of these pieces of equipment makes them ideally suited for numerous types of food preparation, a requirement often placed on the banquet production department. As with steam equipment, floor drainage is necessary for cleaning. It makes sense, therefore, to locate braising pans close to the steam equipment.

As mentioned earlier, the roasting station may be one and the same with the bakeshop, so the ovens selected for most banquet operations should be capable of roasting or baking a wide range of products. Often, a mix of ovens—deck and convection—is chosen to increase flexibility.

BANQUET HOLDING AND PLATING

Banquet foods are typically held in warming cabinets or in the same equipment used for their preparation. For example, soup for a banquet frequently stays in the steam

kettle in which it was made until service time. It is then drawn off into pitchers or a bootleg for service.

A plating station or area is essential for quick service to a large banquet. This can consist of a simple countertop or, in operations where many banquets are served, a special banquet plating cart with heated wells that hold full steamtable inserts. In cases where plating and holding equipment is purchased for banquet service, the pieces should be as portable as possible. Portability will allow the equipment to be removed from the plating area when not needed, thus improving traffic flow in the kitchen. Identify where the plating station will be set during the design phase to ensure that sufficient electric service is brought to that area. Plate dollies and portable heated plate lowerators will help ensure that meals are served at the proper temperature. Banquet carts should be capable of holding food for at least 45 minutes without affecting quality. Some operators choose to plate meals cold and place them in a warming cabinet that is held in a walk-in. For service, the warmer is activated and brings its contents up to serving temperature.

SHORT-ORDER QUICK-SERVICE SECTION

Short-order (quick-service) sections in compact kitchens consist of several stations, all of which are frequently handled by one person. Such is the case in small diners around the world. The cook has every piece of equipment within reach at all times. In larger restaurant kitchens, several individuals may handle short-order sections. For any short-order section to work, the following design elements must be considered:

- *Griddle station.* The griddle station design covered in the à la carte section discussion also pertains to short-order sections. However, in quick-service restaurants, where items such as burgers are prepared in batches, a clamshell top speeds the cooking process. Clamshells can be heated platens (flat steel surfaces between which foods are placed to cook) that swing down and sit atop the food on the griddle, heated hoods fitted with radiant heaters that cook from the top, or a clamshell under which steam builds up to speed cooking. The platens work best when foods are the same thickness throughout. If foods vary in thickness, the radiant hood works best. Panini presses would need space in the design if this popular sandwich option appears on the menu.

- *Fry station.* High-volume quick-service restaurants and diners frequently employ more fryers than à la carte

Figure 5.19
This steam kettle is ideal for cooking sauces or batches of moist-heat-cooked items for banquet service.
(Photo by Joseph Durocher)

restaurants. In many quick-service restaurants, the fryer is one of the two primary pieces of cooking equipment. Often, fryers are ganged together to form a bank of equipment. In such cases—as mentioned earlier—a built-in filter system should be chosen. The fry medium from each fryer can be filtered and pumped back into the fryer with the help of a single filter.

- For extremely high-volume quick-service restaurants, a convection fryer can increase output and provide continuous fat filtration while using less energy per pound of food cooked. Mechanized systems for peeling and cutting potatoes should be used when freshly cut fries are featured, along with mechanized breading equipment.

- *Broiler station.* Pull-out broilers are found in some quick-service restaurants and diners, but frequently the broiler is actually integrated with the underside of the griddle. The alternative is the conveyor broiler or char-broiler, which is typically used to cook burgers or other protein foods.

Toasters are often integrated with the broiler station. Pop-up toasters are intended for low to medium volume, while conveyor toasters are designed for medium to high volume. Conveyor toasters offer the advantage of being able to toast items of varying thickness.

DINING ROOM SUPPORT AREAS

This discussion addresses three support areas that bridge the gap between the back and front of the house:

1. *Display kitchens.* While the display kitchen is actually an extension of the back of the house, its design has a considerable impact on the ambience and operation of the front of the house.

2. *Service stations.* Service stations, situated in the dining areas, enable the waitstaff to take care of tabletop needs without traveling back and forth to the kitchen.

3. *Warewashing areas.* Warewashing—which, in a loose definition, embraces all dish and pot washing—is physically placed in the back of the house, but it greatly influences the efficient operation of the front of the house.

DISPLAY KITCHENS

While not appropriate for all restaurant types, display kitchens have many benefits. The significance of display kitchens is that the functioning of the kitchen is within view of the customer and they provide a shorter travel distance for servers from food pickup to table. Celebrity Chef Wolfgang Puck, when asked, "What do your restaurants add that is special?" responded to Libby Platus, contributor to *Restaurant Hospitality* magazine, "People want entertainment. . . . That's why my restaurants have open kitchens, because they are fun." Puck, with a portfolio of more than 70 restaurants, is an ardent supporter of the open kitchen and consistently includes them in his restaurants. Chef Todd English, who opened Beso with partner Eva Longoria in 2008, also takes advantage of the drama of the open kitchen in their 150-seat restaurant in Los Angeles.

The designers of any type of display kitchen must consider the sight lines from the customers' vantage point. All display kitchens benefit from a clean and well-organized appearance. The area needs an adequate supply of hand- and tool-washing sinks to keep it spotless, and chefs must employ optimal sanitary food-handling practices.

PRIMARY PRODUCTION DISPLAY KITCHEN

Primary production display kitchens can be found in restaurants ranging from diners, where the short-order cooks prepare everything in front of the customers at the counter behind them, to the most expensive steakhouses. Diners have been delighted with the display kitchen in New York City's venerable Gallagher's Steak House, where steaks are broiled over a charcoal fire, since 1927.

In many restaurants that feature pizza and fresh-baked pasta casseroles, customers are entertained by dough-twirling pizza chefs as they "create" their pizzas and then bake them next to casserole dishes on a stone hearth heated by a log fire. In numerous full-service restaurants, customers are paraded past the open kitchen, where they can preview the type of food they will be ordering or catch glimpses of the ongoing cooking as they enjoy their meal.

In cafeterias, many people prefer waiting in line at the short-order or stir-fry station to watch their burgers and sandwiches be prepared to order, or their veggie selection combined with a protein to create a personalized order of stir fry, rather than saving time by picking up batch-processed food.

Taken together, these four images show the
four seasons at Park Avenue restaurant.
(Michael Weber Photography)

The card catalog holds past menus from Public in the entryway of the restaurant, where guests can read them.
(Michael Weber Photography)

The soft fabrics and draped ceiling keep this lounge at Landmark quieter than many lounges.
(Peter Wynn Thompson photographer)

This Swiss cheese wall is in keeping with Bembos super-graphic interiors.
(Jose Orrego Herrera)

Super-graphics are used to tie together the separate floors in each Bembos restaurant.
(Jose Orrego Herrera)

The curved, translucent walls minimize
visual and auditory distraction.
(Photos by Scott Pease)

A mix of seating and tables offers a wide
range of options for Table 45 customers.

The box lighting fixtures are soft thematic elements that help define the ambience of Douzo.
(Greg Premru photographer)

The angled panels above the back bar at Douzo are of visual interest to bar-goers.
(Greg Premru photographer)

These honeycomb elements are used to tie together the three levels of Mercat from the lounge area in the cellar to the main dining floor to this private area on the mezzanine level.
(Photos of Mercat by Frank Oudeman)

The honeycomb helps to define the waiting area on the main floor of Mercat.
(Photos of Mercat by Frank Oudeman)

The strong honeycomb image even ties the interior with the exterior of Mercat.
(Photos of Mercat by Frank Oudeman)

The honeycomb adjacent to the spiral stairs leading to the lounge clearly helps tie the two levels together.
(Photos of Mercat by Frank Oudeman)

The exterior of Punk's Grill creates a visual impact that separates this restaurant from its competitors. *(top)*
(Copyright 2009 Ian Pitts)

This order area with its display cooking and assembly station provides customers a visually appealing environment.
(Copyright 2009 Ian Pitts)

From the order entry touch screen to the gravity-powered food and beverage delivery double helix, technology is visible throughout 's Baggers.
(Klaus Keiner photographer)

The wine walls at Fogo creates a
strong visual image.
(Paul Crosby, pcrosby.com)

The sweeping curves of Fogo
de Chao's exterior clearly
separates this restaurant from
the square box structure above.
(Paul Crosby, pcrosby.com)

For display kitchens to be most effective, nearly all of the pre-preparation should be completed elsewhere. Such tasks as chopping, slicing, pounding, and so on should be performed out of sight of the diners. The pre-prepared raw materials are then assembled for cooking in view of the customer.

As with any à la carte range in the back of the house, efficient pre-preparation is the key to success. Pass-through refrigerators that connect to the pre-preparation kitchen and undercounter refrigeration will facilitate an efficient flow from the back to the front of the house. Compact tabletop automatic-lift fryers reflect a simplicity of design in keeping with display cooking, in contrast with the heavy-gauge, black-iron surfaces of an open-top range with oven.

Another type of equipment worth noting is the rotisserie. Here, cuts of meat are roasted on what is technically a vertical broiler unit. The most elaborate rotisserie units are fitted with black iron, brass, and stainless steel, and actually become a décor element.

FINISHING DISPLAY KITCHEN

Finishing kitchens function like a cafeteria line, where the line personnel plate up previously prepared foods. This technique may be used in a full-service restaurant, but with an extra bit of flair.

Patrons will see the assembly of partially finished meal components being arranged and perhaps placed under a cheese melter for a few moments, removed, garnished, and set on an underliner. Time from placing the order to when it is ready for pickup is less than five minutes. Although no "real" cooking takes place in the display kitchen, guests have the perception that their food is being prepared right in front of them. Microwave ovens, compact convection ovens, or quartz ovens can be used in these display kitchens to speed finishing.

SERVICE-ONLY DISPLAY KITCHEN

The service-only display kitchen is nothing more than a plating area. As with the other types of display kitchens, it assists servers in speeding food to their waiting guests.

Soups and preplated appetizer or salad items are often served from the display kitchen. Other examples include antipasto bars and tapas bars, where food items are displayed for guest viewing and portioned by the service staff. This type does not offer quite as much drama, but guests still benefit from a feeling of involvement.

TAKEOUT DISPLAY KITCHEN

Today, the takeout/home meal replacement (HMR) market can generate significant incremental sales for the restaurant. Seeing items prepared, as well as foods on display in refrigerated cases, entices diners. Takeout/HMR kitchens support two presentation techniques:

1. *Ready to eat.* This is the takeout format common to quick-service operations. In most cases, the limited menu is prepared, packaged, held, and ready to eat when the guest arrives.

2. *Ready to heat and eat.* This format presents fully cooked foods that are held in a refrigerated state. In some cases, the fully cooked foods are held in platters in refrigerated cases, from which they are sold by the pound or portion. Complete meals may be portioned and displayed in refrigerated cases in packaging that can go directly into a microwave or a regular oven.

The takeout/HMR display kitchen must be placed so that patrons do not track through the dining room. The ordering and waiting area for takeout/HMR should not interfere with the flow of traffic in and out of the restaurant. In high-volume situations, the entrance to the takeout/HMR area should be separate from that to the regular restaurant.

At a minimum, the design should include as much self-serve equipment as possible. Portioned hot foods should be held in heated display cases that can be accessed from both server and customer sides. Refrigerated deli display cases should be used to display preportioned cold foods.

SERVICE STATIONS

Service stations, also referred to as server stations and waiter stations, are often viewed by designers as a necessary evil in the dining room—necessary because they enable waiters to provide efficient service, and evil because they have no inherent aesthetic appeal; they can be an ugly blot on an otherwise pure design. The truth is that service stations need not be intrusive obstructions in the dining room if they are carefully conceived and developed in the early stages of the design process. This is particularly important in large operations where servers must travel long distances from the kitchen or in operations where several small

Figure 5.20
This service station incorporates all the elements needed to reset tables.
(Photo by Joseph Durocher)

dining rooms are serviced from a central kitchen. There are no set rules for what should be incorporated into a service station. The design of any station should rely on management philosophy, the menu, and the type of service. In some full-service restaurants, it is appropriate to incorporate an ice bin, water station, coffee and tea burners, roll warmer, and all the elements required to reset tables and hold soiled tableware and linen (Figure 5.20).

The aesthetic design of service stations should be well integrated with the front-of-the-house design.

The aesthetic design of service stations should be well integrated with the front-of-the-house design. In some restaurants, the service station is a finely crafted piece of furniture that blends well with the overall decor and helps segment the dining area. In other restaurants, the service station is integrated with an architectural element that keeps the station hidden from view. In still other design scenarios, the service stations are not situated in the dining room but in the service pickup area immediately adjacent to the kitchen. All of these configurations can efficiently support waitstaff functions without detracting from the overall design scheme. An all-important component of the station is the point of sale (POS), which links the servers and the kitchen.

WAREWASHING AREAS

As mentioned earlier, the placement of the warewashing equipment can significantly affect the efficiency of a restaurant. Placement is simple in a restaurant with a single dining room: just as the server enters the kitchen. When operations have multiple points of service with a central warewashing station, however, the location of warewashing equipment is trickier.

In a complex operation, the number of trips and the amount of tableware brought to the warewashing station should affect the placement of warewashing. Consider a hotel where banquet guests are served from one side of the kitchen and the dining room guests are served from the other. Dishes are hand-carried to and from the dining room. However, service to and from banquet areas is accomplished by carrying dishes on oval trays that are set on tray stands. After service, the trays are moved to the service corridor and placed on mobile racks, which are wheeled to the dish area.

In the above example, although the greater volume of dishes comes from the banquet area, warewashing should be located closer to the dining room because the waitstaff make more frequent trips to and from the dining room service areas. If the use of bus buckets is integrated with dining room service, however (thus limiting server time running back and forth from dining room to warewashing), the location of the warewashing system could change. It is therefore crucially important to consider specific operating procedures when making decisions about the location of warewashing.

Placement of warewashing in other than full-service restaurants is also important. To be most effective, the warewashing in a cafeteria-style restaurant should be located near the cafeteria exit. This may necessitate separating the warewashing section from the kitchen. The alternative is to install a (costly) conveyor system or to use mobile carts where users deposit their trays, which are then brought to the warewashing area by staff.

Dish machines are a costly expense (initial purchase and operating) for any foodservice operation, so the choice of equipment is important. The three classes of dish machines are:

1. *Single-rack machines.* The basic single-rack machine is designed to meet the needs of smaller restaurants. When set up for hot water sanitizing, these machines can clean up to 65 racks of tableware per hour. Newly introduced equipment includes front-loading models that can be easier to install than the commonly used side-loading units. Rack machines are also available for installation in a corner space, with doors that open on adjacent sides. Yet another model offers a tall chamber that makes it possible to wash sheet pans and dishware

in a single, compact machine. A recent innovation allows the user to program the wash time from one minute for glassware to six minutes for heavily soiled items. While most models use hot water to sanitize, low-temperature models use chemicals to sanitize washed wares. This machine can clean roughly 1,500 pieces of tableware per hour.

2. *Rack conveyor machines.* When used to their full capacity, these machines can service all but the largest institutional and banquet facilities. Assuming a continuously loaded standard-size rack, a rack conveyor machine can clean about 200 racks of tableware per hour. Twin-tank rack machines are capable of cleaning up to 360 racks per hour. Useful features on this type of dish machine include a side-loading model that allows for corner installation. This can save up to 20 square feet in the dish room layout. A power unloader pushes racks away from the clean end, which makes it possible for just one operator to handle both ends of the machine. Newly introduced spray heads that improve cleaning and rinsing efficiency (available on some models) have been shown to reduce operating costs by at least 50 percent. Rack conveyor machines can clean—depending on whether they are single or double tank—from 4,000 to 6,500 pieces of tableware per hour.

3. *Flight-type machines.* The largest of all dish machines, flight-type units are capable of cleaning tens of thousands of pieces of tableware per hour. Straight flight-type machines offer the advantage of direct loading of dishes onto pegs, which speeds cleaning and minimizes the number of racks needed to support the operation. A variation on this theme is a merry-go-round dish machine that requires tableware to be loaded onto racks. While most models are equipped with slide-up access doors to each section of the machine, some models can be purchased with hinged, insulated doors that allow the models to be installed in spaces with low ceilings. You can expect these machines—depending on configuration—to clean up to 20,000 pieces per hour.

Determining which type of dish machine is based—in part—on the following calculation:

$$\frac{\text{\# of seats} \times \text{\# of turns per meal period} \times \text{of pieces of tableware per cover}}{\text{Capacity of machine per hour}}$$

Of course, the mix of tableware and the available amount of tableware must also be considered. For example, in a fast-casual restaurant with 300 seats, 3 turns per night, and 12 pieces of dinnerware per cover, nearly 11,000 pieces of tableware will need to be cleaned per shift. A double-tank rack conveyor could wash those dishes in two hours, while the flight-type machine could finish the job in one hour. So, it would seem that the rack conveyor would be the optimal choice. However, if the inventory of tableware is less than that required for a single seating, the rack machine might not be able to keep up with the volume of tableware that needs to be cleaned.

Glass washing is particularly important in bar operations. Consideration must be given to the noise and space required for an undercounter glass washer versus a manual washing system versus transporting the glasses to and from a remote warewashing facility. A key consideration is that the bartender should spend as much time serving drinks as possible—not washing glassware while customers await service.

POTWASHING SECTION

Closely aligned with the warewashing area is the potwashing station. Although the potwashing section may be separated from the dish machine, most operations keep the two areas together because of crossover staffing. In large operations where there is a sanitation supervisor, it is easier to supervise the staff when the stations are closely linked. Another

---

GREEN KITCHEN TIPS

- *Recycling wet waste.* Foods that once went into a garbage grinder need to be collected before being stored and then shipped off for composting. Easy-to-access dump stations in the warewashing and pot areas must be incorporated in the design of the dish breakdown station and adjacent to the pot sink.

- *Recycling dry waste.* Such a practice could necessitate the addition of a single or multiple bins near the dish breakdown area (depending on the requirements of the local recyclers). In some locales all cans, glass, and plastic bottles go into one bin. Installing bins in guest service areas, which are clearly labeled as to what should be placed in them, must also be incorporated in the plan. Bins to collect newspapers and other reading material should also be considered.

- *Energy management monitoring.* One of the greatest advantages of induction cooking is that the unit shuts off when the cooking vessel is removed from the surface of the cooktop. Other pieces of equipment can also be controlled to help reduce energy use. For example, a timer on electric flattops can adjust the kilowatt usage during off-peak periods. Such a function works best on units with digital controls.

- *Cold-water wash.* Low-temperature dish machines have been around for decades, but with rising energy costs, they have become a great alternative to their hot-water counterparts. They function just as effectively as conventional dishwashers but without the added cost of heating the water for the wash or dry cycles. Another benefit of cold-water wash equipment is that it does not dump as much heat and moisture into the dishwashing area.

- *Exhaust heat.* Range hoods are designed to remove the heat and smoke produced during cooking. Hood models that dump outside air at the lead edge of the hood will remove much less of the treated air in the kitchen than those that do not incorporate makeup air into the design of the hood.

- *Captured heat.* Captured heat from the dish machine is another way to conserve energy. The heat recovery system uses waste heat to preheat cold incoming rinse water. The rinse water then flows to the wash tanks, where it is used to clean dishware and eventually dumped with far less energy used to heat water than in other systems. Preheated water is used only when the dish machine is first filled each day.

reason for placing the two operations together is that, in some locales, the pots must be sanitized after washing, and the dish machine is the best place to accomplish this.

The potwashing process may be mechanized through the installation of a motor-driven device that grinds the dirt off the pots. In operations where the volume of pots and pans is substantial, a potwashing machine similar to a single-rack machine can effectively remove food buildup from most trays, pots, pans, and utensils. An alternative to ease the potwashing chore is a wash sink that uses high-powered jets of hot water and detergent. In this case, the cleaning solution, heat, and abrasive action of the pressurized water jets loosen all but the heaviest food buildup.

ENVIRONMENTAL CONDITIONS

The lighting, ventilation, spacing of equipment, types of surfaces, and sound levels all have an impact on the effectiveness of production staff in the kitchen. These environmental factors can also affect employee turnover rates, which, in turn, affect the restaurant's bottom line.

LIGHTING

Direct lighting in the back of the house is desirable but must be carefully engineered. Although sufficient light is needed to differentiate between a piece of flank steak and a piece of skirt steak, too much light can create glare that ultimately leads to eyestrain. When properly angled, however, direct task lighting is practical and energy efficient.

To ensure that food looks its best, use the same type of lamps in the production area as in the dining area. The result is that the cuisine is viewed under the same type of light by the chef as by the diners.

Historically, mood lighting was not important in most kitchens, but its role in display kitchens is vital. Theatrical spotlights, for example, are used to highlight the work surfaces and food arrangements in many display kitchens. Here, the lighting scheme provides adequate illumination for the cooks and a focal point for guests to view their meals being prepared and completed dishes as they await pickup.

VENTILATION

The ventilation system is composed of exhaust and makeup air. Exhaust air is generally removed from those portions of the kitchen where smoke, heat, and steam are created. Building codes, in most communities, require that ventilation hoods be installed over all heat- and smoke-producing equipment. Further, the codes require that fire detection and extinguishing systems be installed as part of the ventilation system.

The comfort level of employees is determined by the amount of air removed from the kitchen. However, for every cubic foot of air removed through the hoods, makeup air must be provided. Makeup air can come from ducting that dumps treated air into the kitchen, the dining room, or both. A negative pressure should always be maintained in the kitchen (more air drawn out of the kitchen than is supplied by makeup air ducts in the kitchen) to ensure that smoke and grease are kept from the dining room.

There are two schools of thought about adding makeup air to a kitchen. The first approach is to add the air evenly throughout the kitchen; the second is to add the air where it is most needed. Fresh air is dumped near the dish machine, in the fabrication area, over the bakeshop, or in other areas where heat builds up. In certain newer hood systems, some of the makeup air is added right at the face of the hood. This limits the amount of air drawn across the vertical face of the hood. A flow of exhaust air that becomes too strong is uncomfortable for the cooks. To control heating and cooking costs, a minimum of conditioned air should be drawn out of the dining room. Dining room air is filtered and heated or cooled, and therefore it is costly if too much is exhausted through the kitchen exhaust system.

ACOUSTICS

Kitchens can be noisy places to work. Too much noise can cause discomfort and create unsafe working conditions, and high noise levels may obscure communications between production and service staff. Ultimately, this process leads to guest dissatisfaction. Sound levels in all workplaces must conform to Occupational Safety and Health Administration (OSHA) standards. In those parts of the kitchen where the noise levels are consistently over 85 decibels, every effort should be made to dampen the sound levels. If that is not feasible, employees working in those areas should get baseline hearing tests, and OSHA standards should be followed.

Noise can be controlled through the careful selection and placement of noise-producing equipment as well as the installation of acoustic treatments. If a dish machine is placed, for operational reasons, near the entry of the kitchen, acoustic controls are needed to prevent the carryover of sound into the dining room. Meat grinders and potwashing stations are frequently removed from central production areas where servers interface with the cooks because they create excessive noise.

Acoustic ceiling tiles are commonly specified in kitchens. Sound-absorbing insulation in the wall between the dish area and the dining room may also be called for. To limit the sound of the dish machine in the rest of the kitchen, a wall separating the dish area from the remaining back of the house can be helpful.

SUMMARY

An operational and managerial understanding of all kitchen requirements is essential before a successful design can be implemented. It may be helpful for management to draw up a wish list of desired features and equipment. In any case, it behooves the kitchen designer to ask many specific questions regarding back-of-the house procedures. Will management serve frozen green beans, or will storage and processing space be needed for fresh beans? Will pies and cakes arrive from the local bakery; will frozen pies have to be baked; or will raw ingredients have to be stored in order to bake breads and pastries from scratch? The answers to these and countless other questions all markedly affect the space and equipment requirements of a restaurant kitchen.

CHAPTER 6

MINI-CASE SOLUTIONS

In previous chapters, we discussed the basic principles of front- and back-of-the-house design. Once these are understood, developing individual design schemes becomes possible. This chapter presents a selection of interesting solutions found in recently opened restaurants.

These case studies have been culled from hundreds of examples to demonstrate the diversity of problem solving involved with restaurant design. However, the design of a restaurant does not begin with the reinvention of the wheel. Good design follows basic principles, and good designers and restaurateurs learn from experience.

In each of the cases, challenges faced by the design team and an explanation of the solutions they created are presented. Each of the solutions was created for an individual foodservice establishment at a particular time and in a particular space. Rather than present just the trendiest restaurants or hottest concepts, which may not have withstood the rigors of the marketplace, we have opted to include a spectrum of both new and seasoned designs that illustrate a variety of architectural, decorative, and operational solutions. We also chose a variety of restaurant types and service styles, from a university cafeteria in New Hampshire to a hip Asian fusion urban outpost in Toronto.

While each case can be studied individually, it is also interesting to note that a number of challenges were common to several of the designs. As we looked at these dining establishments, we asked ourselves such questions as:

- Would an innovative order and delivery system featured in one quick-service mini-case work in other casual dining establishments?

- Is the chef's table concept seen in several of our featured restaurants a harbinger of future design elements, or are chef's tables remnants of the past?

- How will the attention to sustainable design that began before the economic meltdown of 2008 shape the direction of restaurant design in the decades to come?

The answers to these questions—and many more—are unknown. However, we believe that the solutions presented here can offer useful insights and ideas that can be applied to projects moving forward.

10 ARTS *RITZ-CARLTON HOTEL, PHILADELPHIA, PENNSYLVANIA*

DESIGNER: *EDG INTERIOR ARCHITECTURE + DESIGN (DESIGNER)*

ARCHITECT: *MCCALL DESIGN GROUP (ARCHITECT OF RECORD)*

OWNER: *GENCOM; THE ARDEN GROUP*

OPERATOR: *THE RITZ-CARLTON, PHILADELPHIA*

YEAR OPENED: *2008*

NUMBER OF SEATS: *DINING ROOM, 90; PRIVATE ROOMS, 40; BAR, 50*

FOH: *6,000 SQUARE FEET DINING; 3,000 SQUARE FEET LOUNGE*

BOH: *2,500 SQUARE FEET*

SERVICE STYLE: *FULL SERVICE*

MENU: *SEASONAL, ORGANIC, MODERN AMERICAN CUISINE SHOWCASING LOCAL PRODUCE; SEAFOOD FOCUS*

DESCRIPTION

The 100-year-old Girard Trust building includes the Ritz-Carlton Philadelphia, private residences, and 10 Arts, housed in a soaring rotunda that reaches 140 feet. The restaurant offers casual yet elegant fine dining and is targeted to both locals and hotel guests. The bar has seating for 50 people, and, when combined with the lounge, accounts for more than one-third of the front-of-the-house square footage. The dining room accommodates 90 patrons, and private dining rooms seat 40.

CONCEPT/CLIENTELE

The concept is to provide a comfortable environment in what could be seen as an intimidating space—the vaulted atrium of the former Girard Trust Company that was built more than 100 years ago. A sophisticated lounge area offers customers signature beverages and light fare. The restaurant has a full menu of innovative items created by the celebrated chef Eric Ripert,

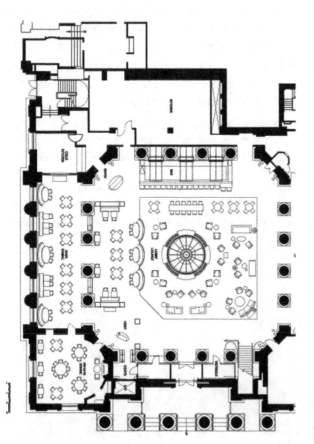

Figure 6.1.1
Floorplan.
(Design by EDG Interior Art & Design)

Figure 6.1.2
An imposing entry lounge area leads to the dining room at 10 Arts.
(Courtesy Eric Laignel)

such as an appetizer of mussels cooked with chorizo and white wine, and an entrée of rabbit paillard served with baby arugula and sweet pea salad with a whole-grain mustard sauce. 10 Arts pushes the envelope a bit more by using organic ingredients, including organic eggs, dairy, and toppings on the breakfast menu. Chef de cuisine Jennifer Carroll, a Philadelphia native and five-year veteran of Le Bernadin in New York City, adds a local flavor to the team and the cuisine.

Billed as an "upscale casual" restaurant with a twist on bistro fare, 10 Arts—pricey though it may be—appeals to a wide customer base. A key aspect of the design, according to the design team, was to create a "signature dining venue for one of the world's premier chefs in this prominent hotel." As was reported in the *Philadelphia Inquirer*, "This is 'Ripert in jeans,'

according to Chef Carroll. We want to be a casual neighborhood restaurant."

DESIGN DIRECTIVE

Described as "haute couture," 10 Arts incorporates fabrics and other design elements originally credited to the noted designer Charles Frederick Worth in the 1800s. A sense of vibrancy and energy and the idea of glowing portals and wine towers provide a modern jewel-like touch, according to the EDG design team. Glass panels shimmer as if they were chatoyant silk fabric. These panels, combined with other design elements—a central seating area, high-boy communal seating at a marble-topped table, and a jewel-toned wool rug—help to create an "impactful, signature moment" for hotel guests and others who are drawn to 10 Arts as a local destination, as stated by the EDG design team.

Figure 6.1.3
The 10 Arts dining room, framed by a glowing glass entry portal, signals serious but unstuffy dining.
(Courtesy Eric Laignel)

Tall, ebony-framed wine towers cosset wines in the center of the lounge/entry area. Surrounding this circular wine tower is a mix of comfortable lounge furniture that sits on a massive carpet that helps to dampen noise levels in the lounge that soars to the vaulted ceiling 140 feet above.

A challenging aspect to this project was the multiple layers of design team members. EDG's design team of seven local and corporate Ritz-Carlton representatives, and chef Ripert's team all influenced the design process. Obviously, such a diverse group needed to maintain careful communications to ensure that all parties were onboard with each design consideration. The EDG team took the lead in the development of feasibility studies that helped to guide the final direction and scope of the project as it went into the design phase.

EDG works with a common objective on all their projects to ensure that each design is "great in its own way." They rely on "design innovation and operational understanding," to help formulate the design direction. The EDG team went from design direction, to developing construction documents, to actual construction, in just 10 and a half months.

UNIQUE IDEA
In the words of the EDG team, "Freestanding glass portals illuminate different aspects of the experience. Their dichroism changes as guests approach or pass each portal." One portal marks the formal entrance to the restaurant. Two others, featuring grids of beveled mirror, conceal private wine lockers.

BEMBOS LARCO *LIMA, PERU*

DESIGNER: JOSE ORREGO HERRERA, CONSULTORA

OWNER/OPERATOR: CARLOS CAMINO AND MIRKO CERMAK

YEAR OPENED: 2007, BEMBOS LARCO; ALL OTHERS, 1991–2009

NUMBER OF SEATS: 91–234, DEPENDING ON LOCATION

BUILDING SIZE: 6,000–10,761 SQUARE FEET, DEPENDING ON LOCATION

SERVICE STYLES: QUICK SERVICE AND TAKEOUT

MENU: CLASSIC QUICK-SERVICE FOOD, MADE TO ORDER FROM FRESH INGREDIENTS

DESCRIPTION

Headquartered in Lima, Peru, Bembos is quite unlike most quick-service restaurant chains—particularly the fast-food transplants from North America. From the high-quality, fresh ingredients used in its menus, to its eye-catching exterior and interior design, Bembos stands out from the competition. This is a deliberate strategy to stand apart from the competitive brand-name fast feeders such as Kentucky Fried Chicken and Burger King.

CONCEPT/CLIENTELE

Based on the low average income of Peruvians—in 2007 it was reported at US$4,000 by the Peruvian Foreign Affairs Ministry—one would expect that there would be a limited demand for restaurants. Yet, when asked about how often

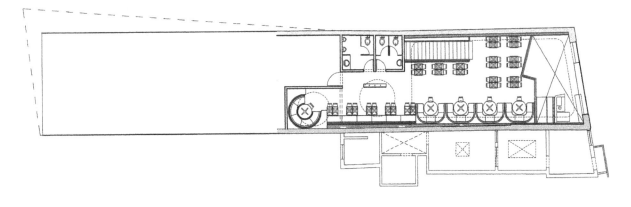

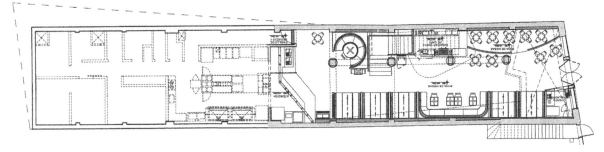

Figure 6.2.1
Floorplan.
(Jose Orrego Herrera)

Figure 6.2.2
Supersized graphic images in this second-floor dining area of Bembos create visual interest.
(*Jose Orrego Herrera*)

residents of Lima eat away from home, Bembos's architect Jose Orrego said residents of Lima go to midlevel restaurants two to three times per week and to more upscale restaurants four to five times per week. Herrera attributes this high level of activity, in part, to the fact that there are not a lot of entertainment options in Lima and eating away from home offers the best way to socialize and entertain friends.

DESIGN DIRECTIVE
When architect Herrera first worked on a Bembos design in the early 1990s, he was given a directive to create "American-look places." The goal was not to create a cookie-cutter prototype for all Bembos units, but rather to

"create unique places that have the essence of Bembos but at the same time be different and attractive," he says.

Herrera needed to consider three operational mandates. First, burgers and other menu items at Bembos are cooked to order and don't sit around in a warmer. Second, the time delay this causes for customers necessitated the inclusion of appealing visual images within the waiting areas as a distraction. The waiting time for customers also contributed to the need to include entertainment areas for children. The third mandate is that there are no cookie-cutter design prototypes for the various Bembos units: each has its own look, although certain commonalities exist.

Figure 6.2.3
Sleek surfaces and curved shapes add architectural flair to the quick-service environment and hint that the fast-food menu is above the ordinary.
(Jose Orrego Herrera)

DESIGN SOLUTIONS

Competing with deep-pocketed North American fast feeders was challenging due to high land values, particularly in Lima. So from the inception of the concept, the Bembos units were designed as multistory restaurants, with areas for children placed on the second level. While vertical travel between floors presents some challenges, it helps to minimize the real estate and construction costs. Further, it has helped Bembos owners to select sites that they would have been excluded from were they tied to single-floor layouts.

UNIQUE IDEA

Architect Herrera created larger-than-life super graphics and sculptures to lend visual appeal and to give each restaurant a unique feel. These include a floating soccer player who seems to have jumped 10 feet high to block a kicked ball, a nine-screen video wall, and a flying mountain biker cruising downhill from a second-floor dining area. Inventive exteriors have varying sized, portal-like windows that create an architectural profile resembling sliced Swiss cheese. Rounded and curved shapes throughout the interiors further distinguish the design. While each of the restaurants designed by Herrera is different, a common palette of colors and design elements link them together. Pictured here is the Bembos in Larco, Peru. It reflects the signature two-level architecture (seen in the floorplan) and the application of super graphics and larger-than-life cartoony characters.

BERKSHIRE DINING COMMONS
AMHERST, MASSACHUSETTS

DESIGNER: LIVERMORE EDWARDS & ASSOCIATES

OWNER/OPERATOR: UNIVERSITY OF MASSACHUSETTS

YEAR OPENED: AUGUST 2006

NUMBER OF SEATS: 800

FOH: 18,500 +/− SQUARE FEET

BOH: 7,500 +/− SQUARE FEET

SERVICE STYLES: COOK-TO-ORDER TAKE-AWAY STATIONS; SELF-SERVE

MENU: PIZZA, DELI, INTERNATIONAL, GRILL, VEGETARIAN, SALADS, STIR-FRY, BAKERY

DESCRIPTION
Berkshire Commons, located on the University of Massachusetts main campus in Amherst, Massachusetts, is situated in the most densely populated residence area on the campus.

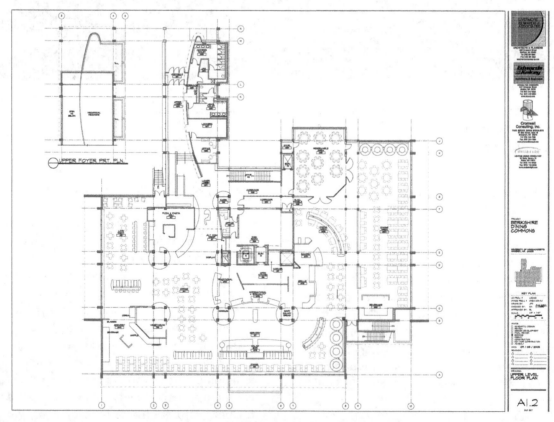

Figure 6.3.1

Floorplan 1.

(Design by Livermore Edwards & Associates)

It provides continuous service from 7:00 am to midnight every day of the school year. Despite the fact that this is a university cafeteria, the team from Livermore Edwards & Associates created a design that delivers a restaurant feel in the seating areas. The high-energy servery has 10 different food stations. The interior is brightened by an expanse of windows that offer views of the campus to the east and the Berkshire foothills to the west. The designers were involved with the project from the early programming and feasibility study throughout all the design and construction phases.

CONCEPT/CLIENTELE

Dining choices at Berkshire Commons include everything from a sushi bar, pasta station,

grab-and-go (prepackaged items for students on the run), and a dim sum brunch. Much of its energy and visual appeal comes from open cooking areas, where fresh food is displayed or prepared in front of waiting students. Opened in 2006, it is a renovation of a dining facility that previously occupied the space.

Customers are drawn from across campus. A core of the Dining & Auxiliary Services client base is freshman and sophomore students, all of whom must sign up for a meal plan.

DESIGN DIRECTIVE

The Livermore Edwards & Associates team was headed by principal in charge, architect Robert Livermore III, along with Brian Amaral, head

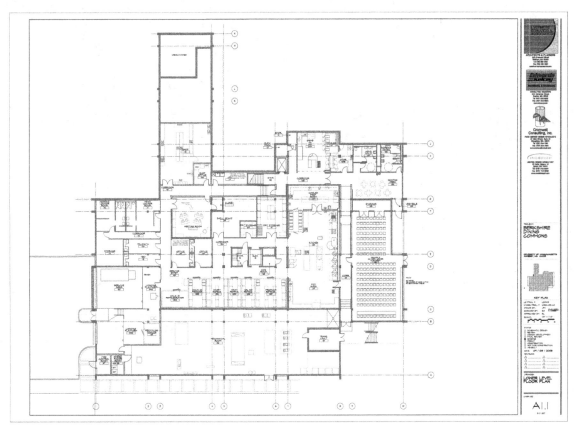

Figure 6.3.2
Floorplan 2.
(Design by Livermore Edwards & Associates)

designer, and Amy Van Lauwei, interiors and furnishings designer. The team worked with Kevin Cromwell, Cromwell Consulting, on the kitchen and display cooking areas. The designers also worked with a fully involved team from Dining & Auxiliary Services at the University, who early on provided "clear guidance as to how they wanted the renovated servery to run, what menu items they wanted to feature, and basic requirements for finishes," says the design team. In support of green initiatives across campus, ongoing roundtables were held with all team members to maximize the sustainable design features within this renovation.

Based on the concept of what Dining Director Ken Toong calls "on-demand" dining, Berkshire's 10 separate stations serve up an ever-changing fare of made-to-order foods that reflect a range of cuisines. The food stations were deigned based on student input. Students also helped to choose the names of the stations—among them, "Veggilicious" and "Taste of Italy."

DESIGN SOLUTIONS
Energy-efficient cooking and storage equipment were incorporated in the food stations wherever

Figure 6.3.3
This grill area in the Berkshire Commons cafeteria is separated from other stations to ensure that students disperse throughout the dining facility.
(Photo by Edward Jacoby)

economically feasible. Some examples of the equipment include Melink hood control systems in all stations but the grill. Low-flow water prerinse nozzles in automated warewashing equipment, water saver controls on the disposer (pot room), and lowest-water-use-per-rack dish machines are examples of the ways in which energy efficiency was integrated into the design.

One of the challenges was to create an upscale restaurant atmosphere with a timeless design that was also durable and easy to maintain. To achieve a noninstitutional aesthetic, the designers included a variety of seating options, ranging from highboy tables and chairs to curved booths. Lighting variety also contributes to a restaurant atmosphere. This includes pendant lighting, pedestal lighting, pendant spotlights, and recessed can lights in the ceiling. Light-emitting diode (LED) lighting on the canopies over the servery stations offers yet another lighting solution.

UNIQUE IDEA
Serving a maximum number of diners was made possible with a circular pedestrian flow that goes throughout the space. It is emphasized by a flooring pattern "pathway" and by the layout of the dining areas. The designers provided a number of stations scattered throughout the space, rather than a contained cafeteria, as can best be seen in the accompanying floorplan.

BLOWFISH RESTAURANT + SAKE BAR
TORONTO, ONTARIO, CANADA

DESIGNER: JOHNSON CHOU INC.

OWNER/OPERATOR: PRIVATE CONSORTIUM

YEAR OPENED: 2004

NUMBER OF SEATS: 63

TOTAL SQUARE FOOTAGE: 3,000 SQUARE FEET

SERVICE STYLES: FULL SERVICE; SUSHI BAR

MENU: ASIAN FUSION

DESCRIPTION

To say that Blowfish Restaurant + Sake Bar is a melding of yin and yang, a blend of Eastern and Western architecture, with fusion cuisine that melds divergent ingredients and cooking styles, is an understatement. Blowfish has a hip, stylish interior inside a structure with a classical exterior. "This methodology of synthesizing, contrasting, and juxtaposing distinct and seemingly opposite elements into a new hybrid aesthetic results in a space that is at once modern and classical, spare and opulent, precious and commonplace," says designer Johnson Chou.

CONCEPT/CLIENTELE

Ownership—an entrepreneurial group for whom Blowfish is the first restaurant venture—has the background that is key to a successful restaurant: finance, marketing, and culinary arts. Not surprisingly, the four partners were actively involved in the design process. They provided a project mandate, research of precedents for restaurant and club design, and design reviews during the planning and construction phases. They were instrumental in defining the brand or image of the restaurant.

Blowfish is a study in contrasts. The lighting in the dining area is punctuated by hanging chandeliers, while the lighting in the bar area relies primarily on can lights recessed into the

Figure 6.4.1
The façade of Blowfish with its classical styling contrasts significantly with the modern glass entry door, signaling the fusion experience to come.
(Photography by Volker Seding)

ceiling above. The seating in the dining area consists of 1950s-style padded chairs, while bar seating looks like upended padded boxes with no backs.

DESIGN DIRECTIVE
The paramount design directive was to create a brand that is a study in contrasts yet works together to create fusion between the French-inspired design elements and the Asian-oriented cuisine. To accomplish this goal, the designers defined four objectives:

1. To create a provocative brand for the restaurant that included a compelling formal and spatial image.

2. To create a unique dining experience amplified by an environment that paralleled and enhanced the experimental characteristics of Asian-fusion cuisine.

3. To create a hybrid, transformable space that would captivate both restaurant and club/lounge patrons, giving it an edge in the highly competitive "King West" restaurant and nightclub district of Toronto.

4. To restore, defer to, and enhance the existing masonry façades of the historic building with minimal, modern interventions.

DESIGN SOLUTIONS
The owners' mandate for a recognizable and memorable interior that reflected a French-Asian influence was achieved with contrasting elements strategically used throughout the space. Custom light fixtures, for example, are contemporary interpretations of the traditional French chandelier, with standard incandescent chandelier bulbs. They are in stark contrast to the sleek tables and clean-lined chairs—reminiscent of the modernist Danish aesthetic—and a metal mesh screen, akin to a Japanese shoji screen, that separates the dining room from the bar. In the words of the design team, "The image of the

Figure 6.4.2
A mesh divider between the dining room and bar limits visual and auditory distraction.
(Photography by Volker Seding)

space is architecturally interpreted as a dialectic of opposites, evocative of the fusion or synthesis of Eastern and Western architecture and their respective forms, materials, textures, and iconography." Guests enter into a spacious entryway from which they can get a snapshot of the inventive design and can view the bar, main dining area, and the sushi bar at the kitchen end of the restaurant.

UNIQUE IDEA
The unisex, four-compartment restroom incorporates a cantilevered hand-washing sink that divides the space in half and provides a must-see for Blowfish patrons. The stainless-steel sink unit is motion activated and can be accessed

from either side. A cantilevered mirror sits above each side of the sink. The design has lead to an unplanned outcome: guests of both genders chat and interact around the sink while waiting for a toilet stall to become available (see photo on page 131).

Figure 6.4.3
Classic-looking chandeliers dress the dining room with sparkle and relate to the classical architecture and French influence. They juxtapose with the clean recessed can lights used in the bar area.
(Photography by Volker Seding)

FOLIO ENOTECA & MICROWINERY
NAPA, CALIFORNIA

DESIGNER: CCS ARCHITECTURE

OWNER/OPERATOR: FOLIO WINE PARTNERS

YEAR OPENED: 2008

NUMBER OF SEATS: 13, ALL AT THE BAR

FOH: 600 SQUARE FEET

BOH: 200 SQUARE FEET

SERVICE STYLE: COUNTER DINING AND DRINKING

MENU: MARKET FORAGING CONCEPT

DESCRIPTION

Folio Enoteca & Microwinery makes a huge design statement in a mere 800-square-foot space. It is part of the Oxbow Public Market, which is located in the "up-and-coming" Oxbow district of Napa, California. This is more than just another wine shop in one of California's best-recognized wine regions. The café offers a menu driven by the seasonal products and artisan foods available from within the Oxbow Market. It is a functioning microwinery where customers can taste and purchase wine or enjoy a glass of wine with a snack at the 13-seat wine bar. Perhaps the most important role for Enoteca & Microwinery is that it markets the wines from Michael Mondavi's Folio Fine Wine Partners, a selection of fine wines from around the world.

CONCEPT/CLIENTELE

Folio Enoteca & Microwinery brings the wine country experience directly into Oxbow Public Market by placing an actual winery within the market walls. The inviting, remarkably efficient space—just 800 square feet—also contains a

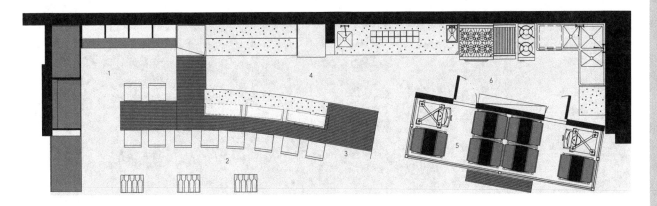

LEGEND
1. WINE RETAIL & MERCHANDISE AREA
2. ENOTECA BAR
3. POINT OF SALE
4. ENOTECA SERVICE
5. MICROWINERY
6. KITCHEN

Figure 6.5.1
Floorplan.

(Design by CCS Architecture)

wine bar, takeout offerings, and a cafe, with a menu driven by the seasonal produce and artisan foods available within the market. Producing 1,200 bottles per year—one white vintage and one red—the microwinery is the first of its kind in Northern California and, at the time of this writing in 2009, the smallest in the United States.

DESIGN DIRECTIVE

The Cass Calder Smith team was headed by Cass Calder Smith and project architect Dera Jill Lamontagne. Folio Enoteca & Microwinery's management team actively reviewed and approved the CCS designs. Suffice it to say, the Mondavi family have deep roots in the California wine industry, dating back to 1919, when Cesare Mondavi—grandfather of Michael Mondavi—moved his family to Lodi, California, where he launched the family's California wine-making empire. Folio Enoteca & Microwinery functions as a marketing spearhead for Folio Fine Wine Partners, a consortium that selects wines from leading vintners around the world. They

assist with marketing, public relations, and sales support.

DESIGN SOLUTIONS

Folio Enoteca & Microwinery incorporates 18 wine barrels used for aging wine in the microwinery. The microwinery itself is glassed in on three sides, with a controlled-temperature environment just as one would find in a conventional wine-aging cellar. The back wall of the microwinery hides the kitchen production area and includes two access doors to the "winery."

The Mondavi family firmly believes that wine education is part of their mission. To that end, two of the barrels in the microwinery are fitted with see-through ends that allow viewers to observe changes in the wine during the aging process. The surface of the wine bar itself is fashioned from clear, straight-grained wood staves that were formerly part of aging tanks at the Folio winery in Carneros, California. The steel framework that defines the microwinery is cantilevered close to

Figure 6.5.2
The compact Folio Enoteca & Microwinery combines self-service tasting and winemaking in one facility.
(Matthew Millman)

Figure 6.5.3
This winemaking area includes fermentation and aging.
(Matthew Millman)

the ceiling over much of the Enoteca bar. This framework holds wood cases in which wine bottles from the Folio collection are displayed. The wine display cabinetry on the back wall of the Enoteca is fashioned from highest-grade Finply plywood. Lead edges of the Finply are trimmed with walnut wood strips. The rich, burnt-orange hues of the stool tops are matched to the color of overhead cabinetry on the back wall of the wine retail area.

UNIQUE IDEA

Folio Enoteca & Microwinery is truly a "message in a bottle." The compact space incorporates many functions—including the microwinery—in a mere 800 square feet. It is a full extension of the Folio Fine Wine Partners collection and its mission is to educate consumers about wine in a fun way.

HI-LIFE EAST *NEW YORK, NEW YORK*

DESIGNERS: WARREN ASHWORTH, ARCHITECT; EARL GEER, DESIGNER

OWNER/OPERATOR: EARL GEER

YEAR OPENED: 2007

NUMBER OF SEATS: 65, DINING ROOM; 20, ENCLOSED SIDEWALK CAFÉ; 35–45, BAR/ LOUNGE

FOH: 1,777 SQUARE FEET

BOH: 378 SQUARE FEET, PLUS 1,400-SQUARE-FOOT BASEMENT

SERVICE STYLE: FULL SERVICE

MENU: CLASSIC AMERICAN GRILLED ITEMS, SUSHI, AND PASTAS

DESCRIPTION

Hi-Life Restaurant & Lounge is a high-energy neighborhood gathering place on the Upper East Side of New York City. It is the sister location to the popular Hi-Life Bar & Grill across Central Park on the Upper West Side of the city. The eclectic interiors decorated with cool vintage items (in the lounge, a retro aquarium does double-duty as the hostess's podium) complement a large, varied menu with more than 100 items. Choices range from traditional starters, such as crab cakes, to spaghetti primavera, to a full range of sushi and

Figure 6.6.1
The internal and external lighting is a draw to customers as they pass by High-Life East.
(Photographs: Bjorg Magnea - www.bjorgmagnea.com)

Figure 6.6.2
While newly designed, the restaurant's eclectic interior incorporates elements from the original High-Life East designed by David Rockwell.
(Photographs: Bjorg Magnea - www.bjorgmagnea.com)

sashimi dishes. Big-band music plays throughout the spaces, reinforcing the feeling of Swing Town in the 1950s.

CONCEPT/CLIENTELE
Owner Earl Geer played a significant role in the design. There had been an earlier and very successful version of this restaurant/lounge—designed by the well-known architect David Rockwell—located in a nearby Upper East Side building that was demolished after the restaurant closed. But before the wrecking ball, Geer salvaged the bar, back bar, signage, paintings, and light fixtures, keeping them in storage for six years while he searched for a new site. His goal was to reinstate the High-Life brand in the new

location. What emerged, according to architect Warren Ashworth, is "a fascinating assembly of objects in a space completely different than their original, and much smaller." While the entire space was designed to attract a young, hip neighborhood clientele, the bar and lounge area were intended to attract a strong bar crowd independent of the restaurant.

DESIGN DIRECTIVE
In this project, the architect did not have free rein to come up with original interior design solutions—the owner knew exactly what he wanted and the design was a true collaboration. However, Geer's directive to reuse elements from his previous restaurant and evoke the buzz of a

youthful neighborhood gathering place with a vintage '50s vibe was compatible with Ashworth's philosophy that comfort, not the architect's ego, is the key to successful restaurant design. In addition, "good design has integrity," says Ashworth. "This translates to one thing: making a space that gives the owner the kind of restaurant they ask for."

DESIGN SOLUTIONS

Because Ashworth had to reinstall salvaged elements into an entirely different and significantly smaller spatial plan, "there were distinct jigsaw puzzle aspects to the project." He made significant modifications to the façade and to the sidewalk café enclosure. However, in other areas, he conserved the useful "bones" and

refurbished and reapplied the elements that Geer specified. This end result "evokes the glamour and the modern verve of post-WWII New York," says Ashworth. "Working closely with the owner and originator of its concept, we designed a space that maximized a modest space and an invaluable existing sidewalk café."

UNIQUE IDEA

Perhaps the most unique aspect of this project comes from Ashworth's uncommon philosophy that "it is the responsibility of restaurant designers to build the owner's reputation, not their own." He worked to ensure that Geer "had room for his creative imagination to soar," while at the same time keeping him from getting so carried away that his ideas became impractical.

HOLLOWAY COMMONS *UNIVERSITY OF NEW HAMPSHIRE DURHAM, NEW HAMPSHIRE*

DESIGNER: LIVERMORE, EDWARDS & ASSOCIATES

OWNER/OPERATOR: UNIVERSITY OF NEW HAMPSHIRE

YEAR OPENED: 2001

NUMBER OF SEATS: 900, DINING; 300, BANQUET; 75, CAFÉ AND LOUNGE

FOH: 11,500 +/− SQUARE FEET (DINING AREAS ONLY)

BOH: 12,000 +/− SQUARE FEET (KITCHEN AND SERVICE AREAS ONLY)

TOTAL BUILDING SQUARE FOOTAGE: 68,000 SQUARE FEET

SERVICE STYLES: COOK-TO-ORDER, TAKE-AWAY STATIONS, SELF-SERVE

MENU: PIZZA/PASTA, COMFORT FOODS, SALADS, GRILL, DELI, VEGAN STATION, DESSERTS, STIR-FRY

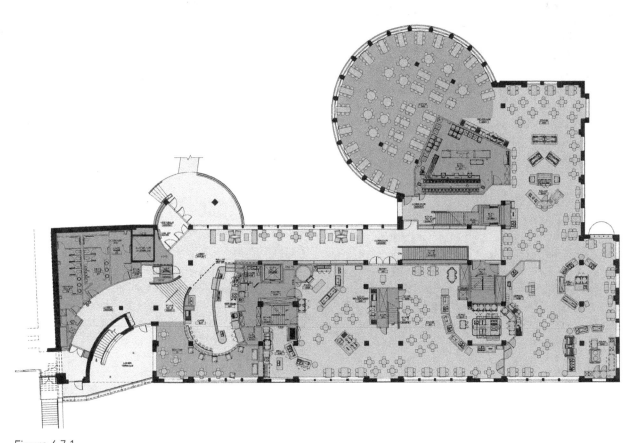

Figure 6.7.1
Floorplan.
(Design by Livermore, Edwards & Associates)

Figure 6.7.2
The oversized windows in the main dining area of Holloway create visual appeal to students and other passersby.
(Photos by Peter Vanderwarker Photographs)

DESCRIPTION

Holloway Commons on the University of New Hampshire campus was, when it opened in 2001, the first new dining facility added to the campus in more than 20 years. At the heart of Holloway is a multistation student cafeteria. The kitchen also prepares food for banquets of up to 300 and provides logistic support to the cash operation called Panache.

CONCEPT/CLIENTELE

The three-level Holloway dining facility is located within Holloway Commons at UNH, which was conceived as a multipurpose building intended to serve all members of the university community. Assistant Vice President for Business Affairs David

May, who was the director of dining when the planning process began, wanted the facility to connect conveniently to another UNH facility called the MUB (Memorial Union Building), which has a fast-food court and serves as the UNH Student Union. The banquet area at Holloway, with seating for 300 guests, became the largest banquet/meeting space run by UNH dining services.

The architectural firm Livermore, Edwards & Associates, which has completed several dozen university dining projects, was responsible for both architecture and interior design. The design team of Robert Livermore III, AIA; Brian Amaral, and Amy Van Lauwe worked with UNH from the initial programming stage through the final completion of the building. During the schematic and design development stages, the design team met with UNH managers and other representatives from across campus to discuss design ideas and solutions.

DESIGN DIRECTIVE

"The design team were given the directive to maximize seating, spread the dining experience throughout the building, and design so as much of the food production as possible would be completed within view of the customers," says David May. The Holloway Commons cafeteria (Ho Co as the students call it) takes up the entire third-floor footprint of the building when one adds the cash operation called Panache. The cafeteria floorplan, with many different food stations, helps to minimize the length of the waiting line at any station to fewer than 10 customers at any point in time. During any given meal period, Holloway has at least 14 food stations in operation, where customers help themselves to everything from beverages to full entrées, or wait briefly for made-to-order grill or stir-fry dishes.

Part of the design directive was to create a cafeteria that would operate when all of the other dining facilities on campus were closed during the summer months, thus leaving Holloway Commons as the one campus dining facility. This move was intended to save the operating costs of running several foodservice operations, and it works because Holloway is situated in the center of the campus. Management also wanted a design that allowed some stations to be closed during extremely low traffic days, further decreasing labor costs.

DESIGN SOLUTIONS

Multiple food and beverage stations ensure that long lines of customers are minimized, and the design of each station contributes to an efficient operation. For example, the stir-fry station—one of the most popular—incorporates a six-foot-long griddle, flanked by a smaller griddle used exclusively for vegetarian preparations, where

Figure 6.7.3
The Euro station is broken into three components, which help to disperse students at this station.
(Photos by Peter Vanderwarker Photographs)

stir-fry cooks combine the vegetables portioned into bowls by students with their choice of protein. While the cook-to-order nature of this station requires the most labor per meal, it works smoothly and the lines usually remain a reasonable length.

A variety of seating appeals to the diverse customer base. Highboy deuces were placed close to food stations yet do not interfere with circulation patterns. The largest dining area incorporates long, standard-height tables in an open, airy space that has floor-to-ceiling windows and a vaulted ceiling. This is the most popular area for students to congregate in large groups, and it is also the loudest. A quieter mezzanine dining area opens to views of the servery below, and also offers reserved seating nooks for group meetings.

Two aspects of the project—the need to join Holloway with the MUB (Memorial Union Building), and the challenges of a steep slope between the buildings—led to an innovative architectural solution. Diners can enter the cafeteria through an internal corridor between the MUB and Holloway that passes through a student mail area, or via an external entrance located down a sloping half-story walkway from the main entrance of the MUB.

UNIQUE IDEA

Nearly every aspect of Holloway Commons was designed with flexibility in mind. Most of the servery equipment is mobile, for example. This allows management the capacity to tweak the design to optimize flow and to reconfigure the space to meet the ever-changing demands of their customers. The six-inch clearance under nearly every piece of servery equipment also facilitates cleaning.

LANDMARK GRILL + LOUNGE *CHICAGO, ILLINOIS*

DESIGNERS: WARREN ASHWORTH, ARCHITECT; CHRISTINA ZIEGLER, DESIGNER

OWNER/OPERATOR: ROB KATZ AND KEVIN BOEHM

YEAR OPENED: 2005

NUMBER OF SEATS: 286 TOTAL; 18, THE CATWALK; 40, BLUE ROOM; 60, MAIN DINING ROOM; 55–60, PRIVATE DINING ROOM; 30–35, VELVET LOUNGE; 25, BLUE BAR, 25; UP TO 125, MAIN BAR

FOH: 11,000 SQUARE FEET

BOH: 3,500 SQUARE FEET

SERVICE STYLE: FULL SERVICE

MENU: QUALITY AMERICAN WITH FRENCH AND ITALIAN INFLUENCES, FRESH WOOD-FIRED PIZZA

DESCRIPTION

From its inception, the Landmark Grill + Lounge was recognized not only for its innovative menu but also for its innovative design. Restaurant reviews called it a "see and be seen hit in the making," with a design that "looks great with food." At Landmark, the food and the design complement each other. Appetizers include choices such as bison carpaccio or sweet corn risotto; entrees span the culinary palate with such items as tournedos of beef with sherry glaze and bone marrow hollandaise and vegetarian

offerings like fried green tomatoes, wood roasted eggplant, jersey milk ricotta, and pickled torpedo onions. The partners are not newcomers to the restaurant business in Chicago, having collaborated on the wildly successful Boka, a fine-dining restaurant located just a few blocks north.

CONCEPT/CLIENTELE

The restaurant is situated within a building that was formerly a theatrical rehearsal space. It is directly across the street from the Steppenwolf performance theatre that was founded in 1974 by Gary Sinise and his two partners. After opening in 2005, Landmark quickly gained a reputation as a hip restaurant and club destination.

Figure 6.8.1
As an homage to the noted Chicago architect Louis Sullivan, the designers incorporated an overscaled arch on the exterior of the restaurant.
(Peter Wynn Thompson Photography)

Figure 6.8.2
A detail of the catwalk balcony in Landmark, which took advantage of what might have been wasted space to create a sexy lounge for people-watching.
(Peter Wynn Thompson Photography)

This was the third restaurant that architect Warren Ashworth (joined by designer Christina Ziegler) created for owners Rob Katz and Kevin Boehm. The owners presented their general concept for the space and the Ashworth design team worked unimpeded from there. It attracts a hip urban crowd with three bars, four dining areas, a catwalk lounge, a private dining room, and a sumptuously decorated VIP room.

DESIGN DIRECTIVE
Since Ashworth and the owners had previously worked together, a level of trust was already established, and the directive to the design team was straightforward: "They told us their general outline for the space and the menu," Ashworth says. A main component of the design directive was to create a cozy and welcoming feeling within the massive space while also conveying drama and excitement.

Ninety-five percent of Ashworth's design plan was approved and implemented. The architect was convinced that Landmark had the potential to be a big hit: he exchanged some of his services for an equity share in the restaurant.

DESIGN SOLUTIONS
As an homage to the noted Chicago architect Louis Sullivan, the designers incorporated an overscaled arch on the exterior of the restaurant. A relief of the world incorporated in the arch is intended to welcome customers. Inside, to help create a more intimate feeling in the bar area and main dining room, the designers added a "catwalk" lounge. The L-shaped catwalk mitigates the effect of the overly high ceilings over the bar; provides additional seating, with an ideal vantage for people watching below; and also offers an additional flow pattern from the entryway to the rear of the main dining area. This sexy catwalk lounge quickly became the talk of the town and maximized return on what could have been wasted space.

UNIQUE IDEA
Two unique ideas were incorporated into the design of Landmark: the use of the color blue in the Blue Bar and Blue Dining Room, and the installation of a pizza-finishing line in the front-of-the-house.

Figure 6.8.3
The pizza bar in the rear of Landmark is lit by a mix of direct and indirect fixtures that create a warm glow.
(Peter Wynn Thompson Photography)

Common wisdom says that blue—rarely the color of food—is not especially conducive to intimate dining. Designer Christina Ziegler knew she could prove this to be erroneous, and so she does. Landmark's Blue Dining Room, a symphony of blue with cream-colored accents, is a comfortable, soothing enclave for fine dining. What first catches the eye in the Blue Bar is a large painting (owned by Ashworth) of a sleeping nude all in varying hues of blue.

The second idea came about in response to the limitations of the existing, cramped basement kitchen, which was not large enough to accommodate the pizza-making operation. Since there was no option to enlarge the back-of-the-house, the designers integrated a pizza-making finishing line into the main bar area. Bringing food production out front adds energy and excitement to the bar area, while also helping to solve the spatial limitations in the kitchen.

MERCAT A LA PLANXA CHICAGO, ILLINOIS

DESIGNER: D-ASH DESIGN INC.

BRANDING AGENCY: KORN DESIGN

OWNER/OPERATOR: SAGE RESTAURANT GROUP

YEAR OPENED: 2008

NUMBER OF SEATS: 209 TOTAL; 159, DINING ROOM; 18, PRIVATE ROOMS; 32, BAR

SERVICE STYLES: FULL SERVICE, BAR SERVICE

MENU: BREAKFAST, LUNCH, AND DINNER ALL INSPIRED BY SPAIN'S CATALONIA CUISINE INCLUDING TAPAS, CURED MEATS, AND CHEESES

DESCRIPTION

Mercat a la Planxa ("on the grill") has received stellar ratings for its food, service, and design since opening in 2008. The restaurant is housed within the renovated Blackstone Hotel—which

Figure 6.9.1
The cavernous quality of Mercat a la Planxa's dining room, with its soaring ceiling and huge windows, is mitigated by tiered seating and curved enclosures.
(Photos of Mercat by Frank Oudeman)

Figure 6.9.2
At the bar, hexagonal latticework—a signature design element throughout the restaurant—ties together the vertical spaces.
(Photos of Mercat by Frank Oudeman)

first opened its doors in 1910—on the south side of Chicago just west of Grant Park and Soldier Field. The hotel is a classic example of French Beaux-Arts architecture. Phrases such as "great atmosphere all around" and "amazing food, spectacular space," pretty much sum up the consensus of reviewer comments. While the restaurant is housed within the structure of a hotel, one reviewer commented that Mercat a la Planxa has such a strong identity that it feels like a restaurant with an attached hotel. Celebrity chef Jose Garces is responsible for the restaurant's Catalan cuisine. Owner and operator

Sage Restaurant Group and the d-ash design team worked closely together on the design concept.

CONCEPT/CLIENTELE

Sage Restaurant Group, owned by Sage Hospitality Resources in Denver, Colorado, was also the project developer. The total project costs for the hotel and restaurant was an estimated $119 million, including $18 million in tax increment financing (used by municipalities to fund projects that will pay for themselves with

Figure 6.9.3
Bare-bulb lighting that hangs from the high ceiling adds sparkle and intimacy, and helps to define the space that leads to the lounge below.
(Photos of Mercat by Frank Oudeman)

increased sales and other taxes) from the city of Chicago, and $15 million in historic tax credits.

Sage Restaurant Group's CEO Peter Karpinski has said that he loves the food, the architecture, and the people of Spain—and this was the driving force behind Mercat's design. The designers maintain a philosophy that it is "more important to be able to translate the vision of the team rather than dictate some stringent design dogma," notes David Ashen of d-ash design. His colorful, see-and-be-seen design for Mercat, with such elements as Spanish tiles around the open kitchen and paintings of a bustling Spanish market, was inspired by a Catalan-influenced aesthetic that evokes the vibrant culture of Spain without resorting to clichés.

DESIGN DIRECTIVE

In addition to creating the feeling of a modern Spanish restaurant that reflected the Catalan menu, the design team also took cues from the historic Beaux-Arts architecture of the Blackstone Hotel, replete with soaring ceilings and expansive windows. The collaboration between the owner (Sage Restaurant Group), the branding agency (Korn Design), and d-ash design "was extraordinary," says David Ashen, "and the restaurant and its success are a direct result of this."

DESIGN SOLUTIONS

The designers were faced with an awkward layout that required guests to enter the restaurant on a cavelike lower floor before traveling up a level to reach a large, open space. Working within the constraints of the building's landmark status, they nevertheless created an asset out of a liability by crafting a multitiered environment with a clear sense of entry, anticipation, and arrival. Now, patrons enter into an intimate bar that is punctuated by a dramatic circular stairway rising to the restaurant above. The stairway is a visual focal point and also adds a sense of anticipation about reaching the dramatic dining room above.

The cavernous quality of the dining room, with its high ceilings and huge windows, is mitigated by tiered seating that allows for a clear view of other tables and outdoor vistas. Multiple Edison bulbs that hang at varying levels from the high ceiling retain drama and sparkle and also keep the space from feeling barnlike.

UNIQUE IDEA

Perhaps the most unique design element is the honeycombed latticework detailing that was used in various locations of the bar and dining room. The hexagonal shape of the latticework, says Ashen, is a symbolic geometry that can also be found in the tiles designed by Catalan Modernisme leader Antonio Gaudi (1852–1926). It is a subtle, almost subliminal theme reference that also makes a strong decorative statement, defines spatial areas, and helps to unify Mercat's multiple levels.

METRO 9 STEAK HOUSE *FRAMINGHAM,* *MASSACHUSETTS*

DESIGNER: JUDD BROWN DESIGNS, INC.

OWNER/OPERATOR: PETER SARMANIAN

YEAR OPENED: 2007

NUMBER OF SEATS: 225 (DINING ROOM)

FOH: 5,200 SQUARE FEET

BOH: 1,800 SQUARE FEET

SERVICE STYLE: FULL SERVICE

MENU: STEAKHOUSE

DESCRIPTION

Metro 9 is a renovation of an existing Irish pub that was transformed into a modestly priced steakhouse. Its classic yet modern design is targeted to a business clientele and a family clientele. The design team was ever mindful that the owner of Metro 9 intended to level the building in just eight short years after opening, but wanted a concept that could live on in other locations. This project was completed within the specified budget with a construction time of less than nine weeks. Metro 9 is incorporated within a larger structure, located in the front quadrant of a multitenant block consisting mainly of medical offices and restaurants.

CONCEPT/CLIENTELE

The multi-unit owner had a definite direction in mind for seating layouts, color, and other interior design elements. Although the property was to be torn down in eight years, the owner felt that the elements of a successful venue could be transferable to other locations.

DESIGN DIRECTIVE

The owner approached the JBD Design team of Judd Brown, ASID, president, design director, Li Qi, senior designer; Manny Sousa, designer, and Jill Saccoccia, designer, with the request to transform the existing pub into a contemporary steakhouse. Because the space was very dated and because the life span of the restaurant was limited, budget played a key role in the renovation. Working with a classic format of rich colors and original artwork, the design team used custom elements to update the atmosphere of a classic steakhouse for a younger generation.

DESIGN SOLUTIONS

The team followed an accelerated design/build process, working with a preselected local contractor with whom they had collaborated on previous projects. This process helped to keep construction costs down and to speed the opening of the restaurant.

As complete demolition was not possible, it was necessary for the design team to work with the existing shell, replace all furniture and fixtures throughout, make modifications to the existing pub-style bar, and turn the intimate pub-style dining spaces into an open dining venue.

The JBD team requested that the interiors not conform to old-fashioned steakhouse design, and they avoided the heavy woodwork and moldings typically found in vintage steakhouses. Items such as decorative wrought iron–style grilles and fieldstone fireplaces in the lounge and dining areas convey the comfort of a classic steakhouse without the clichés, as do the chocolate-colored walls and platinum gray moldings that meet a merlot-colored ceiling.

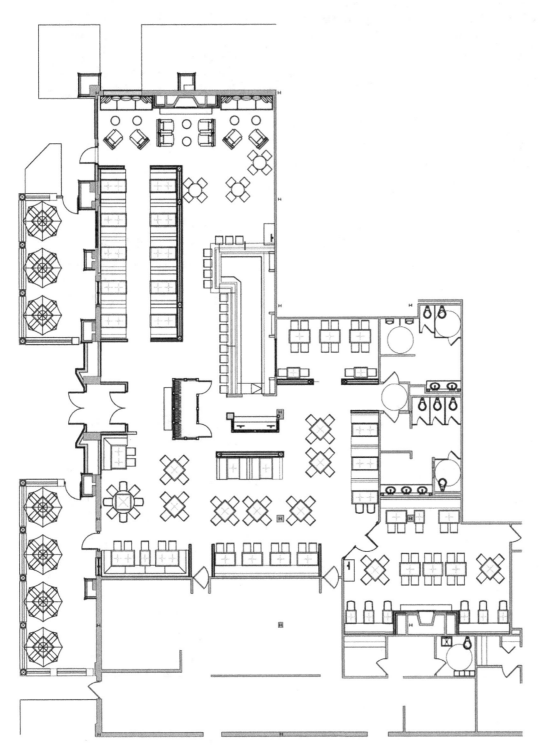

Figure 6.10.1
Floorplan.
(Design by Judd Brown Designs, Inc.)

Figure 6.10.2
The fieldstone fireplace, overscaled leather chairs, and beamed ceiling in Metro 9's lounge bespeak a classic steak-house setting.
(Photography by Warren Jagger Photography, Inc.)

Figure 6.10.3
Throughout the restaurant, the designers transformed a low, sheetrock ceiling with a custom treatment that helps to define spaces and mute noise.
(Photography by Warren Jagger Photography, Inc.)

Figure 6.10.4
The use of wood and leather continues the steakhouse reference into the bar, and the walls were opened up so patrons could view the dining space.
(Photography by Warren Jagger Photography, Inc.)

A space that originally consisted of several intimate dining areas was transformed into two: the main dining room and the bar. In the dining room, copper light fixtures add warmth, there is a mixture of booths and tables, and original artwork includes black-and-white views of the nine cities in the United States targeted for future restaurants—thus, the "Metro 9" name. The new bar, fronted with glass block and high-gloss quartz stone, serves food as well as drinks. Existing cabinetry above the bar was removed, and the walls were opened up so patrons could view the dining space. Fireside furniture in the lounge includes overscaled leather chairs that lend the feel of a living room for both cocktails and dining. The color palette chosen for the space was also not typical of conventional steakhouses.

UNIQUE IDEA

One of the greatest challenges posed by the existing building shell was the eight-foot ceiling, which could not be changed because the space is located in a retail center. (Also, the existing heating, ventilating, and air conditioning [HVAC] and heating systems could not be altered.) In addition to the kinesthetic disadvantage of its low height, the sheetrock ceiling caused sound to reverberate. With a custom treatment of 6-by-12-foot frames, the designers transformed the ceiling into a visual focal point that helps to mute noise rather than amplify it.

PARK AVENUE *NEW YORK, NEW YORK*

DESIGNER: *AvroKO*

OWNER/OPERATOR: *FOURTH WALL RESTAURANT GROUP*

YEAR OPENED: *2007*

NUMBER OF SEATS: *100, DINING ROOM; 171, PRIVATE ROOMS (TOGETHER); 10, BAR*

FOH: *4,500 SQUARE FEET*

BOH: *5,500 SQUARE FEET*

SERVICE STYLE: *FULL SERVICE*

DESCRIPTION

Park Avenue, an ever-changing phoenix that took shape in the shell of the former Park Avenue Café, gives birth with a fresh design as the seasons change. The Park Avenue Café was a long-standing pillar of the Upper East Side dining scene in Manhattan in serious need of revamping. The design team from AvroKO took on the challenge by creating a space that morphs its interior—including lighting, seat cushions, flooring, and ceiling—and its menu four times a year: spring, summer, fall, and winter.

Figure 6.11.1
The Park Avenue bar area, with a view to the summer dining room. The bar serves food as well as drink, and house wines are displayed as part of the merchandising efforts.
(Michael Weber Photography)

▲ Figure 6.11.2
A vine-wrapped statue suggestive of an English garden run amok is incorporated in the spring design.
(Michael Weber Photography)

▶ Figure 6.11.3
Elongated birch branches in this winter setting evoke the cool beauty of the season.
(Michael Weber Photography)

CONCEPT/CLIENTELE

The owners knew that more than seasonal menu changes were needed to ensure year-round popularity of the restaurant. They further identified a goal of creating a destination restaurant, one that would attract not only local patrons from the well-heeled neighborhood, but also a younger downtown crowd.

The resulting concept, with interiors and menu items that change seasonally, "entices diners to come back each season to experience a new taste as well as a new environment," says the AvroKO design team. The cuisine, featuring fresh, locally raised ingredients and proteins, also reflects the popular "food climate" of the day.

The key to the success of this concept was to minimize the time needed for changeover from one season to the next. In the words of the AvroKO team: "Like a theatrical show, a set change must be of both speed and quality,

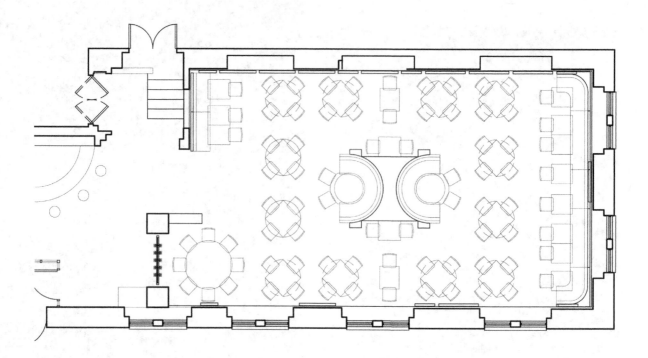

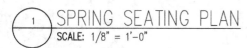

SPRING SEATING PLAN
SCALE: 1/8" = 1'-0"

Figure 6.11.4
Floorplan spring.
(Copyright: AvroKO 2008)

and Park Avenue's design needed to be both polished and malleable."

In addition, each season's shift needed to remain cohesive with the overall look and feel so that it felt comfortable, yet at the same time new, to the restaurant's regular patrons.

DESIGN DIRECTIVE

The design team had to contend with several givens of the restaurant footprint—existing ceiling, existing circulation patterns (for the most part), and existing placement of the bar and the washrooms. So, the design directive came down to reinventing the same dining space four times per year, with reusable "set" designs that

would need only subtle tweaking as time went by. The AvroKO team knew they wanted more than cliché-ridden design elements. Their design mantra became one of "discovery," and they loosely hung their changing "quadripartite" designs using the "physical and sensorial suggestions of 'Captain James Cook's' voyages to four separate regions." They interpreted the regions as follows:

- Summer—Galapagos Islands, with reclaimed whitewashed wood and 40 hand-cast tortoise shells.

- Autumn—Pacific Northwest, with warm woods and knotted rope.

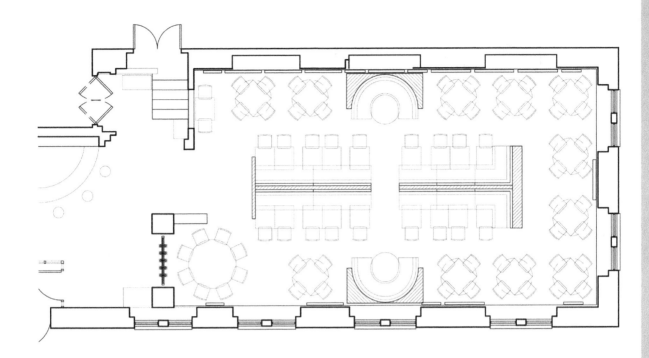

SUMMER SEATING PLAN
SCALE: 1/8" = 1'-0"

Figure 6.11.5
Floorplan summer.
(Copyright: AvroKO 2008)

- Winter—Antarctica, with elongated birch branches, raw leather, and vintage British Navy buttons.

- Spring—Wild New Zealand with elements drawn from an English Garden.

DESIGN SOLUTIONS

The AvroKO team stresses that when a restaurant design needs to periodically change, "more time planning equals less time doing." Flexibility was the key to keeping operational downtime to a minimum.

To achieve a cohesive identity, the designers also worked on the restaurant's graphic and branding materials. For each season, they designed the labels for house wines, the menus, and the marketing collateral in a way that fused all of the elements together across the four seasonal designs.

The target customer was defined as one who appreciates the confluence of great food and design. In the New York restaurant market, where foodies abound and restaurants are too numerous to count, capturing people's attention was part of the challenge. The seasonally changing design created a unique marketing niche for Park Avenue, one that had patrons anticipating new visits as the seasons changed.

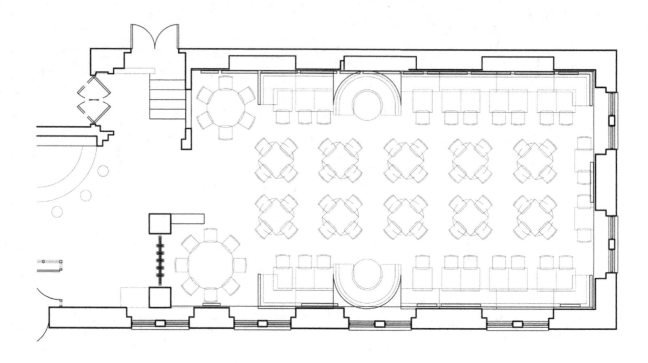

WINTER SEATING PLAN
SCALE: 1/8" = 1'-0"

Figure 6.11.6
Floorplan winter.
(Copyright: AvroKO 2008)

UNIQUE IDEA

It's not always what you see that makes a design unique. While the manifestation of a seasonally changing design at Park Avenue is the obvious creative idea, it would not be possible without an innovative structural set that makes it possible for the restaurant to quickly change its identity. It took the AvroKO team six months of off-site construction to build an elaborate steel wall frame system with custom tracks and separate panels that enable the changeover crew to facilitate a complete makeover in little more than a day. Patrons who enjoy the last lunch of summer on one day can visit again the next night for the first dinner of autumn—with every menu item and every design element changed, from the wall treatments to the seating upholstery to the tabletop linens to the uniforms.

PINK PEPPER *HOLLYWOOD, CALIFORNIA*

DESIGNER: ANTHONY ECKELBERRY

OWNER/OPERATOR: TONY BOON

YEAR OPENED: 2005

NUMBER OF SEATS: 44

FOH: 1,073 SQUARE FEET

BOH: 921 SQUARE FEET

SERVICE STYLE: FULL SERVICE

MENU: THAI CUISINE

DESCRIPTION

At Pink Pepper, design elements meld together as intricately as the Thai cuisine prepared in the kitchen. With a reputation for eye-popping and palate-popping cuisine, Pink Pepper first opened in 1989. Seen here is the substantial redesign in 2005 by Anthony Eckelberry that updates the decor while still reflecting the colorful Thai theme. The restaurant is located on the ground floor of a parking garage.

CONCEPT/CLIENTELE

There is nothing subtle about the decor elements in Pink Pepper. From the carved wooden entry doors commissioned by artisans in Thailand to the intricately designed sculpture of Buddha in the dining room, a distinctive Thai atmosphere attracts a loyal local clientele to this well-known eatery. Wall hangings, folded screens, and an overall rose-hued ambience further promote the thematic design.

DESIGN DIRECTIVE

Within Pink Pepper's interior, theme elements meet modern design, creating the one-of-a-kind contemporary café feel requested by the owner. For example, the entry doors are fashioned from teak wood and hand carved with a traditional Thai motif, but they are set in a contemporary concrete-and-glass wall. Continuing the juxtaposition of Thai-inspired decor with contemporary accents, contemporary Thai paintings contrast with the stainless-steel ducting that weaves its way across the ceiling.

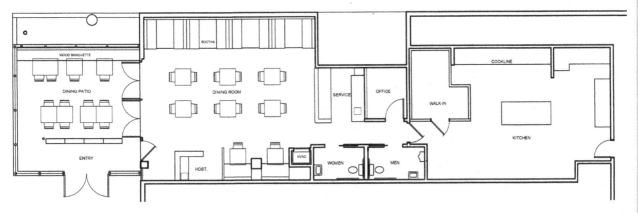

Figure 6.12.1
Floorplan.
(Design by Anthony Eckelberry)

DESIGN SOLUTIONS

As noted earlier, Pink Pepper is located on the ground floor of a parking garage. Faced with a low, suspended ceiling that hid all of the mechanicals above, the designers opened up the room by removing the suspended ceiling. In the redesigned space, an intricate web of ducts for heating, cooling, kitchen exhaust, and makeup air crisscross the ceiling. Designer Eckelberry, who grew up in France, believes that

renovations should reuse the elements of an existing structure in an artistic way, and that is what he did by keeping the HVAC exposed. The ceiling was painted an off-white hue to give it a more finished look. While Pink Pepper's updated decor reflects a fresh new look, "the successive alterations to a structure give a character that is unique to that location and help carry the memory of the place for people who had been there before," says Eckelberry.

Figure 6.12.2
Thai theme elements meet modern design at Pink Pepper. In the dining room, contemporary Thai paintings contrast with the exposed stainless-steel ducting that weaves its way across the ceiling.
(Photography by Anthony Eckelberry)

Figure 6.12.3
Dining room detail: Thai artwork and an intricately carved statue of Buddha express the restaurant's theme.
(Photography by Anthony Eckelberry)

UNIQUE IDEA

The greatest constraint of this design was the cold industrial feel of the parking garage envelope. The designers offset the cold feeling by painting the concrete ceiling and floor, specifying warm teak tables and chairs, and covering booths with an upholstery of traditional Thai patterns. To further warm the space, the bottom half of the plaster walls were covered with a teak wainscoting, with a hand-finished, Venetian mustard-colored paint applied above. These design elements, along with the ceiling treatment with its intricate web of exposed ductwork described earlier, turned what was a stark section of a parking garage into an inviting and pleasing atmosphere for guests.

PUBLIC/THE MONDAY ROOM *NEW YORK, NEW YORK*

DESIGNER: AVROKO

OWNER/OPERATOR: AVROKO RESTAURANT GROUP

YEAR OPENED: 2003, PUBLIC; 2006, THE MONDAY ROOM

NUMBER OF SEATS: 125, PUBLIC; 20–25, THE MONDAY ROOM

FOH: 4,800 SQUARE FEET

BOH: 1,550 SQUARE FEET, INCLUDING 550-SQUARE-FOOT STORAGE/OFFICE

SERVICE STYLE: FULL SERVICE

MENU: AUSTRALASIAN CUISINE SUCH AS GRILLED KANGAROO AND TASMANIAN SEA TROUT, PUBLIC; SMALL PLATES WITH ITEMS SUCH AS GLAZED EEL AND GRILLED KOBE BEEF TONGUE, THE MONDAY ROOM

DESCRIPTION

Public/The Monday Room—owned and operated by the AvroKO design firm—offers two gathering places with different menus and missions, housed in what was a former muffin factory located in the downtown Manhattan neighborhood known as NoLita. Public's dining areas include wide-open rooms for convivial dining, while the adjacent Monday Room (added three years later) is a small, intimate space with a library-like feel intended for a comfortable drink, flight of wine, or light meal. Infused with a hip yet convivial atmosphere that feels like it has always been there, Public fast became a neighborhood icon known for great food: the restaurant was awarded a coveted Michelin Star in the 2009 New York Guide for executive chef Brad Farmerie's inventive Australasian cuisine.

In the words of the design team, Public hearkens back to a time "when institutions could be depended upon for the greater good." This sense of common good informs the architecture, design elements, and graphics. In contrast, The Monday Room "evokes a collective living room." Here, a relaxed atmosphere offers a setting to begin or end an evening. This lounge area—minus a bar—features flights of wine paired with selections of exotic cheeses, glazed eel, and other "appeteasers."

CONCEPT/CLIENTELE

Since AvroKO was also the owner, the designers had the freedom to test and showcase their ideas about food, design, and convivial dining. With a four-month schedule for design and build-out, the team—working with a very restricted budget—set out to create a public space that hearkens back to precomputer times. For example, they lined one side of the entry with Dewey Decimal System card catalogs filled with copies of Public menus since opening in 2003.

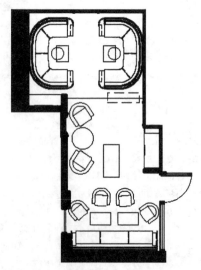

Figure 6.13.1
The Monday Room Floorplan.

On the opposite side of the entry are brass post office boxes that are used for wine storage by the restaurant's regular customers. The Monday Room shares the same outside entry, with an interior door that opens into its much quieter space.

DESIGN SOLUTIONS

One design challenge that the AvroKO team debated in depth was how to create the anchoring effect of a long communal table without losing seating flexibility. Their solution was the design and installation of a long aluminum I-beam that become the base (and backbone) of the communal table. Riding on this beam are six solid walnut, two-person tabletops that can form six intimate deuces or be pushed together for parties of up to 12.

Figure 6.13.2
A tilted mirror offers guests seated at the bar a glimpse of the action in Public's dining room behind them.
(Michael Weber Photography)

Figure 6.13.3
Regular customers store their personal wine selections in brass post office boxes located in the restaurant's entry area.
(Photography by Yuki Kuwana)

Figure 6.13.4
A view of the communal dining
table and the card catalogs, which
are used to store past menus.
(Michael Weber Photography)

UNIQUE IDEA

The team clearly thought about every small
detail of the spatial, decorative, and graphic
design, while at the same time being on top of
marketing details, operational requirements,
and the restaurants' ultimate profitability in
New York's highly competitive marketplace. One
example of how their thoughtful analysis turned
into a unique idea involved their solution for an
innovative takeaway.

A small takeaway, historically a matchbook with
the restaurant's logo and address, typically
functions as a reminder to customers of places
they have visited and might return to. But with
the smoking ban that was imposed in New
York City's public spaces in 2003, the idea of
matchbooks had lost its appeal.

In thinking about an alternative, the design team
wanted to create something "more surprising

Figure 6.13.5
In the washroom, takeaway soaps in the wall display, printed with a branded sticker, are effective merchandising elements.
(Michael Weber Photography)

in form, function, and location—an amusing offering that would catch patrons off guard while remaining memorable and desirable." They next identified the washroom as an intriguing location for guests to pick up their takeaway—a familiar concept to those who abscond with the small amenities in hotel bathrooms. For AvroKO, the idea of small takeaway soaps was also "an ode to the spirit of service and grooming that most midcentury washrooms provided." They purchased bulk amounts of the most basic, utilitarian, plain-Jane soaps they could find, and personalized them with a simple, branded sticker. Stacked on the washroom sinks, they immediately resonated with guests and began disappearing nightly by the purseload.

RED MARLIN RESTAURANT BAR AND TERRACE
SAN DIEGO, CALIFORNIA

DESIGNER: CCS ARCHITECTURE

OWNER/OPERATOR: HYATT REGENCY MISSION BAY, SAN DIEGO

YEAR OPENED: 2008

NUMBER OF SEATS: 220, DINING ROOM AND PRIVATE ROOMS; 30, BAR AND LOUNGE; 80, OUTDOOR

FOH: 5,500 SQUARE FEET INTERIOR PLUS 2,500 SQUARE FEET OUTDOORS

BOH: 3,500 SQUARE FEET

SERVICE STYLES: FULL SERVICE WITH SOME BUFFET FOR BREAKFAST SERVICE

MENU: CALIFORNIA-MODERN CUISINE WITH INGREDIENTS PROCURED FROM LOCAL, ENVIRONMENTALLY RESPONSIBLE SOURCES

DESCRIPTION
Operated by the Hyatt Regency Mission Bay in San Diego, Red Marlin overlooks the Mission Bay Marina and the city of San Diego and boasts some of the most stunning bayside views in San Diego. The restaurant is a short five-minute walk

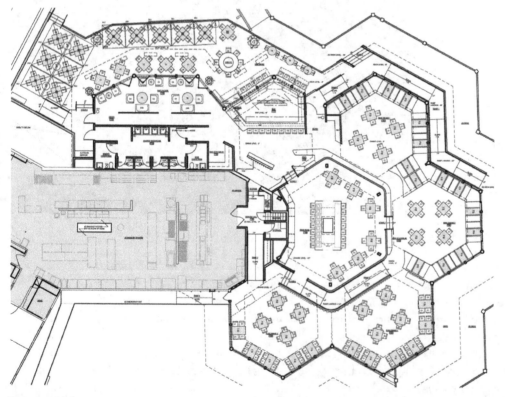

project type
New Restaurant within a Resort

size
6,500 sf interior
2,500 sf exterior (deck and bridge)

budget
$1.5 million

estimated completion
january 2008

contractor
Webcor

Figure 6.14.1
Floorplan.
(Design by CCS Architecture)

Figure 6.14.2
The marina-side view of Red Marlin shows the restaurant's connection with its bayside location. Inside, an elevated seating area gives diners a spectacular waterfront view.
(Matthew Millman)

from the hotel tower and adjacent to the major meeting facilities. Guests can choose from open-air terrace seating, an indoor-outdoor bar, several dining rooms, and Red Marlin's chef's table with its own cooking area. The trend-forward menu focuses on healthy, fresh options that appeal to the mind as well as the palate: beautiful food, simply presented, with an emphasis on sustainable, organic ingredients.

DESIGN DIRECTIVE

CCS Architecture worked with clear directives from the restaurant's on-site Hyatt managers and the owners from Hyatt corporate, all of whom were very involved with the design. Each contributed to the design process in varying amounts. CCS was brought into the project to redesign an existing restaurant venue after a development plan for the major overall hotel renovation was already completed. Since this was

a low-budget renovation, there were a limited number of modifications that could be made to the front-of-the-house and back-of-the-house spaces. For example, the CCS team wanted to install all-new, operable windows and doors to create a greater connection to the outdoors and connect the lounge to the deck. Due to budget restrictions, this aspect of the project was shelved.

DESIGN SOLUTIONS

Nevertheless, the CCS team used their low budget strategically to bring the outdoors in. With a million-dollar view of the marina and the ocean, creating a means to connect the interior with the surrounding deck area was essential. The CCS team repositioned the bar so that it would serve guests seated both indoors and on the deck. It essentially became an indoor-outdoor bar, with an outdoor fire pit warming the

Figure 6.14.3
A central wine room with a community table and a fireplace under a "floating" hood helps to lessen the impact of a high, vaulted ceiling and create an intimate area for groups of friends or business associates.
(Matthew Millman)

space on cool evenings. The restaurant's entry reception area was located between the new bar and the main dining rooms.

The designers also detailed the space in a way that enhances its connection with the bayside location and the Pacific Ocean beyond, with an overall palette of materials that include wood, canvas, and boat hardware to reinforce the marina just outside. The color palette of white, navy blue, and touches of deep red are reminiscent of the glimmering light reflections on the water.

Inside the restaurant, the design team created a central wine room with a community table and a fireplace under a "floating" hood. This focal point

helps to lessen the impact of a high, vaulted ceiling and create an intimate, sought-after area for groups of friends or business associates.

UNIQUE IDEA

To improve customer access to the restaurant, CCS added a new pedestrian bridge that leads from the hotel to the restaurant entry. The new bridge connects Red Marlin to the hotel's renovated grounds and pool area, defining a clear path for hotel guests to walk to the restaurant. The main entrance to the restaurant was relocated, making it easily accessible from the hotel and visitor parking lots. Enabling both hotel guests and destination diners to easily locate the restaurant was critical to Red Marlin's success.

'S BAGGERS® *NÜRNBERG, GERMANY*

DESIGNER: KLAUS KIENER

OWNER/OPERATOR: MICHAEL MACK, HEINEMACK® GMBH

YEAR OPENED: 2007

NUMBER OF SEATS: 105, DINING ROOM; 99, BEER GARDEN

FOH: 6,672 SQUARE FEET

SERVICE STYLES: A NEW KIND OF FULL SERVICE

MENU: REGIONAL GERMAN CUISINE: BURGERS, BRAISED MEAT, POTATOES, VEGETABLES

DESCRIPTION

This is the restaurant that George and Jane Jetson, along with the kids and their dog, Astro, would have rocketed off to for a meal. The melding of creative engineering and software design with innovations in service make this a singular restaurant, one that portends new ways technology could change restaurants in the future. It's not often that restaurants get a patent, but at 's Baggers (which means "potato fritter" in the Franconian German dialect), the heart of the operation is a patented food delivery system developed by HeineMack® GmbH.

Figure 6.15.1
At 's Baggers, the food arrives via innovative spiral tracks that carry food trays from the second-floor kitchen to waiting guests.

CONCEPT/CLIENTELE

There's no doubt that the restaurant's concept appeals to a new generation of tech-savvy diners. At its core is a double-tracked helix—resembling a super-sized double DNA strand—that winds its way down from the second-floor kitchen to the dining room below. The kitchen staff puts containers of food on custom-designed trays and sends them down the helix; then they reach the customer via a doughnut-shaped lazy Susan.

With the helix delivery system as a visual focal point, and touch screen order-entry monitors at the tables, 's Baggers has a futuristic look. The high-tech ambience, however, is tempered with a color palette of warm reds on the tabletops, glowing yellow walls, and a mix of wall-washing light and drop-pendant direct lighting.

At 's Baggers, the system facilitates a full menu, although unlike the traditional full-service restaurant, diners choose items from the touch-screen menu and then order at their leisure without having to wait for a server. Meals are delivered to each guest without the help of waiters or waitresses.

Figure 6.15.2
Diners choose menu items from a touch-screen monitor and order at their leisure. Meals are ordered and delivered without the help of waitstaff.

DESIGN DIRECTIVE

At the core of this design is the delivery system, the order-entry screen, and the software that runs the whole system. The owners refer to the entertainment aspect of 's Baggers as "event gastronomy," although their goal is to provide "the most efficient restaurant system in the world." The order screen can be programmed with an illustrated menu that has details about the food, the restaurant, the restaurant suppliers, even the system itself—far more information than could be included in a standard printed menu. The software can also be set up to support customer loyalty cards and to conduct guest satisfaction surveys.

DESIGN SOLUTIONS

Upon arrival, each guest is given an RFID (Radio Frequency Identification Card), which they insert into the order terminal in front of their seat. Payment can be made via mobile phone or by swiping a debit card, which is then recorded on the RFID chip. As guests leave, they hand the card to the cashier, who swipes it and collects cash if there is a balance.

The system does not eliminate the need for servers, but it does cut down the staffing requirements. At 's Baggers, the waitstaff spend time dealing with the individual needs of each customer, like refilling a beverage or bringing an extra plate, because they are not distracted by taking orders, order entry, and food pickup and delivery.

There are many perks for diners. For instance, they can send e-mails to friends using the touchscreen keyboard while waiting for their orders to arrive. If the recipient of the e-mail comes in to dine within a specified time, both the sender and receiver get a bonus set by the restaurant. A customer loyalty program called "Friends Card" interfaces with the order-entry terminal and rewards guests for frequent visits.

UNIQUE IDEA

It seems counterintuitive to equate less staff with better service, but that is the unique idea behind this innovative technology. The greatest challenge is the initial cost of customizing each system to meet the needs of an individual restaurant or chain of restaurants. The order-entry screens need little modification between one restaurant and another, but customizing the software is an essential and expensive process.

TABLE 45 *CLEVELAND, OHIO*

DESIGNER: *BLUNDEN BARCLAY & ASSOCIATES ARCHITECTS, INC.*

ARCHITECT OF RECORD: *HFP AMBUSKE ARCHITECTS, INC.*

OWNER/OPERATOR: *INTERCONTINENTAL HOTELS/CLEVELAND CLINIC FOUNDATION*

CHEF/OPERATOR: *ZACHERY BRUELL*

YEAR OPENED: *2006*

NUMBER OF SEATS: *130, DINING ROOMS; 20, PRIVATE DINING; 50, BAR*

FOH: *5,300 SQUARE FEET*

BOH: *3,200 SQUARE FEET*

SERVICE STYLE: *FULL SERVICE*

MENU: *CONTEMPORARY PREPARATION OF MEATS, SEAFOOD, AND VEGETARIAN SPECIALTIES.*

Figure 6.16.1
A glass-walled chef's table for eight overlooks the plating area of the kitchen. It sequesters diners while still allowing them to catch the action.
(Photos by Scott Pease)

DESCRIPTION

Table 45, located within the InterContinental Hotel in the heart of the Cleveland Clinic campus, serves hotel guests, patients, and staff from the local medical community looking for an upscale meal or meeting place. The space has a timeless and flexible design geared to the different clientele who frequent the restaurant for breakfast, lunch, and dinner—often over many days.

CONCEPT/CLIENTELE

In its earlier incarnation as a restaurant known as Classics, this hotel restaurant was conceived as a formal dining experience—but it failed to meet sales expectations. The Cleveland Clinic administrators and InterContinental management team retained Chef Zachery Bruell—who had formerly run two very successful Cleveland restaurants—to reopen the restaurant as Table 45 and provide a much more versatile experience.

Architect and principal-in-charge William Blunden, FAIA, who had designed two other restaurants for Chef Bruell, was charged with creating a dining environment targeted to different times of day, different dining occasions, and a variety of clientele. It was important for Table 45 to appeal to the Cleveland Clinic patients and families who stayed at the hotel, sometimes over many days; to the administrators and physicians who came for a business lunch; to clinic patients in wheelchairs enjoying a meal with family; to guests grabbing a quick breakfast before heading over to see a loved one in the clinic; and to destination diners coming from nearby communities to enjoy a special meal. Different spaces, each with its own feel, had to be created within the overall floorplan.

DESIGN DIRECTIVE

Most important, the spaces needed to be flexible. Blunden divided the seating into three main areas, each with its own distinctive feel. He also integrated a unique chef's table for

Figure 6.16.2
The clean architectural look of Table 45 provides a time-less setting suited to a variety of clientele.
(Photos by Scott Pease)

eight directly across from the plating area in the kitchen, offering not only a view of back-of-the-house food production but also an opportunity to talk directly with the chef (and to talk in complete privacy away from other diners).

Table 45 had to be completed in a short time frame of six months for planning, construction, and design. The fact that the restaurant was going into an existing building made it even more challenging because of the limitations imposed by the existing conditions, says Blunden.

DESIGN SOLUTIONS

Blunden incorporated a wide array of seating types and barriers to differentiate dining areas and to provide different levels of privacy. These include (but are not limited to) horseshoe-shaped booths surrounded with frosted glass panels, rectangular two-person booths, freestanding four-tops, and banquettes. The moveable, frosted glass walls that subdivide the main dining area can be configured to define private dining sections. The chef's table is the most intimate space, with a glass wall that completely encloses the action side of the space.

Various forms, including the frosted panels, half-wall divider/planters, and a mix of lighting, create visual interest in the restaurant. Guests enter Table 45 through the bar—the noisiest part of the restaurant—and then move on to increasingly quieter spaces within the dining areas. Natural light brightens much of the space during the daytime, and different-colored placemats and table settings differentiate breakfast, lunch, and dinner meal periods.

Campbell Black, regional director of operations for InterContinental Hotels, assembled a team of roughly 15 hotel managers, clinic administrators, architects, designers, contractors, and the chef, who helped to orchestrate the design. They worked with data about the market, always being mindful of the shortcomings of the previous restaurant that caused it to fail—and were closely involved with the design process from plan development to final construction.

UNIQUE IDEA

While he is a seasoned architect and designer, Blunden has been responsible for only three restaurants—all for Chef Bruell. When asked about this, he said, "What we do for Zach Bruell is not a lot different than what we do for others. We aspire to a classic understatement and don't include things that are not necessary."

TERZO *SAN FRANCISCO, CALIFORNIA*

DESIGNER: CCS ARCHITECTURE

OWNER/OPERATOR: LAURIE THOMAS, OWNER, NICE VENTURES

YEAR OPENED: 2006

NUMBER OF SEATS: 50, DINING ROOM; 20, PRIVATE ROOMS; 20, BAR

FOH: 1,200 SQUARE FEET

BOH: 800 SQUARE FEET

SERVICE STYLES: FULL SERVICE, PLUS DINING AT THE BAR

MENU: MEDITERRANEAN SMALL AND LARGE PLATES, EUROPEAN WINES, TAPAS

DESCRIPTION

Terzo started out as a tapas bar but—while it still has tapas on the menu—quickly became a full-service restaurant offering full-size portions. The name, which means "three," is the third restaurant opened in the San Francisco Bay area by Laurie Thomas, owner of Nice Ventures. With a menu that blends flavors from countries around the Mediterranean and local, high-quality food that is often organic, the restaurant is a hip, popular gathering place for residents of the city's nearby Cow Hollow and Pacific Heights neighborhoods.

CONCEPT/CLIENTELE

Terzo is a renovation of an existing, fine-dining restaurant that had featured gourmet cuisine.

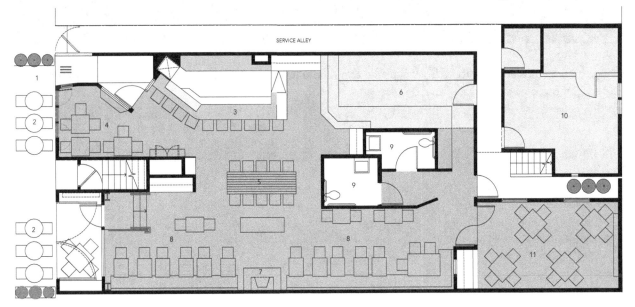

FLOORPLAN
1. ENTRY
2. OUTDOOR DINING
3. BAR
4. BAR DINING
5. COMMUNITY DINING
6. OPEN KITCHEN
7. FIREPLACE
8. MAIN DINING
9. W/C
10. PREP DINING
11. WINE ROOM

Figure 6.17.1
Floorplan.
(Design by CCS Architecture)

Figure 6.17.2
White oak tabletops and a restored brick fireplace add warmth to Terzo's contemporary design, while bare-filament Edison light bulbs give overall illumination.
(Art Gray Photography)

It fills a need for affluent neighborhood residents looking for contemporary dining in a more approachable environment, at a slightly lower price point. The Mediterranean menu, with its use of fresh, local cuisine, reflects the northern California mind-set and appeals to a loyal repeat customer base. Design elements such as a zinc-topped bar and an oak-topped communal table for 10 in the dining room also appeal to the sensibilities of neighborhood patrons.

DESIGN DIRECTIVE

Design principal Cass Calder Smith and project architect Tim Quayle of CCS Architecture took their design directive from the owners, who were involved in every aspect of the process, from the original idea to the design review to the final renovation. The CCS design goal was to create an ambience of modern, casual luxury that would help drive restaurant profit.

DESIGN SOLUTIONS

This was a reuse of an existing space, completed on a limited budget of $800,999. The most visually compelling element is a wine display that stretches 40 feet along one wall of the dining room. The use of white oak tabletops contributes to the warm modernism that is at the heart of the design.

The front part of the restaurant resembles a standard European tapas bar. A custom-made refrigerated display case helps merchandise the small-plate section of the menu by giving guests an enticing glimpse of the items they can enjoy while sipping their drinks. At the far end of the zinc-topped bar, there's an open kitchen for food production. Bar patrons can also sit at tall, white oak tables to eat, drink, converse, and watch the action in the open kitchen.

From the bar, guests continue on into the dining area, where a large communal table centers the room. A restored fireplace adds warmth and the flickering movement of fire, bare-filament Edison light bulbs give overall illumination, and directed pin lights provide task lighting.

UNIQUE IDEA

The designers selectively placed mirrors throughout the restaurant, some in strips and some that cover large surfaces such as the outside of a washroom. These help to open up the compact space and also create a bit of a see-and-be-seen environment. Of particular note is the strip of mirrors above the banquets that are across from the bar, which reflect the ever-changing comings and goings of customers as they enter the restaurant as well as the people seated at the bar.

Figure 6.17.3
Wall-mounted wine displays are a visual focal point in the modern room.
(*Art Gray Photography*)

ZAMPIERI'S HARBOR GRILLE *DESTIN, FLORIDA*

DESIGNER/ARCHITECT: JUDD BROWN DESIGNS, INC.

OWNER/OPERATOR: BRENDA ZAMPIERI

YEAR OPENED: 2006

NUMBER OF SEATS: 275 TOTAL, INCLUDING 70, MAIN DINING ROOM; 45, BOARDROOM; 50, HARBORSIDE ROOM; 50, THE DECK; AND ~60 AT THE SUSHI BAR AND THE LOUNGE BAR.

FOH: 7,500 SQUARE FEET

BOH: 2,500 SQUARE FEET

SERVICE STYLE: FULL SERVICE

MENU: STEAK, FISH, SUSHI, EXTENSIVE WINE COLLECTION

DESCRIPTION

Zampieri's Harbor Grille is a conversion of a space that was formerly a casual waterfront bar into a high-energy, hip steak and seafood restaurant. It is located on the lower floors of a luxe condominium complex that is adjacent to the ~50-slip Destin Yacht Club and Marina in the Florida panhandle.

Figure 6.18.1
Large, tilted mirrors in Zampieri's Harbor Grille dining room provide a view of the marina to diners who do not face the water.

(Photography by: Jack Gardner Photography)

CONCEPT/CLIENTELE

This was a conversion of an existing space, so the overall floorplan was not changed. The kitchen remained as originally built, but the dining and bar seating areas were rearranged. The concept was to create a steak and seafood restaurant with a more modern vibe, unlike others in the Destin marketplace, that would appeal to members of the yacht club, residents in the condominium above, and others who live or vacation in the area.

DESIGN DIRECTIVE

Judd Brown, president and design director of Judd Brown Design, Inc. and three of his designers—Li Qi (senior designer), Manny Sousa, and Jill Saccoccia—took on the challenge to convert the existing casual waterfront bar into a "new, young, hip restaurant, unlike the typical male-dominated power steakhouses." A further directive was to depart from the typical Florida color scheme. The design team responded to the owner's directives by coming up with custom solutions that fit the space and appealed to the new generation of clientele that the owner wanted to attract.

DESIGN SOLUTIONS

To begin with, there was a very large wine room that had been used in the previous incarnation of the space, which the designers relocated to the mezzanine dining area adjacent to booth seating. The existing multipanel folding wall that opened to the boardwalk adjacent to the marina had to be removed due to hurricane compliance issues. It was replaced with a two-foot-high solid wall base on which was placed a window wall capable of withstanding hurricane-force winds.

Always working with the goal of creating a "bright, fresh new look that would run contrary to many of the steakhouse restaurant interiors in the marketplace," the design team decided to reject not only the dark, heavy look of the old-fashioned steakhouse, but also the blue,

Figure 6.18.2
A black and red zebra print carpet and contemporary hanging light fixtures with red shades are typical of the design elements that help the restaurant depart from a traditional steakhouse look and attract a younger clientele.
(Photography by: Jack Gardner Photography)

aqua, and teal hues typically found in waterfront restaurants. They did include elements to reference and reflect the restaurant's waterfront setting, such as a wall of cascading water that flows down a black granite slab, and angled mirrors that provide a clear view of the marina to diners who do not face the water. But their color palette of red, black, and chocolate brown makes the space feel more like a modern gathering place than a staid steakhouse or conventional seafood restaurant.

Seating materials include a mix of faux alligator prints in chocolate and ebony and high-sheen red vinyl. A mix of floor coverings ranges from a black and red zebra-print carpet in the dining areas, to sisal-like carpet in the sushi bar that opens to an outside deck, to red-lacquered hardwood floors in the bar/lounge.

Zampieri's Harbor Grille spans three levels: the sushi bar on the boardwalk level, the dining room on the main level (upstairs), and the bar/lounge on a level that is roughly eight feet above the dining room. A cabaret/entertainment area was

also requested by the owner, so the designers positioned both the sushi bar and the bar/lounge to have clear sight lines to the southwest corner of the main floor, where a grand piano sits on a raised platform.

UNIQUE IDEA

The original bar that sits in the restaurant was built in the 1970s. While functional, its golden oak paneling and stained-glass elements had an old-timey look that dated the entire facility. The design team applied black glazing stain on the woodwork, thereby updating the look without having to bust the budget with a costly replacement.

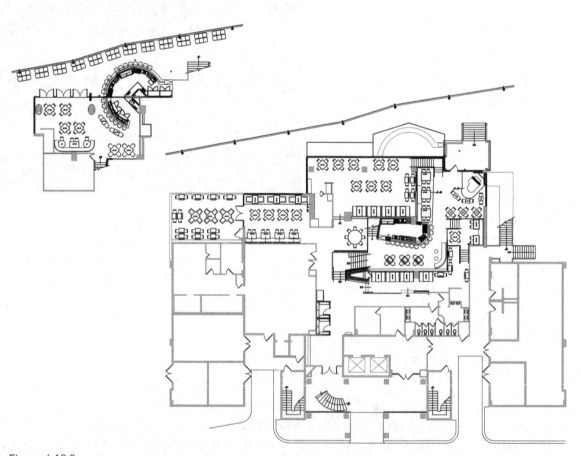

Figure 6.18.3
Floorplan.
(Design by Judd Brown Designs)

DOUZO BOSTON, MASSACHUSETTS

DESIGNER: DARLOW CHRIST ARCHITECTS

OWNER/OPERATOR: HLC GROUP

YEAR OPENED: 2006

NUMBER OF SEATS: 138

FOH: 2,800 SQUARE FEET

BOH: 1,700 SQUARE FEET

SERVICE STYLES: FULL SERVICE, SUSHI BAR, AND TAKEOUT

MENU: MODERN JAPANESE CUISINE, SPECIALIZING IN SUSHI

DESCRIPTION

Located in Boston's Back Bay, Douzo—which translates to "please come in"—offers a calming aesthetic for dining. The liberal use of white, black, and shades of brown, with small splashes of red and a mix of patterned wall hangings and seat fabrics, creates a thematic yet subtle dining environment. The contemporary Japanese cuisine, with such items as foie gras sushi and an entrée of black cod miso yaki, is complemented by the room's soft lighting and neutral colors.

CONCEPT/CLIENTELE

The Darlow Christ design team—Catherine Christ, project designer; Peter Darlow, principal in charge; Wendy Grunseich, project manager; and Lynette Suslowicz, interior designer—worked with Douzo's owners from the restaurant's inception. Every detail, from concept development to the selection of interior elements, was carefully thought out with the operational goals and objectives in mind. Located in a fashionable residential neighborhood in Boston, the restaurant needed to attract a hip, urban clientele.

DESIGN DIRECTIVE

The designers were inspired by modern Japanese aesthetics and by the chef's innovative cuisine. Their goal was to create a stylish interior that would resonate with the young, upscale residents of the neighborhood.

The resulting design uses soft thematic elements but avoids obvious clichés. Folded stainless-steel panels that float above the bar display calligraphy that spells out four themes—eating, drinking, happiness, and togetherness. The designers also created giant "light boxes" on the ceiling—the largest of which

Figure 6.19.1
The calligraphy on four stainless steel panels that float above Douzo's bar spells out the restaurant's themes of eating, drinking, happiness, and togetherness.
(Photography by Greg Premru)

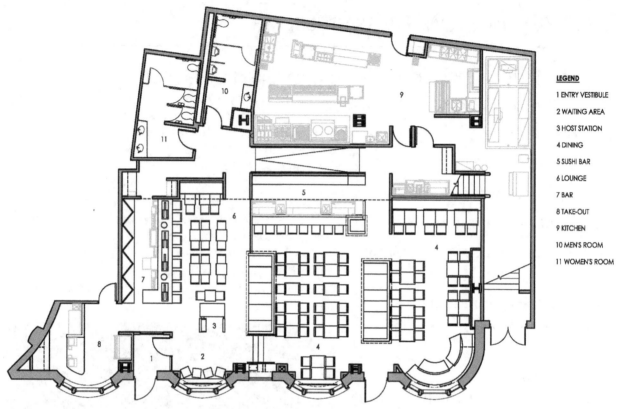

Figure 6.19.2
Floorplan.
(Design by Darlow Christ Architects)

LEGEND
1 ENTRY VESTIBULE
2 WAITING AREA
3 HOST STATION
4 DINING
5 SUSHI BAR
6 LOUNGE
7 BAR
8 TAKE-OUT
9 KITCHEN
10 MEN'S ROOM
11 WOMEN'S ROOM

measures 13.5 feet long, 4.5 feet wide, and 4.5 feet high—whose glowing geometric forms define dining areas and add the suggestion of traditional Japanese design (see photo in color insert).

DESIGN SOLUTIONS

The footprint of Douzo is a modest 4,500 square feet, but the ceiling is 18 feet high. The height led to two significant design solutions: First, a mezzanine level was added to house support areas (office, storage, and mechanicals). Second, the high ceiling made it possible for the Darlow Christ team to create the geometric light boxes that provide overall ambient lighting throughout the space.

Another challenge was to incorporate multiple access/egress points. Due to the constraints of the building shell, deliveries have to arrive through the parking garage, and an egress stair that functions as a fire escape had to be incorporated into the design. The designers also added an interior access door that could be used by the building's other tenants. In addition, an interior ramp that was required to meet Americans with Disabilities Act (ADA) accessibility requirements (to the restrooms) was designed so that it could also double as a service corridor from the kitchen to the bar.

UNIQUE IDEA

As noted earlier, the design team created custom-designed light boxes to provide an overall illumination and to help break up the high-ceilinged space. Fashioned from mahogany, with simple linear fluorescent tubes inside, these floating, glowing elements became visual focal points in the restaurant's interior.

CHAPTER 7

SPEAK OUT ON DESIGN

Much can be learned from those who are involved with restaurant design on an ongoing basis. Owners must effectively communicate their concept to designers and work closely to ensure that it is correctly interpreted. Owners not only have to be involved during the creative and construction phases of a project, but they also continue to interact with the design and architecture after the restaurant opens. Chef-owners have the added challenge of creating menus and food presentations that work with not only the back-of-the-house equipment but the front-of-the-house design elements. Designers and architects are charged with translating the owner's concept into a layout and environment that supports the restaurant. Once in operation, the managers on the floor are charged with making the designs work. There are times when the "as built" designs continue to evolve over the years.

To gain insights into how various members of the design team think, we interviewed a mix of restaurant design experts. They all agreed that two elements are essential to the success of any front- and back-of-the-house design: ongoing communications during the design process, and an efficient layout.

While there are several threads that weave through each of these interviews, we are pleased to note that each of our interviewees bring different ideas and perspectives to the table. Readers should note that designing a restaurant is not a rote procedure, nor is it informed by absolutes. Rather, it is an ongoing organic process where input from many parties leads to the desired end. While egos can come into play, those design teams that respect the contributions of each team member are often the most successful.

DAVID ASHEN

PRESIDENT
D-ASH DESIGN INC.
NEW YORK, NEW YORK

David Ashen and his team at d-ash design marry creativity with functionality across many markets, ranging from restaurants to retail to educational facilities. The firm began making its name in restaurant design in the mid-2000s and by 2009/2010 had about a dozen restaurant projects opening or in development.

Q: What constitutes good restaurant design? From a design perspective? From an operational perspective?

A: Good restaurant design does two things: it transports the guest to another place, providing a retreat from reality for a short period of time; and, if it works well, allows the staff to service the guest with ease and in an unobtrusive manner. Neither element can live alone.

From a design perspective, good design is very subjective. However, I do believe that a successful design upholds the strategic direction of the restaurant and creates an environment that supports the cuisine and does not overpower the dining experience. In a restaurant, the food, not the room, should be the star. However, the two should live in harmony.

Q: Does good design mean expensive design?

A: Money buys neither taste nor good design. There is a new restaurant that opened in my neighborhood recently (called Buttermilk Channel), and the owners had one-tenth of the budget that I typically get from my clients to spend on building out the space. Yet the result is a very pleasant environment that is both comfortable and functional. While there are no memorable moments in the design of the space, there are also no huge mistakes, and more importantly, the design supports the food, which truly is the star here. People wait in excess of an hour to get seated. On the other end of the spectrum, I believe that when a guest spends significant money on a meal, they also

Figure 7.1
David Ashen.
(Frank Oudeman)

expect a special environment, and this must be considered in the development of any new restaurant.

Q: From a historical perspective, has restaurant design become more important to the overall success of a restaurant during the past 10 years?

A: In certain cases it has. In major cities such as New York and Los Angeles, it has become the norm that star chefs get paired with star designers. The bet is that the higher the star power, the higher the chances of success. People will go to a restaurant just to see the latest design of a superstar like Phillipe Starck or David Rockwell. If the service and food isn't good, they won't go back, but for the mega-restaurants, the star-power design is an expected cost of entry.

Q: Aside from star power, do you see any other restaurant design trends?

A: What I see in the United States, in the big cities at least, is a better understanding of what good design really is. I hope that the trickle-down theory works here and we start to see good design spread through the country. Just as Target has made good design accessible to middle America through its partnerships with Issac Mizrahi and Michael Graves, I hope that middle America will begin to get quality design in their strip mall restaurants.

Q: How can restaurateurs best work with designers to create a successful restaurant design? What advice would you give to operators about working with designers?

A: First and most important, the operator/owner should have a clear idea of the food they are going to serve and the type of customer they want to attract. I believe a strong strategic foundation is essential, so if the owner/operator can afford to include a branding or marketing expert, that would help. Don't expect the restaurant designer to develop the strategy; most can't. Also, spend time with the designers visiting other restaurants, eating, sharing what you like and don't like, and discussing what works (or doesn't) while you are in the experience. See as much as possible.

Q: What was your most challenging restaurant project, and what factors made it most challenging?

A: Our most challenging project was our most recent, Urban Farmer at The Nines, a hotel in Portland. The client wanted to create a destination restaurant that had a

Figure 7.2
Working sketch of Mercat a la Planxa in Chicago, Illinois, the first ground-up restaurant designed by d-ash design.
(Frank Ouderman)

separate identity from the hotel; however, the space allocated for the restaurant was in the back of a nine-story atrium lobby on the eighth floor of the building. Not only does the customer have to come off the street and up to the eighth floor, but they must also go through the lobby of the hotel in order to get to the hostess stand. The dictate from our client was to create a sense of separation and intimacy within a grand open space—all without building walls.

Q: What are the greatest strengths of your firm, and why?

A: We are very good at taking a marketing or brand strategy and translating it into an environment that creates a unique customer experience. Our strength is in our ability to collaborate with owners and their other creative teams and create a three-dimensional visualization of the idea. Also, because of my background in Human Factors Engineering, we are very good at creating spaces that work for both the staff and the guest.

Q: What is the relationship of design to food and service? To what extent does/should the menu influence the design?

A: In our work, there is a direct relationship between the menu and the design. The client usually does not have the specific items on the menu developed when we begin our design, but we definitely have a general direction. We always begin our design process by pulling images that describe our concept, and the images are a direct result of the direction of the cuisine.

Q: Is a strong graphic image important?

A: Yes, I do believe in developing a strong graphic and branding package. It is more than just a graphic image; it is a comprehensive package that outlines all points of communication with consumers and customers. I have learned from my experience with retail brands that a strong graphics and communication package helps build consistency and connections to customers.

Q: How closely do you generally work with a foodservice consultant? At what phases in the project? Do you ever interact with the chef?

A: Each client works differently. Usually, we like to work with a foodservice consultant as soon as we have an initial design scheme developed. It is important to have a system of checks and balances. The stronger the client team, the stronger the final product; so if we have access to a foodservice consultant and the chef, we are able to create a more successful design. However, often the chef is not on board until the design has been almost fully developed.

Q: Your firm is known for creating interesting design solutions that are also practical for the operator. What is there about your approach to the design process that makes this happen?

A: First and most important, listen to the client. We are very good listeners and even better at distilling the relevant information. Second, my very pragmatic training in Human Factors Engineering provides an understanding of human psychology and basic principles in designing around how people use things. I always consider how a design will make someone feel, how they will move in the space, and how all the operational issues will be addressed.

Q: Please discuss two examples of your firm's top restaurant designs from the past five years and why you feel they are important.

A: Mercat a la Planxa in Chicago was our first ground-up restaurant. The collaboration between the owner (Sage Restaurant Group), the branding agency (Korn Design), and our office was extraordinary, and the restaurant and its success are a direct result of this. Urban Farmer was the second restaurant we did with Sage, and it was our most surprising restaurant project. The expectations were not high because of the challenges posed by the location (see above), and therefore it allowed us a certain amount of freedom to test some ideas regarding private and public space. It ended up to be a great success and proved that large obstacles can sometimes be overcome.

Q: How has restaurant design changed since you've been in the business? What kinds of innovations or changes have happened in terms of design elements like lighting, color, seating, and acoustics?

A: In the short time I have been in the business of designing restaurants, design has definitely become a major element of the dining experience. The environment and its uniqueness are becoming as important as the food, and designers and owners are becoming more sophisticated in how they use light, color, and materials. There are many more options available to us in regard to furniture and materials that allow for inventiveness without breaking the bank. As technologies advance, lighting (types of lights and controls) and sound systems become more affordable and, therefore, more accessible, allowing the designer more tools for affecting the environment.

Q: What are the most important trends in restaurant design today? Will they last?

A: I think one of the biggest changes in restaurant design is the merging of the restaurant and the lounge/nightclub. Restaurants like Buddakan (in Philadelphia and New York) have created a new typology, creating a destination that is not about the food, but more about the total experience. People no longer go to dinner and then to a club (or lounge) for after-dinner entertainment; they now look for a complete experience at one destination. New restaurant designs are providing multileveled experiences that allow for choice. I believe that in a down economy, people will search for value in how they spend their leisure dollars and that this trend will continue to grow.

Another trend that I see is that more restaurants are serving small plates of food (family style); sharing is in today and probably will be for a while. Restaurants are being designed to accommodate this with more communal and lounge seating. I think we will see more restaurants with less conventional seating in the future.

Q: How is sustainable/green design influencing today's restaurant landscape? How do you think it will influence restaurant design in the next decade?

A: Green design has become more of an influence in our hotel restaurants. We have just completed two restaurants in hotels that are aiming for LEEDS certification and we had to really think about the materials we were using. It is not that difficult to make the interior green in regards to materials. Lighting has been more of a challenge, but we are finding that every month there are more energy-efficient products coming out to fill the void. The other interesting thing to think about is waste and how that is dealt with. In our new restaurant in Portland, we will be composting some of the organic waste, and in order to do that, we had to think about storage and workflow in a different way. Fortunately, Portland is one of the few cities that is encouraging composting and has regular trash pick-ups for organic matter. Other cities should look to Portland as an example of what can be done on a government level to encourage communities to become more sustainable.

There is no doubt that sustainability will influence all design in the next decade. We are running out of resources, and it has become a necessity to look at alternatives to how we live. I think the Slow Food movement will also pick up steam and will have an effect on restaurant design.

Q: Any additional forecasts for the 2010 decade?

A: The 2010 decade will see us coming out of the worst economic situation in almost 80 years. In the short term, I believe that simple design and food will be the norm. However, once we emerge from the recession, I think there will be a rebellion of sorts, a new era of decadence that almost certainly will emerge from a period of frugality. How that will manifest itself is yet to be seen. However, I do believe that there will be a new vibrancy and extravagance in color, materials, and ingredients that will bring a new breath of life into restaurant design.

WARREN ASHWORTH

PRESIDENT
WARREN ASHWORTH,
ARCHITECT PLLC
NEW YORK, NEW YORK

Warren Ashworth has been a practicing architect specializing in restaurant design since 1980. Prior to establishing his own practice in 2004, he partnered with renowned architect Larry Bogdanow for 24 years and was involved in the design and construction of more than 125 restaurants. Ashworth, who is also known for his residential design, says that "the very private aspects of that work continue to inform the very public aspects of restaurant design."

Figure 7.3
Warren Ashworth.
(Peter Wynn Thompson)

Q: What constitutes good restaurant design? From a design perspective? From an operational perspective?

A: Integrity. Good design has integrity. This translates to one thing: making a space that the gives owners the kind of restaurant they ask for. It means knowing when to say no, to yourself and to the owner. It means making decisions that answer the need specified, but putting in the grace notes that let the place sing.

Operationally—that is a harder question to answer. Some of it comes from instinct, some of it comes from skill and experience. I will make one generalization, though: Symmetry is a disaster operationally and design-wise. Never resort to symmetry as a planning motif. It has nothing to do with how to run a restaurant.

Q: Does good design mean expensive design?

A: No, in fact, a restricted budget often produces a stronger design than a fat one. It encourages creative use of materials, finishes, and unusual found objects. More than that, there is a subtle relationship to the business side as well. Discerning customers are aware of excess. While they may be quite willing to pay $35 for an appetizer knowing it has foie gras in it, they are less inclined to pay $35 for an appetizer to underwrite leather ceilings.

Good value design may mean making use of some existing materials in a space. It always means discussing if something adds value. A wooden bar top that costs $4,000 does the same job as the under-lit, cast-glass bar top that costs $30,000. They both hold up customers and their drinks. But if that glass bar top draws more customers in, more often, *and* keeps them there, it may be well worth the difference. Lastly, good value design also means using materials that will make the customer comfortable rather than make the place photograph really well for the architect's portfolio.

Q: From a historical perspective, has restaurant design become more important to the overall success of a restaurant during the past 10 years?

A: Perversely, while the answer to this question is undoubtedly yes, I do not necessarily think this is a good thing. Now that restaurants in Las Vegas have become the paradigm for the design world, many restaurants wind up far too reliant on layers of "wow." People are gob-smacked by the image of an assistant sommelier clipping on belaying gear to climb 40 feet for a bottle of wine. But, what happens in Las Vegas should stay in Las Vegas. In the real world, we architects and designers should be walking that tightrope between simple delight and razzle-dazzle, between homey and hip, between comfortable and contrived.

Sometimes, an effort to create "atmosphere" actually ruins the atmosphere of a restaurant. In 1984, New York restaurateur Danny Meyer sat down with my former partner and myself to interview us about designing his first restaurant, Union Square Café. One of the very key things he said was, "I do not want a restaurant where someone walks in and says, 'Wow, who designed this place?'" He wanted a restaurant that felt like it had always been there, a place where no architect had ever trod. Union Square Café has stood up well to that unusual measure, and Danny's success reminds me how important it is not to overdesign.

Q: What do you foresee for restaurant design in the 2010 decade?

Figure 7.4
Exterior sketch of Landmark in Chicago, Illinois, with an overscaled arch that references famed Chicago architect Louis Sullivan.

(Design by Warren Ashworth)

A: My hope is that the "realignment" (I love that word) of wealth that started in 2008 will also realign the restaurateur's view of what is important to the customer. Even Applebee's has stated publicly that they need to get back to concentrating on their food. The truth is that with good food, great staff, and fair value, you can open a restaurant in a garage! Just put in some good lighting—always spend on lighting—and you could have a very successful place.

Q: How can restaurateurs best work with designers to create a successful restaurant design? What advice would you give to operators about working with designers?

A: Start by finding an architect or designer who listens, rather than one who tells *you* right away what you need. Then, you want to communicate to that person the restaurant that is in your head. But, I have had many clients who cannot do that—they don't have such an image (because they have been busy with the business plan) or they don't want to influence what *I* will come up with. Fine, no problem. What we *really* need to know about you are things you might feel are incidental: describe a dining room, in a house or in a restaurant, that you go back to and why; describe a building you like; describe your favorite chair. Bring us images from magazines you have torn out; logos that you like; matchbook covers you have collected; attractive menus you have swiped; photos from books of specific projects that caught your attention. Use circles and arrows to point to what attracts you.

And don't forget to tell us *what you don't like.* This is often just as important. Tell us about restaurants you find unattractive, colors and patterns you stay away from. Let us know your peeves. These help us a lot when offering choices.

Q: What was your most challenging restaurant project, and what factors made it most challenging?

A: My most challenging restaurant project was for TGI Fridays, working with my former partner Larry Bogdanow and in close collaboration with a well-known foodservice consultant. TGI Fridays came to us looking to revamp their tired units. But we found that it was extremely difficult to introduce new ideas into an existing, static corporate culture. There were too many departments weighing in on our design proposals and we had a sense, from early on, that this was a futile exercise. We visited many units and made many proposals, but in the end, corporate scrapped the plans, changed their advertising, and carried on as before.

Q: What do you think is your firm's best design, and why?

A: Landmark Grill + Lounge in Chicago would have to be the answer. For an architect, the harder the problem, the more interesting the solution. Landmark had myriad problems: The main space had a huge, inhospitable barn-like interior; the rest of the place (11,000 square feet) was built on a total of *six* different levels; there was too much natural light in the main room; there was *no* natural light in much of the balance of the space; the entry was set well back off the main sidewalk and felt hidden; and there was a very strict budget. But, on the plus side, we had two great clients.

Q: What makes a great client?

A: A great client is someone who is experienced in the restaurant and/or bar business. The value of experience cannot be emphasized often enough—if clients don't have it, they better have a foodservice consultant or I will not take the job. A great client is someone who knows what they want; it is someone who makes decisions when choices are presented and who sticks by those decisions; it is someone who trusts their consultants enough to give them the latitude they need, yet stays constantly aware; and it is someone who is gracious under pressure.

Q: What is the relationship of design to food and service? To what extent does/should the menu influence the design?

A: I have to say that in my experience, the menu often comes later. We always know at the beginning what the general food focus is, but it is very rare that the menu is mapped out before the plans are finished. I think, in fact, it is sometimes the other way around. A menu might be influenced, even slightly, by the design. The reason for this is that the chef is often not hired until construction is well under way. A chef may take the job because they like what they see and like the management. Then, taking a cue from what is going on around him or her, they work their own creative magic.

Q: Is a strong graphic image important?

A: I would put excellent graphics up there with lighting as one of the most important features in a restaurant, whether it is a chain or an individual unit. The graphic image helps cement an identity. Human beings are attracted to a strong identity, as are dogs to parking meters.

Q: How closely do you generally work with a foodservice consultant? At what phases in the project? Do you ever interact with the chef?

A: Foodservice consultants are great. I consider myself lucky if I land a job with one. I will often try to convince a client to bring one on board, if there is not one already. Starting from the very beginning of a project, often before a space is selected, a foodservice consultant helps an owner with the big picture. They consult on the business side, the graphics, the menu, the marketing, the uniforms, the catering, the hiring, the branding, and the integration of the design.

I have designed a handful of restaurants for chefs. It is a different approach to design. Unlike with other restaurateurs, I barely have to concern myself with the back of the house. Chefs are aces at understanding the operation, circulation issues, and delivery times. But most significantly, chefs always have their restaurant in their mind's eye, and sometimes that image is very, very clear, which is great. After all, they have spent many intimate years making notes about what they like and dislike (usually the latter) in other places. When they come to me, they have finally found backing, support, and enthusiasm from others. Working directly with chefs is always a pleasure because of the directness of the connection with the food. With a chef, there is never any question of what is most important.

Q: Your firm is known for creating interesting design solutions that are also practical for the operator. What is there about your approach to the design process that makes this happen?

A: Working briefly in restaurant kitchens in my youth gave me a good feel for how important a smooth operation is. I have a strong sympathy for how hard this business is. I know many restaurateurs who work long, long hours for a little profit. They remind me of farmers or fishermen. I look at them and wonder what drives them to do this, season after season, for such modest returns. My job is to make their lives easier any way I can. Of course, I want to give them a restaurant that customers love and want to come back to—but I also want to give them a place where the pastry chef's dacquoise does not end up in the pot sink, for lack of a clear path; where the hostess does not contract hypothermia from gusts of arctic air, for lack of a vestibule;

and where the house manager can't dim the lights consistently for lack of centralized dimmers.

The key for the designer is to ask questions. It is not necessary to interview the pastry chef, the hostess, and the house manager, but it is essential to learn what employees are anticipated to staff the restaurant, what their roles and stations are, how many shifts there will be, and what supplies and storage they need.

Q: How has restaurant design changed since you've been in the business? What kinds of innovations or changes have happened in terms of design elements like lighting, color, seating, and acoustics?

A: Las Vegas not withstanding, restaurant design has not really changed. It is about the same thing it always was: letting people feel special, while making them comfortable. As it ever was, the goal is to create an individual statement that appeals to many. And the best designers are always going to strive for a timeless feel. Innovations abound, but honestly, the customer does not want to be too aware of them. While there are many wonderful new ways of lighting tables, ordering food, and cooking food, the customers at the table will be happy with candles, a server who memorizes their order, and great food well prepared.

Q: What are the most important trends in restaurant design today? Will they last?

A: Every few months the hospitality magazines focus on new trends for the coming year in much the same way that *Women's Wear Daily* tries to identify what will be hot next season. Sometimes they are right, sometimes they are wrong. I honestly feel that good designers and architects do not concern themselves with trends. What is important is to be aware of what is being done in the trade, and who is doing what and where. A good example is open kitchens. Innumerable publications covered the "trend" of open kitchens—how they were coming east from California and going to change the restaurant scene forever. Well, open kitchens did come east, and many people experimented with varying degrees of openness. But they have not radically changed the restaurant landscape. They have made it richer, just as the invention of MR-16 light bulbs made the world of lighting choices richer.

BILL AUMILLER, AIA

PARTNER
AUMILLER YOUNGQUIST, PC
CHICAGO, ILLINOIS

Bill Aumiller and Keith Youngquist founded their eponymous firm in 1980. Their focus is to provide foodservice operators an effective way to communicate their vision through innovative architectural design. Aumiller Youngquist has designed more than 350 different concepts and more than 1,500 restaurants. They approach each project with the goal of rethinking the design process and creating spaces with unique identities.

Figure 7.5
Bill Aumiller and Keith Youngquist.
(Eric Wentworth illustration, wintercrowstudio.com)

Q: What does successful restaurant design mean to you? What is the single most important key to good restaurant design?

A: The primary role of any restaurant is to nurture the customer. This obviously pertains to providing nourishment for the patron's physiological well-being, but we feel it also involves nurturing their psychological and emotional well-being as well. To this end, we try to create a physical environment that complements the food concept and the dining experience.

The single most important step in effective restaurant design is developing a functional floorplan that provides for smooth and timely service from the operational side, while delivering an enjoyable dining experience for the customer. If this is not done skillfully, the interior design is always straining to overcome the shortcomings of the spatial layout.

Q: Do you think that, to remain competitive, restaurants must offer an architectural "experience?"

A: Aumiller Youngquist has been practicing experiential design since our inception, thanks to the influences of some of our initial clients such as Chicago concept developer Rich Melman of Lettuce Entertain You. Authors Pine and Gilmore (*The Experience Economy*) simply defined and explained what we had been doing intuitively. We thoroughly embrace their theories and continue to apply them to our work.

Currently, we are seeing the importance of experiential design expanding beyond the fine-dining and casual-dining segments. The paradigm is shifting, and customers are beginning to demand full dining experiences in the quick-service and fast-casual segments of the industry as well. They are no longer willing to purchase a simple, cheap commodity for lunch or breakfast.

We have also seen a transition from individual experiences to group experiences. Following September 11, 2001, we began to see more and more people gathering at restaurants not only to eat, but also for the social interaction. They derive comfort and strength from participating in the camaraderie of a larger social group. In light of the worldwide economic crisis that began in 2008, we would anticipate this trend to continue.

Q: What does theme design mean to you?

A: This topic hits a hot button for us. We typically find that "themed" restaurants result in a superficial, unfocused, fragmented, and incomplete design statement with very little personality. We try instead to develop conceptually strong restaurant designs. We feel that a strong, well-defined concept results in a focused, integrated, complete design statement with a full personality.

For example, Tucci Benucch was an Italian restaurant located in the Avenue Atrium shopping center on Michigan Avenue in Chicago. A simplistic account of its *theme* would describe it as a rustic country Italian restaurant. Our *design concept* would describe it as a rustic Italian farmhouse to which the patron would be welcomed at the front door by the farmer's wife and shown to a table in one of the dining rooms. The dining rooms would each be designed as a different room in the house, ranging from the mudroom to the living room, bedroom, and, of course, the country kitchen. Our intent was to give the customer a break from the kinetic, brash surroundings of the shopping center and present them with a quiet and intimate haven, a little bit of home away from home.

Q: Does good design mean expensive design?

A: No, neither cost of construction nor cost of design services needs to be expensive. However, without quality design, the construction cost of the project is liable to increase, and inefficiencies in the planning process will likely lead to higher operating expenses and less-than-optimum seating counts. Without strong, functional planning, the kitchen staff and the service staff are likely to be strained, resulting in a higher turnover and requiring a larger staff to fill the gap of improper planning.

Good design results in a focused solution that concentrates construction spending where it will be most effective. Good design also eliminates potentially expensive decorative and architectural elements, selected on a whim, that do not contribute to the stated design concept.

Q: Will design continue to be an important element in the overall success of a restaurant in the 2010 decade?

A: We believe that as long as the economic downturn continues, budgets will become much more limited, even as design continues to become ever more important to the overall success of a restaurant concept. It will be more vital than ever for designs to stay focused and cohesive, eliminating as much waste as possible from the design treatments and the budget.

Q: What usually gets in the way of successful designer/restaurateur collaboration? How can they best work together?

A: The biggest obstacle to a successful collaboration is poor communication. The restaurateur needs to clearly express to the designer his expectations, goals, food concept, market segment, check average, style of service, preconceived design ideas, and, most importantly, budget. In turn, the designer needs to listen carefully to what the

Figure 7.6
At Del Frisco's Steakhouse in New York, a dining balcony takes full advantage of the high-ceilinged space by adding a mezzanine level for additional seating over the bar. The restaurant design also accentuates the view out to the Rockefeller Plaza cityscape through 30-foot-high windows on three sides.
(Credit Mark Ballogg)

owner has to say. Where information is lacking, the designer needs to guide the owner through the thought processes needed to arrive at a cohesive set of goals for the project.

Q: What advice would you give to students or operators about working with designers?

A: *Communicate.* Students should ask questions and listen to the answers. They should try to absorb as much information as they can from experienced designers in what is a very complicated genre. Operators must provide the designer with as much information as possible on their preferences and requirements, including any preconceptions with regard to the interior design of the space. Next, operators should listen to what experienced designers have to say. After all, operators hire designers for their input and expertise. It is perfectly all right to disagree with your designer as long as you talk it out and come to an informed and mutual conclusion.

Q: How do you keep coming up with fresh ideas? What usually inspires the concept? Please share a few examples of your designs that you feel have been most successful, and why.

A: We typically draw our initial design inspiration from the food concept. To this we add market, geographical, and existing building influences, as well as the owner's personality if applicable to the situation. As long as restaurant owners keep coming up with creative and new food concepts, we can continue to develop fresh and exciting designs.

A good example would be the Del Frisco's Steakhouse space on 6th Avenue in Manhattan. The food concept was a traditional high-end steakhouse with some contemporary twists. The design concept of the original Del Frisco's space in Dallas was a traditional, English men's club feel with a touch of Victorian influence. It had a very interior focus. But in New York, the Rockefeller Plaza location boasted spectacular, 30-foot-high windows on three sides with wonderful views of the front plaza, as well as Radio City Music Hall, the Simon & Schuster Building, Fox News, and, most importantly, the constant traffic up and down 6th Avenue. It was the ultimate New York space. So the decision was to build a New York Del Frisco's instead of a Dallas Del Frisco's in New York. Utilizing what the site offered, we embraced the extroverted nature of the space and accentuated the view out to the plaza and street for all of the restaurant patrons. Our concept reflected more of a New York attitude that brought the idea of see and be seen to a new level.

Another example is the foodservice facilities for the Museum of Science and Industry in Chicago. The existing facilities were a hodgepodge of operations ranging from a cafeteria that hadn't been touched in decades to a downtrodden Pizza Hut. The image this displayed was totally unsuitable for a facility that is always updating its exhibits. Our concept statement had four primary points: (1) *inspiring*: a stimulating exchange of museum knowledge that would fill visitors with anticipation; (2) *interactive*: fresh food stations, to inspire culinary genius through demonstrations; (3) *real and educational*: utilizing state-of-the art technology and media for provocative displays, demonstrating the science behind the food; and (4) *nurturing*: balancing the guests' cognitive development with their physiological well-being by giving them space to reconnect with each other. With these departure points for the design, we proceeded to develop a facility that was much more aligned with the museum's goals and that reflected the modernization that had gone on in other parts of the facility.

Q: What is the relationship of design to food and service? To what extent does/should the menu influence the design?

A: We try to not lose sight of the fact that a restaurant is a business, one that sells food and the experience of consuming that food. If the design concept does not blend with the food concept, the public is going to be confused. An over-the-top design for a casual dining restaurant, for example, will likely cause customers to feel a little intimidated, and they may even come to the conclusion that they can't afford to eat in the establishment.

Likewise, the design concept and the food concept have to be compatible. A few years ago, I consulted with a brewery in Bavaria that built restaurants and leased them to independent operators, whose restaurants had a variety of menu offerings. The developers took pride in giving me a tour of some of their restaurants, starting with a traditional Bavarian concept. The next restaurant was an Italian food concept, but it was housed in a traditional Bavarian interior. We proceeded to look at Greek, American, and Asian concepts all housed in traditional Bavarian spaces. It was a very confusing day, at the end of which I had to ask in advance what type of food concept we would be looking at next.

Q: Which design team members (outside your organization) are most important to the success of a restaurant?

A: We try to assemble as much of the design team as we can during the predesign phase and keep them involved throughout the design process. This includes members of the ownership team such as the chef, general manager, and operations manager. It also includes all out-of-house consultants such as graphic designers, lighting designers, acoustic engineers, and kitchen design consultants. By having this group of people on board during the planning stage, concept development stage, and preliminary design stage, we hope to keep the team focused and on target. People who are involved in the development of the design concept are much less likely to become a deterrent as the process moves forward.

Q: How has restaurant design changed since you've been in the business? What kinds of innovations or changes have happened in terms of design elements like lighting, color, seating, and acoustics?

A: I think we have continued to see the importance of a well-planned interaction between the kitchen and the dining areas. This began with the advent of display kitchens back in the 1980s. More recently, we have seen the influx of more and more textural options for surfaces, as well as the development of good-looking surfaces that are easy to maintain. We have also seen flooring trends move from carpeting to hard surface materials during the 1980s, and now back toward the use of carpeting. Most important, we have seen huge changes in the importance given to proper lighting, as well as an increase in the number of lighting options available. If the lighting design is ineffective, then a good design has no chance of becoming an outstanding design.

Q: How did the economic downturn of 2008 affect the restaurant design industry?

A: Since the middle of 2008 we have seen the biggest slowdown in restaurant construction since our firm was incorporated in 1980. Typically, the restaurant industry has been relatively recession-proof, but that was not the case in this recession. Independent restaurateurs couldn't get financing or were afraid to attempt a new project in the midst of uncertainty. Public companies pulled back on expansion and concentrated on same-store sales to please their shareholders. Even well-capitalized, privately held chains watched the economy and waited for real estate prices to bottom out, putting their restaurant development on hold. This slump was like nothing we had seen before.

Q: How is sustainable/green design influencing today's restaurant landscape? How do you think it will influence restaurant design in the next decade?

A: With the recession that began in 2008, the restaurateur's first thought was of survival, and they abandoned many of their altruistic and green initiatives. The exception was where the sustainable design could actually save the owner money in the short term as well as the long term—for example, to-go packaging manufactured with recycled paper or low-e glass windows to help reduce air conditioning costs, Operators also began to implement income-generating green programs, such as selling used fryer oil to recycling companies.

I think that when the economy recovers we will see a renewed interest in sustainable and green design. Our natural energy resources are limited. As a result, kitchen manufacturers will continue to develop more efficient equipment, and there will likely be development of alternative energy sources as well, such as utilizing solar power to heat water for use in public restrooms. As manufacturers continue to find cost-effective methods to use recycled materials, there will also be an accelerated movement toward using sustainable building materials.

Q: What will be the most important trends in restaurant design in the 2010 decade?

A: I think we will see considerable consolidation in the casual dining market and increased demand for fast-casual concepts that provide a dining experience at lunch, dinner, and breakfast. I believe we will also see growth in the breakfast market, with concepts becoming a little more sophisticated than they have been in the past.

Good design is timeless. Restaurateurs will continue to want spaces that invite their customers to gather and socialize, seeking comfort and camaraderie with the rest of the community. In the short term, I think spaces will become simpler and less ostentatious, underscoring the delivery of good value for the patron's dollar.

WILLIAM A. BLUNDEN, FAIA

WILLIAM A. BLUNDEN AND ASSOCIATES ARCHITECTS CLEVELAND, OHIO

Award-winning architect Bill Blunden is what you might call a boutique restaurant designer. Over the course of a distinguished architectural career, he has designed three very successful establishments for noted chef-operator Zachery Bruell, most recently Table 45 at the InterContinental Hotel on the Cleveland Clinic campus—a space that needed to function for different times of day, different dining occasions, and a variety of clientele.

Q: What constitutes good restaurant design, from an aesthetic perspective?

A: Good design is good design. It relies on the ability to utilize space, natural and artificial light, scale, and proportion to support the intended uses of the space. In a restaurant, these intentions seem to me to be multiple. You want to create a space that has energy but still allows for intimacy. It should provide choices for people, from the single diner to the couple, from groups of friends to groups of business associates.

Each one of those uses requires a different response from the architect, but they must all somehow be integrated to create to a sense of place, not just fragmented spaces. Certainly, a restaurant is a combination of theater and gallery, as well as dining. It should allow people to see others and be seen as well as provide privacy for those who desire it. The designer needs to orchestrate these varying needs in a way that creates an environment that has personality and energy, and provides a setting for a memorable experience.

Q: Does good design mean expensive design?

A: Absolutely not. Good design is about creating a visual environment that supports and enhances an experience. This can be done with the most common of materials. It is the inventiveness of the designer in responding to the

Figure 7.7
William Blunden, FAIA.
(Photos by Scott Pease)

particular needs that creates good design. You could make a marvelous restaurant out of just drywall and some glass. It goes back to the fundamentals—and the fundamentals of design don't cost money. The charge to the designer is to respect the budget and apply those fundamentals in ways that enhance, reinforce, and support the activities going on in the space.

Q: From a historical perspective, has restaurant design become more important to the overall success of the restaurant?

A: I don't think it has become more important, but it may not have always been applied at such an intentional level. More restaurants are being designed now, as opposed to just being put together. I do think the bar has been raised

Figure 7.8
Among the seating options at Table 45 in Cleveland, Ohio, are private dining spaces enclosed by frosted glass, with bands of clear glass that allow diners to see the rest of the room without sacrificing their own privacy. *(Photo by Scott Pease)*

and that it will continue to be raised because the competition is more intense and the public is expecting more.

Q: How can restaurateurs best work with designers to create a successful design?

A: The most important thing is to establish good communication with one another, which must continue throughout the project. I have always used large-scale physical models (as opposed to computer models) to illustrate design options to clients. Restaurant operators must be as explicit and definitive as possible about their expectations. That includes who their patrons are and how they view

their restaurant compared to the competition. They should know the architect they are hiring and the kind of work he or she does; if that work does not meet their expectations, they need to find a firm whose previous work does.

Q: It is obvious that you work well with chef Zachery Bruell. What insights have you gained from that relationship?

A: Designers must ask probing questions and must be very good listeners. In listening, we gain an accurate understanding of the issues, which enables us to interpret them in creative ways so that the solutions we arrive at respond to the realities of the unique challenges of each project.

Q: Who were your most important collaborators on Table 45?

A: The chef, the hotel's director of food and beverage, the general manager of the hotel, and the assistant general manager of the hotel, as well as all the contractors. In order to have a project of high quality, it is a team effort, and every member of the team brings talent that adds to that quality. All the pieces must be there.

Q: What factors made the design of Table 45 challenging?

A: It is a restaurant housed in a major hotel located on a major medical campus, which is part of a cluster of high-profile cultural institutions in University Circle, just east of the center of downtown Cleveland. The restaurant serves the larger metropolitan area, the Circle area, and the hospital campus. Some of the patrons are patients staying in the hotel, sometimes for extended periods; others are visiting patients or are from the city or suburban communities. All of them come to Table 45 to enjoy a special dining experience.

It is always challenging to design a restaurant that serves both lunch and dinner because the atmosphere required at lunch, in my view, is very different from the atmosphere desired for dinner. The mood of the restaurant at lunch is brighter, more open. The integration of natural light in the space for the lunchtime crowd is essential. The evening meal needs a softer mood, although still infused with energy.

As well, the schedule for the design and construction of Table 45 was very compressed, with the design being done in three months and the construction being done in three months. It was an intense effort, with quality never compromised. The fact that the restaurant was going into an existing building made it even more challenging because of the limitations imposed by the existing conditions.

Q: What is the relationship of design to food and service? To what extent does/should the menu influence the design?

A: The relationship of design to food and service is synergistic. There is a constant shifting between which is the star and which is the supporting cast. When one enters a restaurant, there is an immediate impression of the quality of the environment. That quality has to be supported with equal quality in the service, the food presentation, and the entire meal. All of these combine to make the remembered experience, and that remembered experience is the life-blood of the restaurant.

As for the menu influencing the design, I believe it is wrong to focus on that because menus change. The environment should be one that can be flexible, accommodating change. This allows for new ideas about food, whether they are about new cooking methods, innovative presentations, or the menu items themselves.

Q: Do you feel that there is a place for theme design in the restaurant design market today?

A: Theme design does not interest me, but there is always going to be a place within restaurant design where it is desired. That does not mean, however, that in order to have an Italian restaurant, you must have red-checked tablecloths, exposed brick on the wall, candles, and wood chairs. If you do a theme restaurant, it is important for it to be as authentic as you can possibly make it—but the downside to theme design is that it has little flexibility to accommodate market shifts and new ideas.

Q: How has restaurant design changed since you have been in the business?

A: The biggest change in restaurant design is that people are now much more sophisticated in their judgments, of both the design and the food. Today's diners compare the environment to every other restaurant they have experienced, just as they compare the food. Expectations are definitely heightened. This drives the designer to search for new ways to accommodate and delight patrons, adding flexibility and choices.

At Table 45, for example, I made several private dining spaces enclosed by frosted glass, with bands of clear glass that allow diners to see the rest of the room without sacrificing their own privacy. Moveable frosted glass walls were used to subdivide the main dining area, offering a larger private dining section when desired. We used both natural and artificial lighting to create different moods within different sections of the restaurant. The restaurant was designed so that it became progressively quieter as one walked through the spaces. A variety of seating options included stools looking into an open kitchen, two-top and four-top table seating, banquettes that skirt the edges of the main dining space, a chef's table within the back-of-house kitchen, open horseshoe booths that form the perimeter of the main dining room, and the enclosed booths with the frosted glass.

There are so many choices and moods that people can have a different experience each time they come: a total of five zones for dining and drinking. The restaurant's background color is neutral: a soft off-white, with warm brown leather in the dining room and black leather in the bar. Natural maple on tabletops, accent walls, and the bar itself combines with the leather and the chrome of the chair frames to create a feeling of warmth that still has contrast and sparkle. Color was introduced through artwork and the diners themselves.

Q: Do you feel that the economic downturn that began in 2008 will have a long-term negative impact on the restaurant design industry?

A: The long-term impact on restaurant design will not be negative but may change the way we think about restaurants. Being challenged to do more with less always has the potential of leading to better design. We need to stay open to new ideas and new ways of doing things, be flexible in our responses, and be realistic in our expectations. If we do this, we can still create wonderful and exciting new places, even in hard times.

CASS CALDER SMITH, AIA, AND LEV WEISBACH, AIA

DESIGN PRINCIPALS
CCS ARCHITECTURE
SAN FRANCISCO, CALIFORNIA,
AND NEW YORK, NEW YORK

Established by Cass Calder Smith in 1990, CCS Architecture has become known for its innovative restaurant designs. Rooted in a modernist aesthetic,

the firm always aims to create a singular sense of place by following a clear architectural process of synthesizing ideas, experiences, and inspiration.

Q: What constitutes good restaurant design?

A: First, a restaurant needs to have a clear concept about what it is intended to be. You can't have good architectural design without a concept. Then it needs to have the right feel for what it's intended to be. This often is related to how the

Figure 7.9
Cass Calder Smith and Lev Weisbach.
(CCS Architecture)

Figure 7.10
Exterior sketch of Terzo in San Francisco, California, a modern and warm neighborhood wine-bar restaurant with a calm vibe.
(CCS Architecture)

design expresses the perceived level of luxury—older places typically expressed formal versions of luxury, and newer places are about more casual interpretations of luxury.

Then the restaurant needs to express the feel of its owner or chef, like clothing on a person, but in relation to the context. Places need to live up to customer expectations as well. So a destination restaurant needs to be dramatic and have a wow factor. A small neighborhood place needs a calmer design.

The design needs to complement and create a reference for the cuisine—that's what keeps people's perceptions in sync. For example, a barbecue restaurant should be somewhat rustic, like the food. And as in all buildings, the architectural fundamentals of space, light, outlook, and form are important.

Q: What is good restaurant design from an operational perspective?

A: The design must efficiently accommodate the flow of service as it relates to food and beverages being picked up and delivered. After that, it's all about materials and finishes that can endure a cattle drive.

Q: The Folio Enoteca in Napa, California, is unique because it is a microwinery and tiny restaurant within a food market. What inspired your design, and to what extent was the design shaped by the owner and location?

A: The proximity to the Napa region inspired us. We had only 800 square feet in a market setting, yet the space needed to express its function as a microwinery in addition to its function as a place to drink wine and eat food. The other design inspiration is that the project needed to be "branded" so that the owner's company came to life as an entity that is more than a wine label. So this led us to the deep red colors and the merging of the wine barrels with modern materials.

Q: Please share some examples of good value design.

A: The first restaurant CCS designed was Lulu, in San Francisco. It was a very low-cost project, but it was very strong as a design. The concept for it was clear—a piazza in a warehouse with a working fireplace. Lulu's design is straightforward, restrained, and elemental. It was, and continues to be, epic after many years of operation.

Generally, the architect's early, low-budget projects bring out the most creative efforts. Frank Gehry's early work was his most creative, and it was dirt cheap. There are many examples of this in industrial design as well. Think of all the Eames products or denim jeans. One of the most salient aspects of good design and especially good value design happens when design is restrained. This means keeping things more simple, which leads to sophistication.

Q: From a historical perspective, has design become more important to the overall success of the restaurant during the past 10 years? If so, do you think this trend will last into the 2010 decade?

A: Yes, very much so, and yes, we think the importance of restaurant design will last into the 2010 decade. Restaurants are more competitive than ever, and so the bar keeps rising for design, food, service, etc. It's not rising to finer or more expensive, but to unique and more creative.

Q: How can restaurateurs best work with designers to create a successful restaurant design? What advice would you give to operators about working with designers?

A: Successful projects of any kind are the result of a great collaboration between designer and client. Restaurateurs need to be clear about what they want and disciplined in being consistent about that. Designers need to be good listeners. Then they both need to be able to debate and discuss without taking anything personally. It is a very good thing for restaurateurs to take their designers on tours to visit restaurants they like or don't like. This should include having a meal, so everyone is eating and experiencing the restaurant together. Most of our best restaurant projects have included this, and we were able to see through the eyes of our clients. It makes the designer more inspired to deliver.

Q: What was your most challenging restaurant project, and what factors made it most challenging?

A: Perhaps the most challenging project was La Mar Cebicheria Peruana, a Peruvian seafood restaurant in San Francisco that opened in 2008. It is located on the Embarcadero pier, one of multiple buildings that all have landmark status (and the accompanying design constraints). The clients were Peruvian, so we had long-distance communication to deal with. The space was large—11,000 square feet—and plans included an outdoor deck, large dining room, and bar/lounge area. We had a tight budget and a short schedule. On top of this, everyone's expectations were extremely high. But all involved rose to the challenge, and in the end the restaurant opened to a great buzz for both food and design.

Q: What is the relationship of design to food and service? To what extent does/should the menu influence the design?

A: Food, service, and design are totally dependent on each other. They not only need to relate to each other, but they need to be in the same pitch so that that they end up in harmony.

Q: How closely do you generally work with a food-service consultant? At what phases in the project? Do you ever interact with the chef?

A: All projects have foodservice consultants. They start with us in schematic design while we get the kitchen, bar, and back-of-the-house areas in place. We work with chefs a lot, as chef-owners are frequently our clients.

Q: Your firm is known for creating interesting design solutions that are also practical for the operator. What is there about your approach to the design process that makes this happen?

A: We like to take problems and make the most out of them. It's a style of problem solving. We also really like to see our projects work well operationally. Our clients appreciate it and always hire us for their next projects.

Q: Please provide a few examples of your firm's "top designs" from the past five years and why you feel they are important.

A: Let's break these down into epics—think big production movies—and indies—as in independent films with a small budget. In the epic category we have:

- La Mar Cebicheria Peruana—an instant San Francisco landmark where we merged a modern sensibility within a historic set of buildings on the water.
- Perbacco—here, we really created a place for downtown San Francisco that's totally in tune with the location.

In the indie category:

- Terzo—a stylish, modern, and warm neighborhood wine-bar restaurant with a calm vibe.
- Townline BBQ—here, we nailed the concept of a road-house as the setting for barbecue. The recycled wood materials and the utter casualness of the place is really strong.

Q: How have your thoughts about restaurants changed since your first restaurant design project back in 1990?

A: [Cass Calder Smith] My experience has made me into a veteran foodie rather than a novice. It has also made me very appreciative of a good restaurant because I know how hard they are to create. I have also taken great restaurant design ideas and used them for other project types.

Q: What are the most important trends in restaurant design today? Will they last?

A: The open kitchen is still a big deal, but it's shifting to visible kitchens as opposed to totally open kitchens, due the challenges of noise control. Acoustics has definitely become more important. The community table is huge and we think here to stay—it's a response to the casual lifestyle we all live.

Q: Any forecasts for the 2010 decade?

A: Due to the economic downturn that began in 2008, fewer new restaurants will be built. But the ones that are built will be better. We will continue to see places that are smaller and more casual, due to the public hangover related to big places that are driven by star chefs.

Q: How is sustainable/green design influencing today's restaurant landscape? How do you think it will influence restaurant design in the next decade?

A: Some clients want to have LEEDS [Leadership in Energy and Environmental Design]-certified establishments. Their interest is tied to their concern for the environment and also so they can utilize the certification for marketing purposes. The restaurant industry in general is using more and more organic and sustainable food, and therefore they want their projects to be in sync with this—which means we use sustainable materials whenever possible. One of the most common of these sustainable products is reclaimed lumber: for example, we used reclaimed hickory in Lettus: Café Organic, and reclaimed barn wood in Firefly Grill and Townline BBQ.

In the next decade, manufacturers will come out with more and more restaurant products that are sustainable. The next wave of products will probably be about energy usage and air quality. We expect to see kitchen equipment that is more energy efficient and grease exhaust systems that are better at grease capture to prevent pollution, adding to what is already on the market in terms of various types of ultraviolet filter hoods and smog-hog exhaust air cleaning systems. We are starting to see solar panels used on restaurant roofs to generate electricity and to produce hot water, and we expect this to continue and expand.

CATHERINE CHRIST AND PETER DARLOW

PRINCIPALS, DARLOW CHRIST ARCHITECTS INC. CAMBRIDGE, MASSACHUSETTS

Since its inception in 1992, Darlow Christ Architects has grown into a midsized firm of architecture and design professionals, large enough to handle major projects, yet small enough so that principals Catherine Christ and Peter Darlow are involved and accessible to clients. With a philosophy of creating designs that function as marketing tools, DCA has been involved with about 50 restaurants.

Q: What does successful restaurant design mean to you?

A: At Darlow Christ Architects, we consider a restaurant design successful if the concept differentiates the client from their competition and if the architectural design strengthens the connection to that overall concept. From an operational perspective, the design needs to provide a sense of organization, control the flow through the space, and respond to the specific challenges of the site.

The key is achieving a balance among the architectural imagery, the functional necessities, the construction/code limitations, and the budget—all while reinterpreting the restaurateur's vision and, ultimately, creating a financially successful business venture.

Figure 7.11
Catherine Christ and Peter Darlow.
(Photo Credit: Greg Premru)

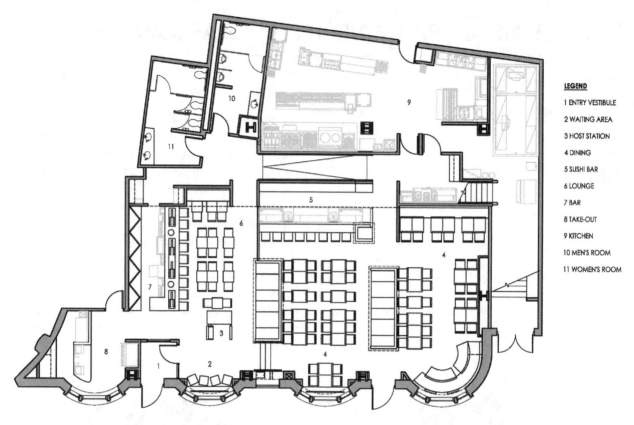

LEGEND

1 ENTRY VESTIBULE
2 WAITING AREA
3 HOST STATION
4 DINING
5 SUSHI BAR
6 LOUNGE
7 BAR
8 TAKE-OUT
9 KITCHEN
10 MEN'S ROOM
11 WOMEN'S ROOM

Figure 7.12
Floorplan of Douzo in Boston, Massachusetts., a contemporary Japanese restaurant with a calm, modern dining environment that has subtle theme references.
(Darlow Christ)

Q: Do you think that, to remain competitive, restaurants must offer an architectural "experience?" If so, what are the components of an architectural experience?

A: The competition at almost all price points has become intense, and often the architectural experience is the deciding factor on where those entertainment dollars are spent. The design of the flow through the space, the changing viewpoints, the differing experiences at the lounge, the table, and even the restrooms contribute to the overall architectural event.

Q: What does theme design mean to you? Does theme have a place in the design of restaurants in the 2010 decade?

A: Our designs are heavily conceptual—meaning that we always start with a strict, definable concept from which we build all parts of the project. We consider a design "thematic" when that concept is recognizable by the guest, but a concept does not need to be obvious to qualify as good design. However, we also believe that it is important to go

beyond trends and make the design goals specific to the individual restaurant. In some cases, a "themed" restaurant may be the appropriate design choice.

Q: Does good design mean expensive design?

A: You often get what you pay for in regards to functional design items such as equipment, MEP [mechanical, electrical, plumbing] systems, and durable finishes. However, creating an effective image involves eliminating all but the essential elements that reinforce the concept. Therefore, there is no reason that a *good* design should increase the cost. Rather, a *poor* design is often wasteful due to a more-is-better philosophy.

Q: Do you feel that design is still an important element in the overall success of a restaurant? Will this continue in the 2010 decade?

A: The experienced restaurant guest has come to expect a certain level of architectural design. This expectation will probably increase in the next decade. The challenge will be to find inventive ways of using materials, lighting, and details to exceed the anticipation.

Q: What usually gets in the way of successful designer-restaurateur collaboration? How can they best work together?

A: When the designer-owner relationship breaks down, it is often due to unrealized or unrealistic expectations attributed to construction costs or to special limitations of the space and/or building codes. It is important that the designer keep the operator abreast of these items continuously as the project proceeds. It seems obvious, but communication is still the most effective way to work well with a client.

Q: What advice would you give to operators about working with designers?

A: Operators should define their business goals and trust their architect to have their best interests at heart. Pulling together a restaurant is extremely complex and needs collaboration as a team.

Q: Your firm is known for its innovative designs. How do you keep coming up with fresh ideas? Please share a few examples of your designs that you feel have been most successful, and why.

A: Since our main objective is to brand our projects, we first try to find the element that will set this project apart. We may start with three or four initial thoughts based on the cuisine, the delivery, the location, or the owner's goals. From these, we do extensive research to edit our ideas into one definable concept. We take this concept and apply it to the layout, the finishes, and the details, and coordinate it with the graphics, the furniture, the lighting, and so on.

For an Asian restaurant near Boston, we worked with the concepts of feng shui. The goal was not only to make a design that respected the tenets of the ancient Chinese philosophy, but that actually expressed them in three dimensions. For this, we researched and narrowed our focus to the expression of the five elements. We divided the space according to the typical grid of feng shui and held to the materials and colors that were appropriate for the direction on the grid. For example, the dining room was *metal* supported by *earth* so we used soft browns and off whites accented with silver. We commissioned an artist to create a metal "bird" screen designed to interpret the idea of good fortune created by a rising flock of birds.

In another example, an urban sushi bar explored the ideas of folding. We studied the heritage of folding in Japanese culture and chose to interpret the meaning in our design. We created four expressions of this concept: flattening a folded object to reveal its creases, denying the fold by offsetting a folding panel, breaking a folded shape into layers, and cutting away the folds altogether.

In both of these examples, it was not necessary to make the concept obvious, but, as in most of our work, the effect of holding to a given concept has proven positive for the success of the restaurant.

Q: What is the relationship of design to food and service?

A: The typical model is a three-way relationship of food to service to atmosphere. If any of these is lacking, there is a possibility of failure. We tell our restaurant owners that the architectural design can bring the client into the space but cannot overcome food or service that is below the guest's expectations.

Q: How closely do you generally work with a kitchen design consultant? What other design team members are critical?

A: We generally begin with a kitchen consultant immediately after we have a schematic plan. We feel that it is important to get their expertise on the team as early as possible. In addition to the MEP/structural engineers, whose interface is crucial to a successful architectural design, the graphic designer is extremely important. We work very closely with graphic designers to develop not only the menus, but oftentimes graphic elements that are incorporated into the architecture. We also like to use artists to add another layer of richness and interest to our projects. Instead of hanging artwork, we prefer to integrate the art into the architecture. We give artists the basic concept but want them to use their own skills to interpret it.

Q: How has restaurant design changed since you've been in the business?

A: When we first started in restaurant design, most of the restaurants were living room–style interiors where the goal was to make you feel comfortable and at home. Spaces were human scale, with familiar finishes. Then, some designers began to add more dramatic moves—not yet thematic. Often, this was done through scale, color, or other contrasts. Gradually, finishes began to be more interesting, and we saw restaurants where the use of a particular finish became the concept. Recognizable theme restaurants emerged with the explosion of themes in retail. Currently, pure theme restaurants have given way to more subtle explorations of conceptual designs.

Q: What will be the most important trends in restaurant design in the 2010 decade?

A: The decade will probably begin with the continuation of the green movement through the use of simpler design and of recycled or earth-friendly finishes. New lighting technologies will play a large part. But then, for the same reason movie-going increases in a down economy, the visual experience may become more theatrical, more removed from daily reality.

Q: Speaking of green design, how is it influencing today's restaurant landscape?

A: Currently, green philosophies in restaurants are apparent mainly in the specification of materials, but we are seeing more designers expressing the underlying ideas of sustainable design through flowing space-shaping forms, natural textures, and organic imagery. Also, many items that make a project sustainable happen behind the scenes in the building systems and the back-of-the-house areas. After the economy went south in 2008, budget constraints limited the use of certain green products and systems but, in the next decade, demand in the marketplace will probably make these more cost competitive.

RON KOOSER, FFCSI (FELLOW FOODSERVICE CONSULTANTS SOCIETY INTERNATIONAL)

PRESIDENT AND COO
CINI•LITTLE
INTERNATIONAL, INC.
WORLD HEADQUARTERS:
GERMANTOWN, MARYLAND,
WITH OFFICES WORLDWIDE

The foodservice consulting and design giant Cini•Little International, established in 1971, has designed countless kitchens for restaurants, hospitals, stadiums, corporate dining, and more—virtually every type of foodservice facility. President and chief operating officer Ron Kooser (based in Chagrin Falls, Ohio), who grew up in the foodservice industry, says that "it always comes back to being able to create an environment where people can enjoy the foodservice industry, either as an owner, worker, or customer."

Figure 7.13
Ron Kooser.
(Copyright © 2009 Ian Pitts)

Q: What does successful restaurant design mean to you?

A: There are all the usual definitions: efficiency, comfort for the workers, easy to clean, flexibility, and so on. But to simplify the definition, it is the function of the image designers to get the customers into the restaurant, the job of the image and kitchen designers to meet the expectations of the customers by serving their needs while in the restaurant, and the kitchen designer's task to get them out as quickly and conveniently as possible, so the next customer can be served. That is how a restaurant can be successful and continue to operate in today's market, assuming the operators know how to control costs and run a business. This probably sounds like a very technical definition, but it is true, and it is true for any style or type of restaurant.

Q: What is the key to good back-of-the-house design?

A: Ideally, of course you want to design the kitchen around a menu, but we all know that the menu a restaurant opens with is not going to be around very long. So oftentimes, the kitchen must be designed to serve a very generic menu. The successful restaurant kitchen should be able to adapt to menu changes, while always providing the products and environment needed for timely food production and service.

Timing (the pace of service) is a very important influence on kitchen design. If the concept calls for a fairly low check average, for example, then customers are going to have to be served quickly yet comfortably, so there can be more customers served in another seating.

Timing can be impacted greatly by the degree of interactivity the customers have with the kitchen. This can vary

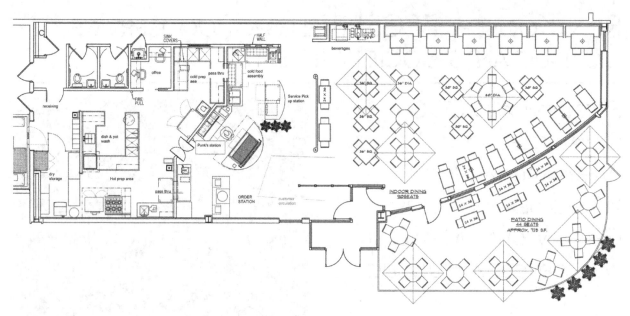

Figure 7.14
The flooplan for Punk's Backyard Grill in Annapolis, Maryland, where the concept is that customers relax in an environment that feels like their neighbor's backyard while Punk cooks their burger.
(Cini•Little)

from a full-service chef's table in the middle of the kitchen to customers ordering their meal at a counter, to ordering via a touch screen at the table, to gathering food at a service counter and taking it back to the table, or to selecting food from a buffet self-service. It is all a matter of providing the customer with the level of activity they are expecting to participate in, or pay for, in the restaurant.

The single most important key to good kitchen design is for all players on the team to understand their parts in achieving the goals of the project. Everyone, including the architect, engineers, interior planners, chef, etc., have to understand the concept, buy into it, and understand the part they each play in achieving it. It like a football team that is built around a running game and some of the offensive line is better at pass blocking than run blocking. The entire team has to work together to create a winning combination.

Q: Do you think that the popularity of the chef's table will continue? Do you see any new trends connecting customers with the back of the house?

A: We have to ask ourselves what "chef's table" means—it can have different definitions based on the restaurant concept. Is sitting at a counter watching and talking to the

cooks considered a chef's table, or does it have to be in the kitchen? How about a stir-fry operation with customers selecting their ingredients to be prepared in front of them by the chef?

I think that people enjoy the connections with food, and we will continue to see new concepts. At Punk's Backyard Grill in Annapolis, Maryland, for example, the concept is that customers relax in an environment that feels like their neighbor's backyard, enjoying a cold beer under an umbrella while Punk cooks their burger. People get to watch Punk cook for them in a place with a very simple menu concept, compared to some of the high-priced, celebrity chef operations popular before the 2008 economic meltdown.

Q: Does good kitchen design mean expensive design?

A: Good kitchen design does not have to be expensive, but the concern about sustainability and green design, along with the price of utilities playing a bigger part in the cost of running a restaurant, translates into higher costs. Funding may not be available for the additional up-front expense of green products.

Another cost factor that must be considered is the incorporation into the design of an open kitchen. When the public can see what is going on in the kitchen, it must meet all of their expectations—not only for cleanliness, but also in terms of showing off a professional image. Used equipment, while it might function well enough, may not be appropriate.

Food safety applications, while necessary, also add to the back-of-house cost, as do adequate and properly positioned cold storage, blast chillers, and similar items—all worth the initial investment in the long run.

Q: What is more important to the overall success of a restaurant, the kitchen design or the front-of-house design?

A: You really can't separate the kitchen design from the rest of the restaurant in terms of restaurant success. This goes back to my opening statement: get them in, feed them, and get them out so you can take care of more customers. The customer has to feel good throughout this entire process. People have certain expectations about the restaurant that must be met, or exceeded, in order to get them to return, and also to tell others about their experience. They don't want to be confused by the image, service, menu, or overall experience—all of these must be coordinated and delivered as anticipated. If the image says quick service, the kitchen had better be designed to deliver quick service. If the image says casual, the kitchen and menu had better be positioned to respond to that image in a manner that meets customer expectations.

Q: What usually gets in the way of successful kitchen designer–restaurateur collaboration? How can they best work together?

A: Misunderstandings of what is expected from each party is usually the most difficult challenge to overcome If a restaurateur has never worked with a professional kitchen designer, they likely do not know what to expect. If a kitchen designer hasn't worked with an experienced restaurateur, it will also be difficult to get them both on the same page. The chef or restaurateur with limited experience is likely to have a lack of understanding about different methods of operating, different equipment and applications, no knowledge about how building codes impact the planning process, and so on.

Q: What advice would you give to students or operators about working with kitchen designers?

A: It certainly makes it easier if the kitchen designers have experienced the real-life issues of working in a kitchen, rather than being equipment salesman. When we started Cini•Little almost 40 years ago (then Cini-Grissom), nearly all of the other "kitchen designers" out there were equipment salesmen. That was one of the reasons we started out on this adventure. Since then, the professional foodservice consultant has become a reality, and their experience has increased to a level that enables them to provide layouts and designs that meet the needs of operators and chefs.

Q: With the advent of celebrity chefs, we've also seen the advent of stage-set kitchens. Is the concept of the kitchen as a stage something you have seen in the kitchens that Cini•Little designs?

A: Yes, the same kind of kitchen stage sets that are being built for celebrity chefs in restaurants are being built in colleges, hospitals, and other foodservice venues. Cooking suites are not limited to high-end restaurants. We are designing them into all kinds of foodservice operations, along with tandoori ovens, rotisseries, char grills, and other visible cooking islands.

JOSE A. ORREGO, SCHOOL OF ARCHITECTS FROM PERU

CEO
CONSULTORA METROPOLIS
S.A.C
LIMA, PERU

Architect Jose Orrego is CEO of Metropolis, based in Lima, Peru. During the past 20 years, the company has developed hundreds of commercial and residential projects, including more than 90 restaurants. "We design environments that help our clients to reach their goals," says Orrego. "At the same time, we recognize that our designs must go beyond the function; they must enrich the lives of the people in a positive and meaningful way."

Figure 7.15
Jose Orrego Herrera.
(Eric Wentworth illustration, wintercrowstudio.com)

Q: What constitutes good restaurant design?

A: A good design is one that manages to make the food served taste better, and assures the customer a memorable experience.

Q: Does good design mean expensive design?

A: A good design does not necessarily have to be expensive, but it should arouse all the senses. Color and light are two fundamental factors to enable the box that contains the restaurant to be converted into a space for the gastronomical experience. A contemporary restaurant starts off with a script, one that tells a story, and the ambience is part of that story. This practice helps to minimize costs.

Q: How important is design to the overall success of a restaurant chain?

A: Our office has worked for 20 years designing the premises for the most successful hamburger chain in Peru—Bembos. Our Bembos projects have become known for introducing vanguard concepts to the traditional fast-food venue. Our starting point for any restaurant design is to define the period of time in which it must be current.

Experience has told us to set the life period of a restaurant to seven or eight years before the concept becomes exhausted.

For us, the concept of a chain restaurant must be more abstract than textual. The Bembos units, for example, are not cloned projects that repeat themselves ad infinitum. We keep some design elements common to all the restaurants, so that each is recognizable as part of a chain, but each restaurant provides a unique design experience. Customers know this, and look forward to being surprised by each building.

Each time a new restaurant opens, customers look to see what is new, and there is an increase in sales. When existing restaurants have completed their seven- to eight-year cycle, they are remodeled with new concepts, and sales typically increase up to 30 percent. We have discovered that design sells when it creates enthusiastic customer expectations.

Q: What do you foresee for restaurant design in the 2010 decade?

A: The new generations have become more refined design consumers, and the Internet has helped them to

Figure 7.16
Bembos Asia Exterior: Each Bembos unit has a distinct design identity that departs from fast-food clichés.
(Jose Orrego Herrera)

become very visual. Restaurants are leaving theme concepts behind, and restaurant design is evolving into gastronomical experiences that excite sight, smell, hearing, taste, and touch in order to make the experience memorable. Restaurant designs must have an anthropological component that interprets the new necessities of the urban dweller and also responds to the next generation of consumers.

Q: How can restaurateurs best work with designers to create a successful restaurant design? What advice would you give to operators about working with designers?

A: The main problem is that restaurateurs think that it is enough to deliver good food at a good price. Historically, this was true—people's main motivation to visit a restaurant was to eat good food. In the near future, this will no longer be the case. Why go to a restaurant just for the food when you can find any exotic product to cook in your own kitchen (with plenty of continuous cooking instruction from the media), and good-quality pre-prepared food to eat in the comfort of your own home?

What people can't get at home is the ritual of dining as a celebration, in a unique space.

Q: What was your most challenging restaurant project?

A: It is a continuing challenge for us to reinterpret the model of fast-food restaurants. This concept for Bembos has evolved many times. We are constantly proposing hypotheses of how fast food should look for the 21st century. Our latest concept is that restaurants allow several experiences in one building, not just to sit and eat but to enter and eat a hamburger in one place, then eat a dessert in another area of the restaurant, and finally top off the meal with a coffee while watching the children play in yet another area. This gives people an experience, not just a meal.

Q: What do you think is your firm's best design, and why?

A: Our latest project (Bembos Javier Prado) for the Bembos restaurant chain is an eye-catching building that has been treated with a skin of geometrical figures based on a fractal composition. This architectural treatment has been a huge draw and has helped the restaurant to develop a loyal base of repeat customers.

Q: What is the relationship of design to food and service?

A: A design means more than just developing pretty restaurants. The menu is a fundamental starting point of the restaurant's concept. From the technical area [back of the house] to the variety of menu items, through the internal and external image of the building: all elements have to be consistent.

Q: Is a strong graphic image important to the marketing effort of chain restaurants?

A: One of the major marketing challenges today is that it is very difficult to be heard, if everyone yells at once. The restaurant's graphic image must be strong because our culture has conditioned us to respond to clear and identifiable graphics.

Q: Your firm is known for creating interesting design solutions that are also practical for the operator. What is there about your approach to the design process that makes this happen?

A: The starting point to all our designs is that the restaurant must function from an operational perspective. From there, we turn our attention to the aesthetic development of the building. We start with the layout, resolving the function of the kitchen and the service areas. From this point, working with foodservice consultants and owners, our art begins—distributing tables in an efficient way, creating ambience, and finally building the container that will give the restaurant its image.

Q: Please discuss two examples of your firm's top designs and why you feel they are important.

A: The Bembos restaurant chain is a concept we are very fond of because of the opportunity to create a new category of fast food. Another restaurant, Panchita, is a casual dinner restaurant, dedicated to Peruvian dishes from the prestigious chef Gaston Acurio. In this project we had the opportunity to transfer the ambience of the Peruvian estates to a restaurant concept that can be repeated and exported to other cities.

Q: How has restaurant design changed since you've been in the business?

A: Restaurant designs have become more sophisticated over the last decade. All aspects of the interior (and in many cases the exterior) are now controlled by the design. Lighting and acoustics are two of the main elements that have evolved and become more effective. The use of lighting is a fundamental resource, and just as we can select a wine to match the meal, we select lighting to match and enhance the meal.

Another important concept is the exposure of the kitchen as a part of the restaurant, trying to achieve a type of honesty in regard to the kitchen and its integration with the customers. And the restaurant is now an experience, with different table layouts that offer a different experience within the same restaurant.

In the case of quick-service restaurants, I think they are becoming less fast, because people are discovering that it is important to take a moment to eat well.

Q: Any forecasts for the 2010 decade?

A: There has to be a vision of developing restaurants for a new generation of consumers who get their culture from the Internet and look for places where they can connect on a sensory level.

DREW NEIPORENT

FOUNDER
MYRIAD RESTAURANT GROUP
NEW YORK, NEW YORK

Restaurant impresario Drew Neiporent has been in the business for more than 30 years. His company, Myriad Restaurant Group, has operated several dozen restaurants over the past 20 years and partnered with such notables as Robert De Niro, chef Nobuyuki Matsuhisa, and architect David Rockwell.

Q: What does good restaurant design mean to you?

A: Good restaurant design is when front of the house and back of the house work together efficiently and the guest derives the benefit.

I believe that lighting is the most critical element in the front-of-the-house design. It is the most theatrical aspect, and it is what creates the wow factor.

Q: What are the most important design elements from an operational perspective?

A: You have to allot enough space for all of the necessary back-of-the-house functions, including the areas for storing tableware and equipment for the waitstaff. The problem is always limited space and where to put everything, but the design goal has to be to make the job of the server easier.

Q: Does good design mean expensive design?

A: Design tends to be expensive these days. The owner has to make it clear right from the beginning how much money is available per square foot. Every design element has to be budgeted. The design team should come into meetings ready to identify where they want to spend money.

Every time I collaborate with a new designer, they seem to be interested only in the aesthetics. It's easy to overspend. We spent $18,000 on one piece of art that could also have been a shelf. Overall, the owner doesn't want to look at any one thing and say it was a mistake.

Q: From a historical perspective, has restaurant design become more important to the overall success of a

Figure 7.17
Drew Nieporent
(Courtesy of Robert Leslie, 2008)

restaurant during the past 10 years, and do you think this trend will last into the 2010 decade?

A: Absolutely. We live in such a busy time: People are influenced by façades. You can knock off the look of a competitor but not the taste of the food. Some owners try to just use a gallon of paint to indicate a change, but that isn't very convincing.

Q: How can restaurateurs best work with designers to create a successful design?

A: Try to make the mission statement as clear as possible. If the project is a redo, talk about the history and the sense of place. Keep some of the spirit of the old design and at the same time try to transform it. Identify what worked in the existing space and try to keep it—and don't let the designer obliterate your ideas.

Figure 7.18
Corton, the latest addition to the Myriad family of restaurants, emerged from the New York City space that Myriad formerly operated as Montrachet.
(Courtesy of Robert Leslie, 2008)

When you're working from a clean slate, it is a lot easier. For example, when I looked at the blank space that would become Nobu, I saw that the original concept had the sushi bar in the back of the room. I moved it to the middle of the restaurant, where it became the stage and has been quite successful.

As a client, all you can do is tell your designer what you are looking for. From there, you listen to his or her proposed design treatments. Typically, you choose a designer based on their previous work. It's like hiring a coach—you want the head coach of the team that won the Super Bowl, not the assistant coach of the team that lost.

Q: What other advice would you give to operators about working with designers?

A: Make sure to remember that as the client, the ultimate decision rests with you. Don't allow the passive-aggressive nature of a designer to change the direction of your project. The operator needs to have a strong personality, and always has the final say. Designers should be involved in every part of a design. Whether you give them the right to make the final choice is another story.

Q: What was your most challenging restaurant project and what factors made it most challenging?

A: Nobu 57. With 13,000 square feet on two levels, figuring out where to place each element in the design became a real challenge. And we had lots of partners, which led to lots of opinions. While the owner has the final say, control of the design discussion goes to different people at different times.

My recommendation is to choose financial partners who are not too involved with the design. Make sure that they have patience and confidence in your abilities. In my experience, the ideal business partners have been hands-off because they believed that I know what I'm doing.

Q: Which restaurant designers have you most enjoyed working with and why?

A: Many of our restaurants have been collaborations with the Rockwell Group. The original Nobu opened great avenues between us and David Rockwell. David is not pretentious. While he has a strong personality, he ultimately respects our opinion so much that when he has a problem he will compromise.

Sometimes I love a battle. At the end of the day, you don't want it to be an "I told you so" moment. For example, I thought Nobu 57 was going to be a problem because the foyer had a wind tunnel effect. A simple solution was to take out the revolving door and it works fine.

Q: What is the relationship of design with food and service?

A: Design, food, and service have to work synergistically with each other. Noise reduction and space between tables are essential for staff and customer comfort. Color affects the look of food and the look of people: all these elements must be considered for a harmonious design.

Q: To what extent does/should the menu influence the design?

A: Clearly, the menu needs to be in place for the back-of-the-house design. Typically we bring on the chef quite early. Sometimes the chef comes on as a partner. The menu will absolutely affect the selection of tableware.

Q: How closely do you typically work with a food-service consultant?

A: Every step of the way. These days, the kitchen consultants are the people who understand the new equipment and what is needed for new cooking techniques such as sous vide.

Q: What is there about your approach to the restaurant design process that leads to creative and practical design solutions?

A: What is most important is to honor the space in which you are working. Remember that these spaces are restaurants, not museums. It takes the combination of good, practical back-of-the house design and the aesthetics of the front-of-the-house design to create an interesting and efficient restaurant.

Q: How has restaurant design changed since you've been in the business?

A: I think that design was not as important to the success of restaurants built in the early to mid-1990s. With limited money, we were able to design something that worked— in part, by taking what was there and retrofitting it for our needs.

Today, design has become a little schizophrenic. Too many designs are nothing more than a mish-mash of elements that don't necessarily work together. French designer Philippe Stark has influenced design in a positive way, but when his ideas are copied or dumbed down, they don't have the same resonance. We have seen too much of the Las Vegas effect on design.

DAVID SHEA, OWNER-PRINCIPAL, AND TANYA SPAULDING, PRINCIPAL

SHEA, INC.
MINNEAPOLIS, MINNESOTA

Shea, Inc., is a Minneapolis-based marketing and design firm that describes itself as "collaborative, confident, holistic, quick, and witty." A staff of architects, interior designers, graphic designers, and marketing experts provide concepting and design for roughly 20 to 30 restaurants annually, with particular expertise in design solutions that support the restaurant's message and strengthen the brand.

Q: What constitutes good restaurant design?

A: A good restaurant design stems from an understanding of the business opportunity, the target audience, and the desired brand experience. From there, the most successful designs ensure that the brand is executed flawlessly in all points of contact from entrance to lighting to seating to tabletop to restrooms. In addition, good design ensures that there is a perfect balance and flow between design and operations and one is not compromised for the other.

Q: Does good design mean expensive design?

A: Never. Actually, good design means using resources in the areas that will have the most impact, and sometimes the best designs are the least costly. For instance, many restaurants spend a lot of money on design elements in the ceiling.

Figure 7.19
Tanya Spaulding and David Shea.

Figure 7.20
The interior staircase at Barrio in Minneapolis, a casual restaurant with a menu inspired by the "street foods" found in and around Latin America.
(Tim Davis, conphoto.net)

Frankly, most customers will notice lighting fixtures or brightness of the light, but rarely does the ceiling have an effect on their experience (unless it's overdesigned and noticed for that reason). It's vital to spend money in places that will enhance the overall experience for customers. Ultimately, restaurant designers need to focus on the way the design details affect the customer experience and create appropriate solutions.

One of our recent projects, Brasa Rotisserie, presented the challenge to renovate an old gas station in an urban residential neighborhood within an extremely tight budget. We chose to take advantage of the former service station features that are atypical to a restaurant, such as the large garage doors that were once used as car service bays. Inside, we created an intimate space where the customers are almost part of the cooking experience, and the large garage doors open to let the tables spill out onto the patio, making this a unique and popular neighborhood destination. Our

budget was well less than $500,000 in all, and Brasa has become one of the most profitable restaurants per square foot in the entire region.

Q: From a historical perspective, has restaurant design become more important to the overall success of the restaurant during the past 10 years? Do you think this trend will last into the 2010 decade?

A: The market has grown tremendously in the past 10 years, putting more and more competition on the street. It challenges all restaurateurs to create a memorable, quality experience, and while the design is a vital component *within* that experience, design can also very much be the driving force *behind* that experience.

Q: How can restaurateurs best work with designers to create a successful restaurant design? What advice would you give to operators about working with designers?

Figure 7.21
The Barrio Logo conveys the brand's high-energy vibe.
(Tim Davis, conphoto.net)

Figure 7.22
Brasa, a low-budget renovation of an old gas station in an urban residential neighborhood in Minneapolis, became a popular and profitable neighborhood restaurant.
(Photo by Tim Davis, conphoto.net)

essence of their brand name and achieve ways to evolve and extend them into varying environments. Some examples of these have been Rick Bayless and the creation of Frontera Fresco (a fast-casual concept taking inspiration from Frontera Grill in Chicago), and Marcus Samuelsson and his evolution from fine dining into burgers with Marc Burger.

Q: What do you think are your firm's most successful designs, and why?

A: Shea's most successful designs are the restaurants that have become long-term profitable businesses that stand the test of time. Our best designs are not trendy but focused on delivering a great experience that can grow and evolve. One example includes La Belle Vie in Minneapolis. It was a restaurant we moved from one city to another into a historic space. Our design was simple, allowing the elegance of the original architecture to shine, and we enhanced the space with sophisticated, understated furnishings and great lighting. In the three years since the move, revenues have grown substantially each year, and the bar has become one of hottest destinations in the region.

Q: What is the relationship of design to food and service? To what extent does/should the menu influence the design?

A: The menu is a key component in creating the brand—a restaurant concept and brand cannot be created without at least a menu direction. Design, food, and service are the key components of a solid and successful concept. Each one has equal importance, and all three have to work

A: In our case, we need to work together with the operator to establish the restaurant brand, its point of differentiation, and the desired impression upon customers before any design begins. We also need to have a solid financial budget and an agreement of the key areas where the money should be spent. We stress with our operators that the goal is to create a successful business, not just a trendy design. Great restaurant design is so much more than the latest and greatest products, finishes, and fabrics. Great design means customers have a great experience and operators achieve business success. Designers should never begin a project without a budget and brand direction that makes sense for the opportunity. We would urge operators to make this the most important challenge for their designers.

Q: What was your most challenging restaurant project, and what factors made it most challenging?

A: The most challenging projects have been working with well-known celebrity chefs in which their name has become a brand. Our challenge in these cases is to understand the flawlessly together and reinforce each other in order to create a successful experience.

Q: How closely do you generally work with a foodservice consultant? At what phases in the project? Do you ever interact with the chef?

A: It is vital to establish a relationship with both the chef and the foodservice consultant/kitchen designer from the very beginning and work closely with them throughout the project. The menu items are a necessary component in building the brand and must be understood when determining the location, size, and layout of the kitchen. If these elements are not understood from the beginning and incorporated into the overall design solution, you run the risk of design competing with operations. A good designer will always create with the most efficient operations in mind.

Q: Your firm is known for creating interesting design solutions that are also practical for the operator. What is there about your approach that makes this happen?

A: Our approach is inclusive of design, food and beverage service, and operations from the very beginning and throughout the entire process. Our design is collaborative with the owner, the staff, the consultants, and the contractors. We make sure to get perspective from the chef, line cooks, bartenders, waitstaff, and all other front-of-house staff to ensure that the design is practical for their individual roles and that it creates good operational flow. We engage consultants early so there are no hidden costs or surprises in the building process. Once we consult all the stakeholders and we all agree upon the overall impression we want to create, we are able to come up with really smart designs.

Q: What role do graphics play in the overall restaurant concept?

A: Graphic design ultimately needs to be integrated into the overall design and not thought of as a separate category. It is important in every restaurant, regardless of size or scale. Good design is establishing a brand and executing that brand in all points of contact, and that includes signage, wayfinding, menu design, and takeout packaging as well as marketing and promotions. How a brand is seen outside of the actual space is equally important to the impression customers will have of the restaurant. If menus, signage, packaging, and marketing are designed as separate components from the space, there is the great risk that there will be a disconnect for customers.

If graphics are overlooked, restaurateurs are missing out on an extremely important opportunity to create the desired experience.

Q: Please provide two examples of your firm's top designs from the past five years and why you feel they are important.

A: There are two projects that rise to the top for completely different reasons. The first is Barrio, a casual sit-down establishment by a James Beard–nominated chef, with a menu inspired by the "street foods" found in and around Latin America. This concept has redefined "casual" by offering a top-quality experience in a relaxed setting. The design and atmosphere allows guests to unwind, relax, and interact. The menu offers products that are convenient and of the highest quality, at price points that allow customers to visit with frequency. In these difficult economic times, we focused on what customers want *now,* and it has been wildly successful. We feel this gives us a tremendous opportunity to roll out the concept nationwide. It simply works so well on all levels.

The second design is the Midtown Global Market. It is a collection of about 40 to 50 food concepts within a market environment. The market provides an opportunity for entrepreneurs, small businesses owners, and chefs of many cultures to come together and provide a dynamic series of quality food options. Our design has great function in its overall flow and use of seating and common areas, and it allows the personalities of each individual concept to shine through. This was successful because it was the first of its kind in Minnesota and it has had tremendous exposure and success.

Q: How has restaurant design changed since you've been in the business?

A: For Shea, restaurant design has always been centered on creating successful consumer environments. Twenty years ago, this was a novel approach, but today the market has shifted to have a better understanding of this concept. In terms of materials, we place a lot of emphasis on lighting in order to enhance the overall experience. Products are evolving with more options and better quality. Green design is certainly becoming the norm, and more restaurateurs are finding long-term benefits of designing with eco-friendly materials and operationally efficient equipment.

Another big change over the past five years has been the increasing popularity of celebrity chefs and the public's fascination with restaurants and food. In working with celebrity chefs to create environments, it is a fun challenge to inject their personality and celebrity into the space while still focusing on creating a great experience.

Q: You mentioned that green design is becoming the norm. What do you foresee for the next decade?

A: Sustainable and green design has significantly changed the restaurant landscape and is now an expectation in every project, especially as materials continue to improve. Elements must be chosen with effectiveness, performance, and sustainability in mind. All designers must adopt these practices in everything they do. It is not a trend, it is a shift in the entire retail marketplace.

Q: What are some other directions in restaurant design today?

A: There aren't any overwhelming new trends, but there are several shifts in restaurant design that will likely continue. In addition, the market has shifted a bit to creating bar areas that are more integrated into the overall experience, where the bar is selected as a preferred place to dine due to its energy. It is no longer just a place to wait for a table. Also, more and more kitchens are being brought from the back and exposed to the diners, allowing more interaction and offering a theatrical dining experience.

Q: Any forecasts for the 2010 decade?

A: Until the economy rebounds, we will continue to see that "casual, comfortable, and approachable" is the dominant paradigm. Even formal restaurants are converting to more casual ways to ensure that they are approachable and not intimidating. In this same vein, eating at the bar area of a restaurant is becoming increasingly popular because it's a fun and less formal way to enjoy the food. With customers being more and more mindful of how they spend their money, it will be vital to give a great value for their money at all levels from fast-casual to sit-down dining.

JAMES WEBB

PRINCIPAL
WEBB FOODSERVICE DESIGN
CONSULTANTS, INC.
TUSTIN, CALIFORNIA

Founded in 1990, Webb Design focuses on the long-term operational requirements of foodservice operations, including energy consumption, fixture and equipment maintenance, and overall service and customer flow patterns. Three separate design studios within the company offer commercial kitchen, cook-chill, and commercial design specialties.

Q: What does successful restaurant design mean to you?

A: If there were a magic formula to successful restaurant design, we would all be rich. To the restaurateur, a successful restaurant is a place that is profitable and brings people together to celebrate life and its journeys and, of course, the enjoyment of culinary delights created by the owner or chef. The restaurant doesn't have to be "designed" to perfection but must have a balance or synergy that creates a unique energy between the restaurant staff, dining space, kitchen, and customer. It balances style, uniqueness, authenticity, soul, character, flavor profiles, presentation approach, ethnicity, and cultural contours. On the other hand, a restaurant can be so pristinely designed that the design itself pulls soulful energy out of the picture, creating a stark hollow environment without a personality.

Assuming meticulous design techniques are in place, the single most important key to good restaurant design is the ability to blend the client's personality and soul with the space, keeping the project budget in mind at all times.

Q: What defines the operational success of a design?

A: There are many factors to consider when evaluating the operational success of a restaurant. The restaurant must flow in a logical form, giving the staff ultimate efficiency in

Figure 7.23
James Webb.
(Courtesy of James Webb)

movement from the dining areas to various kitchen functions. Many owners tend to cut corners when purchasing equipment, as budgets come into play during the course of the project. From an operational perspective, budget cutting can be disastrous, as there are many things to consider when selecting operationally efficient equipment. Well-planned and -selected equipment can save operators significant dollars over relatively short periods of time, paying for the investment quickly.

Quality equipment certainly makes a difference in food cost by increasing yields, producing more consistent products, and giving higher throughput rates. Custom-fabricated stainless steel is often thought of as expensive and is substituted with lesser-quality fabricated items. The cost

CAL STATE
FULLERTON

Conceptual Rendering-Exhibition/Chef's Portico/Euro

WEBB

Figure 7.24
Conceptual rendering of a stylish servery station that signals the experience of made-to-order, high-quality food by an exhibition chef.
(Courtesy of James Webb)

of real estate and workflow efficiency is far more expensive than the difference in cost of well-designed custom fabricated fixtures versus "buyout" products. Well-designed and -placed custom fixtures are more efficient, last longer, yield more storage, and are easier to maintain and clean. Balanced exhaust and air-conditioning systems are critical to the success of an operation, as they bring the operator significant savings by reducing heating and air-conditioning costs, as well as providing an environmentally friendly atmosphere for clientele.

Q: Do you think that, to remain competitive, restaurants must offer an architectural experience?

A: There is not an absolute formula for restaurants to remain competitive by offering an architectural experience. In fact, many patrons are not architecturally sophisticated and therefore do not appreciate the various nuances offered in architecturally "perfect" environments. It definitely can be argued that great design is appreciated by all—if even

in the subliminal sense. The successful architectural experience includes a balance of lighting, sound, comfort (or not), color, temperature, materials, and the engagement with food. Basically, all the human senses must synchronize in a way that allows the customer to feel appropriate in the space. Successful restaurants that are not professionally designed but have the magic working for them can still offer an architectural experience, just maybe not a sophisticated one.

Q: Does creating an architectural experience have a place in the design of today's noncommercial foodservice operations?

A: All foodservice customers, in any environment, deserve an experience. Today's customers expect it—and they are surrounded by competing experiences every day in the retail environment.

Q: Have your clients been asking for more or different food stations than a decade ago? What is driving those requests?

A: Our clients are looking for authenticity, ethnic fusion, and fresh, made-to-order food items. Customers want to participate with the food experience and feel they are ordering products with high value, that have a high degree of freshness and customization. Quick food that is freshly prepared in an exhibition style is important. It is shouldered by grab-and-go food having the appearance of being prepared on premises and on the same day of purchase.

Q: What usually gets in the way of successful designer-operator collaboration? How can they best work together?

A: Many designers don't listen to the operator and really hear what the operator wants or needs. Designers can proceed in their own world and not communicate the needs of the operator in the design. This can lead to frustrating design sessions and make projects very difficult. Designers must practice the art of listening and patience.

Q: What advice would you give to students or operators about working with designers?

A: Make sure the designer understands what is wanted. Have them repeat what was discussed in meetings. Operators must participate in meetings and voice opinions. Do not settle for something not liked.

Q: Your firm is known for its innovative designs. How do you keep coming up with fresh ideas?

A: We are constantly involved with food, trends, focus groups, and the young emerging customer. We are actively involved in industry trade conferences and participate regularly in industry events. Traveling and visiting all types of hospitality venues provides food for thought and keeps the mind fresh.

Q: What is the relationship of design to food and service? To what extent does/should the menu influence the design?

A: The menu is part of the personality of the space and the operator. Plate presentation and style of service are also very important in beginning the formation of a design.

Q: What is the relationship of the foodservice consultant and the restaurant designer?

A: Our firm has both kitchen and interior design studios. We feel this is very important because form and function must fuse together. The kitchen consultant must be involved in the beginning phases of design to opening day, as kitchens and other support areas are linked closely with the dining spaces. They must work efficiently and offer the balance discussed earlier. Interaction with the chef is crucial to providing a complete design package and should never be ignored. Chefs can be finicky and difficult to understand at first, but they offer artistic and functional approaches that must be heard.

Q: How has restaurant design changed since you've been in the business?

A: Certainly, energy use and sustainable design have become important. Exhibition kitchens with high display value are more popular than ever. Food is in front of the customer on all levels.

Q: What will be the most important trends in restaurant design in the 2010 decade?

A: The emerging customer is from a new generation that wants it all now. They are multifunctional and expect an authentic experience in a social, see-and-be-seen setting.

As well, in the near future, electronics and computer technology will manage menu ordering systems for customers. More convenience, freshness, and versatility in the menu offerings will be expected.

Q: When will the restaurant design industry climb out of the effects of the economic downturn that began in 2008? What new challenges will design teams face in the 2010 decade?

A: The industry will rebound when consumer confidence is raised. More attention will be paid to energy conservation and environmental/sustainable design. Sustainable design is the forefront of the industry. It involves energy, ergonomics, throughput, food quality, and, ultimately, profitability. It is here to stay and will become more sophisticated and expected. The Millennials are already expecting it.

CHAPTER 8

RESTAURANT DESIGN: PAST, PRESENT, AND FUTURE

Looking Back

Those of us who have been living the restaurant design scene since the late 1970s have seen some dramatic changes. Back then, there wasn't much diversity in restaurant design. Most establishments were targeted to the high-end restaurant goers, the low-end fast-food customers, or youthful diners looking for a good time. Design styles included formal, traditional hotel restaurants where jackets and ties were required; brightly colored fast-food interiors with fixed-seating, plant-filled rooms known as fern bars; and memorabilia-filled theme eateries.

It wasn't until the 1980s that restaurant design became a topic of public conversation. The design aesthetic began to change with the introduction of postmodern architecture and a lighter look with clean aesthetics that appealed to broader markets; 1950s-style diners came back in vogue. Bentwood chairs that required less floor space and made seating more flexible came into widespread use and thematic elements were toned down. Theme didn't die, but it often became more subtle and more complex with evocative references rather than stock clichés. Lighting choices and applications were expanded to create dramatic stage sets that were supported by sound systems that reverberated off the hard-surfaced interiors in the newly introduced see-and-be-seen theatrical restaurants. An expanded use of colors from deep hues to light pastels seemed to pop when lit by new light sources.

This was the birth era of professional restaurant design, when well-established—and several up-and-coming—architects were first called upon to create signature restaurant environments. Many of their designs exposed the structural components of the surrounding building. Design solutions were metaphorical as well as functional in an effort to stimulate people's perceptions and imaginations. Straightforward architectural treatments, such as the use of levels to define seating areas, became commonplace in restaurant interiors.

The gap between fashion and restaurant design grew smaller. Style was crucial, but the restaurateur had many choices. Like fashion, restaurants often reflected a kind of mix-and-match mentality.

The momentum that began in the 1980s catapulted design forward to where today's restaurants not only reflect the latest design directions, but often create them. Here's a look at past trends still shaping restaurant design today.

1990 to 2009

In the 1990s, texture became an important design element. Building walls were often stripped down to their rough-textured, unfinished surfaces such as concrete, brick, stone, wood, or metals. Noted artists and craftspeople were engaged to create signature design elements. Consumers expanded their culinary palates and became more demanding about food, and designers responded by paying more attention to the center of the plate (COP) and design elements—and in some cases, created quieter environments with softer light levels that complimented both people and cuisine.

As innovative cuisine and fresh, local food became a national obsession, more and more restaurants included display kitchens that brought the back of the house up front, and also became a new form of entertainment. The staid design of traditional hotel restaurants began to morph into innovative dining environments, with numerous hotels outsourcing their dining spaces to "celebrity chefs," who opened restaurants with contemporary designs that would have been an anathema just a few years before. Cookie cutter was out, fashion was in, and a new generation of restaurant-goers avidly sought the most stylish new places. By the end of the 1990s, restaurant design had blossomed into a bona-fide profession, and design became a critical marketing tool in virtually every type of establishment.

Kitchens also changed as the movement away from frozen to fabricated-on-site took hold. Individually quick frozen (IQF) portions of frozen steak were replaced with Cyrovac™ packed wholesale cuts that needed to be trimmed and cut into steaks on-site. This fabrication required additional kitchen pre-preparation areas. With the increased emphasis on COP, a new American cuisine began to emerge that drew from the geographic and ethnic diversity of the United States. Chefs scoured the width and breadth of the country to find all manner of American-grown exotica. Hydroponic gardens made it possible to serve tasty tomatoes in the dead of winter in frigid northern states. Nouvelle cuisine—with its roots going back to World War II—gave way to architectural food presentations, with larger portions displayed on an ever-increasing array of dinnerware shapes, colors, and textures. Vertical food presentations displayed fresh and exotic ingredients in artful sculptural forms.

DEMOGRAPHIC CHANGES

Demographic changes significantly affected restaurant design during these two decades, as aging Baby Boomers (born 1946 to 1963) entered an era of changing physical abilities and their offspring, Generation X (born 1964 to 1981), entered the workforce and became active restaurant customers with their own design preferences. As Boomers—who had spearheaded the move to frequent dining out—climbed into their 50s, they began to expect certain elements of comfort, pampering, and convenience from the dining environment. High light levels that made it easy to read the menu and move around the restaurant, seating that was easy to get in and out of, acoustic treatments

that allowed for comfortable conversation, and take-home packaging for leftovers were design characteristics of restaurants targeting this huge demographic segment. Starting in 2006, the first generation of Boomers began early retirement, many with sizable retirement incomes that allowed them to continue to dine out often—but this changed for many with the collapse of the financial markets in 2008, when retirement portfolios invested in the market took a huge hit. Although Boomers like to be pampered, restaurant price points once again became critical for them.

Gen X grew up accustomed to dining out because many of them were raised in two-income homes where away-from-home dining was more the rule than the exception. They like to enjoy themselves, expect instant gratification, and are the first truly tech-savvy generation. Unlike their parents, they had no problem tolerating the high noise levels and low light levels of the popular gathering-place restaurants that proliferated from 1990 to 2009. Most significant, they look for each restaurant to provide more than a good meal in comfortable surroundings. They want a dining experience geared to socializing with their friends and one that meets their technology needs for strong cell phone signals and wireless Internet access.

By 2005, the Gen X population of 25 to 34 years old was significantly lower than it had been in more than two decades. The decrease of population in this group had a negative impact on the entry-level labor pool and on the pool of college-trained managers who serve as the backbone management staff in many types of restaurant operations. However, until the economic downturn that began in 2008 caused a crumbling housing market, Gen Xers were earning more money (adjusted for inflation) than those of the same age just a decade earlier.

It was also during this time period that a new generation began dominating the workforce—and became the largest consumer group in the history of the United States. Generation Y (born 1981 to 1995 and also known as the Millennials) wants it all—now. They were new to the workforce at the start of the 2000 decade, but were not interested in working their way up the ladder. They were taken care of by Mom and Dad throughout their college years, expected to have employment offers come to them (rather than having to hunt for them) while still in college, and carried a significant amount of student loans (Figure 8.1).

Gen Y is the first generation of techno whiz kids who can text their friends and order dinner at the same time. They prefer informal, fun restaurant environments. They

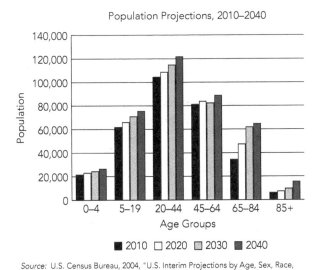

Population Projections, 2010–2040

Source: U.S. Census Bureau, 2004, "U.S. Interim Projections by Age, Sex, Race, and Hispanic Origin," http://www.census.gov/ipc/www/usinterimproj/

Figure 8.1
Population Projections 2010 to 2014. In the 2010 to 2040 decades, Generation Y will become the largest consumer group in the history of the United States.

are also the most environmentally conscious generation, for whom green design and sustainable menus are important criteria when eating out.

THE ECONOMIC DOWNTURN

The challenge with any commentary about the economy is that it depends on what is meant by "good"—not to mention that the recession and financial collapse that began in 2008 changed economic forecasting forever. By 2009, the stock market free-fall, the crumbling housing market, the scam artists who milked billions of dollars out of investors, the bank failures that led to unprecedented government bailout packages, and the continuing wars in Iraq and Afghanistan wrung the last vestiges of confidence that many Americans had in the economy. We do know, however, that the economy cycles over time, so it seems safe to say that (without a significant increase in dependence on fossil fuel or other unforeseen events) the economy will rebound.

The financial services industry is likely to regroup and reposition itself with new industry and government guidelines to prevent a repeat debacle. It is important to remember that in the early 1990s, the real estate market took a similar—perhaps worse—tumble that led to the government's formation of the Resolution Trust Corporation and a $50 billion plan funded with government-issued bonds

to help bail out a troubled financial services industry and commercial real estate that had been foreclosed upon.

It is the confluence of economic conditions—rising prices, increased unemployment, and a stock market downtown—that fueled the more recent reaction to the subprime real estate woes. Without question, large numbers of consumers relied on short-term debt and real estate investments that they could not afford over the long term.

Such uncertainty put pressure on restaurant sales in 2009. Customers downscaled their away-from-home dining expectations even as many restaurants were forced to increase prices due to their rising operating and food costs.

Although people had less disposable income, the popularity of culinary shows such as *Top Chef, Gordon Ramsey's Kitchen Nightmares, Throwdown with Bobby Flay,* and many more kept Americans interested in food, and helped the restaurant industry remain solvent. However, with less disposable income, people went out to dine less often, to less expensive restaurants, or to operations where they could choose items that could be shared.

THE EXPERIENCE ECONOMY

In our last edition, we referenced the "experience economy" philosophy of Joseph Pine II and James H. Gilmore in their 1999 book *The Experience Economy: Work Is Theatre & Every Business a Stage* (Harvard Business School Press). They said that we were entering a new age of economic output in which experiences rather than goods and services would form the basis of commerce. They proposed five key principles of experience design:

1. Theme the experience.
2. Harmonize the impressions with positive cues.
3. Eliminate negative cues.
4. Mix in memorabilia.
5. Engage all five senses.

The tenets of the experience economy remained strong in restaurants through the 2000 decade, with stalwart theme operations such as the Hard Rock Cafe, the Rainforest Cafe, Olive Garden, and the Outback continuing to thrive, and newer midpriced theme operations such as Longhorn Steakhouse and Texas Roadhouse coming onto the scene. What seemed particularly important to success was engaging people's senses with an ever-changing array of culinary treats and interactive experiences—for example, tasting the wine samplers offered at Olive Garden, or being entertained by the line-dancing service staff at Texas Roadhouse.

ENVIRONMENTAL ISSUES

By 2009, most restaurants had converted all of their refrigeration systems to non-chlorofluorocarbon (CFC) refrigerants. While some—wishing to be good corporate citizens—converted to further minimize their impact on the ozone layer, others converted due to the rapidly escalating cost of CFC refrigerants used to recharge systems that had leaked.

As for solid waste, consumers increased their awareness of solid waste issues and restaurants followed suit. By 2009, some quick-service operations finally began to shift to biodegradable packaging. Local legislation also forced new restaurants—and in some cases existing ones—to clean the air leaving their exhaust systems. Continuing legislative action all but prohibited smoking in most restaurant interiors in the United States.

Concern about water usage—fresh and waste—forced many restaurateurs to install equipment that used less water in all areas of the restaurant. Controlling water usage was also important because municipalities significantly increased charges for water and for processing wastewater to meet state and federal regulatory standards. Design modifications in back-of-the-house ware-washing and potwashing equipment enabled them to operate more efficiently, with less water usage. In the front of the house, some restaurateurs installed waterless urinals in the men's rooms. Some also started to use gray water for landscape irrigation around the restaurant grounds.

As we predicted in our last edition, the increased cost of electricity was mitigated by the introduction of more efficient lighting, including compact fluorescent and light-emitting diode (LED) bulbs and fixtures. Systems that captured waste heat to preheat municipal water further improved the energy efficiency of many restaurants.

As for cooking technologies, there was not a significant improvement in electric or gas efficiency. Our forecast in the previous edition of better insulation in ovens and around steam kettles did not happen. Waste heat from refrigeration systems did not get captured to preheat water or to temper makeup air. However, there is no reason why such energy-saving practices could not be utilized in the future.

GREEN DESIGN

We forecasted in the previous edition that designers would stop using wood harvested from old-growth forests, and that softwoods and farmed hardwoods would be used increasingly in restaurant design. We also predicted that designers would start using more recycled materials for building and furniture design.

These forecasts came to pass, and more. Not only did such practices as the use of recycled materials become commonplace, but the 2000–2009 decade saw a major sea change in terms of consumer awareness of, and demand for, green and sustainable practices. What began as a trend became a movement, and new standards were quickly developed. By 2005, green design was given a big boost from growing concerns over global warming, coupled with sticker shock at the pump, numerous documentaries—most notably Al Gore's Oscar-winning work, *An Inconvenient Truth*—and the fictional movie *The Day After Tomorrow*.

Concerns about the energy consumption of buildings and about carbon footprints grew exponentially. The U.S. Green Building Council (USGBC) reported in 2008 that buildings were responsible for 72 percent of electricity consumed in the United States (Source: Environmental Information Administration, 2008 EIA Annual Energy Outlook). Those same buildings—when heated with carbon-based fuels—created a huge carbon footprint. And the waste created by construction/demolition sites further reinforced the negative costs of buildings on the environment. By the end of the decade, Leadership in Energy and Environmental Design (LEED) standards—which were first conceived in 1994—were quickly becoming the benchmark for sustainable architecture and design.

FOOD SAFETY

By the late 1990s, numerous food poisoning outbreaks had heightened consumer concern about the U.S. food supply, and in the first half of the 2000 decade lead and melamine—both connected with cancer in humans—were found in foods imported from China.

Salmonella in poultry and peanut butter, coliform bacteria in water supplies, antibiotic-tainted water in freshwater supplies, and reports of tainted foods being imported from overseas opened consumers' eyes and spearheaded moves to ensure food safety in restaurants. Hazard Analysis Critical Control Points (HACCP) grew increasingly important and became a corporate mantra in all manner of chain operations.

The Centers for Disease Control and Prevention estimated recently that 76 million Americans are affected by foodborne illnesses each year, and 5,000 die from those illnesses. From a design perspective, building security, temperature-sensing equipment, and even an awareness of the materials-handing practices of suppliers have become issues of concern in the past decade.

MICRO FACTORS
REDESIGNED CHAINS

The early 2000s saw an explosion of redesigned chain restaurants—quick service through midpriced family dining. This was due in part to the fact that the furniture, fixtures, and equipment of restaurants built in the 1970s and 1980s had become worn out. But many also needed design updates in order to meet growing consumer expectations. Some quick-service chains went beyond aesthetics and reconfigured units to increase drive-through business and expand self-serve beverage offerings.

LABOR SHORTAGES

Labor shortages in these decades forced restaurateurs to modify the layout and choice of equipment in their operations in an effort to increase staff productivity. By placing more service responsibility in the hands of customers, operators—particularly in the quick-service sector—were able to trim costs in an effort to maintain profitability. We did not see the introduction of as much automated kitchen equipment as we had expected. While the robotic chef that appeared several times at the National Restaurant Association show in Chicago in the 2000 decade drew huge crowds, early adopters have been few and far between. However, advances in front-of-the-house technology that improved labor productivity and guest services were significant.

Restaurateurs increased their use of preprocessed foods, such as washed and bagged salad greens that were ready for plating. In some cases, the salads were prepared to the exact specifications of the restaurateur and vacuum-packed to ensure a seven-day shelf life. Onions, shallots, and garlic along with carrots and potatoes that were peeled, cut, and ready for cooking helped keep labor costs at a minimum. Labor savings coupled with smaller capital investments—no need to install costly washing and drying equipment for salad greens, for example—boosted the use of these preprocessed foods.

RESTAURANT SALES

The National Restaurant Association reported industry sales of $379 billion in 2000 and expected 2008 sales to rise to $558.3 billion (in current dollars)—an increase of 47 percent over eight years, with an annual average of 5.9 percent growth rate in sales. Two-income families were expected to be a prime contributor to this growth; and in fact, takeout sales benefited in nearly all market segments during the 2000 decade (Figure 8.2).

However, by the end of the decade the world economy had become so toxic that all but a few restaurants were feeling the impact. Some turned to discount pricing to spur business, while several chain operators closed units that were marginally profitable. Stock prices of many well-known

39 Years of Restaurant-Industry Sales: 1971-2009

This chart shows the sales growth of the restaurant industry since 1971, when the National Restaurant Association first issued its annual forecast. Here you can see the growth in the number of dollars spent each year, and that number adjusted for inflation.

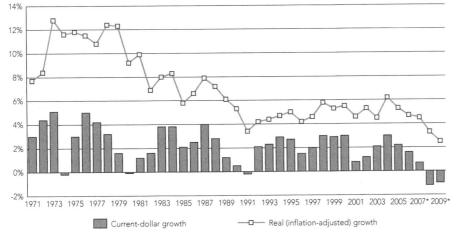

Figure 8.2
This chart shows the sales growth of the restaurant industry since 1971, when the National Restaurant Association first issued its annual forecast. Here you can see the growth in the number of dollars spent each year, and that number adjusted for inflation.

* Growth rates are estimated for 2005 to 2007 and projected for 2008 and 2009. Providing final estimates for restaurant-industry sales from previous years is an ongoing process. The National Restaurant Association's Restaurant Trendmapper offers updated sales estimates as they become available. Visit www.restaurant.org/trendmapper to learn more.

Source: National Restaurant Association

restaurant companies plummeted with the release of each quarterly report, and sales suffered in nearly every market segment.

Nevertheless, new restaurants continued to open. In a February 27, 2009, article in the *Wall Street Journal* titled "Grand Openings in Grim Times," writer Katy McLaughlin reported that such notable chefs as Jean-Georges Vongerichten, Thomas Keller, and Wolfgang Puck were making multimillion-dollar investments in new restaurants. In February 2009, chain restaurateur Ed Doherty, Doherty Enterprises, opened a mega-restaurant in Philadelphia reported to have cost $12 million. During the recession, celebrity chefs and restaurateurs were able to secure real estate at 10 to 15 percent discounts due to their notoriety. Further, they pressed suppliers to reduce prices on tabletop and other design elements. The bottom line was they felt they could succeed with lower fixed costs.

As predicted by many economists, an upward path out of the recession relied on the confluence of numerous macro and micro factors. A decrease in unemployment was most important. When people went back to work, they would no longer draw from unemployment insurance coffers, and their buying power would be plowed back into the economy—and into dining out.

COMMISSARY OPERATIONS

As predicted in our last edition, chain restaurants—large and small—developed commissary operations to take advantage of automated labor-saving equipment that contributed to a decrease in the cost of labor per portion of food served. These centralized facilities also contributed to improved consistency and made it possible for chain restaurants to expand their menu offerings without overtaxing production staff or their equipment. By centralizing production of bakery products, sauces, soups, and produce, chain operators were able to decrease capital investments and labor costs at the individual restaurant level.

COOK-CHILL SYSTEMS

Cook-chill programs were expanded beyond large cafeteria operations. Ice bath chillers that dropped temperatures of packaged, cooked food from 190 degrees Fahrenheit down to less than 40 degrees Fahrenheit in a matter of minutes made it possible to implement cook-chill programs in all but the smallest restaurants. Cook-chilled menu ingredients were integrated in commissary operations and helped to decrease the stress on line staff during peak service periods.

CODE REQUIREMENTS

A self-imposed desire to obtain LEED certification on new and renovated structures placed extra pressure on designers, architects, and restaurateurs during the 2000 decade. Architects and designers engaged special consultants—specialists in sound and technology, for example—to ensure that the resulting designs operated most effectively. While most of these specialists were not required by building officials, they were essential to the design team.

FRONT-OF-THE-HOUSE DESIGN

In our last edition, we asked the question, "What will the guest contact area of restaurants look like?" The colors, shapes, and forms of restaurant interiors mirror the fashions of the time. Architectural trends also influence design, and interiors of the 1990 and 2000 decades were inspired by their architectural shells. In the late 2000s, however, there was a new shift from lavish and expensive restaurant showpieces to equally creative, but more relaxed, toned-down designs. Designers increasingly learned about restaurant operations and created interiors that were as practical as they were pleasing to the eye.

SMALLER SPACES

Land costs, rent, and the price of materials continued to escalate during this time period. Building material costs skyrocketed after the devastation created when Hurricane Katrina came ashore, and new construction projects in California, Nevada, and Florida brought thousands of condominiums and freestanding home developments online.

Menu prices were forced to increase due to escalating food costs—particularly the costs of those products that relied on grains like wheat and corn. The only savings came in new construction of some quick-service restaurants, where drive-throughs decreased the amount of floor space needed for guests to wait to place their orders. While the space needed to queue up lines of cars must be considered, the number of parking spaces needed shrinks when more customers choose the drive-through versus sit-down option.

FASTER TURNOVER

Turnover has become an important goal since our 2001 forecast. Guest pagers sped guests from the bar to their table, which increased the potential of turning seats over faster. Those operations that adopted table management software were able to identify their top-producing servers and alerted floor supervisors of delays. And order- and pay-at-the-table technology further increased table turns.

LABOR-SAVING FEATURES

The order-entry technology mentioned earlier helped with labor savings in both the front and back of the house. Also, an increased reliance on display cooking for banquets and buffets helped save labor costs.

EASY MAINTENANCE

Ease of maintenance continued to be important, with hard materials like wood, metal, and stone finding their way into designs that once might have sported paint, wallpaper, or fabric finishes. Brass, while still in use in some places, was often replaced with other materials due to its high maintenance costs. Newly developed synthetic materials that were durable yet easy to shape and install also came into vogue.

RESTROOM SANITATION AND DESIGN

We can't really say that restroom construction has changed significantly. However, new technologies did improve sanitation and also addressed issues of sustainability. Hands-free soap dispensing, handle-less infrared faucets, and high-speed hand dryers improved sanitation and reduced reliance on paper towels and the attendant clutter that they produce. These practices also led to labor savings because employees did not have to check the status of the waste cans and paper towel supply. Perhaps the greatest addition to restrooms came from the high-speed hand dryers that quickly dry hands in much less time than their predecessors.

Poured concrete floors—some of them acid washed—minimized maintenance issues and contributed to overall sanitation. One-piece molded sinks and counters eliminated cracks and crevices where dirt and germs could breed. In many new operations, the toilets and urinals became self-flushing, and some operators installed water-free urinals that reportedly saved more than 40,000 gallons per fixture per year.

ENVIRONMENTAL COMFORT

Restaurant-goers and reviewers continued to complain about noisy restaurants. Numerous articles in the press as well as consumer survey results cited noise as the number one complaint about restaurants during the 2000 decade. More closely packed seating arrangements and the continued use of hard surfaces contributed to overbearing sound

levels in many restaurants—a significant challenge for Baby Boomers who were beginning to deal with hearing issues. In addition, low light levels in many restaurants—in part driven by efforts to save electricity—often made it difficult or impossible for older diners to read the menu.

DESIGN DIVERSITY

Design diversity continued to be an important trend. From the late 1990s to the late 2000s, restaurateurs reached out to newbie designers in an effort to obtain true individualism that was not derivative of other restaurants. This is evident by the list of designers whose work is represented in Chapter 6—many of whom are new to the industry since the last edition of this book was published.

THE PAST AND PRESENT BY RESTAURANT TYPE
QUICK SERVICE

The newly dubbed "quick-service" restaurants continued to shed the images of standard fast-food prototypes and often received as much design attention as pricier full-service places. Consumers experienced increased accuracy at many drive-throughs, with order screens that allowed them to view each order as the cashier entered it—so it was easy to note mistakes and modify orders before driving away after paying for a chicken sandwich but receiving a burger. Order-entry kiosks in some quick-service restaurants placed order-payment responsibility on customers, decreasing the amount of staff needed at the pickup counter. Increased use of credit, debit, gift, and company cards sped transactions and minimized change-making errors.

Some fast feeders switched to flexible seating options rather than seats bolted to the floor. Play centers for children continued to be designed in fast-food operations both domestically and internationally.

FULL SERVICE

Particularly after the economic downtown that began in 2008, we started to see an increased popularity of full-service restaurants with a good price-value relationship of food and design. Interiors showed creative use of materials, finishes, graphics, and other interior elements without breaking the bank. (Figure 8.3.)

Smaller spaces and the relaxed atmosphere of a neighborhood hangout became hallmarks of popular places. Tabletops got smaller as well, and there was a significant increase in

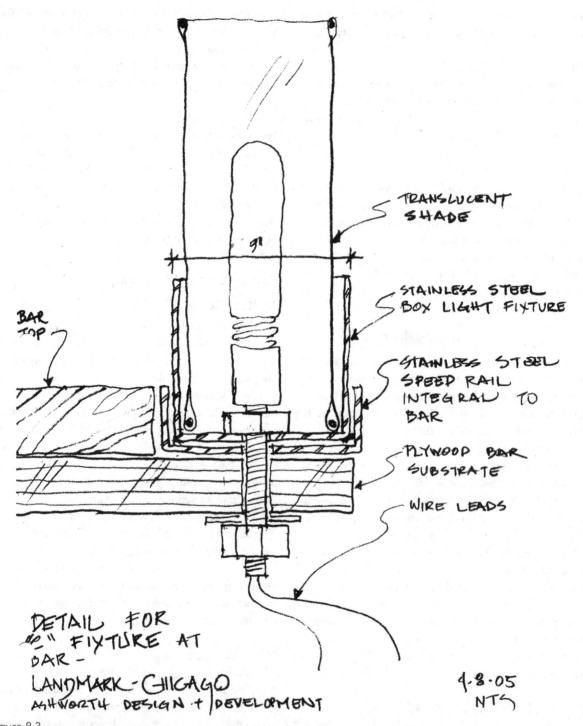

TRANSLUCENT
SHADE

STAINLESS STEEL
BOX LIGHT FIXTURE

STAINLESS STEEL
SPEED RAIL
INTEGRAL TO
BAR

PLYWOOD BAR
SUBSTRATE

WIRE LEADS

BAR
TOP

DETAIL FOR
"e" FIXTURE AT
BAR -
LANDMARK - CHICAGO
ASHWORTH DESIGN + DEVELOPMENT

4·8·05
NTS

Figure 8.3
A creative solution integrates light fixtures with the bar design at the Landmark Grill + Lounge in Chicago, designed by Warren Ashworth and Christina Ziegle.

the use of natural and recycled materials. Communal tables continued to be popular elements in many seating arrangements, attracting large groups or single diners.

The open kitchen remained popular in many full-service restaurants, as consumers became "foodies" in increasing numbers and sought out the venues of celebrity chefs. As well, with an ever-expanding consumer interest in wine, designers incorporated creative wine displays and cellars that customers could view from the dining room or waiting areas.

Hotel restaurants eschewed the staid formal dining room and opted for distinctive designs that appealed to hotel guest and locals alike. Theme—sometimes referred to as "concept" and often expressed without clichés—tied together the design in all areas of the restaurant, from entry to restroom.

CAFETERIA

Corporate cafeteria spaces did not shrink as a result of telecommuting. In fact, savvy companies saw their cafeterias as a key draw in hiring and retaining employees. For example, Google™ added free meals to its employee benefit package, enjoyed in brightly lit and comfortable spaces. Many institutional cafeterias converted their stale straight-line cafeterias to scramble serveries where cooked-to-order items were the norm rather than the exception.

BANQUET

Growing numbers of restaurateurs allocated space for private function rooms, sometimes with their own kitchens, for parties and events that ranged from birthday celebrations to corporate meetings. Many of these spaces were multifunctional, with Internet access and support for audio-visual presentations.

TAKEOUT

We saw some dedicated space added to restaurants for home meal replacement (HMR) offerings during the 1990s and 2000s, but not nearly as much as expected. That said, takeout sales expanded, with most of the menu item assembly and packaging taking place in the kitchen.

BACK-OF-THE-HOUSE DESIGN

We've discussed design changes that resulted from macro and micro factors and how front-of-the-house design changed as a result. Let's take a look at back-of-the-house design changes in general terms and then by segment.

SMALLER SPACES

Productivity per square foot of kitchen space continued to be important, and multifunctional pieces of equipment such as combination ovens helped with that productivity. Preprocessed, custom-tailored items such as diced potatoes or slivered carrots that arrived in ready-to-use sealed bags further supported smaller production areas.

IMPROVED WORK ENVIRONMENT

Kitchens continued to be hot, steamy, and all too often smoky places in which to work. In our previous edition, we predicted air conditioning and quieter equipment coming to restaurant kitchens but have seen little improvement in these environmental areas.

SANITARY ENVIRONMENT

Perhaps the most significant advancement during these decades was the expanded use of materials that resist bacterial growth. These included everything from antimicrobial products that were embedded in items like cutting boards and knife handles to the various components on slicing machines. Not much progress was made in floor improvements to create a more sanitary environment, however. Our forecasts about air curtains on reach-ins and digital alarms that alert when doors were left open did not come to pass.

MODULAR EQUIPMENT COMPONENTS AND CONSTRUCTION

The inclusion of on-board diagnostics in equipment ran out of steam early in the first decade of the new millennium due to cost factors. And we did not see components that could be used to upgrade the burner output of range-tops. There was, however, an increase of modular equipment that ranged from steam tables to combination ovens mounted on wheels, to facilitate cleaning and reconfiguration of the kitchen space. A variety of compact, portable pieces of kitchen equipment helped to increase kitchen flexibility and allow more menu options to be served in remote locations.

IMPROVED COMMUNICATIONS

Communications between the front and the back of the house improved significantly during these decades, in part due to technology such as order printers and order displays on monitors that included a total of all items needed from a given station. Managers and supervisors in many operations stayed in touch with staff using lightweight radio frequency–based earphones. Servers also used the earphones to relay messages to the kitchen and floor management. And waist-mounted bill-payment systems that printed a hard copy of a charge right at tableside showed great acceptance by customers and management.

AUTOMATED TASKS

When we wrote the last edition, we thought that the tightened labor market and customer expectations of consistently prepared foods would easily justify the cost of automated systems, including robotics. But we saw no burger patties being dispensed onto conveyor griddles, carbonated beverages auto-dispensing, or French fry cooking and portioning driven by point of sale or order kiosks in the front of the house. What is particularly surprising is that many of these automated components have been around in one form or another since the early 1990s.

LOOKING FORWARD: THE FUTURE

As Yogi Berra once said, "It's tough to make predictions, especially about the future." But if we don't make predictions, we won't be pushing the envelope and giving our readers something to ponder over in the years to come. We'll admit up front that we're bullish on the restaurant industry and the role that design and architecture plays in successful restaurant design. So here is what we see for the next decade.

PURCHASING LOCAL

Local sourcing of commodity items and foods that are custom grown for an individual restaurant or an entire chain will become ever more popular. In part, the high

---

THE ECONOMIC CRUNCH

During the writing of this edition, we saw the greatest economic downturn since the Great Depression. The confluence of elements that left nearly every element of our domestic economy and those of countries around the world in disarray confounded world leaders and posed significant challenges to all industries, including the restaurant, design, and architectural fields.

In April 2009, the American Institute of Architects Work on the Board monthly business survey reported that after steep declines during the fourth quarter of 2008 and first quarter of 2009, architecture firms were beginning to see a small uptick in business conditions, particularly in terms of inquiries for new projects. However, how a turnaround would manifest itself in terms of restaurant construction and design was a point of disagreement. Some professionals (see Speak

Out on Design interviews, Chapter 7) saw a return to the days of heavy restaurant design spending and highly individualistic interiors to retain a competitive edge, while others believed that restaurants would be hard-pressed to support the over-the-top designs that made such places as Aureole in Las Vegas and Buddakan in New York City extremely popular in the 2000 decade.

One thing industry observers agreed on was that people would continue to eat out, although perhaps less often and more frugally. Rather than go out for dinner and movie, or dinner and a club, people were starting to go to the restaurant/lounge for an evening's entertainment. Instead of traveling to the big showy gathering place and spending a small fortune to eat the cuisine of a celebrity chef, some were frequenting comfortable restaurants with a neighborhood vibe and good food. In this difficult economic environment, good design became more important than ever to attract customers and keep them coming back.

cost of fuel to transport foods across the country—or from overseas—will make such transport uneconomical. There's also the high carbon footprint to consider. In some locations, a resurgence of the "kitchen garden" or green roof garden will allow herbs and vegetables to be grown on the premises. In such cases, with appropriate landscaping, this practice could also lead to an inviting al fresco dining or snacking environment.

Purchasing locally reduces the amount of food miles needed to bring food from field to table. With shorter supply lines, there is less chance of food contamination, and storage spaces can be reduced in size as deliveries—particularly for smaller restaurants—can be made daily.

NUTRITION IMPERATIVE

By 2012, some forecasters are predicting global food shortages on an unprecedented scale. In part, grain products that are redirected to fuel production will drive those shortages. In addition, climate changes have added to drought conditions and water shortages in areas that were once productive agricultural sites, further challenging our traditional nutrition sources. And as emerging economies improve their income levels, they spend increasing amounts of money on food. These food expenditures place significant demand on global food prices. The era of cheap food in the United States is gone forever.

So what does this have to do with design? Perhaps we'll see on-site aquaculture ponds added to the restaurant site, producing everything from plump, fresh mussels and king crab to the highly nutritious tilapia fish that are well suited to any size aquaculture operation.

In the first six years of the 2000 decade, tilapia consumption in the United States increased almost sixfold. Nearly 75 percent of all tilapia production was located in Asia, but much of that production could be local, perhaps in tanks in the basement of a restaurant. Most important is that tilapia can be grown without antibiotics or other chemicals, and they are more efficient converters of food to body mass than the meats and poultry common to restaurant menus.

While we're not suggesting that a "fish pond" in the basement of every restaurant is feasible, it is a metaphor for restaurateurs to rethink their nutritional ingredient sourcing and reconsider how those ingredients travel, get stored, and eventually arrive on the center of the plate in front of the customer.

GREEN AND SUSTAINABLE DESIGN

We believe the importance of green design will grow exponentially, as the Millennial generation fuels the leading edge of sustainable practices and the public at large becomes fully aware of how buildings consume resources. Much has been written about "green" restaurants. While some believe that going green is nothing more than a fad, we predict that sustainable, green practices will significantly affect restaurant design in the coming decade. Green and sustainable considerations will influence the full range of furniture, fixtures, and equipment—energy sources, lighting elements, kitchen equipment, and the materials chosen for seating, flooring, and wall coverings among them.

GREEN CONSTRUCTION

Green construction was simmering in the wings at the turn of the millennium and gained momentum in the late 2000s. The Green Restaurant Association, with roots that date back to 1990, became a focal point for sharing information about green and sustainable practices. The USGBC, with its LEED rating system, certification process, and LEED resources helped the movement from conventional to eco-friendly construction and operational practices to progress. The concept of LEED certification was publicized in the media and became a consideration in the minds of restaurant design teams. As of this writing in early 2009, growing numbers of restaurants were being built to LEED standards, but many owners were foregoing the certification process until their restaurants became profitable enough to justify the expense for certification.

In fact, while some LEED components can be costly, others can be incorporated with minimal added expense. Such was the case in a green McDonald's built in Savannah, Georgia. In a March 2008 article in *QSR* magazine, Lori Hall Steele reported that owner Gary Dodd was bullish about the green features of his new McDonald's. The design includes windows all around the building to take advantage of passive solar loading and brighten the interior with natural daylight. Storm water that runs off the white, sun-reflecting roof (which also kept the interior cooler in hot summer months) was used to irrigate plantings around the outside of the restaurant. Bicycle racks and reserved parking spaces for low-emission vehicles were among low-cost additions that made the design green-friendly.

Green construction and operations coupled with LEED certification are said to decrease operating costs by as much as 9 percent. While the up-front costs—frequently as low as 3 percent above conventional construction—are higher than conventional construction, the payback can be analyzed with a simple break-even analysis. Most important, any ongoing savings due to the inclusion of LEED elements in the structure will help to bring more dollars to the bottom line over the life of the restaurant.

Sustainable energy sources are no longer limited to fringe eco-friendly restaurants but mainstream restaurants as well. The Chipotle Mexican Grill restaurant in Gurnee, Illinois, won a protracted battle with town planners in late 2007 to install a wind turbine that would power the restaurant and sell any surplus power to the electric grid. Scaled-down wind turbines are suited to any size restaurant, and with costs below $60,000 per unit, paybacks in saved energy costs could be realized in less than 10 years; after that, the savings became pure profit. Of course, the greatest challenge continued to be local residents who didn't want the technology creating noise and scaring birds in their neighborhoods.

The U.S. Environmental Protection Agency (EPA) has highlighted dozens of restaurant chains that are using as much as 20 percent of their energy from sustainable sources. Starbucks is one such company that has earned Green Power Partnership points for its wind power energy usage that totals over 185,000 kWh per year. While wind turbines can raise local concerns, restaurateurs have begun to employ next-generation solar panels that are integrated into the roofing material in some locations, and with increased use of this technology, it may become cost effective even in colder locations like the Northeast.

By the middle of the 2010s the cost of building using green materials and techniques will be on par with conventional construction methods of the mid-2000s. As an extra incentive, operating costs per square foot of these buildings will be lower than the conventional counterparts, and the savings compound year after year. We also expect that both state and federal tax incentives will decrease the overall cost of installing elements that contribute to sustainability.

Build Right

While LEED certification is highly desirable, it may be out of reach for some projects. This doesn't mean that restaurateurs, designers, and architects should ignore aspects of sustainable design even if their project will not lead to some sort of LEED certification.

For example, insulated concrete forms (ICFs) and spray-on foam insulation are two building options that can benefit many restaurants. The ICFs lock together, and when filled with concrete they are rigid, durable, and provide an exterior barrier that significantly improves the insulating qualities of exterior walls. While not as effective, sprayed-on foam is another way to improve the thermal quality of external walls.

Similar applications for insulated poured ceilings, multipane windows, and nontoxic waterproofing are three additional sustainable building solutions without complete LEED certification, and there are many more options for building right.

Green Operations

Going green will increasingly impact the way restaurants do business. Designers will select sleek water carafes that bring filtered water to diners rather than bottled water. While space will be required to hold all of those carafes, significantly more space would be needed to store cases of bottled waters. Going green also involves going local, which means that a restaurant's source of ingredients comes from a nearby family of suppliers who, if the restaurant runs out of an ingredient, can get that ingredient to the operation is a short period of time.

Many restaurants will employ green record keeping that starts as a data file when an employee fills out an online employment application, or when the chef adds a new menu item that calls for a new menu ingredient. The data trail for employees will be integrated into the employee personnel records, and for the new ingredient the specifications will be automatically integrated in all of the standardized recipes used in the restaurant. Such simple moves will decrease data entry costs and minimize paper usage that is common in traditional record-keeping systems.

It's hard—perhaps impossible—to eliminate all waste from a restaurant. What counts is what is done with that waste. One simple example is the reuse of spent fry medium for use as heating fuel and for vehicular fuel. New technologies will develop to economically convert what would otherwise be a waste into a fuel source.

Designers will have to incorporate spaces for recycled containers where metal, glass, and plastic can be stored. And food wastes will no longer get ground up and flushed down the drain. They will be compacted and taken away to biomass gas production facilities, with each ton of waste yielding a refund to the restaurant and a plethora of energy-saving by-products.

The University of New Hampshire has already created a cogeneration plant on campus that is fueled by renewable, landfill methane gas generated by Waste Management of New Hampshire at their recycling facility some 13 miles from the university. By 2009 UNH had gone off the natural gas grid, and when the co-generation plant is not overtaxed, the plant has been able to sell electricity to the grid. The use of landfill methane gas yields an estimated savings of 67 percent compared with natural gas or oil, with an expected payback by 2020.

Eco-friendly packaging that can go directly into the compost bin where it decomposes in a matter of weeks has helped to decrease the negative impact of foodservice containers. Additionally, disposable plates fashioned from spent sugarcane and drinkware made from cornstarch have also become important in an eco-sensitive environment. Informed operators have developed marketing campaigns around the use of these new packaging materials to promote their sensitivity to sustainability.

WATER ISSUES

While initial installation costs are higher than tank-dependent counterparts, on-demand tankless water heaters save a great deal of energy over their useful life. When properly sized, these water heaters can deliver a constant supply of hot water set to whatever temperature is needed. For restrooms and hand washing, temperatures should not exceed 106 degrees Fahrenheit, whereas a tankless water heater that connects to the dish machine can be set at 140 degrees Fahrenheit or higher. Unlike heaters with tanks far from the point of use, these water heaters can be installed within a few feet of the point of use. This practice will minimize the amount of water that is wasted while a customer or staff member waits for hot water to reach the faucet head.

Waste heat recovery systems will be integrated in everything from prewarming makeup air to prewarming water used in dish machines. Water that used to be dumped down the drain will increasingly be used to preheat water that flows into the wash or prerinse tank of dish machines. Such practices will lower energy bills, improve cleaning of tableware, and decrease overall water consumption. We had predicted in our previous edition that waste heat from refrigeration systems would get captured to preheat water or to temper makeup air. While this forecast did not happen, we still feel confident that manufacturers will ultimately figure out how to capture this heat before it is vented away or dumped down a drain.

Gray water—water from hand sinks or employee showers—will be used for irrigation, particularly in restaurants with significant landscaping or green roofs. In most cases, gray water needs to be treated before being reused, but the cost of this treatment is far less than the cost of using fresh municipal water.

RECYCLING

We touched on recycling in the Green Operations section earlier. The truth is that restaurants can begin with a simple recycling plan that grows over time. However, for such a plan to succeed, management must first determine what is recycled by the local municipality or waste removal firms. While some recycling plants accept nearly any type of plastic, some will only accept #1 and #2 plastics. When it comes to glass, some recycling plants require the glass to be separated by color, while others dump all glass together.

In part, how the recycled materials will be reused impacts how and what the recyclers will accept. For example, glass that will be ground and used as aggregate in asphalt does not have to be sorted, whereas glass that will be melted and used to create other glass elements must be sorted. The same holds true for all other items that are recycled. Management must determine what and how items will be recycled and then work with the designers or architects to ensure that sufficient space is planned to hold recyclables prior to pickup.

LIGHT RIGHT

We predict a marked reduction in the use of incandescent bulbs—perhaps as much as a 60 percent reduction. Such a reduction will significantly conserve energy when the incandescents are replaced with more energy-efficient light sources. Compact fluorescents will become the replacement bulb of choice. In addition to their energy-saving characteristics, some fluorescent bulbs will burn up to 10,000 hours, thus reducing the cost of relamping a restaurant.

Fluorescents will be joined by an increased amount of LED lighting. As the cost of colored LEDs drops, manufacturers can produce light sources with different, and warmer, hues that are appropriate for front-of-the-house illumination. Conventional ceiling fluorescents will continue in use, particularly in kitchen areas, as they are very efficient for overall lighting.

ARCHITECTURAL RECYCLING

In keeping with the green movement, a growing number of restaurants will be built within existing shells, in both free-standing structures and in building complexes. Such is the case for a Newick's Seafood restaurant in Concord, New Hampshire, that gave life to a shuttered Smokey Bones building that was slated for demolition. Such adaptive reuse can save construction costs and energy costs, and minimizes the amount of materials sent to landfills. In fact, the U.S. EPA, in their report *Characterization of Building-Related Construction and Demolition (C&D) Debris in the United States*, estimated that 136 million tons of C&D waste were generated each year. That figure is quite significant, particularly when compared to the 209.7 million tons of municipal solid waste generated each year (U.S. EPA Report 530/R-98-007) in the United States.

GLOBAL DEVELOPMENT

A growing number of designers and architects will work beyond the borders of their home countries. The global energy crunch will force them to utilize local building materials, thus saving transportation costs. We also see these increased transportation costs and the devalued American dollar as a deterrent to importing materials and furniture from overseas. So, we predict, "buy local" will become the credo for designers, whether they are working in their hometowns or halfway around the world.

MARGINAL SITES

Over the next decade, operating margins will continue to tighten due to rising operating costs, taxes, and other direct expenses. Algorithms for site selection that worked well from the 1970s until the 1990s may no longer work, particularly in domestic settings. Designers will have to create restaurants that may not have optimal vehicular traffic or pedestrian traffic and—as seen in countries like Japan—will be asked to create blockbuster restaurants several stories above street level. For some, that may be an overwhelming challenge, but we look at the Adam Tihany–designed Per Se restaurant housed on the fourth floor of the Time Warner Center at Columbus Circle in New York for inspiration, as well as the Bembos chain in Peru that builds two-story restaurants to make it possible for them to build on a smaller plot of land in a desirable area.

SEAMLESS TECHNOLOGY

The skyrocketing success of the Internet, personal computer games, and other chip-based technologies leads us to believe that we will see significant advancements in the use of technology in the restaurant industry, and many of those technologies will build on the design and architecture of the space.

Consider, for example, the 's Baggers restaurant in Germany (see mini-case in Chapter 6). Technology is at the core of the concept, from entering orders on a touch screen that sits in front of diners, to the use of the screen to type e-mails to friends, order food to go, or gather information about local attractions—this restaurant depends on technology throughout.

While the classic architectural still-shot is a compelling visual in design magazines, diners will be more discerning about choosing a restaurant in the future, and a single picture is not as compelling as 360-degree views of a restaurant. In the coming decade, we'll see more restaurants incorporate 360-degree views of each of their dining and drinking spaces that will be available on the Internet.

We'll even go so far as to say that potential customers will be able to do a float-through, as they would in Second Life, where they will spot a table that they like. They'll be able to click on the table and check its availability for next Thursday evening at 7:15. If it's available, they will make a reservation online and receive a confirmation e-mail that they will present to the host/ess when they arrive. The reservation data will already be in the table management system and can include items that the customer preorders during the reservation process. This seamless marketing, purchase, and delivery system truly is the wave of the future.

Second Life and similar Internet sites will increasingly be used to solicit customer likes and dislikes as part of the design process. In the late 2000s, for example, Second Life was used to help formulate the conceptual design of the Aloft Hotel chain, which was a vision of W Hotels and part of the Starwood family of hotels. In effect, the Aloft Hotel chain was designed for and (in part) by the hip clientele who frequent these hotels. Second Life was also used as part of the design formulation for pubs in the United Kingdom. The way it works is that each viewer creates an avatar, which becomes his or her online persona while on the site. During the design process, input can be offered in real time when members of the design team are online or at other times of the day.

Techno-Marketing

Designers need to acknowledge that the Millennials and others who have cell phones with Internet connectivity will increasingly use their handhelds to search for restaurants on the Web. Restaurant owners will be pressed to create subsites of their restaurant site that are designed for smaller screens and—in many cases—slower access speed.

Highs and Lows

From dining in the depths of the oceans to dining in the sky, offbeat settings that have a significant "wow" factor will continue to offer experiential dining experiences to the subset of clientele looking for something new and different. For example, dining in an underwater space that has wild fish swimming around a domed dining area provides an ongoing kaleidoscope of changing "decor" at the Hilton Maldives Resort & Spa, which sits five meters below the ocean's surface. It offers a 270-degree view of sea life in this part of the Indian Ocean. The dining area is encased in a clear acrylic shell adjacent to a vibrant coral reef.

On the other end of the spectrum, dining in the sky can be an impressive setting for special events. The Dinner in the Sky organization provides a platform with 22 seats into which customers are strapped and a space inside the open rectangle in which chefs—tethered to the platform—assemble food courses and serve them to the high-flying guests. The unit, with a full load of guests, staff, and food, weighs roughly seven tons. Once loaded, the platform is whisked up to 180 feet above the ground by a crane that is designed to lift up to 200 tons (Figure 8.4). The concept originated in Belgium and by 2009 became available in over 16 countries worldwide. Dinner in the Sky offers diners a bird's-eye view of local landscapes or cityscapes.

Hit All of the Senses

We first noticed the importance of aroma many years ago, when we were writing the first edition of *Successful Restaurant Design*. We were at the Horton Mall in San Diego and were drawn into a cinnamon bun shop by the tantalizing aromas that hit our noses as we passed. We sat outside the shop enjoying our cinnamon buns while watching the behavior of other shoppers. We estimate that 85 percent of those who intended to walk by were drawn into the shop by the irresistible smells of cinnamon and baking bread (as we were) and emerged in a few minutes munching on their purchases.

So, what was there about this shop that made it so special? The key was scent. The proprieters vented the exhaust air from the ovens that baked the buns out into the outdoor walkway in front of the shop.

This would be difficult to do in an interior restaurant, but we believe that scent is one of the most neglected design elements. Clearly, the scent of baking bread attracts

Figure 8.4
Dining with a view: Dinner in the Sky can accommodate 22 high-flying guests for a meal up to 180 feet above the ground.
(Copyright 2009 All rights reserved. Dinner in the Sky LV)

customers—and the smell of garbage or aged seafood repels them.

As mentioned in earlier chapters, the air is so purified in most dining spaces that arriving customers are not enticed by appealing aromas that effectively whet the appetite. We predict that a growing number of restaurant designs will integrate technologies to disperse signature aromas through the ventilation system of the restaurant dining areas. Further, we may see a return of tableside cooking in high-end restaurants, which infuses the air with the aroma of food as it cooks.

FRONT OF THE HOUSE

Restaurants will increasingly incorporate separate rooms that can be used as small function rooms, or opened to accept overflow from the main dining spaces. Technology will continue to improve turnover rates. By allowing customers to preorder, order from the table, pay at the table, and—perhaps—robotic servers may also contribute to improved turnover rates. New materials will be easier to maintain, yet will have a feeling of luxury.

Most important, new materials and technology in restrooms will ensure the perception of good sanitation. The sweet aroma of waterless urinals, coupled with hands-off soap dispensing, water faucet flow, and high-speed hand dryers, when coupled with auto-opening doors, will ease fears that some people have of public restrooms. When coupled with a hands-free hand sanitizing dispenser at the exit door of the restroom, the package is complete.

As mentioned earlier, noise is the biggest complaint for many customers. Advanced sound-dampening technology—similar to that used in Bose headphones—will be integrated into dining spaces. Customers will be able to dial up the level of sound dampening that they want at their tables, and the system will work its magic automatically.

BACK OF THE HOUSE

We need to see a vast improvement in the efficiency of the equipment and systems in the back of the house. While speed seems to have been the driver in past decades, we have reached a turning point where speed at the expense of higher energy costs is not a viable solution. The equipment manufacturers—like some automobile manufacturers—will have to undergo a radical rethinking to create more energy-efficient equipment that is as appealing as the Toyota Prius without significantly increasing the selling price.

This will be a tough order for some equipment manufacturers. If one manufacturer steps up and builds—not a really hard thing to do—a more energy-efficient oven or steam kettle, it will grab more than its own share of the market, and others will follow.

CONCLUSION

As economic conditions improve over the next decade, many of the challenges faced in the previous decade will disappear, but new ones will arise. We should see a return to good times—although not quite as good as in the go-go 1990s—under the presidency of Barack Obama and his successor. Much of the future rests on the policy decisions that Congress and the executive branch put forward over the near term. As we have seen, biodiesel is not the panacea that Congress thought it was. In the middle of the last decade, the diversion of corn to energy production had a ripple effect through the economy and the price of food around the world.

Perhaps the single most important trend that we see for the future decade is that designers and architects—along with restaurant owners—will become increasingly concerned about the environment. The "green" train has left the station, and those who are not aboard will be left in the dust. Green has moved from being a cost to an investment to a mandate—that can actually save money while helping to preserve the planet.

INDEX

Restaurant names appear in **boldface** type, *ci* refers to the color insert.